MELODRAMA: STAGE PICTURE SCREEN

Melodrama
STAGE PICTURE SCREEN

Edited by

JACKY BRATTON, JIM COOK, CHRISTINE GLEDHILL

BRITISH FILM INSTITUTE

bfi

BFI PUBLISHING

First published in 1994 by the
British Film Institute
21 Stephen Street
London W1P 1PL

The British Film Institute exists to encourage the development of film, television
and video in the United Kingdom, and to promote knowledge, understanding and
enjoyment of the culture of the moving image. Its activities include the National
Film and Television Archive; the National Film Theatre; the Museum of the
Moving Image; the London Film Festival; the production and distribution of film
and video; funding and support for regional activities; Library and Information
Services; Stills, Posters and Design; Research, Publishing and Education; and the
monthly *Sight and Sound* magazine.

British Library Cataloguing-in-Publication Data.
A catalogue record for this book is available from the British Library.

ISBN 0-85170-437-9
      0-85170-438-7 pbk

Cover by Design & Art
Cover still from *Suspicion* (Alfred Hitchcock, 1941)
Typeset by Goodfellow & Egan Ltd, Cambridge
Printed in Great Britain by Page Bros Ltd, Norwich

Remembering Jan Shepherd

1942–1993

*Her energy and enthusiasm for melodrama
fostered a lasting dialogue between theatre and film,
overcoming illness to bring melodrama as
performance alive for us all*

CONTENTS

PART 3　REVISIONS

PART 4　POLITICS

FOREWORD AND ACKNOWLEDGMENTS

Inspired by the exciting convergence of interest in melodrama over the last decade between specialists in theatre studies, art history, music and film, we felt it appropriate in 1992 to explore and extend these convergences through the forum of a first international and interdisciplinary conference on melodrama. That we were able to secure for the conference eighty papers from twelve countries meant that this aspiration was well and truly realised, and our first and immense debt of gratitude must go to all of those who gave papers. They constituted the Melodrama Conference and without their collective contributions this volume would not exist. Confronted with the intricate and complex work of turning such a conference into a book of manageable proportions, we felt it appropriate to select papers which most directly reflected the interdisciplinary and transformational concerns of the Conference manifested in the four keynote papers which head each of the sections of this volume. We are particularly indebted, therefore, to the thirteen colleagues who agreed to undertake the exacting work of transforming their oral presentations into essays for publication.

A further debt of gratitude is owed to the people (primarily but not exclusively BFI staff) who worked so hard to make the conference happen: Nicky North, joint Conference Co-ordinator; Lea Jacobs (University of Wisconsin–Madison, USA) and Tana Wollen who (along with Nicky North and ourselves) made up the organising committee for the event; Alpa Patel and Kathleen Luckey, who held everything together administratively for ten months and, with Jacintha Cusack, Anita Miller and Yvonne Salmon, ensured the smooth running of the event itself.

Central to the Conference and to its pleasures were the three programmes of 'Victorian Nights' – film screenings held at the National Film Theatre. Advice on the structure of these and programme booklet research for them was carried out by former students of a BFI extramural evening class on melodrama: Guy Barefoot, Caroline Dunant, Frank Goodman, John Peregrine, Fere Shahbakhti and Nick Wall. This group also organised seasons of screenings at the National Film Theatre in 1988 and 1990 and thus contributed substantially to a growing public awareness of the pleasures of melodrama.

At the planning stage of the Conference, Colin MacCabe, as Head of BFI Research, approved a travel grant for Christine Gledhill to visit North America to research film and theatre archives.

Finally, our thanks to all those in BFI Publishing who helped prepare the book's publication.

Jacky Bratton, Jim Cook and Christine Gledhill

NOTES ON CONTRIBUTORS
AND EDITORS

Guy Barefoot is a PhD student at the University of East Anglia, working on a thesis provisionally entitled 'Ornament and Crime: Hollywood's "Victorian" Melodramas 1944–50.' He was a member of the Melodrama Research Group which in 1988 planned the seasons of 'Hollywood as Melodrama' at the National Film Theatre and organised the accompanying exhibition 'The Melodramatic Imagination: From Victorian Stage to Hollywood Screen' at the National Theatre, and which in 1990 organised seasons of British Melodrama at the National Film Theatre.

Jacky Bratton is Professor of Theatre and Cultural History at Royal Holloway, University of London. She has published widely in nineteenth-century areas, including most recently articles on clog-dancing and cross-dressing in the music halls, and a book on theatre and the British Empire, *Acts of Supremacy* (Manchester University Press, 1992).

Peter Brooks is Tripp Professor of Humanities and Chairman of the Department of Comparative Literature at Yale University. His publications include *The Novel of Worldliness* (Princeton University Press, 1969); *The Melodramatic Imagination* (Yale University Press, 1976); *Reading for the Plot* (Knopf, 1984); and *Body Work* (Harvard University Press, 1993).

Nick Browne is Professor of Critical Studies in the Department of Film and Television at UCLA. He has edited *The Politics of Representation: Perspectives from Cahiers du Cinéma 1969–72* (British Film Institute/Macmillan, 1990) and *American Television: Economies, Sexualities, Forms* (Gordon & Breach, 1993), and is author of *Film Theory: An Historical and Critical Perspective* (China Film Press, 1993). An earlier version of this essay appears in Nick Browne et al., *Modern Chinese Cinemas: Forms, Identities, Politics* (Cambridge, 1993).

Jim Cook was the co-ordinator of the Melodrama Conference with Nicky North. From 1973 to 1993 he worked in the Education Department of the British Film Institute with a special responsibility for organising and teaching film and television courses for adults.

Caroline Dunant is an art historian, film studies graduate, and author of a novel and verse picture-book for children. She was a member of the Melodrama Research Group which in 1988 planned the seasons of 'Hollywood as Melodrama' at the National Film Theatre and organised the accompanying exhibition 'The Melodramatic Imagination: From Victorian Stage to Hollywood Screen' at the National Theatre, and which in 1990 organised seasons of British Melodrama at the National Film Theatre. She is currently writing *The Guide to Children's Cinema and Video* to be published by Bodley Head in 1994.

Caryl Flinn teaches Cinema Studies at Innis College, University of Toronto. She has published articles on film, feminism, and sound in *Screen, Wide Angle* and *Cinema Journal* among others, and is author of *Strains of Utopia: Gender, Nostalgia, and Hollywood Film Music* (Princeton University Press, 1992).

Jane Gaines is Associate Professor of Literature and English and Director of the Program in Film and Video at Duke University, North Carolina. She recently published *Contested Culture: The Image, the Voice, and the Law* (British Film Institute/University of North Carolina Press, 1991). 'Fire and Desire', her essay in this volume, is part of a longer project entitled *Other Race Desire: Early Cinema and Empire.*

Daniel Gerould is Lucille Lortel Distinguished Professor of Theatre and Comparative Literature, Graduate School, City University of New York. His publications include *Witkacky: Stanislaw Ignacy Witkiewicz as an Imaginative Writer* (University of Washington Press, 1981); *Melodrama* [editor] (New York Literary Forum, 1980); *American Melodrama* (Performing Arts Journal Publications, 1982); *Guillotine: Its Legend and Lore* (Blast Books, 1992); *The Witkiewicz Reader* (Northwestern University Press, 1992).

Christine Gledhill was Editor of Study Materials in the British Film Institute's Education Department and is now Principal Lecturer in Media and Cultural Studies at Staffordshire University. She edited and contributed essays to *Home is Where the Heart Is: Studies in Melodrama and the Women's Film* (British Film Institute, 1987) and *Stardom: Industry of Desire* (Routledge, 1992).

David Grimsted teaches history at the University of Maryland and is the author of *Melodrama Unveiled: American Theater and Culture 1800–1850* (University of California Press, 1987). He is currently completing the first volume of a two-volume study *Beneviolence: Democratic Rioting 1828–1861.*

Tom Gunning teaches Film History and Theory at Northwestern University, Illinois. He is the author of *D. W. Griffith and the Origins of*

American Narrative Film (University of Illinois Press, 1991) and of numerous articles on early film. He is currently working on a book on early cinema and the experience of modernity.

Chuck Kleinhans teaches in the Radio/TV/Film Department at Northwestern University, Illinois. A founding co-editor of *Jump Cut*, he made the video *Postcards from Nicaragua* and recently completed *Continuous Entertainment*, a video anthology of his Super-8mm films. He frequently writes on independent documentary and experimental film and video.

Barbara Klinger is an Associate Professor of Comparative Literature and Film Studies at Indiana University. She has published in *Screen, Wide Angle* and *Cinema Journal*, and is the author of *Melodrama and Meaning: History, Culture and the Films of Douglas Sirk* (Indiana University Press, forthcoming).

Richard Maltby is Senior Lecturer in American Film at the University of Exeter. He has edited *Dreams for Sale: Popular Culture in the Twentieth Century* (Harrap, 1989) and is the author of *Harmless Entertainment: Hollywood and the Ideology of Consensus* (Scarecrow Press, 1983). He is currently completing *Reforming the Movies: Politics, Censorship, and the Institutions of the American Cinema, 1908–1939*, to be published by Oxford University Press, and *Hollywood Cinema: An Introduction*, with Ian Craven, to be published by Basil Blackwell.

Martin Meisel is Brander Matthews Professor of Dramatic Literature at Columbia University and Vice President for Arts and Sciences. His publications include *Shaw and the Nineteenth Century Theater* (Greenwood, 1976) and *Realizations: Narrative, Pictorial, and Theatrical Arts in Nineteenth-Century England* (Princeton University Press, 1983).

Laura Mulvey is Senior Lecturer in Film Studies at the University of East Anglia. She has co-directed six films with Peter Wollen and is the author of *Visual and Other Pleasures*, a volume of essays published by Macmillan in 1989. A book of her essays is to be published shortly by the British Film Institute.

Jane Shattuc is an Assistant Professor of Film at Emerson College, Boston. She has written articles on melodrama, Fassbinder, and postmodern Film. Her book *Television, Tabloids and Tears: Fassbinder and Popular Culture* is forthcoming.

Simon Shepherd is Reader in Drama at Nottingham University. He has written on Renaissance drama, Joe Orton, and seventeenth-century women writers. With Peter Womack he is currently working on a history of English drama from the Middle Ages to the present day.

INTRODUCTION

JACKY BRATTON, JIM COOK AND
CHRISTINE GLEDHILL

This anthology, a distillation from the wide range of papers offered at the Melodrama: Stage Picture Screen Conference, highlights the protean nature of melodrama, its cultural role in mediating socio-political change and its interdisciplinary critique. Together these essays seek to 'catch' melodrama as it shifts between forms, cultures and decades and as it is reconstituted in successive interacting socio-political contexts and critical disciplines. Although a diverse range of concerns are represented, a number of shared or complementary preoccupations emerge in reading across its sections. It is a mutual concern with history and cultural context which brings theatre studies, art history, film studies and musicology into contact. Not least of the gains of this encounter is the recovery of cinema's relation to its melodramatic inheritance, which has opened up new ways of putting questions to mainstream cinema. Yet equally, cinema's status as a twentieth-century medium of mass entertainment in which melodrama comes to reside offers a retrospective view of nineteenth-century melodrama as an agent of modernity. A combination of history and a shared Freudian interest in the language of the body and the psychodynamics of familial relations lead to a re-posing of the issue of personalisation so frequently condemned as a key feature of ideological domination in popular culture. Rather than displacing the political by the personal, melodrama produces the body and the interpersonal domain as the sites in which the socio-political stakes its struggles. The political implications of this shift become clearer in those essays which raise issues of audience or look at the use of melodramatic structures by non-Western or ethnic minority film-makers. In this context, the notions of excess, sensation, spectacle and affect by which melodrama is most commonly characterised become key terms in a debate about how the form engages with and processes the complexity of modernity and the politics of cultural change.

Debates

Peter Brooks's *The Melodramatic Imagination* has been a foundational text in theorising the genre, not only providing a model of 'classic' melodrama based on French theatre from 1790 to 1830, but by making links to the

Freudian narrative of the psyche and building a bridge whereby film could be reconnected to its nineteenth-century precursor. The influence of Brooks's work is felt throughout this anthology but in this section in particular his model is refined and debated. In his paper, which opened the conference, Peter Brooks applies Foucauldian theories of the body to his earlier conception of melodrama. Maintaining that the French Revolution marked a new moment of personal accountability through the body, he argues that 'the hystericised body offers the key emblem' in the convergence of melodrama and psychoanalysis. The performative rhetoric of melodrama – the acting out of moral statements by way of affirming their truth – literalises the new centrality of the body as site of meaning, leading to 'an aesthetics of embodiment'.

Simon Shepherd addresses two aspects of this rhetoric which have given rise to subsequent oversimplification. First, against the assumed simplicity of melodrama's ethical emotions and fantasy solutions, Shepherd argues that melodrama displaces tragedy because it is better suited to express the complexities of modernity. Melodrama's characteristic triangular relationships and high points of suspense construct deliberately problematic patterns which recognise its solutions as attempts to impose order on what is ultimately disorderly. Focusing not on pair-bonded resolutions but on explorations of personal history, identity, violence and the family romance, the plays are structured around a repeated set of oppositions – person and institution, truth and law, feeling and categorisation – which cannot be finally resolved. Secondly, since the plays Shepherd discusses were successes of the English Regency stage, he suggests that their quest for identity and a newly understood place in society manifest a structure of feeling which relates not to the French Revolution but to Reform agitation and English Radicalism.

The issues both of historical context and of melodramatic self-reflectiveness are taken up by Jacky Bratton who, contesting critical orthodoxies, asserts the importance of audience response and of neglected aspects in the writing of English Regency melodramas: their comic characters and their range of verbal languages. The relation between melodramatic comedy and melodramatic excess is often ironic or parodic, a balance, moreover, which stage writers and performers attuned closely to their particular audiences. Sophisticated games with melodramatic style and meaning might be played in both Patent and East End theatres, but with different class meanings. Thus melodrama of the early 19th century responded to the diverse political and class consciousness of its audiences with very varied voices.

Simon Shepherd and Jacky Bratton both challenge the presumed simplifications of melodramatic excess – stressing the reflexibility of many melodramatic strategies – and insisting on the historical specificity of its particular manifestations. Tom Gunning treads similar territory but taking as his focus the work of André de Lorde, the seminal playwright of the Grand Guignol, at the end of the 19th century. From this perspective he seeks to modify Brooks's conception of excess. Brooks, he claims, "'tames' spectacular excess by defining it as 'expressive'" and consequently regards the form as decadent as soon as excess begins to separate from its significant motive, to be pursued as an end in itself. Gunning, on the other hand, argues for a more historically flexible model based on 'a dialectical interaction between moral significance and ... non-cognitive effects, thrills, sensations'. In the mid-19th century 'sensation' becomes a keyword of the popular culture of modernity; in melodrama physical and emotional sensation replace moral cognition as the objective of the pictorial tableau. André de Lorde's plays, far from striving to manifest the moral occult, expose the inadequacy of all modern discourses that pretend to discover a moral universe. Their endings 'display a vertiginous image of order destroyed and discourse rendered meaningless' – a logical consequence of a form which emerged 'from a world in decay' where excess was necessary because the signs of virtue were becoming unrecognisable.

All four essays challenge, refine and extend the insights of *The Melodramatic Imagination*, applying the perspectives of cultural materialism and Foucauldian theories of the body to melodrama beyond Brooks's original boundaries to reveal its place in structures of feeling elsewhere and at other times.

Transformations

While the four essays collected in 'Transformations' are similarly attentive to differing historical moments and cultural contexts, the focus here is less the nature of melodramatic meaning than the diversity of its manifestations and the formal mechanisms which facilitate its transformations across media, historical periods and national cultures. This section opens up the relation of melodrama and modernity, demonstrating the degree to which it becomes the form both to register change and to process change, in particular mediating relations between a lost but problematic past and the present.

Martin Meisel's opening paper demonstrates the flexibility of melodrama's language in an account of its structuring tropes – light and dark; picture and motion; focus and panorama; succession and recurrence – 'scattered chiaroscuro', capable of engaging cognitive and affective response across a range of forms. By examining Dumas's novella *The Corsican Brothers*, along with its subsequent stage and, later, cinematic adaptations, Meisel shows how combinations of these paired features both organise melodrama's conditions of perception (its visuality) and render individual 'realisations' distinct (transformed) through formal and contextual variation. The 1939 film version shows the strain in modernising a nineteenth-century text when it is no longer possible to believe in 'a genuine congruence between reality and its representations' nor in a providential 'coherence in things and events'. On the other hand *noir* detective fiction, exemplified by *Farewell My Lovely*, suggests that the 'more determined will' and 'specialised consciousness' of the private eye is capable of holding together melodrama's 'scattered chiaroscuro', making this genre the 'living heir of nineteenth-century melodrama'.

Caroline Dunant exemplifies Meisel's emphasis on the heightened visuality of melodrama in a case study of the melodramatic in the work of 'Olympian' painters such as Sir Lawrence Alma-Tadema. Her initial focus is on the consonance between the group's project of clarifying a rapidly changing present through the construction of an ideal but 'realistic' past and melodrama's vocation, according to Peter Brooks, for 'uncovering, demonstrating and making operative the essential moral universe in a post-sacral era'. Yet in the appeal they share with melodrama to the popular, the immediate and the sensuously emotional, and in their mass circulation through improved reproduction techniques and popular magazines, these paintings are products of modernity and anticipate their own imminent transformation into the biblical and epic melodramas of cinema's second decade.

This mediation between past and present and transformation across cultures provides the focus of Guy Barefoot's analysis of the way the concepts 'melodrama' and 'Victorian' cross centuries and continents. Pursuing *East Lynne* through a trajectory of 'persistence, rejection and revival' as the immensely popular Victorian novel succeeds equally in its British and American dramatised and filmed versions, Barefoot shows how this trajectory (which includes changing critical evaluations of the text) both sustains the text's longevity and transforms it formally and thematically. *Gas Light*, on the other hand, began as a conscious contribution to contemporary critiques of the Victorian. Consequently, while stimulating through successive theatre and film adaptations a popular interest in 'Victoriana', it differs in the degree to which it rejects or positively engages with the melodramatic or Victorian according to version and country of production. Thus Barefoot brings to light some of the processes by which melodrama as a nineteenth-century form survives and is transformed in different national twentieth-century contexts.

Where Martin Meisel and Guy Barefoot pursue melodrama from Europe to America, the final essay in this section looks at the reverse transatlantic movement of melodrama's return from Hollywood to Europe. In examining the influence of Douglas Sirk on the New German Cinema director Rainer Werner Fassbinder, Caryl Flinn's specific focus is on transformations taking place at the level of music. Music in melodrama is an often 'moving' but elusive component of melodramatic effect. By drawing on recent film theory's arguments about melodramatic excess, Caryl Flinn proposes that music in Hollywood melodrama, like other non-verbal signs, stands in for language's inadequacies. By contrast, she argues that music in New German Cinema is self-reflective, drawing attention to its sources of citation rather than claiming unmediated expression. Linking such arguments to historical determinations, Flinn suggests that, rather than the notion of hysterical excess, Freud's concept of melancholia better explains the difficult relation of such music to its past sources, a relation which, she argues, is consonant with the social and cultural context of the 70s when film-makers like Fassbinder strove to come to terms with history.

Revisions
Through their considerations of discrete transformations of 'melodrama' across forms and histories, the essays in 'Transformations' indicate the productivity of what Ben Singer has described as the term's 'semantic sprawl'. 'Revisions' is concerned with the impact of the widening of his-

tory and theory suggested by this 'sprawl' on film theory's initially more constricted use of the term. As Laura Mulvey's opening piece suggests, melodrama entered film studies in the 70s to serve particular theoretical needs. Since then a new concern with history and production context has not only changed the driving questions of the discipline but permitted acknowledgement of cinema's inheritance from other aesthetic forms. In particular the notion of 'excess', understood as a mode of distanciation and ideological critique practised by an intelligentsia, is relocated in the production and reception contexts of popular culture. In different ways these essays all ask the question posed by Jane Shattuc: 'what happens if we read melodramas "straight" – the way they were intended to be read?'

In reviewing the entry of melodrama into film theory, Laura Mulvey suggests that, whereas the 'melodramatic' nature of Hollywood had been legitimated as authorial *mise en scène*, or taken up in structuralist readings of the western and gangster genres as mythic treatments of the public (and male) sphere of history, the domestic melodrama which focuses on the private space of home and female concerns depended on feminist theory and psychoanalysis for its decipherment. Crucial was the concept of displacement which read the excesses of *mise en scène* as symptoms of irreconcilable contradictions. Mulvey, however, challenges the critical restriction of melodramatic psychodynamics to the private sphere. Drawing on Freud, and citing the long history of melodrama, she suggests that its popular 'narrative structures, psychic scenarios and character figurations' constitute a pool of 'mnemic symbols' which through repetition become social, serving collective fantasies that register social and political contradictions. Thus a seemingly ahistorical film like *Magnificent Obsession* enables '"ordinary people", us, to stop and wonder or weep, desire or shudder, momentarily touch[ed by] "unspeakable" but shared psychic structures' through which the political contradictions of 50s America reached its audience.

In challenging authorial conceptions of excess through a focus on industrial marketing categories, Barbara Klinger indirectly suggests how collective fantasies are reprocessed and circulated in popular culture. Against academic genre classification she poses the industrially generated, historically specific 'local' genre which cuts across and reorganises the field of existing genres, categorising films for popular consumption. Thus the 'adult film' of the 50s draws the domestic melodrama and other genres into a new alignment, resemanticising 'sensation' for a film industry trying to cash in on the period's contradictory mixture of sexual liberalisation and repression in response to changing conditions of production and reception. While claiming 'adult' status, excess as sensation serves both male and female fantasy, combining increased female sexual display for a male spectator with the confessional revelation of romantic and psycho-sexual problems aimed at female audiences.

Jane Shattuc explicitly positions herself with those audiences and against the academy's notion of excess as ironic distance from a popular involvement identified as false consciousness. The real object of distanciation, she suggests, is emotion. The interaction of melodramatic emotion and popular consciousness in the case of *The Color Purple* becomes dou-

bly contentious in the adaptation of a black feminist novel by the white
male film industry. Citing the contradictory reactions of black men and
women and white feminists and drawing on arguments by Fredrick
Jameson and Patrocinio Schweickart, Shattuc proposes that all melodramas produce a double hermeneutic: a positive one which draws on the
emotional power of authentic liberatory aspirations ('Celie's narrative as a
metaphor for feminine transcendence of patriarchal control'); and a negative one which recuperates the Utopian impulse in complicity with an
oppressive ideology (the 'scapegoating of the black male'). The political
importance of tears, she argues, lies not simply in the fact of recuperation
but in ideology's necessary staging of the Utopian aspiration to which it
attempts to provide an answer. It is, therefore, important for feminists to
read the 'reason of emotion' in order not to throw out the aspiration with
the ideology.

Chuck Kleinhans raises similar questions when he asks why in the 80s
an independent, UCLA-trained African-American film-maker should
choose from the range of aesthetic modes now possible within the post-
modern aesthetic field to make *God Bless Their Little Hearts* as a realist
domestic melodrama. In exploring this question Kleinhans challenges
excess not only for its imputed value as a distancing device but as an anti-
realist strategy. If the domestic melodrama's integral relationship with
realism makes its particular manifestations eminently contingent and
hence quickly outmoded, this contingency nevertheless finds its flash-
points in 'social commonplaces' and its emotional affects in a 'profound
psychological resonance in the audience of its time'. The heuristic value
of this recognition, Kleinhans suggests, requires a re-evaluation of the
intersection within the popular forms of Western capitalism of the familial
and the social.

This proposition is illuminated by Nick Browne's concluding examination of how the category of melodrama might be applied in post-liberation
Chinese cinema. For both Western and non-Western melodrama, the
melodramatic is equated with effect, which in turn implies a source of
emotion in or around the person. The different understanding of the person in Western and Chinese cultures, however, produces quite different
articulations of melodramatic conflict: whereas in Western melodrama the
social can be accessed only through the personal, in Chinese culture the
person is a function of the social, a point in a network of 'conventions,
social relations, transactions within the group'. Thus, if the choice of
domestic melodrama in *Bless Their Little Hearts* is in part due to the fact
that familial relationships in capitalism constitute one of the few authentic
expressions of the social, in *Hibiscus Town* the social order becomes the
oppressor of those who transgress the 'unauthorised assertion of individual choice'. Here we have not domestic but political melodrama, centring
not on familial crisis but on a trial of the Cultural Revolution which
exposes the victimised relation of the personal to the social.

Politics

The cultural materialist concerns of this anthology lead in this final section to an explicit confrontation between melodrama and politics in terms

6

of both the politics of melodrama and the melodrama of politics. The conventional conception of melodrama is of a bourgeois and quietist form but Daniel Gerould, in an exploration of the symbiotic relation of melodrama and revolution in France and the USSR, brings to light a subgenre of melodrama which demonstrates its capacity to promote social change. While the plays by Pixérécourt which founded the genre functioned to recuperate the French Revolution in the interests of bourgeois hegemony, later playwrights used melodrama's confrontations between the dispossessed and the powerful to put the people on stage in re-enactments of the betrayed Revolution as mass spectacles which sent threatening signals to the authorities. Indeed, nineteenth-century revolutionary struggles led to the overspill of theatre into what Gerould calls 'paratheatrical activities' whereby political agitation and education took on melodramatic theatrical forms. Such practices were consciously embraced as political and aesthetic choices in the post-Revolutionary USSR by both theatrical and film practitioners, breaking down the distinction between politics and theatre still further. Gerould sees in the potent metaphor of the orphan a reason why Soviet practitioners preferred the failed proletarian Commune of 1871 to the successful bourgeois Revolution of 1789, for it provided a melodramatic revolutionary scenario that could support a teleological happy end in the 'last-minute recognition that the triumphant Russian Revolution of 1917 is the long-lost child of the Commune'.

The kinship between melodrama and politics, however, could be exploited to reactionary ends, as David Grimsted shows in a study of the chronicling of their actions by mid-nineteenth-century American vigilantes. Comparing a representative stage melodrama and chronicle, Grimsted notes that the myth of Eden – fall, retribution and redemption – animates both, but that 'the comic middle' of stage melodrama is absent from vigilante writing, thus eliminating the irony that would reveal the self-deception of 'the wordy moralism of melodramatic rhetoric'. Analysing the 'shady politics and patent racism' of another example, Grimsted suggests that vigilante writing reverses melodrama's implicitly Marxist view of class and hierarchy, championing wealth and property against the 'scum' and 'rabble' that make up the majority. The vigilante chronicle, therefore, uses the powerful formulas of melodrama to justify 'a complacent equation of social position with moral worth' which is both seductive and damaging to American political life.

Richard Maltby's essay on the relations between progressive reform and the early film industry focuses on the emergence of a new popular form as itself subject to a melodrama of cultural and political struggle. Pointing to the repression involved in nineteenth-century American melodrama's figuration of class and racial conflict in terms of rape, whereby woman is used both to withstand the sexual assault of depraved masculinity and to deny her own sexuality, Maltby shows how, with capitalism's increasing commodification of leisure and desire, the female image shifts from being a restraint on desire to its stimulant. New entertainments involving female display – dance halls, cabarets, music halls and cinema – threatened to release sexual pleasure from its geographic and private confines in the red light districts. The resulting 'white slavery panic' of the early 20th century explained prostitution as an assault on 'native-born agrarian purity' by the 'foreign urban panderer'. Cinema, in many cases developed by foreigners, found itself caught up in a politically motivated melodrama, in which it was wilfully 'misrecognised' as panderer rather than reformer. Consequently, it fought for its place in bourgeois society by developing a moralised narrative structure, paradoxically restaging in films such as *Traffic in Souls* the very scenario of white slavery which had fuelled the panic in the first place.

Given early melodrama's reactionary treatment of race, Jane Gaines's concluding essay on the African–American Oscar Micheaux's *Within Our Gates* returns to the politics of the form, resituating the film within the scandal of its reception which focused on one brief lynching sequence. Combining textual analysis and a culturalist perspective, she argues that Micheaux's particular use of cross-cutting changes the meaning of the lynching from a brutal degradation to the rhetorical encouragement of 'righteous indignation in the black spectator'. Reversing the criticism that Micheaux's work displays a politically reactionary 'double consciousness', she argues that his 'maverick style' could produce for his disenfranchised audience meanings which are radically different from those available to a white middle-class audience. Trapped inside history and a bourgeois black consciousness as he inevitably was, Micheaux's achievement in using the melodramatic mode to transform and make strange dominant forms is historically and culturally the only possible negotiation of an oppressive hegemonic structure that he could have made.

This anthology suggests, then, through its historical, formal and cultural analyses, melodrama's key role in modernity as a mediator of social and political change through the diverse and personalised forms of popular culture. A growing understanding of this role is emerging from the meeting of disciplines and cultural histories around the topic of melodrama, and is challenged by perspectives brought to bear from non-Western or ethnic minority cultures. At the conference itself the need was signalled for a more determined widening of horizons and proactive engagement with the different modes of the melodramatic wherever it works through the engagement with modernity of decolonialising cultures. It is to be hoped that this volume will act as a stepping-stone in this project.

PART 1
DEBATES

MELODRAMA, BODY, REVOLUTION

PETER BROOKS

Encountering this audience of experts in film, I find myself thinking about other resonant encounters set up by the occasion. There is, for instance, the encounter of Henry James with Adolphe Dennery's melodrama, *Les Deux Orphelines*, which he reviewed in its New York production in 1875 and which he found a bad rendering of the original, but none the less 'worth seeing simply for the sake of sitting in one's place and feeling the quality of a couple of good old-fashioned *coups de théâtre* as your French playwright who really knows his business manages them'.[1] Then there is Griffith's encounter with the French Revolution, which curiously is not part of Dennery's play, set at an unspecified date in *ancien régime* France (with some indications that revolution must be in the offing). In choosing to set *Orphans of the Storm* at the outbreak of the Revolution, Griffith as it were pays unconscious tribute to the moment of origin of the imaginative mode he so effectively exploits, making the 'storm' a central metaphor not only of a crucible of modern history (and with repeated references, in the titles, to its unfortunate replay in the Bolshevik Revolution) but also of an enabling condition of modern representation. The encounter of silent cinema with melodrama was perhaps a simple inevitability, but Griffith inscribes it, by way of the Revolution, in his text. Finally, in the intersections of Griffith's cinematic style, melodrama, the Revolution, we have a key encounter of the body with meaning, giving us a key representation of a modern aesthetic of meaning embodied.

The idea I want to explore here is something like this: silent cinema revives a certain semiotics of the body which first made its appearance in melodrama – or proto-melodrama, since the name was not then coined – at the moment of the French Revolution, which itself calls into being a new valorisation of and attention to meanings inscribed on the individual body. The first part of my sentence may be a simple truism: silent cinema must use the body in expressionistic ways, as the vehicle of meanings that cannot otherwise be conveyed. And it is by now well known that silent cinema in general, and Griffith in particular, reaches out to melodrama for the stylistic features that allow meanings to be conveyed without words.[2] But what may still need exploration is the way in which the aes-

11

thetics of mute expression is related to a more general aesthetics and politics of bodiliness, and what these have to do with the Revolutionary moment, with the 'storm' into which Griffith plunges Henriette and Louise. Let me, then, give some attention to the storm, and its practices of the body, before coming to terms with Griffith.

The work of Norbert Elias (in *The Civilizing Process*) and Michel Foucault (especially *Discipline and Punish*), however different in premises, converges in the sense that the modern body is subject to increased control and discipline: from table manners to prison regimes, from the public covering of bodily parts to the new architecture of domestic privacy, modernity brings a new sense of the limitations imposed upon the uses of the body.[3] The French Revolution marks a symbolic, and a real, nexus for a new controlled and self-controlled autonomous body, since the person – that relatively new concept, so much indebted to Rousseau, the individual, which could only, finally, be identified by way of the individual body – was held accountable in new ways. As historian Dorinda Outram has argued, this new autonomous, disciplined, stoic body was 'of vital importance to its users and its audience at a time when the first use in French history of state terror on a mass scale was demonstrating how, on the contrary, in reality the body was frail, vulnerable, ultimately disposable'.[4] Under the Revolutionary regime, the individual had to account for his body, take responsibility for it, in starkly changed conditions. Consider in this context the conclusion of the Revolutionary leader Saint-Just's famous *Rapport sur les suspects incarcérés* of 1794, which ends with the decree: 'The Committee of General Security is invested with the power to liberate patriots in prison. Any person who asks to be freed will give an account of his conduct since 1 May 1789.'[5] This summons to individual responsibility for one's actions, the imperative of self-surveillance, as it were, is a corollary of the accountability of individuals to the power of the state, of the state's claim over persons. The result of this claim was, notoriously, what Simon Schama has described as 'the body count' of the Reign of Terror: one pays for the failure to account fully for one's actions with one's body.[6]

Jacobin oratory, for all its abstraction, frequently implicates the body in this manner. Saint-Just again, in his 'Report on the Necessity to Declare Revolutionary Government until the time of Peace':

> There is no prosperity to be hoped for so long as the last enemy of liberty shall breathe. You have to punish not only the traitors, but even those who are indifferent; you have to punish whoever is passive within the Republic and does nothing for her: for, from the time that the people manifested its will, everything that is opposed to it is outside sovereignty; everything that is outside sovereignty is enemy.[7]

A process of demarcation is under way here, one that results in making any non-adherent to Jacobin politics potentially dispensable, liable to elimination. Saint-Just further declares: 'What constitutes a Republic is the total destruction of everything opposed to it' (p. 192). Bodies are on the line, and rhetoric receives an immediate translation into action exercised

12

on the body. As Foucault writes, speaking of penologists of the Revolutionary era, 'As soon as the crime has been committed, without loss of time, punishment will follow, putting into act the discourse of law and showing that the legal Code links not only ideas, but also realities.'[8] The guillotine represents an abstract notion of judgment embodied in an exemplary machine for the punishment of bodies.

This insistence on bodiliness is strikingly in evidence in one of the more bizarre and macabre episodes of the Revolution, the disinterment of the bodies of the kings of France from the Abbey of St Denis. In the process of extirpating the criminal idea of monarchy, the Revolution discovered that it needed to get rid of what the journal *Les Révolutions de Paris* called the 'impure remains' and the 'vile bones' of past monarchs.[9] During October 1793, the desacralisation of kings reached its apogee. The bodies of those mythic figures from the past, including the monarch dear to every French heart, Henri IV, and including the Sun King, Louis XIV, were exhumed and thrown into quicklime in the common pit – the fate also of Louis XVI after his execution in January of the same year. Even Saint Louis ended up in this grave of commoners. It may be a strange comment on the enduring charisma of the anointed body of the king that, even inanimate, it had to be destroyed, effaced, reduced to nothingness. Regicide was somehow incomplete until the substantial body left behind at the passing of kings was wholly eliminated from the new regime of virtue. The positive gesture complementary to this act of eradication was, of course, the transport to the Panthéon of the bodily remains of those intellectual precursors of Revolution: Voltaire in July 1791 (shortly after the king's attempted flight ended at Varennes) and Rousseau, belatedly, in October 1794, following the demise of the Jacobin Republic for which later historians so often held him responsible.

October 1793 also saw the execution of Marie-Antoinette, following a trial in which her crimes against the Republic were made to appear inextricably linked to her sexual immorality. Accused of insatiable 'uterine furores', of liaisons with both men and women, the *Autrichienne*'s alleged conspiracies with the enemy were matched by her supposed attempts to debauch and ruin the Bourbon males, not only her husband but also her son, the Dauphin. The *enragé* Hébert managed to introduce into the prosecution the claim that she initiated the Dauphin into incestuous games and masturbation, thus seriously damaging his health. In the generalised need to read crimes as bodily, where women were on trial there seemed to be a specific need to place criminality squarely on their sexuality. They were aristocrats, thus libertines – both Agrippina and Messalina, in the classic rhetorical accusation – thus lacking in the modesty and fidelity characteristic of good *petite bourgeoise sans-culotte* wives, thus out of their place, thus driven by an ungoverned ambition finally attributable to an ungovernable sexuality. Much excellent recent work on women in the Revolution (by Lynn Hunt, Joan Landes, Sarah Maza, Dorinda Outram, for example) has made us aware of the peculiarly relentless exclusion of women from the radical renovation that ought logically to have furthered their liberation. The Republic of Virtue did not conceive that women should occupy public space; female virtue was domestic, private, unas-

13

suming. As Dorinda Outram writes: 'The same arena which created public man made woman into *fille publique*.'[10] It was October 1793 that also
saw the defeat of revolutionary radical feminism, as the feminists were
beaten, literally, by the proletarian *poissardes*, and the Convention went
on, early in November, to order the closure of the women's revolutionary
clubs. Mme Roland went to the guillotine and, shortly before her, Olympe
de Gouges, the author of *Les Droits de la femme et de la citoyenne* (1791),
as well as the anti-conventual play *Le Couvent, ou les voeux forcés* (1790).
As Chantal Thomas has noted, Marie-Antoinette, Olympe de Gouges and
Mme Roland were grouped together by the *Moniteur Universel* as examples of unnatural women:

> Marie-Antoinette … was a bad mother, a debauched wife, and she died
> under the curses of those she wanted to destroy. . . . Olympe de
> Gouges, born with an exalted imagination, took her delirium for an
> inspiration of nature. . . . The Roland woman, a fine mind for great
> plans, a philosopher on notepaper, the queen of a moment … was a
> monster however you look at her. . . . Even though she was a mother,
> she had sacrificed nature by trying to raise herself above it; the desire
> to be learned led her to forget the virtues of her sex.[11]

Political women, scribbling women, debauched women: they all come
together as examples of 'the sex' out of control, needing the ultimate correction in order to conform to what Saint-Just calls the '*mâle énergie*' of
the Republic.

Even more than these three women, the danger of the sex in politics
was represented, as Chantal Thomas also has shown, by Charlotte
Corday. Stabbing Marat in his bathtub brought clearly into the symbolic
arena the hand-to-hand combat of denatured female aristocrats – indulgents, federalists – and male friends of the people. For her judges, she
was simply a 'monster' in female guise, something like an example of
demonic possession, to which women traditionally were most prone. In
the subsequent cult of Marat, Charlotte Corday is present only in that
gash in Marat's breast, a kind of displaced representation of her woman's
sexe: her sex as wound on the martyred man. David's famous painting
says it all: the ecstatic face of the martyr, the drops of blood on the
immaculate sheet, the quill pen still grasped next to the kitchen knife
fallen on the floor, the bathwater become a pool of blood – all these
elements suggest the intrusion of an ungoverned female sexuality on a
life dedicated to the higher cause. The male body has been made to pay
for the primal drives of the woman's body. At the same time, Marat's
apotheosised body has gained a realm to which the woman's body has
no access.

It is through David's painting that Charlotte Corday's letter, written in
order to win an audience with the great man, has been immortalised. We
can still decipher it today: '*Il suffit que je sois bien malheureuse pour avoir
droit à votre bienveillance*' ('The simple fact of my misfortune is my claim
to your benevolence'). The letter makes of the Friend of the People a victim of his very benevolence, here ignobly practised upon by a consum-

mate hypocrite. The letter is all the more perfidious in that its language of Rousseauian sensibility belongs to the repertoire of the good guys, not the villains. It is in fact a sentence typical of those spoken by the virtuous characters in melodrama – the genre that had not yet been so christened in 1793, but which had already seen its proto-examples on the stages of Paris: Boutet de Monvel's *Les Victimes cloîtrées* of 1791 is often considered the first melodrama.

October 1793 saw the staging of the representative melodrama of the Terror, Sylvain Maréchal's *Le Jugement dernier des rois*, which opened to great acclaim at the Théâtre de la République (formerly the Théâtre-Français) two days after the execution of Marie-Antoinette. 'There is a fit spectacle for republican eyes,' gloated Hébert in *Le Père Duchesne*.[12] The Comité de Salut Public ordered 3000 copies of the printed text, and the Ministry of War then signed up for 6000, to send to troops at the front in order to kindle their republican zeal. But the best measure of the success of the play may be the fact that the Comité de Salut Public, at a moment when gunpowder was one of the most precious commodities in France, granted the petition of the Théâtre de la République for 'twenty pounds of saltpetre and twenty pounds of powder' needed to produce the volcanic eruption that ends the play, and kills off all the monarchs of Europe – the 'crowned villains' – that it has assembled on a desert island.

Jacques-Louis David's *Marat assassiné*.
Courtesy of Institut Royal du Patrimoine Artistique.

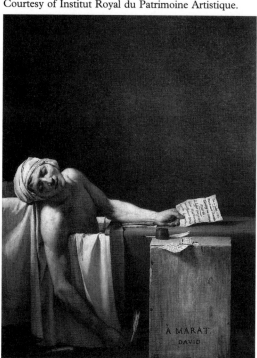

Le Jugement dernier des rois, a 'Prophecy in One Act', envisions a Europe in which the *sans-culottes* of all the nations have risen up against their monarchs, deposed them, and brought them, under the watchful eye of an international *sans-culotte* police force, to a desert island, where they find a virtuous old Frenchman, who was cast away on the island because he dared to protest against the abduction of his virginal daughter by royal courtiers. He lives in a hut set against a boulder, on which he has inscribed the motto: 'Better to have as neighbour/A volcano than a king./ Liberty ... Equality.' The castaway has made friends with the savages who paddle over in canoes from a neighbouring island, who are naturally noble and, once instructed by the castaway (acting on the example of Rousseau's *vicaire savoyard*) come to join him in worship of the sunrise. The *sans-culottes* lead in the deposed monarchs one by one: George III of England, Francis II of the Habsburg Empire, Frederick-William II of Prussia, Ferdinand of Naples, Vittorio-Amedeo III of Savoy, Charles IV of Spain, Stanislas-Augustus of Poland, Catherine, Empress of All the Russias, plus the Pope. Predictably, they fall into monarchical – that is to say, the worst possible – behaviour. George tries to be released on the grounds of his insanity; Charles of Spain implores the Pope to solve their difficulties by performing a miracle; Catherine tries to lure Stanislas into an amorous tryst in a cave. They fall to squabbling over a crust of bread, and the stage is littered with broken sceptres and crushed crowns. Their dissension is ended by the eruption of the volcano, and they descend in flames into the open trap of the theatre.

Maréchal's play, in any sober view, is pretty silly stuff, but it is animated by Jacobin rhetoric of both sensibility and ferocity, virtue and terror, in a theatrical form that demonstrates why melodrama was the artistic form created by the Revolution – perhaps its only enduring cultural creation. It indeed suggests that saying that melodrama was the artistic genre of the Revolution is nearly a truism, since revolutionary public speech itself, as my examples from Saint-Just suggested, is already melodramatic. Charles Nodier would later claim that 'Melodrama was the morality of the Revolution,' by which he meant that it is inherently a democratic form, in which the humble of the earth stand up to overbearing tyrants and express home truths, about the value of the good heart, the sanctity of the domestic hearth, the essential moral equality of all and the fraternity of the virtuous, and win through to see villainy punished and virtue rewarded, in spectacular fashion, in the last act.[13] Refining Nodier's words, we might say that melodrama is the genre, and the speech, of revolutionary moralism: the way it states, enacts, and imposes its moral messages, in clear, unambiguous words and signs.

Subtlety is not the mode of *Le Jugement dernier des rois*, nor of any other melodrama. Its world is the world-turned-upside-down of carnival. The kings are in chains, the *sans-culottes* reign supreme, handing down sentences both just and inflexible, and stated with all the high moral sententiousness of melodrama. There are all the sonorous clichés of Jacobin rhetoric, both the denunciations of *ancient régime* rulers for sexual immorality as well as tyranny – 'Was there ever a nation that at the same time had a king and had decency?' asks the leader of the *sans-culottes* –

and the fulsome praise for the domestic as well as civic virtues of the *sans-culottes*, 'who earn their bread by the sweat of their brow, who love work, who are good sons, good fathers, good husbands, good friends, good neighbours, but who are jealous of their rights as they are jealous of their duties'.[14] As in all melodrama, people are characterised in unambiguous epithets: 'venerable old man!' 'brave *sans-culottes!*' 'crowned monsters!'. Home truths are emphatically announced: 'these savages are our elders in liberty: for they have never had a king. Born free, they live and die as they were born.'

Like the oratory of the Convention, the rhetoric of the play – indeed, the play itself – is performative, seeking by the power of an ever more violent word to impose the Jacobin republic on a recalcitrant reality. *Le Jugement dernier des rois* in effect says: 'Be it enacted that there are no more kings.' But between that rhetorical moment, the fictive moment of the play itself, and its realisation stand all the foreign armies and the internal traitors, the hoarders, the federalists, the indulgents, and so on. As the rhetoric of denunciation at the revolutionary tribunals needed not merely to inculpate but to destroy, to create the rationale for elimination, so here, once all the monarchs have been lined up on stage, the leader of the *sans-culottes* draws up his bill of particulars that will lead to their bodily elimination:

It's for the service of this handful of cowardly brigands, it's for the whim of these crowned villains, that the blood of a million, of two million men, the worst of whom was worth more than all of them, was spilled over every inch of the continent, and beyond the seas. It's in the name or by the order of this score of wild beasts that entire provinces have been devastated, populous cities changed into piles of ashes and corpses, innumerable families raped, stripped bare, reduced to famine. … Here they are, these butchers of men in time of war, these corruptors of the human species in time of peace. . . . Nature, hasten to finish the work of the *sans-culottes*, breathe your fire-breath on this refuse of society, and plunge kings forever into that nothingness from which they never should have emerged.

If in the world outside the stage the performative is enacted by the guillotine, the purgation of those who cannot understand that there is no middle ground between virtue and terror, on-stage 'Nature' is under the command of rhetoric, and the volcano promptly erupts to destroy the kings, consuming their very bodies.

We are, I think, forcibly impressed again and again by the 'bodiliness' of revolutionary language and representation, the need to conceive the revolutionary struggle in both a practice and a language which hold the body ultimately responsible, its position within the scheme of things the necessary measure of success or failure. One can hence see in the revolutionary moment the origins of what we might call an aesthetics of embodiment, where the most important meanings have to be inscribed on and with the body. This is, I would argue, a relatively new phenomenon in the history of literature, one that in many ways finds its precursor in the very man so often held responsible for the Revolution, Rousseau, who in his *Confessions* gives a dramatically new role to the body (his own body) as a prime determinant of his life's meanings, and the way the narrative of that life has to be constructed: as, for instance, in the marking of his body in his childhood punishment at the hands of Mlle Lambercier, which, he tells us in a passage which seemed particularly prescient of Freud, determined his sexual orientation and even his character for the rest of his days. This is not to argue that the body is unimportant in literature before the late 18th century: many examples come to mind, from the Greeks onwards. Certainly in *ancien régime* France the body, be it the tortured body of the criminal or the sacred body of the king, is very much a part of everyday life and symbolism. But the *ancien régime* body belongs to a traditional system, a product of both Christian and popular cultures, that is taken for granted. It is when this traditional system is evacuated of meaning by the Revolution that a new aesthetics of embodiment becomes necessary. The loss of a system of assigned meanings is followed by one where meanings must be achieved, must be the product of an active semiotic process in which the body is newly emblematised with meaning. The body in early Romantic literature, and thereafter, assumes a new centrality as a site of meaning; during the Revolution, in the popular genre of melodrama, we have a kind of literalistic realisation of this new importance of the body as the site of signification.

The melodramatic body is a body seized by meaning. Since melodrama's simple, unadulterated messages must be made absolutely clear, visually present, to the audience, bodies of victims and villains must unambiguously signify their status. The bodies of the virtuous victims are typically subjected to physical restraint. Boutet de Monvel's *Les Victimes cloîtrées* offers a final act in which the heroine and the hero are confined in the deepest cells of a convent and a monastery respectively, in representation of the evil power of the monks who act at the behest of the aristocrats. They will be liberated by a republican mayor, draped in his tricolour sash, in a clear dramatic gesture of freeing the body from oppression. One has a similar use of sequestration in the *in pace* of a convent in the unfortunate Olympe de Gouges's drama *Le Couvent, ou les voeux forcés*, and there are numerous other examples. The body sequestered, enchained, unable to assert its innocence and its right to freedom, becomes a dominant element of melodrama that endures long after the Revolution, that indeed appears consubstantial with the genre. Guilbert de Pixérécourt, the first undisputed master of the genre, returns again and again to the situation in such plays as *Le Château des Appenins*, *Les Mines de Pologne*, *La Forteresse du Danube*, *Latude, ou trente-cinq ans de captivité*: the titles alone suggest the nightmarish Gothic spaces in which the virtuous are confined. Furthermore, none of these melodramas can reach its denouement until the virtuous bodies have been freed, and explicitly recognised as bearing the sign of innocence. This sign is often, notoriously, inscribed on the body itself, in the form of a birthmark or other stigmata, or an emblem worn on the body since childhood: marks and emblems that eventually permit the public recognition of the virtuous identity. *La croix de ma mère*, the token that eventually establishes identity

18

(as with Louise's locket in *Orphans of the Storm*), indeed has become proverbial as the sign of the melodramatic recognition scene. The final act of melodrama will frequently stage a trial scene, as in some revisionary version of the revolutionary tribunal, in which the character of innocence and virtue is publicly recognised through its signs, and publicly celebrated and rewarded, while the villain is bodily expelled from the social realm: driven out, branded as evil, relegated to a space off-stage and outside the civilised world.

Melodrama constantly reminds us of the psychoanalytic concept of 'acting out': the use of the body itself, its actions, gestures, its sites of irritation and excitation, to represent meanings that might otherwise be unavailable to representation because they are somehow under the bar of repression. Melodrama refuses repression or, rather, repeatedly strives towards moments where repression is broken through, to the physical and verbal staging of the essential: moments where repressed content returns as recognition, of the deepest relations of life, as in the celebrated *voix du sang* ('You! my father!'), and of moral identities ('So you are the author of all my wrongs!'). It is, of course, in the logic of melodramatic acting out that the body itself must pay the stakes of the drama: the body of the villain is publicly branded with its identity, exposed in a formal judgment scene, then, if not put to death in hand-to-hand combat, driven from the stage and banished from human society; while the body of persecuted virtue is at first expressionistically distorted, as in a hysterical conversion, then is rewarded, fêted, married, and emblazoned with all the signs of the public recognition of its nature.

It is in the context of melodrama's constant recourse to acting out, to the body as the most important signifier of meanings, that we can understand the genre's frequent recourse to moments of pantomime, which are not simply decorative, which in fact often convey crucial messages. *Le Jugement dernier des rois*, for instance, has that apparently somewhat superfluous group of noble savages with whom the Europeans can communicate only in gestures – but without misunderstandings, since 'the heart's the heart in all countries'. Their presence attaches the play firmly to the origins of melodrama in pantomime. They offer a set of visual messages, pure signs that cannot lie, the undissimulated speech of the body. In an important moment of the play, these savages instinctively express their horror and loathing for the kings of Europe in bodily language, representing before our eyes the right, unprejudiced, non-verbal, visible reaction to the fact of tyranny. And as the genre develops, one finds many more highly elaborated examples of the mute role, which is often the bearer of the most sublime messages in the play. I have elsewhere discussed the instance of the mute Eloi, in Pixérécourt's *Le Chien de Montargis*, who faces the excruciating experience of standing trial for a crime he did not commit while unable to defend himself verbally. His gestures and bodily postures constantly evoke a realm of higher law and truer judgment in which he will be vindicated. Much late eighteenth-century reflection on the nature of language and its origins tends to the view that gesture is the first and ultimately the most passionate form of communication, that which comes to the fore when the code of verbal

Orphans of the Storm. Courtesy of The Museum
of Modern Art/Film Stills Archive.

language lapses into inadequacy. As Marmontel put it, 'It is especially for
the most impassioned moments of the soul that pantomime is necessary.'[15]
Only the body can speak for the soul at those moments.

Which brings me back to Griffith, and his elaboration of an expressionistic aesthetics of the body within a thematics of the French
Revolution, as if in intuitive understanding that here lies the inception of
the imaginative mode and its expressive repertory that he was so successfully to exploit. Griffith's cinema is indeed technically similar to that bas-
tard form that precedes and prepares melodrama, *pantomime dialoguée*, in
that the intertitles offer a skeletal structure of verbal meanings which the
film enacts and embodies. The intertitles are quite like those banners and
placards that are often presented in *pantomime dialoguée*, the display of the
semantics of a situation, which often simply doubles the message the
audience can deduce from the mute action itself. Henry James, I mentioned, singles out two *coups de théâtre* in Dennery's play as especially
worthy of note. Both are preserved in Griffith's film. One is the moment
when Pierre finally goes into revolt against Jacques, with the words: 'As
you say yourself, we come of a race that kills!' This needs intertitling,
since it is not semanticisable through gesture alone – though what is none
the less most memorable in the scene is Pierre's expression of manic joy

20

and defiance, and his bodily movement of self-assertion, his casting off of years of subjection.

The other *coup de théâtre* noted by James needs no words at all. It is the moment when Henriette in her apartment recognises the voice of Louise, singing in the street. In *Orphans of the Storm*, this develops as a major sequence. As Henriette converses with the Countess, Louise appears in a long view, at the very end of the street, groping her way forward, forcing herself to sing under La Frochard's command. Henriette's face meanwhile begins to register recognition, almost as if preconsciously. Then Henriette begins to tremble, her whole person seized with the drama of discovery. The scene then unfolds in the mode of panic action, as Henriette leans from the window, with gestures of yearning, hope, desperate seeking. The spectator has the impression that she may precipitate herself bodily into the street, while in the street the blind Louise casts about for the source of the voice calling to her.

It is a moment when the bodies behave nearly hysterically, if by hysteria we understand a condition of bodily writing, a condition in which the repressed affect is represented on the body. Indeed, Griffith's cinema is always on the verge of hysteria, and necessarily so, since hysteria gives us the maximal conversion of psychic affect into somatic meaning – meaning enacted on the body itself. The psychic overload, the hyperbole of the moment, is then confirmed by the arrival of the soldiers to arrest

Orphans of the Storm. Courtesy of The Museum of Modern Art/Film Stills Archive.

Henriette and throw her into prison, by means of the *lettre de cachet* obtained by the Count, her suitor's father. This serves, of course, only to increase and justify an aesthetics of hysteria, since there can be no discharge of the overwhelming affect, as Henriette and Louise are again separated – and also the recognition which is on the verge of taking place between the Countess and Louise is again delayed.

I argued in *The Melodramatic Imagination* that there is a convergence in the concerns of melodrama and of psychoanalysis – and, indeed, that psychoanalysis is a kind of modern melodrama, conceiving psychic conflict in melodramatic terms and acting out the recognition of the repressed, often with and on the body. Now I have become convinced that the hystericised body offers a key emblem of that convergence, since it is a body pre-eminently invested with meaning, a body become the place for the inscription of highly emotional messages that cannot be written elsewhere, and cannot be articulated verbally. Hysteria offers a problem in representation; Freud's task, from the *Studies on Hysteria* onwards, is learning to read the messages inscribed on the hysterical body, a reading that is inaugural of psychoanalysis as a discipline. Griffith appears to understand that whoever is denied the capacity to talk will convert affect into somatic form, and speak by way of the expressionist body. It is worth noting in this context that the birth of modern psychiatry also dates from the French Revolution, notably in the work of Philippe Pinel, who was appointed chief physician for the insane at Bicêtre in 1793, then took over the hospital of the Salpêtrière in 1795.[16] Pinel's therapies are highly dramaturgical stagings of bodies that are speaking of affects that cannot be discharged other than through bodily enactments.

The hysterical body is typically, of course, from Hippocrates through Freud, a woman's body, and indeed a victimised woman's body, on which desire has inscribed an impossible history, a story of desire in an impasse. This description applies as well to Griffith's bodily enactments of moments of emotional crisis, and in general to the moments in which melodrama distorts the body to its most expressionistic ends. A fine example in Dennery's play comes just before Pierre turns on Jacques and kills him, when Henriette and Louise are finally together in La Frochard's den, but Henriette has fainted and Louise stumbles on her unconscious body without at first recognising it. As the stage directions in Dennery's play make clear, this is the moment when recognition between the long-separated orphans begins to dawn through Louise's touching of Henriette's body which, in its very unconsciousness, carries the freight of the drama and its impending dénouement.

One more example, and I shall be ready to conclude. This comes from Griffith's version alone. It comes when Henriette is in the tumbrel, on the way to the guillotine, and makes her last farewell to Louise, who is in the street – the sequence formally titled, as a kind of set piece, 'The Farewell'. As she leans from the tumbrel for a last embrace from Louise, and their lips meet and are held long together, Henriette's body appears to be in an almost impossible position, tilted from the cart, rigid, already nearly inanimate, like a mummy or a puppet, a bleached image, *pallida morte futura*. It is a pure image of victimisation, and of the body wholly seized by affec-

22

tive meaning, of message converted on to the body so forcefully and totally that the body has ceased to function in its normal postures and gestures, to become nothing but text, nothing but the place of representation.

As a coda to my reflections on the aesthetics of embodiment deriving from the Revolution, encoded in melodrama, and renewed by the silent cinema, let me evoke very briefly one of the most remarkable redramatisations of the Revolutionary body in our own time, Peter Weiss's play, *The Persecution and Assassination of Jean-Paul Marat as Performed by the Inmates of the Asylum of Charenton Under the Direction of the Marquis de Sade*. In the debates between the two protagonists, Marat keeps returning to the urgency of his writing, the need to compose his call to the people, whereas Sade opposes to this the irreducible claim of the body. As Charlotte Corday stands over the bathtub, Sade speaks: 'Marat/forget the rest/there's nothing else/beyond the body/Look/She stands there/her breast naked under the thin cloth/And perhaps she carries a knife/to intensify the love-play.'[17] When Corday finally delivers her blow, the resulting tableau of Marat dead is designed to mimic David's painting, which Sade's speech has now explicitly invested with the sexuality we noted in it. But this does not occur before Sade has continued his reflection on the body:

> Marat/as I sat there in the Bastille/for thirteen long years/I learned/that this is a world of bodies/each body pulsing with a terrible power/each body alone and racked with its own unrest/In that loneliness/marooned in a stone sea/I heard lips whispering continually/and felt all the time/in the palms of my hands and in my skin/touching and stroking/Shut behind thirteen bolted doors/my feet fettered/I dreamed only/of the orifices of the body/put there/so one may hook and twine oneself in them.[18]

Weiss's Sade takes us back through revolutionary embodiment to the body itself, no longer the bearer of messages, no longer the token in political struggle, but the ultimate integer that politics cannot touch, yet that informs all politics because it demands a deeper psychic revolution that political revolution ignores. Sade ends his speech: 'Marat/those cells of the inner self/are worse than the deepest stone dungeon/and as long as they are locked/all your Revolution remains/only a prison mutiny/to be put down/by corrupted fellow-prisoners.'[19] We are, of course, in the madhouse at Charenton, in a world of hystericised bodies only barely held in control by the wardens and nurses. Weiss makes us reflect on the history of embodiment that seems so much a political and aesthetic legacy of the Revolution, makes us see that the affective representations performed on and with the body at the last bring us back to the body itself: to imprisonment, constraint, repression, and the problem of desire. Griffith, too, inevitably brings us back to the body as the ultimate, and ultimately mysterious, signifier of the deepest, unarticulable meanings.

Notes

1. Henry James, 'Notes on the Theatres: New York', in Allan Wade (ed.), *The Scenic Art* (New Brunswick: Rutgers University Press, 1948), p. 24. For

parts of this paper, I have drawn on published material of my own: 'The Revolutionary Body', in Bernadette Fort (ed.), *Fictions of the French Revolution* (Evanston: Northwestern University Press, 1991), pp. 35–53; and chapter 3 of my *Body Work* (Cambridge, Mass.: Harvard University Press, 1993).

2. See, in particular, the fine study by Robert Lang, *American Film Melodrama: Griffith, Vidor, Minnelli* (Princeton: Princeton University Press, 1989).

3. See Norbert Elias, *The Civilizing Process*, trans. Edmund Jephcott (2 vols; New York: Pantheon, 1978 and 1982), and Michel Foucault, *Suveiller et punir (Discipline and Punish)* (Paris: Gallimard, 1975).

4. Dorinda Outram, *The Body and the French Revolution: Sex, Class, and Political Culture* (New Haven and London: Yale University Press, 1989), p. 81.

5. Saint-Just, 'Rapport sur les suspects incarcérés' (26 February 1794), in *Oeuvres choisies* (Paris: Gallimard/Idées Poche, 1968), p. 192.

6. See Simon Schama, *Citizens* (New York: Knopf, 1989), especially chapter 17.

7. Saint-Just, 'Rapport sur la nécessité de déclarer le gouvernement républicain jusqu'à la paix' (10 October 1793), *Oeuvres choisies*, p. 169.

8. Foucault, *Suveiller et punir*, p. 112.

9. See the fine account of this episode given by Emmet Kennedy in *A Cultural History of the French Revolution* (New Haven: Yale University Press, 1989), pp. 206–12.

10. Dorinda Outram, *The Body and the French Revolution*, p. 127. See also Lynn Hunt, *Politics, Culture, and Class in the French Revolution* (Berkeley and Los Angeles, University of California Press, 1984); Joan B. Landes, *Women and the Public Sphere in the Age of the French Revolution* (Ithaca and London: Cornell University Press, 1988); Sarah Maza, 'Remarks for Yale Symposium, "Representing the French Revolution",' 7 October 1989 (unpublished MS).

11. *Le Moniteur Universel*, 19 November 1793, translated and cited in Chantal Thomas, 'Heroism in the Feminine: The Examples of Charlotte Corday and Madame Roland', in Sandy Petrey (ed.), *The French Revolution, 1789–1989* (Lubbock, Texas: Texas Tech University Press, 1989), pp. 79–80.

12. Cited in Marvin Carlson, *The Theater of the French Revolution* (Ithaca: Cornell University Press, 1966), p. 177.

13. Charles Nodier, Preface to Guilbert de Pixérécourt, *Théâtre choisi*, 4 vols (Paris and Nancy, 1841–3).

14. I quote from the first published edition of *Le Jugement dernier des rois* (Paris: C.-F. Patris, L'an second de la République Française, une et indivisible). Translations are my own. My complete translation of the play is printed in *Yale Review* 78,4, 1990, pp. 583–603.

15. Marmontel, *Supplément* to the *Encyclopédie*, vol. 4, s.v. 'Pantomime' (Paris and Amsterdam, 1777). On this question, see *The Melodramatic Imagination*, chapter 3.

16. On Pinel, see Jan Goldstein, *Console and Classify: The French Psychiatric Profession in the Nineteenth Century* (Chicago: University of Chicago Press, 1987).

17. Peter Weiss, *The Persecution and Assassination of Jean-Paul Marat as Performed by the Inmates of the Asylum of Charenton Under the Direction of the Marquis de Sade*, English version by Geoffrey Skelton, verse adaptation by Adrian Mitchell (New York: Pocket Books, 1966), pp. 128–9.

18. Ibid., pp. 130–1.

19. Ibid., p. 131.

PAUSES OF MUTUAL AGITATION

SIMON SHEPHERD

There is a pause of mutual agitation when Eugenia is left alone with Bertrand in Dimond's 1809 melodrama *The Foundling of the Forest*. So too there is one when Inspector Morse learns from Lewis about the connection with the woman he once loved in the 1992 episode 'Dead on Time'. Such moments are marked by specific performance elements: the foregrounded look, created as much by the operation of face and neck muscles as by camera; the entry, or noticeable change, of music.

When Inspector Morse's neck muscles tighten, they indicate recognition of his personal involvement in the logic of the narrative. The 'private' aspect of his police work is what melodrama, supposedly, wants to play upon. For melodrama is typecast as a form interested solely in gut reaction, in emotional thrill which has no social significance. Tragic emotion, by contrast – or by Aristotle – is linked to the correctly managed body politic, and it is that contrast with tragedy that has shaped accounts of the emergence of melodrama, which is portrayed as degrading the connection between performance and civic society. The buskins of Oedipus are replaced by the neck muscles of Morse. But Morse is at least a real detective, whose activity will establish a clear distinction between innocence and crime. In that outcome the detective story, together with its parent, melodrama, declares its role in civic society as a fantasy of morality and justice. It is to this role that Peter Brooks ascribes the popular appeal of melodrama when it first emerged in the chaotic world of Revolutionary Paris. His account of the form thus sidesteps the constraining contrast with tragedy and finds a serious public role for melodrama's interest in tales of personal truth.

Brooks's hugely influential work has acquired the status of orthodoxy, but that orthodoxy, for which Brooks is not personally responsible, has suppressed a couple of details. First, that the conditions for melodrama's emergence in Revolutionary Paris may not be assumed to be identical in Regency London, so something of the connection between melodramatic form and society still remains to be told. And second, the concept of ethical fantasy accepts rather than questions that element of melodrama which has always been most notorious, namely the apparent simplicity of

25

its emotions, its gut reactions and thrills. Morse's neck muscles, however, are not intrinsically more simple than a pair of buskins. And at a particular point in our cultural history they make a truth that buskins cannot articulate. That truth is embodied in those moments where agitation pauses, suspended, frustrated not solved, as a character recognises that what comprises the mutual is both intimate and threatening. The fact that Morse's neck muscles have instant meaning shows how well learnt is the cultural message for which Eugenia's body was developing the vocabulary.

What she has yet to dread

In that pause in *The Foundling of the Forest* Bertrand has revealed himself to Eugenia, the woman who, in the past, he had been ordered to kill. Now, penitent and despairing, he tells her that he comes 'to serve and save you'. She asks what new terrors await her. After the exit of her female guardian, there follows the pause. Then Eugenia invites Bertrand to tell her what she has 'yet to dread'. For Eugenia the period of anonymous refuge is over; the past has found her, and in so doing indicates her destined future. She re-enters a narrative sequence in which she has no control over her life. The agitation is her body showing itself engaged by the narrative. For Bertrand, his knowledge of past and possible future compels him into a necessary relationship with Eugenia. His agitation comes not so much from his feelings for *her*, which have already been

John Thaw in 'Dead on Time', *Inspector Morse*, 1992

26

shown in his posture of supplication, as from the unique knowledge he has, about both her and the man who threatens her. When Eugenia and Bertrand recognise each other's identity, they come to know that they are positioned, as if objects, within a sequence of events potentially outside their control.

The agitation can be said to show the body in relation to knowledge, the subject becoming object (Brooks's account of muteness is useful here, although it remains trapped within its ethical assumptions). The acting of early melodrama required the body to be able to show not so much transparent emotional expressivity as the processes of coming to knowledge, of recognition and realisation. One of the much-used words is 'apprehension': the Eugenia performer has to gaze at Bertrand 'intensely with apprehension'. The individual body is marked or moulded by the structure of causality that determines its existence. This requirement, or indeed inscription, of the body is indicated epistemologically in the interest in theories of body types, where moral predispositions are supposed to have specific physical characteristics. This somewhat mystificatory twaddle was to develop into the trendy science of phrenology. (It may be paralleled, of course, in melodrama's development of a moralised and psychologised stage music; one of the earliest uses of such music was by Thomas Holcroft who translated Lavater's *Physiognomical Bible*.) Such theories insist that the body is never situated in an innocent naturalness, free of acculturation. Its physical features themselves derive from and are scripted for a role within the relationships of morality and power.

Whereas eighteenth-century acting had deployed a gestural language which was often explicitly self-referential, operating on a pattern of repetition and difference, melodrama repositions this language within a new sort of narrative. It thereby produces a foregrounding of the moments of coming to knowledge, of 'apprehension'. For a dramatist as theatrically competent as 'Monk' Lewis, transparent expressivity was the problem. The written text of *The Castle Spectre* (performed 1797) is full of discovery and recognition, but there is almost an embarrassment around emotional expression, which is resolved in a camp self-knowingness: 'I clasped Percy to my breast, and my heart caught a spark of that fire which flames in his unceasingly!' 'Caught fire, lady!' By contrast, Dimond seems to have been interested in fixing these expressive moments: two years after *The Foundling* he developed what became the familiar technique of living pictures in his 1811 drama *The Peasant Boy*.

The agitation between Eugenia and Bertrand is mutual. The dramaturgy requires the guardian, Monica, to exit. She goes upstairs, which prolongs her departure and marks her difference from the other two. Their history requires that Eugenia face Bertrand alone, a regular condition of human agency in early melodrama. She is asked to find a saviour in the man who once threatened her. Just as she begins to trust him, and at the moment he swears an oath to protect her from Baron Longueville, one of Longueville's henchmen, followed by the Baron himself, silently enters the cottage unobserved by any except the audience. Thus when Eugenia says to Bertrand 'Rise! your penitence wears nature's stamp, and I believe it honest,' she is moved by the natural truth of his emotion and

27

The Foundling of the Forest (Dimond, 1809)

is at the same time more vulnerable than she has been hitherto. The point of arrival at a sense of trust is also a point of extreme danger. Eugenia's appearance of agency, standing over and judging Bertrand, is actually a moment of subjection to forces outside her control. It is a classic moment of 'melodrama suspense', selected by the publisher as the title-page illustration. Its format was to be enthusiastically repeated in figures appearing at doors, at windows, through trees, behind seemingly solid walls. All the time a pair of eyes gazes into the private space, unexpectedly, without invitation, putting it under observation. Had Hamlet been a person of melodrama he would not have got away with all those soliloquies unwatched. Renaissance drama was worried and fascinated by the individual's capacity to be both centred and yet outside the dominant. Melodrama shapes so many of its terrors around the irresistibility of the gaze, endlessly repeating the fears of a society in which surveillance had become one of the modes and metaphors of power.

By having Eugenia face her would-be assassin now as her saviour, *The Foundling* uses a topos of early melodrama in which a quest for knowledge, or a bid to escape, leads to a confrontation with that which is most dreaded. Again it is a scenario which stages the limitations or horrors of agency, where you find violence in what you had always thought of as refuge, recognise yourself in what you planned to destroy, discover the other in your own history. The instability of Eugenia's new bond with Bertrand is marked by more than the Baron's secret entry, for when Bertrand asks how she escaped the murder attempt, it brings back memories for her: 'My dream of confidence dissolves, and now I turn from thee again with horror! Again I view thy murderous poniard reared to strike – again my wounded infant shrieks upon my bosom, and the fiery gulf yawns redly at my feet!'

In the *Inspector Morse* episode they had to use flashback to show the car accident and fire. But the flashback operates to keep past horrors in the past: it may be present onscreen, but it is cognitively framed as flashback. It does not, notably, disrupt the integrity of the bodies who remember. By contrast, the Eugenia performer calls on techniques of the body which were derived in part from the rigours of eighteenth-century mime. Thus Eugenia, who had stood with assurance over Bertrand, is now seen to relive herself standing on the edge of flames holding a wounded child. The same body can shift between, as it were, Weimar poise and pantomime gesticulation. Such shifts were in line with post-Diderot performance theory, in which acting technique took priority over spontaneous feeling. Melodrama method was uniquely equipped to deal with restagings of remembered incidents.

When memory is thus re-enacted in the body, the tension between determination and agency is located in the physiology of the person. Thus the wonderful scene in Buckstone's 1826 melodrama *Luke the Labourer* when Luke has arrived to gloat over the farmer's imprisonment for debt, only to find him released; sight of him produces in Luke a reliving of the events that cause him to hate the farmer, namely the death of his wife in an ill-maintained farm cottage. Luke's vengeful authority transforms into the victimised body, his compulsion to re-enact reversing his proposed relation of power to the farmer. Eugenia, like Luke, like so many in Buckstone's and Pitt's dramas of the 1840s, is subject to a personal history that always shapes her. That history shakes her body in the pause of agitation.

In a drama of sentiment Bertrand's feeling of pathos would guarantee his benevolence towards Eugenia. For Eugenia, however, the penitent Bertrand is also the dagger-bearing Bertrand. He is always his past. By contrast in, say, Thomas Morton's *Zorinski* (1795) the central figure is about to execute the king; suddenly he is moved by a vision of himself as traitor, and he thereafter supports the king. Emotional change can change history. In *The Foundling* Bertrand attempts to reassure Eugenia by telling her the narrative of the past (and thus taking control over it), but the audience knows that all the reassurance is circumscribed by the hidden presence of Longueville. That the audience has a knowledge temporarily unavailable to the characters is, of course, a stock situation in melodrama. It is constitutive of 'suspense'. The audience longs for the moment at which the characters will speak its knowledge: this will be a moment in which everything seems to be coherent, known, ordered, a plenitude perhaps. Melodrama works to produce and block desires for this plenitude. By now it is a familiar form of narrative organisation: why, though, might it have been favoured at this period?

Legs of headless frogs

The eighteenth-century culture of sensibility tended to propose that the operation of true emotion would produce a society of benevolence, in that common humanity only needed to free itself of artificial and institutional constraints in order to articulate its natural bonds. While 'feeling' was thus constructed in a fantasy of social order, late eighteenth-century science was discovering feeling as a part of the constitution of living creatures, located within a nervous system outside the control of the conscious mind: the legs of headless frogs twitch. The discovery of 'feeling' has a potentially democratic flavour to it not only in that it privileges so-called common humanity above class difference but also in that it locates truth in deeply felt emotions rather than in the discourses of dominant institutions. In repeated narratives of early melodrama a villain will try to organise circumstantial evidence in order to use law to achieve his aim. This procedure is usually defeated by an irruption of truth produced from real experience and emotion. All these terms are, naturally, ideological. What is here is a structure of feeling about the individual in relation to law, where the conflict is produced as nature versus institution. Law is the crucial institution because it is seen to address individuals from outside them, to turn subjects into objects by inventing narratives about them. The institution is class-based, so the truths claimed by its narratives authorise control by an often corrupt dominant. The organisation of suspense not only foregrounds the tension between differing knowledges and narratives, but more importantly it also specifically cathects the irruption of natural truth into the apparent logic of law.

Early melodrama suspense seems to be produced within the same structure of feeling which sets the terms of Regency radicalism, with its political analysis predicated upon an ideology of reform and clean-up rather than class conflict (Calhoun, 1982). There was campaigning for universal suffrage against a state machine figured as 'Old Corruption'. In William Godwin's novel *The Adventures of Caleb Williams* (1794) there is a sense that the institutions of society, and in particular law, cannot and will not hear the truth of the yeoman's son. The conflict is imaged as an established and largely faceless institution versus youthful enterprise and initiative (although this crosses over with a sense of class in Godwin's Jacobinism). Specifically, Caleb's voice is disallowed by gentry magistracy. A few years later Godwin's close friend and political ally Thomas Holcroft adapted for the English stage a French drama of a man made mute – literally disallowed – and misunderstood by genteel society. Holcroft's play was very successful, and was the first to call itself a 'melodrama'. Later plays which have that label did not necessarily share the deliberate political project of Holcroft and Godwin but, as Anastasia Nikolopoulou argues (1990), the ideological ambiguity of a genre such as outlaw melodrama speaks the contradictions of a fragmenting artisan consciousness, its Utopianism and nationalism. The leading activists of Regency oppositional politics were often artisans, as were a number of those who rioted in 1809 when the management of Covent Garden explicitly tried to price the lower classes out of the auditorium. That riot over access to fictions would seem but one way of confirming that the

30

shape of early melodrama, however fantastic, was produced within the same structure of feeling as shaped the terms of the current political conflict.

Godwin's hero finds himself caught in a contradiction. Caleb is temporarily sheltered by a gang of robbers who see themselves as the enemies of 'society' and reject its values. This attitude troubles him, however, for he merely wants society to be reformed by hearing, and being able to hear, his truth. He thinks that the correct unfolding of the narrative of truth will integrate him into society, whereas it can never integrate the robbers. This is, however, mistaken; for when Caleb has an opportunity to speak his truth he cannot face its consequences. He is, he realises, already implicated in what he wants to denounce. The act of truth-speaking will not alone lead to a reformed society composed of fulfilled individuals. Caleb's coming to manhood, his arrival at a public voice, are part of a process founded on law and violence. His justification to the world can only be effected through law; but he also has to learn that once he has set law in motion he cannot stop it, even though he might wish to. His public utterance of his real self is bound by the rules of an institution outside himself. He can never again have the innocent security from which he started. His fulfilment is structured around what he lacks.

Godwin's handling of truth narrative and suspense is useful as a reminder that the point of arrival need not be a point of plenitude. These uncertainties about the outcome of 'suspense', which are uncertainties also about universal suffrage in a class-divided society, inhabit a number of melodramas. When suspense points towards order as its conclusion, it offers to organise, to make sense of, indeed to make orderly that which has been violent or wild. In *Caleb Williams* the meaning of Caleb's truth will put an end to the violence emanating from Mr Falkland. On the other hand, it will have no effect on either the robbers or Mr Falkland's corrupt agents. There is a problem about the extent to which natural truthfulness can cure violence, a problem that marks the demise of the sentimentalist fantasy of a society ordered by benevolence.

The wild child
Truthfulness seeks to speak of that which has been hidden. It finds itself compelled to narrate of origins, of the true originating relations between people. The narrative of origins also works as a process of categorisation, where final order is the image of categories correctly filled. As such this process is informed by the epistemological shape of much late eighteenth-century science. Like that science it finds itself facing manifestations of feeling or vitality which escape available categories (the frogs' legs again). The early melodrama narrative promises order based on democratic truth and correct categorisation. At the same time it worries about the limits of truth and that which may not be categorised. Its modes of ordering the subject are aware that the subject may not be totally ordered.

A narrative is set in motion by Baron Longueville, who wants to kill the orphan Florian in order that he may have for himself Geraldine, the niece of the rich de Valmont. Florian is favoured by de Valmont, who discovered him while wandering the country after losing his own family in a fire.

De Valmont now wants Florian to marry Geraldine. Florian's praise of him spells out the issues here: 'Friend! protector! more than parent! the beings who had called me into life denied my claim, and you performed the duties Nature had renounced. Ah, sir! I am thoughtless, volatile – my manners wild; but, from my inmost soul, I love, I reverence, I bless my benefactor!' The speech is packed with key terms arranged in a set of oppositions: true justice and parenthood, morality and nature, benevolence and wildness. After he has experienced the collapse of father-hood in the 'normal' process of country-house life, de Valmont has to re-establish paternity as an act of choice and planning in the face of natural wildness. The adopted son is consciously evaluated where the natural son would have unproblematised privileges. What neither knows at this time is that they are biologically son and father. Florian will be the last to know, and then only after a process in which he first has to discover his mother.

But this is a different, and rather more important, narrative, set in motion not by the Baron but by 'nature'. Early on, Florian is lost: 'I was found in a wood when a baby, and have just lived to years of discretion to be lost in a wood again.' His horse had bolted just when he was thinking delightedly of 'his' Geraldine. His mental focus on her 'image' is ruptured by rain and increasing storm. Just as he thinks he is to be rescued, 'a vivid flash of lightning at that instant gleams upon the path before him, and displays the figure of Sanguine, masked, with an unsheathed poniard, advancing between the trees'. The romantic daydream is replaced by a real threat – from a faceless man with a naked weapon. In the next scene Florian comes across a cottage where the door is opened by a 'wildly dressed' 'Unknown Female', who 'on seeing Florian, recoils with trepida-tion – he catches her hand, and forcibly detains her'. Florian has found his mother.

Florian is subject to two pressures. The Baron surrounds him with murderers when he wants rescuers, isolates him socially. For the fiend-like Longueville Florian is important because of his attachment to Geraldine. 'Nature' or chance moves him outside country-house society, dislocates his attachment to Geraldine, and impels him towards discovering his mother.

The process of establishing the identities of the real family is repeatedly blocked by the strength of the feeling which recognition produces. Early in Act III de Valmont is brought a letter written by Eugenia, which tells him she escaped the fire. De Valmont's reaction is to threaten vengeance: 'In the delirium of his passion, he draws his sword, and strikes with it as at an ideal combatant' and collapses, convulsed. When Geraldine and Florian appear, 'He grasps the scroll and points to it emphatically, but cannot articulate.' Similarly, when Eugenia kisses Florian's hand she sud-denly gazes at it 'and a tremor pervades her whole frame'. That tremor has to last until the end of this section: when Florian asks her to 'pro-nounce my parents' name', she 'attempts to enfold him with her arms, but faints as he receives the embrace'. Her inability to speak is, on Peter Brooks's model, evidence of her truth: the body takes over from words as the reliable guarantor of meaning. But for Florian, as for the audience, the moment is wonderfully frustrating. It is no good its being true (the audience guesses that already): the important thing is that he hear it, that order can be re-established.

Bound to his mother's fate
In each case that which needs to be said cannot be said. It is prevented by what is disorderly – mad or delirious. The closer the logic moves towards an ordering based on correct category, on identity, the more it moves further away because of the potential for disorder within those identities. That disorder is derived pretty directly from the histories of the subjects. The characteristic rhythms of melodrama suspense articulate the tension between personal history and personal possibility. Expressed 'biologically', the nervous system has a vital logic of its own which defies categorisation; wildness is always present *within* civilisation in a way which Florian's scheme of key terms never realises. Furthermore, that wildness needs to be there, for it scuppers the Baron's plot, as he understands: 'Florian, by what wild chance at such unwonted hour I find you on this spot, admits not of inquiry now.' That wild chance eventually leads to an ending which attempts to fix the interpersonal relations in a stability figured by the uninterrupted eloquence of the father and a triangular family tableau with de Valmont at the centre. This is the promised order which had been forced to be suspended by the operations of passion. Florian greets his father: 'My parent – my preserver! twice has existence been my father's gift.' To which de Valmont replies: 'My forest prize – my foundling boy!'

De Valmont's pleasure in his forest prize seems to know none of the fear that a similar sort of child meant to the benevolist philosopher Diderot: 'If your little savage were left to himself and to his native blindness, he would in time join the infant's reasoning to the grown man's passion – he would strangle his father and sleep with his mother' (from *Le Neveu de Rameau*, quoted in Roach, 1985). But for Florian and his mother a previous triangle has been animated by something like Diderot's violence. As the villainous baron tried to carry off Eugenia, he was stopped by Florian. Longueville fights back, and Eugenia is taken away. At this moment she declares her identity: 'thy mother blesses thee – long-lost, late-found. Behold! she struggles now to bless her child, and now she dies content!' Florian 'rushes madly upon the baron, who parries the assault – then, in an agony of despair, casts himself at his feet.' The moment at which the mother is identified coincides with the son's failed assault on the older man, which results in the son also adopting a position of vulnerability with regard to that man. The violence proceeds in a different direction from that in Diderot's image, the source of it being the man who acts the role of 'bad father' in the narrative. But schematically both images are familial triangles in which violence replaces the supposedly normal love relations.

The stable de Valmont triangle comes after the baron's, and so replaces it but without necessarily cancelling its possibility. As the de Valmont triangle is set up on stage, it has little sense of a fullness which is natural, or even unproblematic. Florian leads a 'trembling and uncertain' Eugenia into the arms of de Valmont. For Geraldine there is no place in the triangular order, her relationship with Florian (and his identity as lover)

33

excised by the family romance. When de Valmont invites Eugenia to greet in Florian 'our mutual image', the son is not stepping into the place of patriarchal masculinity. He has imaged his mother by submitting his body to a more powerful man, just as he has imaged his father precisely by failing with his – what shall we say – weapon. The tableau that offers at last to fix true identity cannot find mutuality that is free of possible agitation.

In this respect *The Foundling* shares anxiety with plays written before and after. Thomas Holcroft's popular *Tale of Mystery* of 1802 shapes itself around, and fantasises solutions to, a repeated set of oppositions: person and institution, truth and law, feeling and categorisation. It ends by taking those oppositions within the individual, as determinants upon subjectivity. In its final image forces of law are about to seize the villain. He is cradled in the arms of the brother he once mutilated and made dumb. Pleading for them both is the young woman who has discovered that one of the brothers is her, as it were, castrated father, and that the man of whom she had a sexual dread is her uncle. The Jacobin Holcroft terminates the action here, in an unresolved stand-off between law and a loving, violently triangular family. In 1835 John Haines wrote a triangle into his title, *My Poll* and *my Partner Joe*. In the final scene the friend whom Harry had suspected of having a relationship with his wife is brought in dying. He confirms Mary's innocence and 'pulls their hands together, joins them and dies across them'. Harry and Mary 'rush into each other's arms, recollect themselves, and kneel in prayer by the side of Joe'.

Staged in these ways, points of arrival are not necessarily points of achieved stability. The triangle complicates, or even withholds, the balanced mutuality of pair-bonding, always potentially producing the agitation that it seeks to hold in check. The structure of the triangle institutes within itself the pattern of frustration and fulfilment that characterises the suspense narrative. Florian cannot, in gender terms, be a mutual image of both father and mother. The selves that Harry and Mary recollect are defined by the third point of the triangle. The energy of their mutual rush is suspended, not cancelled, by the stasis of the prayer, since it remains always potent in the performers' bodies. But it is never shown again.

In so far as these triangles are concerned with both gender and identity, they take a cultural place alongside Gothic tales of male rivalry, haunting, female victimisation. Their production speaks of a society that satisfactorily and pleasurably imaged crisis as distortion and transgression of supposedly normal bondings. The marital and familial relations which apparently promise stability are shadowed by their always almost-achieved subversion. Thus the precise location of Diderot's supreme virtue, in the private space of the family, can no longer guarantee to deliver the goods. The modern world has its own pet name for the shadow cast by Diderot's wild child – Oedipus – and his appearance here is not unexpected. After all, Gothic and melodrama have been very regularly aligned with the script of psychoanalysis. Elsaesser (1972) says that 'Freud was later to confirm' that melodrama supplied the 'dynamic motifs' of 'depth-psychological phenomena'; Brooks finds structural similarities between melodrama and psychoanalysis; Sedgwick (1985) identifies features of the

Oedipal family foregrounded in Gothic fiction. Viewed in this way, Gothic novels and early melodrama become the parents of modern culture's wild child.

Their mutual image

Eugenia is in fact saved, not by her male relatives, but by Bertrand, the disaffected servant of a tyrannical aristocrat. His rebellion against aristocratic social relations leads to an acceptable solution, in that it limits the baron's fiend-like plans. It is as if Bertrand's action has an ease and clarity because he is outside the trammels of family. The end of the play, however, is not really interested in the baron's power; suspense narrative tends to abjure ease of action and to be interested precisely in trammels. The crises of the story of the foundling's origins operate by problematising gender roles at the point of discovery of familial bonds. It is specifically these elements which are produced as theatrical excitement. The crisis of Florian's first appearance had a gendered structure. The threat from a dagger-wielding man came after he had experienced delight in an imaginary vision of his female lover. That dagger-wielding man is faceless; the single most important feature in his identity is thus the revealed weapon. Florian is back in the wood where he originated, but now, as he says, at the 'years of discretion'. That discretion has a necessary logic in which the son has to look on at a father who is unable either to brandish his sword or to articulate, and where the son's passionate concern to preserve his mother leads in her sight to his self-humiliation before another man.

The psychic tensions of the triangular relationships give a charge to the rhythms of suspense narrative. In the one in *The Foundling* the climactic points of suspense show recognition, agency and affirmation blocked. The blocking produces for the audience an inversion of the (ideologically) proper relationships, which if correctly identified would be a source of stability. The emotion that should be articulated within familial relations inhibits their formulation. Imminent recognition of another produces loss of control of self. The approach of order is accompanied by reversals into confusion. Suspense narrative teaches us to be suspicious of states of innocence and satisfied by the imposition of correct categories. Its narrative shape conducts us from one position to the, necessary, other. Even poor old Morse has to discover the woman he nostalgically loves is at present involved in a crime.

If the narrative form can be shown to articulate something of the structure of feeling of its culture, then the relations which share their rhythms with that narrative may also be explicable. Elsaesser (1972) argues that melodrama 'served as the literary equivalent of a particular, historically and socially conditioned *mode of experience*. Even if the situations and sentiments defied all categories of verisimilitude and were totally unlike anything in real life, the structure had a truth and life of its own'; 'a body of techniques' was turned into 'a stylistic principle that carried the distinct overtones of spiritual crisis'. The notion of 'literary equivalent' can uncover social concerns masquerading as something different on-stage: thus, for Elsaesser, 'the metaphorical interpretation of class conflict as sexual exploitation and rape'.

35

Viewed as literary equivalent for something, the enactments of the process of arriving at recognised gender or family identity might be about coming to occupy a proper place in society. That concern was politically exemplified in Regency culture in agitation about suffrage and fair taxation. An inherited ideology of benevolence was under pressure from, indeed cracking up in the face of, the violence produced in the operation of law-courts and taxation systems. The 'wildness' was clearly endemic, deep within the structural organisation of a no longer benevolent society (not that it ever really was). The possible structure of feeling here might produce as a metaphorical interpretation of itself the image of achieved family stability only barely containing, if not openly compromised with, its potential for violence. And that family stability discovers its precarious, necessary complexity outside the moral simplicity of Holcroft's forces of law or Dimond's wicked aristocrat. Certain sorts of moral or social ideology are revealed to be incapable of explaining the family unit, which is itself not so much refuge from as product, and producer, of the violence of moral and social order. Discovery of the truth of that family's romance in turn takes its shape from the rhythms of a narrative in which coming to identity always involves encountering lack.

These sorts of arguments might explain, eventually, why the popular theatrical and narrative forms of the early 19th century were so insistently organised around concerns that have later been described as 'Oedipal' or 'depth-psychological'. While it cannot be said that those concerns emerge for the first time in this period, it does seem that it was early melodrama which played a major part in arranging those concerns into a narrative form which is readily recognisable, and indeed natural, in our own culture. One of the things that seems most familiar about that narrative is that it suddenly freezes into moments of agitation that is necessarily mutual, where a condition of mutuality is indeed agitation.

My thanks are due to John Fletcher for discussing this essay with me.

Bibliography

Barker, Clive, 'A Theatre for the People' in K. Richards and P. Thomson (eds), *Nineteenth-Century British Theatre* (London: Methuen, 1971).

Brooks, Peter, *The Melodramatic Imagination* (New Haven: Yale University Press, 1976).

Buckstone, J.B., *Luke the Labourer* (London: Cumberland's Minor Theatre, 1828–43), vol. 2.

Calhoun, Craig, *The Question of Class Struggle* (Chicago: Chicago University Press, 1982).

Dimond, William, *The Foundling of the Forest* (London: Cumberland's British Theatre, 1826–61), vol. 40.

Elsaesser, Thomas, 'Tales of Sound and Fury: Observations on the Family Melodrama' (1972), in C. Gledhill (ed.), *Home Is Where the Heart Is* (London: British Film Institute, 1987), p. 43.

Godwin, William, *Caleb Williams* (1794) (London: New English Library, 1975).

Haines, John T., *My Poll and my Partner Joe* (1835) in M. Booth, *Hiss the Villain* (London: Eyre & Spottiswoode, 1964), p. 87.

Holcroft, Thomas, *A Tale of Mystery* (1802) (London: 1824).

Kaplan, E. Ann, 'Theories of Melodrama: A Feminist Perspective', *Women and Performance*, vol. 1, no. 1, 1983, pp. 40–8.

Lewis, M.G. 'Monk', *The Castle Spectre* (London: 1818).

Morton, Thomas, *Zorinski: A Play* (London: n.d.).

Nikolopoulou, Anastasia G., *Artisan Culture and the English Gothic Melodrama 1780–1830* (unpublished PhD thesis: Cornell University, 1990).

Roach, J.R., *The Player's Passion* (Newark: Delaware University Press, 1985).

Sedgwick, Eve K., *Between Men* (New York: Columbia University Press, 1985).

Williams, Raymond, *Modern Tragedy* (London: Chatto & Windus, 1966).

Williams, Raymond, 'Social Environment and Theatrical Environment', in Williams, *Problems in Materialism and Culture* (London: Verso, 1980).

THE CONTENDING DISCOURSES
OF MELODRAMA

JACKY BRATTON

The critical refusal to take melodrama seriously, which Peter Brooks pin-pointed as stemming from a profound unease with its excessive rhetoric, has been dissipated, in the wake of his revaluation, by a concentration on its non-verbal signs. Licensed by Artaud's somewhat romantic enthusiasm for Romantic melodrama as the last authentic theatre in Europe, critics and performers (though perhaps not audiences) have become enthusiastic about the form as a 'central fact of modern sensibility'.[1] However, the revival of its nineteenth-century texts has not so far been very successful, for two closely connected reasons. The first is the contin-ued distrust of the words of the early melodramas, their extreme and excessive speech. This results in performances which charge the lines with gratuitous cheap irony (as in the National Theatre *Ticket-of-Leave Man*, 1981), drown them in operatic music (Riverside Studio *The Bells*, 1992) or simply jettison them in favour of texts newly (and distantly) derived from nineteenth-century novels (*Lady Audley's Secret*, Lyric Hammersmith, 1992, and as toured by Gloria). This seems, especially in the first case, to be a defence against the laughter that it is feared they will provoke. And laughter is the second aspect of the plays that has been overlooked and misconstrued, from *The Melodramatic Imagination* onwards. Twentieth-century ears hear the apparent naiveté, the huge sim-plicity of nineteenth-century melodrama's voice as irresistibly comic; if the melodramatic mode is indeed still part of our sensibility, we must be com-mitting the cardinal melodramatic sin of distorting its message when we try to suppress that laughter, or misunderstand its meaning. In their own time early melodramas easily accommodated the comic response, without embarrassment; it was, indeed, vital to the genre, as it should be to our understanding of it.

By confining his analysis to the pre-1840 'classic' plays of France, before what he regards as the 'decadence' of the form set in, Brooks avoided texts in which the comic element is too overt to ignore. In England, from its eighteenth-century beginnings, and increasingly as the form became dominant, comedy was a major element. The figures who carry the serious weight of the Manichean polarities of melodrama's moral world, especially the villain and the heroine, have no psychological complexities or ambiguities; but alongside them, the countryman who is the villain's unwilling assistant and the maid who shares the heroine's distresses may voice a quite different, more 'natural' and certainly more mixed response to the drama. In assessing these plays as discursive projects, it is their articulation of comic and serious voices which needs to be understood.

My intention, however, is not to reveal a flaw in melodramatic texts, through which another layer of unconscious, repressed meanings might be detected; rather, the contradictions highlighted by examining their different voices are read as deliberate mediations, the means whereby a consensus is tacitly negotiated, and ideological and hegemonic work is done. I wish, in Bakhtin's terms, to assert that the melodrama is heteroglot; to claim that it is, as he claims for the novel, 'a *system* of languages that mutually and ideologically interanimate each other'.[2] I should like to make the same claim for these plays that he does for the novel, that in them 'a conceivably dominant literary language and mutually contending extra-literary languages ... are striving to move from the realm of everyday oral discourse to that of literature';[3] and, moreover, these contending languages are socio-ideological, they operate not only in the play's literary form but in its social being.

British melodramatists used comedy from the beginning, and added it to the French texts they translated. They employed the conventional figures of current practice, mostly low comic servants, whose appearance in high comedy or in tragedy goes back to pre-Restoration drama via the deliberate stratifications of character introduced to purify the protagonists in sentimental comedy. These figures are absorbed without a break into the more innovative dramaturgy of sensational or Gothic melodrama such as Colman's *The Iron Chest* (Drury Lane, 1796), Lewis's *The Castle Spectre* (Drury Lane, 1797) and Dimond's *Foundling of the Forest* (Haymarket, 1809). Servant characters conventionally present a broader, coarser version of a love plot, or scenes in which a comic man scrambles for self-preservation and incidentally or even accidentally achieves heroic feats; a clear instance in melodrama is the figure of Varbel in John Philip Kemble's *Lodoiska* (Drury Lane, 1794). In early melodrama the plot will often, as in the case of *The Foundling*, be mechanically unaffected if the comic figures are omitted: but the inclusion of their sceptical and pragmatic voices is nevertheless a significant modification of the romance. As in Jacobean and Caroline tragi-comedy, they modulate audience response to sensational and emotional high points, channelling sceptical responses. Sometimes, as in, for example, Holcroft's elaboration of the old servant Fiametta in his translation of Pixérécourt's *Coelina*, the comic figures also further the radical aspects of the Romantic project by exhibiting a truer, more 'natural' morality in the lower class, whose pure sensibility is presented as at once comic and admirable.

These early melodramatists might be regarded in some sense as Romantics, though their work for the stage is inevitably shaped as much by genre and by the material conditions of the theatre as by that tendency. Holcroft's radicalism emerges into his plays chiefly in a philosophical form, in relation to the nature of evil; Dimond, also a marginalised figure, was rather a rakehell than a reformer; Lewis wrote on the edges of Romanticism at its most radical stage, but he was always a sceptic about its effects, prone to deliberate demystification and an almost obsessive undercutting of his own horrors, in case they should be taken seriously. All three worked within the mainstream of theatre, selling to the patent house managers, and frankly interested chiefly in the earning power of their plays. John Philip Kemble, himself such a manager, was perhaps the most pragmatic of all, creating and staging *Lodoiska* as a deliberate exercise in box office (a 'species of intellectual prostitution', Hazlitt called it).[4] Each of them might, therefore, be consciously or unconsciously subverting the form that he was using for its popular pulling power. The effect of reinforcement or subversion between the various ideological levels of their work depends upon how the laughter works in the text; and that in turn depended, nightly and moment by moment, on the relationship between the stage and the audience.

To understand the importance that lower-class comic characters developed in English melodrama, one must take account not only of succeeding writers' positions but also of the growing differentiation of audiences in the rapidly expanding London theatre in the first half of the century. Melodramas differ, and not merely in terms of their artistic distinction. The plays which were acceptable to the widest audiences, performed at the Theatres Royal, at the English Opera House, the Olympic and the Adelphi make a particular balance between serious/heroic and comic voices, creating class statements acceptable to their higher-priced seats. The audience profile changes as one moves away from the mixed-class venues around Covent Garden, via the price and licensing war being waged on the south bank during this period, to the new theatres being built on the fringes of London and in the City. Whatever the pretensions of these latter places at their inception, they tended to survive by truncating their price structure, with few prices rising into the middle-class bracket, and anything from a few dozen to three thousand cheap seats. Melodramas tailored to these venues, rarely printed or exported to the fashionable theatres, became the site for the reappropriation of the lower-class character and the comic perspective that he or she provides in a different, genuinely heteroglot voice offering active ideological resistance.

Michael Booth[5] pinpoints the interlarding of comic and serious in melodrama as a glaring instance of the 'popular' nature of the form, evidence that it was intended for uneducated audiences who had no use for 'depth and subtlety' and would not feel any incongruity or recognise any irony in the juxtaposition of high drama and pathos with solo comic turns and farce. Yet on inspection, it appears that it is in the plays written for the Theatres Royal and the other fully licensed houses, whose mixed audiences included the leaders of culture in the pit and the leaders of fashion in the boxes, that these disjunctures are most evident. In, for example, the several dramatisations of Scott's novel *The Heart of Midlothian* that were staged in 1819, Dumbiedikes becomes the chief comic role. In Thomas Dibdin's version for the south bank house, The Surrey, he is an integral part of the action, used to direct and modify audience response to the potentially unsympathetic Puritanism of David and Jeanie Deanes; in the operatic version by Scott's personal friend Daniel Terry with music by Henry Bishop that was staged at Covent Garden, John Liston played Dumbiedikes as a comic turn, complete with knockabout slapstick and dame impersonation, with little interaction with the principals.

There is a significant relation between the low social and moral status of the comic character, and the high standing of the comic actor who performed the role. It was the work of admired comedians such as Frederick Robson, John Liston and Robert Keeley to present the Theatre Royal audiences with impersonations of lower-class men as servants or petty tradesmen, vignettes of character comedy creating a harmlessly idiosyncratic vision of the worker at the service of his betters, where his pretensions could be firmly controlled by laughter. Keeley created the timid and greedy servant Fritz, for example, in Peake's version of Mary Shelley's *Frankenstein* (*Presumption*, English Opera House, 1823), who has remained useful in most subsequent dramatisations as a means to control nervous responses to the monster.

Keeley also played the apothecary Dolittle in Caroline Norton's *The Gypsey Father*, a social problem melodrama written for Covent Garden in the wake of the success there of Jerrold's *The Rent Day*, 1831. Stories of poverty and oppression in modern England were potentially offensive to parts of the Theatre Royal audience even in the flush of radical enthusiasm leading up to parliamentary reform in 1832, and Dolittle is an outstanding example of the way in which the melodramatic comedy acts to modify the absolute and egalitarian morality of the mode. He and his apprentice appear chiefly in three scenes at the beginning and again at the end, framing the play with a farcical satire upon lower-class pretension. The apothecary is 'pert and ignorant', more inclined to serve rich customers than poor ones, and particularly droll because he has a strong interest in his profession and has risen to independant practice by his own efforts. He is used to bring about the happy ending fortuitously: called to tend a poor man who has been stabbed in a domestic conflict in a starving family, he incorrectly certifies his death and so precipitates a wrongful arrest, an error which can then easily be rectified by the reporting of the truth. The dispossessed poor fighting over scraps of food made up a sufficiently harrowing spectacle for Fanny Kemble to remark: 'What a terrible piece! what atrocious situations and ferocious circumstances! ... But, after all, she's in the right; she has given the public what they desire. . . . Of course it made one cry horribly.'[6]

The public with whom she saw the play consisted of a thin house in pit and gallery, but 'dress circle and private boxes full of fine folk'. Their enjoyment of being made to cry horribly must have been considerably facilitated by the distancing. of the story of desperate poverty within a comic frame of *petit bourgeois* incompetence.

Fanny Kemble is also interesting on the subject of *Victorine*, a modern play which the Parliamentary Select Committee investigating the state of the drama in 1832 made something of a touchstone of promising new work. Kemble appreciated the nuanced 'realistic' performance of Elizabeth Yates, excelling in the third act where she is old and in distress and degradation. There was a weary look of uncomplaining misery about her, an appearance as of habitual want and sorrow and suffering, a heavy, slow, subdued, broken deportment, and a way of speaking that was excellent.[7]

She also, however, thought the play's happy ending perfectly appropriate, and added with no apparent sense of incongruity a tribute to the leading comedian: 'Reeve is funny beyond anything; his face is the most humorous mask I ever saw in my life.'[8] She obviously read the piece as a melodrama, where the intercutting of high morality and low humour is a central dynamic, and the outcome is the recognition and restoration of innocence. The committee members, by contrast, deplored the interpolation of comic material into what they wished to see as evidence of a revival of tragedy,[9] a theatrical breakthrough on which legitimate modern drama might be built when the licensing laws had been changed to permit the development of more small theatres like the Adelphi.

Victorine's author/translator J.B. Buckstone knew better than did the committee how an Adelphi melodrama needed to address its audience. The theatre catered very specifically to West End pleasure-seekers, often men out for the evening in groups or escorting a lady, rarely in families, sometimes alone. Its appointments were spartan, with a large pit of old-fashioned benches, and a single tier of boxes, few of them private; its programme often lasted five hours. An important part of the audience came in at nine o'clock, at half price, and consisted of young men in the middle of a night on the town, who dropped in to see the climax of the main piece and stayed for the farce with which the bill ended before going on to the other houses of entertainment that the Strand (where the theatre stood) offered after midnight. This audience was served from 1830 by a small permanent company under the direction of Fred Yates until his early death, and then from 1844 of Celine Celeste and Benjamin Webster. O. Smith, one of its long-serving members, described the company as succeeding because of its tight-knit co-operation and familiarity with each other and their audience; the managers found or commissioned plays specifically to exploit the company's mutually supportive skills. After the leading women performers – Elizabeth Yates, until her husband's death, and then Celeste herself – the most important members of the company were probably the comedians: John Reeve, J.B. Buckstone, Fanny Fitzwilliam, and later Edward Wright and Paul Bedford. These all fostered a frame-breaking, direct relationship with the audience:

Mr Reeve is one of those who invariably shake hands with their auditors at the commencement of a piece, and keep up a kind of social communication with them, until the curtain drops. When our hero has an aside speech to deliver, he pops it at the pit, as if anxious to divide the joke with them, and seems really to wink at the house, whilst he is cajoling the opposite character on the stage.[10]

Reeve gagged his way through plays, never learning his lines, never even trying to 'divest himself of his personal identity', working on 'interpola-

tions on the text, communications with the house'.[11] In the next generation Wright took over this special relationship with the Adelphi audience,
and at a time when public taste was reacting strongly against such licence
he maintained an enthusiastic following for the kind of comedy that relied
on nods and winks and innuendo, working a *louche*, immoral, comic per-
sona which no other respectable theatre any longer welcomed or indeed
tolerated.[12] Accommodating both Elizabeth Yates and John Reeve,
Buckstone deliberately combined two French sources to create *Victorine*,
and was proud of his success in not only interjecting a farcical episode
but lacing its characters into the high drama.[13] The result is shot through
with juxtapositions that create ambiguous responses.

The basic story is very simple. The poor but honest embroideress
Victorine is betrothed to a poor but honest upholsterer Michael; she has,
however, a pair of poor, cheerful but less than honest friends, Alexandre
and Elise, who egg her on to take advantage of a great opportunity – she
has a rich admirer, the landlord of the tenement where she lives. She
retires to bed at the end of the first act, to make up her mind overnight
between the two offers; and in the final scene of the play she wakes to
choose in favour of poverty, honesty, marriage and the upholsterer. The
rest of the text, the larger part, consists of her dream, in which she makes
the other choice, the choice of 'freedom': a musical education, an apartment of her own, and a man who 'does not seek to put any restraint'
upon her, and does not offer her marriage. This, of course, is the meat of
the drama, in which Elizabeth Yates had the opportunity to act out all the
roles of the fallen woman from idle dissipation and spoilt regret to penury
and crime. And she did this in the company of the comic performers: not
only her ne'er-do-well friends, but also a plump and uxorious jeweller,
Bonassus, on whom the idle trio play a practical joke. This was the John
Reeve role; Buckstone himself appeared as Bonassus's servant.

The main part of the play is thus bracketed off from the stage world in
which melodramatic absolute morality must be seen to prevail. It presents
a fantasy in which, to be sure, the necessary moral lessons which will
enforce the choice of honesty in the last scene are eventually delivered,
but which actually engages the audience for three-quarters of its time in
the exploration and, more importantly, the enjoyment of the opposite
choice. Their complicity is constantly managed by means of the comics:
Fred Yates and Fanny Fitzwilliam as the low-life friends of the heroine (to
whom she remains entirely loyal throughout, as they sink into more and
more outrageously criminal activities) and Reeves and Buckstone as the
duped husband and his absent-minded man. Their 'vaudeville' is purely
farcical, involving concealments, mistaken identities, complex entrances
and exits and the endlessly receding prospect of indulgence in food and
sex. In it not only Reeve and Buckstone, but Fitzwilliam and Elizabeth
Yates herself flirted and teased and teetered on the brink of seduction on
stage.

The printed text does not, of course, include Reeve's gags, but it has
its surreally suggestive moments. Reeve as Bonassus says to Alexandre,
played by Fred Yates and well known to the Adelphi audience as
Elizabeth Yates's husband,

I shall admit of no other topic but Mrs Bonassus and her excellent qualities. I'll treat you to some of her preserves, you shall taste her sweetmeats and her jam – oh! her jam. [*Smacking his lips.*] You unhappy wretch; why don't you get married and taste your wife's jam?

He is later embarrassed by Elise (Fitzwilliam) telling Victorine 'do look at Mr Bonassus's legs!' He hides behind a table, and she presses the point: 'You have a very – very handsome calf!' Bonassus responds defensively, 'Mrs Bonassus always admired me for my calf,' at which Victorine joins in, saying 'Then she *is* a woman of taste,' to which Bonassus replies with the clincher: 'You'll say so when you see her bell-ropes.' The delivery of 'her [pause] bell-ropes' is precisely the kind of line upon which a world of suggestion hung in nineteenth-century dialogue. The reaction of the Adelphi audience to such triggers, Reeve's 'wink at the house', can be imagined; and the 'opposite character on the stage' at this moment is the melodrama's heroine, who at the end of the scene will revert to high drama, dropping a letter of rejection from her aristocratic keeper from her nerveless hand and exclaiming 'Ruined! Ruined!' The moment is charged with the ambiguity of the whole play: it is by the pragmatic morality of the comic world that she is 'ruined' at this point, by the loss of her finan- cial support; in the native world of the heroine, she was ruined long since. But using the full repertoire of melodramatic rhetorics – music and tableau as well as the verbal claptrap – the scene demands the audience to empathise with and applaud a woman who, in terms of the dominant voice of the moment, is an unrepentant sinner whose disastrous present circumstances are doubly her own fault. Not only has she succumbed to the temptation of wealth and become a kept woman but she has also, out of boredom and dissatisfaction with that powerless position, behaved capriciously and ungratefully towards her keeper. She collapses into the arms of Alexandre, her husband (Fred Yates).

The Adelphi texts, then, which speak with the voices of the author, the author as performer, and of certain others of the performers as impromptu authors and as pre-existing personae, are by no means as empty of irony as Booth's dismissal of the potential of scenic juxtaposition suggests. Here the disjunctions that are to be negotiated are between the moral high ground that melodrama claims and the more pragmatic tacit understanding of the world shared by the pleasure-seeking West End audience and their stage favourites. When the negotiations actually involve the mediation of a middle-class morality to a predominantly working-class audience, more obvious demands on the heteroglossia of the genre are made.

In, for example, George Dibdin Pitt's *First Friendship*, a successful and repeatedly revived play at the East End theatre the Britannia, Hoxton (1848, 1852 and 1860), there is a very clear interplay of at least four voices, constituting a negotiation with British imperialism. While fulfilling all the ideological tasks of military melodrama, interpolating the working man in the Britannia audience as a British hero, the play negotiates a space for a quite different self-perception by its use of juxtapositions, and especially of comic scenes and characters. Contrasting models of the hero are embodied in the characters of Colin, marked out for heroism the moment he utters his first lines in humble but impeccable English, and his boyhood friend Kenneth, who cannot shake off either his machismo independence or his Scots accent. Across their lifelong argument the play projects the lighter voice of Jimmy, comic cockney soldier, speaking for anti-heroic pragmatism and comfortable survival. Finally, Sarah Lane, manager of the theatre and leading performer, contributed a running commentary on the debate in the character of the heroine's maid and Jimmy's sweetheart, a woman of little education but high literary pretensions chatting extempore with the audience and composing an unintentionally mock-heroic poem about the ignominious military career of her beloved.[14]

I do not mean to suggest that G.D. Pitt, the writer, or Sarah Lane, the manager and performer, were attempting a deliberate subversion of heroic rhetoric, presenting a critique that would discredit the British patriotic line; indeed, the audiences' acceptance of themselves as potential soldiers of the Queen was probably facilitated by the way the melodrama presented it. The play admits that soldiering is not all glory; a volunteer will meet with oppression, is likely to end up disabled or dead, and will certainly have to suppress his natural independence and at least pretend to obey the rules in order to have a quiet life and get a few drinks inside him. It does not, or need not be taken to, say that patriotic sentiments and the pursuit of glory are therefore undesirable or untrue. Both things are true; their counterpoint is the energy of the drama, the stage languages 'mutually and ideologically interanimate each other'.

Sarah Lane's character in *First Friendship* makes comic use of literary artifice and romantic pretensions, talking about the heroines of novels and composing a poem, and at one point echoing Shakespeare's joke about the paucity of extras on the stage, where half a dozen men must be supposed an army. There is clearly an expectation that the Hoxton audience would pick up and relish such references to the difference between art and life, and the conventions of fiction. My final example is of a melodrama that seems to me to demonstrate even more clearly such self-reference and humorous sophistication which we recognise in modern popular art, but have not so far admitted as possible in earlier periods.

Ruth, or the Lass that Loved a Sailor, by Edward Richardson Lancaster, was produced at the Royal Standard Theatre in Shoreditch in 1841, a few years after the 2000-seat, lavishly equipped local theatre was built. It was successful enough to find its way into print, unlike most of Lancaster's work. His only other printed play is an extravaganza rejoicing in the title of *The Devil's Daughters; or, Hell's Belles*. The most striking aspect of both that play and *Ruth* is their deliberate theatrical artificiality, their self-referencing, their disdain for any constricting obligation to realism or rationality. *Ruth* is set in 'olden times' in an archetypal English village and an ancient manor house replete with secret panels; its language is archaised, literary, not only deliberately distanced by the usual inclusion of songs, but also strewn with snatches of verse and archaic exclamations. The characters repeat to each other increasingly gnomic and detailed rhyming prophecies that are recalled to them by the hero's actions, and about to be fulfilled. A highly self-conscious plot presents the characters and motifs of the domestic melodrama absolutely undiluted, without even a minimal displacement: they are innocent village maid, her good old father, the wicked squire, the dispossessed sailor hero who returns, the peasant villain who repents, the maid at the inn and the comic peasants.

The hero reappears unwittingly in the village of his birth and carries out a series of rituals, from rechristening a local landmark with sea water to sitting in the chair of his long-lost father, all signalled as significant by versifying bystanders. The coded, highly charged emblems of the melodrama are represented here by a series of domestic objects, especially three similar hats; sensational struggles and complex misunderstandings depend upon their manipulation:

> Here is the murdered seaman's hat; my old eyes cannot decipher them, but there are characters inside which, no doubt, reveal the owner's name ... 'Michael Lancewood' ... How! that too, was the name of our late lord. This, then, must have been the youth who was stolen away in his infancy. Neighbours – Lancewood of Belville Green lies murdered in his own inheritance. [*A general expression of contending interests. The scene closes on the picture.*][15]

It is striking that this deeply characteristic melodramatic moment of astonishment is distanced for the audience not only by its being made to hinge upon a humble hat, but also by their possession of prior knowledge that Lancewood is alive and well. When the scene opens again, it is to show Lancewood putting on the hat of the man who really was the corpse in the previous scene, before he is arrested by a group of stupid yokels.

Similarly, the set-piece combats between the rightful heir and his villainous uncle are so framed in comedy that their melodramatic force cannot but be qualified by the juxtaposition. Sir Walter speaks out his villainy in as stark and extravagant a manner as ever embarrassed a critic; but his rejection of repression does not disturb, because it is constantly mediated by acknowledgment of its conventionality. The climactic conflict takes place in '*the inmost fastnesses of the forest*', during a terrific storm. The audience is introduced to this locale by the comic characters, who have just dug up a mysterious chest, and speculate knowingly about its likely contents before they vacate, to allow Sir Walter and his men (who are wearing masks, for no perceptible reason beyond the enhancement of their horrific appearance and possibly the disguising of over-used extras) to haul on the pinioned Lancewood. Challenged as to the strict legality of his proceedings, even given that he is a magistrate, and asked to return to the highroad via the Mandrake's Hollow, the villain exclaims, ''Tis strewn with millstones – dead men's bones bleach the road. The ashes from the grave would blind me as I walked, and I should become scorched by the very glare of hell!'

To this the very understandable response of the old retainer is, 'What frenzy is this?'; but Sir Walter knows his own guilt. At the climax of the final battle '*a thunderbolt strikes the Mandrake's Hollow, and exposes a skeleton*' – the bones of his victim – and he proclaims his crime and drops dead. The comics re-enter with the inevitable papers from the old chest that prove Lancewood's identity, and the curtain drops on a tableau outlined against perfectly gratuitous red fire. These extremities are handled with such gusto, such a switchback motion between apparently deliberate exaggeration and knowing, heavily signalled bathos, that one is tempted to see them as the 1841 equivalent of high camp; the suspicion becomes stronger at every climax of the action.

The first act ends conventionally with the fight in which the lone sailor defeats a deluge of enemies singlehanded, and it is managed so as to stress its symbolic, anti-realistic qualities. Lancewood is shown into a bedroom in what he does not yet know to be his own house. As Ruth leaves him there, '*Characteristic music*' announces the arrival of the villain and his cohorts '*from underground*'; they are actually propelled upwards on to the stage through a trap, as if direct from hell. Then Lancewood, contemplating a portrait of his father, checks out the latest hat he has put on and finds that it has a label announcing that it belongs to Sir Michael Lancewood – his 'own name with a title added!' The first of the villains, complaining that it is 'dark as hell', assails him; Lancewood works his way through them, up to the point of defending himself against all four at once with a sword in each hand before leaping to safety through a window into '*highly brilliant flood of moonlight*'. This is the end of the act. In immediate juxtaposition (allowing for an elaborate scene change) comes a sunlit scene of 'rural fête' at which, as the curtain rises, another fight is taking place, two countrymen in a bout of single-stick, with the comic, Pipps, commentating on the action, and the second comic, Dobbin, making himself into a funny picture by looking through a horse-collar. The parody of the foregoing scene, its deliberate inversion, is unmistakable.

What I am trying to establish in this case is not that the melodramatic devices which it deploys with such exuberant ease are actually presented to the Royal Standard audience as parody. They are, I think, not to be taken entirely seriously all the time; the audience is expected to recognise the standard tropes, and to enjoy them on several levels, relishing both the turns of the plot and their own expertise in anticipating those turns. This participatory pleasure is not therefore intended to discredit the moral assumptions on which the fable is based. These are, in fact, shown to operate powerfully in the triumph of good over temptation to evil that runs alongside the spectacle of lost heirs and wicked squires. This strand culminates in the penultimate scene, when Martin Tareseed, Ruth's rejected admirer, who has been truculent and obstructive to the course of justice and true love throughout, speaks out his grievance to her and asserts his determination to have her. His language, significantly, is different both from the comic mummerset of the villagers and the flowery literary rhetoric of heroine, hero and villain: he speaks in northern dialect, for which no realistic justification is offered, and which would seem to be purely symbolic, defining his roughness, his humble station and his ultimate honesty.

In a speech whose biblical periods seem designed to be taken very seriously, offering a threat and also eliciting sympathy for his sufferings, he tells her she has refused me, and I've still been kind; thee hast injured me, and I'm willing to return good for evil; thee looked black on me, when a smile would have bought my soul; thee brought home a stranger, and bid him welcome, to my very face; thee spurned me like a beggar's dog; thee taxed me with murder; thee heaped injury upon wrong – yet I lov'd thee on, and love thee still.

This is a quite different tone of solemnity from the elaborately self-conscious stage language of the rest of the play. It could command serious attention, generating a real tension about the outcome – which is that he threatens to rape her and destroy the letter that will save the hero, and she '*gradually unfastens*' his fingers from it, talking of their childhood; he exclaims, 'Thee hast conquered,' no doubt to the cheers of the audience for the power of innocence and the nobility of the poor man. Yet while this idealism is acknowledged and reinforced, the rest of the play is nevertheless a kind of joke about such literary fantasies. Their deliberate elaboration, and the including of comic juxtaposition and inversion, is a form of jokey self-confidence about the genre, a shared acknowledgment, between the dramatist and the audience, that the play is only an artefact, that its purpose is the telling of a story, by means of certain stage techniques – stylised language, lighting effects, trick scenery, and the actor's skills of declamation and fighting – that are self-conscious, even intertextual, self-referencing within the audience's knowledge of the genre.

Most critical commentary on nineteenth-century melodrama speaks from a position of assumed superiority: modern tastes find it funny, and suppose its pre-modern audiences did not. There is no reason, however, beyond presentist or élitist prejudice, to assume that the classically educated gentlemen who frequented the Adelphi, or Shoreditch audiences made up of 2000 skilled artisans in such trades as silk-weaving, cabinet-making and toy manufacture, a settled and independent urban population created over several generations by immigration from all over Europe, were culturally or theatrically naive. They were surely just as able as we are to use melodramatic storytelling to engage in 'an active, lucid confrontation' with the loss of sacred certainties, and deliberately and repeatedly to reassemble a moral structure from the debris of desacralised signification. If we acknowledge the place of laughter in melodrama, and the consequent possibility that its texts, even 150 years ago, were being read as multidimensional, then we may extend the discovery of 'clear-sightedness and authenticity' which Brooks regards as at stake in our culture to these plays and their audiences.

Notes

1. Peter Brooks, *The Melodramatic Imagination: Balzac, Henry James, Melodrama and the Mode of Excess* (New Haven: Yale University Press, 1976), p. 21.
2. M. Bakhtin, *The Dialogic Imagination: Four Essays by Mikhail Bakhtin*, ed. Michael Holquist, trans. Caryl Emerson and Michael Holquist (Texas: University of Texas Press, 1981), p. 47.
3. David Danow, *The Thought of Mikhail Bakhtin* (London: Macmillan, 1991), pp. 51–2.

4. Quoted in Herschel Baker, *John Philip Kemble* (Cambridge, Mass.: Harvard University Press, 1942), p. 190.
5. Michael Booth, *English Melodrama* (London: Herbert Jenkins, 1965), pp. 35–6.
6. Fanny Kemble, *Records of a Girlhood* (New York: Henry Holt and Company, 2nd ed. 1883), p. 412.
7. Ibid., p. 507.
8. Ibid., p. 508.
9. See, for example, John Payne Collier's evidence to the 1832 Parliamentary Committee, where he cites (para. 304) '*Victorine*, which I suppose everybody has seen with very great pleasure. It is a well-conducted piece (I do not speak of the introduction of Bonassus); it has a most unexceptionable moral.'
10. *Oxberry's Dramatic Biography*, New Series, vol. 1 (London: George Virtue, 1827), p. 190.
11. Ibid., p. 198.
12. See Edmund Yates, *Edmund Yates, His Recollections and Experiences*, 2 vols (London: Bentley, 1884), pp. 197–8.
13. See his preface to the play, printed in vol. viii of the *Acting National Drama* (London, n.d.), from which quotations here are taken.
14. For a more detailed discussion of this play, see J.S. Bratton et al., *Acts of Supremacy* (Manchester: Manchester University Press, 1991), pp. 27–33.
15. Quotations are from the edition printed in *Dicks Standard Plays*, no. 495 (London, n.d.).

THE HORROR OF OPACITY

The Melodrama of Sensation in the Plays of André de Lorde

TOM GUNNING

> You think that when you die, you go to
> heaven. You don't. You come to us.
>
> *The Tall Embalmer in 'Phantasm II'*

Peter Brooks's seminal re-examination of melodrama reopened interest in what had seemed for several generations a dead genre (at least in terms of academic attention) by switching focus from character psychology to an essential semiotic drama. The scale on which twentieth-century theatrical theorists weighed melodrama and found it lacking balanced itself on complex, fully developed characterisations. Such critics claimed that characters in melodrama were limited to Manichean presentations of virtue and vice which allowed no development or nuance of ambiguity, but Brooks revealed that the drama of melodrama lay not in character but in signs. While the essential nature of vice and virtue might be unalterable and eternal in the world of melodrama, drama occurs as the villainous character cloaks himself in the signs of virtue and besmirches innocence with the appearance of vice. Melodrama reaches its climax less by the triumph of virtue than by 'making the world morally legible'[1] as truth shines through all repression.

For Brooks, melodrama reveals itself as a play of signs, moving from their eclipse by the powers of evil to their final visibility and acknowledgment. Melodramas, rather than being plays of blood and thunder, sound and fury, are in fact dramas of significance, and even *signifiance*, the construction of meaning. Finding his ideal model of melodrama in Pixérécourt, Brooks defines the form in terms of its legibility and moral order. Although Brooks affirms melodrama's essential relation to forms of excess, this excess is for him an excess of meaning, or expression, which must muster energy to break through the repression occasioned by a false play of signs.[2]

Brooks's concept of communicating excess allows him to re-examine the deficiencies of melodramas as literature. What carries meaning in melodrama is not simply the verbal text but a host of other registers of signs, as if, as Brooks puts it, words were inadequate to express the moral truth of melodrama's project.[3] Although Brooks acknowledges melodrama's birth from the spirit of music and claims that music aided the legibility of melodramatic action,[4] the key signs are visual, exemplified by the tableau. This halting of stage action so that it forms a 'stage picture' at a particular moment of dramatic intensity and significance transforms action into an instance of meaning. For Brooks the tableau exemplifies 'melodrama's primordial concern to make its signs clear, unambiguous, and impressive',[5] providing 'the opportunity to see meanings represented, emotions and moral states rendered in clear visible signs'.[6]

This reorientation has opened up melodrama's wide-ranging significance for theatre and film history. However, Brooks places his redefinition within rather narrow historical limits, locating the decadence of this melodramatic ideal in the 1830s.[7] Therefore, if the concept of melodrama holds significance for a later period of theatre history and for the whole history of film, we shall have to deal with changes and mediations. Further, the later history of theatre and film bring other aspects of the melodramatic tradition to the foreground. The 'moral occult', the hidden power and significance of virtue which Brooks situates as the ruling aspect of melodrama,[8] may be only one side of the melodramatic tradition, and should be balanced by another aspect, that of the thrill or sensation.

Brooks associates the decline of melodrama around the middle of the 19th century with the pursuit of new categories of thrills and the cultivation of excitement and suspense.[9] Undoubtedly, the pursuit of thrills had been a founding element of melodramatic dramaturgy from Pixérécourt onwards.[10] Brooks in effect 'tames' this spectacular excess by defining it as 'expressive', a process of rendering meanings unambiguous and impressive. However, Brooks's notion of the decadence of melodrama indicates that excess can become separated from its significant motive and be pursued as an end in itself, aimed towards affects (excitement, suspense) rather than cognitive and moral significance. Melodrama might be best seen as a dialectical interaction between moral significance and an excess aimed precisely at non-cognitive affects, thrills, sensations, and strong affective attractions. The very longevity of melodrama as a form demands a historical treatment in which the proportions of this combination as well as the specific nature of the significances and thrills it offers must be specified for each period and each dramatic form.

For Brooks, the melodramatic tableau exemplifies the moral occult and the form's drive towards meaning: the stage action achieves such clarity that it need only arrest itself to convey its significance. A term from the Anglo-American melodramatic tradition could serve as its complement on the side of thrills: the 'sensation scene'. Around 1860 the term 'sensation' migrated from its primary meaning of the evidence of the senses to describe the centre-piece of a new form of theatrical melodrama. The term can be briefly defined as a scene whose spectacular appearance and technical virtuosity was devised precisely to thrill the audience.[11] Dion Boucicault seems to have popularised both term and practice, and Frank Rahill lists some of his more famous sensation scenes: the flaming river boat in *The Octoroon*; the hanging of Achmet in *Jessie Brown*; the burning of the house in Five Points in *The Poor of New York*; the storming of the sponging house in *Formosa*; the horse races in *The Flying Scud* and *The Jilt*; the sinking ship in *Daddy O'Dowd*.[12] From this list we can recognise that the sensation scene required not only the resources of the spectacle stage, but an explosive, even chaotic, measure of excitement and motion, a rather large scale, and, to guarantee its impression, an attention to verisimilitude. 'Sensation is what the public wants,' Boucicault was quoted as saying, 'and you can't give them too much of it.'[13]

Sensation referred to a particularly intense, even overwhelming experience. The new theatrical use of the term targets the spectator as the key in this modernisation of melodrama, focusing on the effect of the scene, its powerful assault on the senses of the audience. The term 'sensation drama' soon became a term for the genre itself, indicating the key role the sensation scene played in its structure and financial success. The *Oxford English Dictionary* quotes Thackeray as writing in 1861: 'At the theatres they have a new name for their melodramatic pieces, and call them "Sensation Dramas".' Although the term seems to have begun in the theatre, the later part of the 19th century soon saw the 'sensation novels' of Wilkie Collins, and the sensation press. One could argue for the term being one of the keywords of the popular culture of modernity.

Brooks's moral occult and the effects of the sensation scene do not exclude each other, since the strong impression of a sensation scene could conceivably express a moral order. Rather, the contrast between the two lies in the way they address an audience. Brooks's melodramatic dramaturgy cannot function without a moral order. The effect of the sensation scene need not contradict such an order, but it does not depend upon it. The sensation drama addresses itself directly to the body and senses. It is physical and emotional sensation rather than moral cognition that counts.

This change in address derives from broad historical changes as well as evolution within theatrical form. Changes in audiences, the technological evolution of stagecraft, and the economics of theatre management all contributed to the sensation drama. But more broadly this transformation of melodrama responds to changes in late nineteenth-century life. Commentators on the sensation drama constantly noted its pursuit of the contemporaneous. A commenter on the sensation novel in the British journal *The Quarterly* said in 1863:

> Proximity is, indeed, one great element of sensation. It is necessary to be near a mine to be blown up by its explosion; and a tale which aims at electrifying the nerves of the reader is never thoroughly effective unless the scene be laid in our days and among the people we are in the habit of meeting.[14]

When the author compares the proximity of the contemporary with an explosion, he coincidentally also cites a frequent example of a sensation scene. The sensation drama presents the modern environment as a series of shocks, filled with assaults on the senses. Late melodrama's fascination with the urban milieu and its staging of the wonders and disasters of technology shows that this entertainment based in sensations both portrayed and helped mediate the new abrasive experience of modernity.[15]

If Pixérécourt, emerging from the French Revolution, stands as Brooks's model for the melodrama of the moral occult, the complementary exemplar of a theatre of sensation appears in the Third Republic about a century later. André de Lorde was the seminal playwright of the Théâtre du Grand Guignol, the theatre of horror which opened in Paris in 1897, and for which de Lorde wrote over a hundred plays from 1901 to 1926.[16] Grand Guignol as a theatrical genre could be seen as a late survival of melodrama as well as its final decadence in Brooks's terms: a theatre entirely dedicated to the evocation of sensations and the undermining of moral order. De Lorde's plays pursue a deliberate modernity, making use of the most contemporary technology and locales – the telephone, the motor car, the X-ray, the operating theatre and the examining rooms of Salpêtrière. The undermining of the moral occult plays an essential role in the modernity of this theatre, as ethical drama becomes replaced by a conflict between official discourses which are shown to be inadequate in creating a moral universe. De Lorde's plays engage with a series of contemporaneous experiences and discourses, providing a fine example of the transformations of melodrama as it entered the 20th century.

Grand Guignol often inverts melodramatic traditions, returning to a Sadean universe in which vice is rewarded and virtue suffers horribly. A number of de Lorde plays explicitly reverse melodramatic topoi. For instance, David Belasco's 1893 play *The Girl I Left Behind Me* could still recycle the final sensation scene that Boucicault introduced in *Jessie Brown* in 1858, in which besieged defenders of a stockade prepare to kill their womenfolk rather than let them fall into the hands of the non-white attackers (Muslim rebels in *Jessie Brown* and Native Americans in Belasco's play). This murderous (not to mention sexist and racist) act in both plays is interrupted at the last moment as the women hear the arrival of rescuing troops.

In *Le Dernier torture*, 1904,[17] de Lorde recycles the cliché in a more contemporary setting, a French consulate in 1900 Peking besieged by Boxer rebels intent on ridding their country of foreign devils. As the situation looks hopeless, D'Hemelin, the consul, decides he must kill his daughter Denise rather than have her undergo torture and rape. As the Boxers scale the walls, Denise calls for her father to save her. Holding her close, D'Hemelin fires his pistol. Clinging to her dead body he hears the sound of a bugle, as allied forces arrive and rescue the beseiged Europeans. The curtain lowers slowly as D'Hemelin lets his daughter's body fall and stutters madly, 'Saved, saved.'[18] De Lorde does more, though, than simply reverse the ending. Not only does this last-minute rescue fail, its failure causes the destruction of the family, daughter dead and the Occidental patriarchal authority driven mad.

De Lorde's dramas push the excess of melodrama towards these dark endings which not only do not reveal a moral occult, but actually display a vertiginous image of order destroyed and discourse rendered meaningless. In this theatre the pursuit of sensation not only runs counter to a moral order, but the dominant sensation of horror results partly from this destruction. How, then, did de Lorde define this modern sensation, the *frisson* for which the Grand Guignol became so famous? In a self-reflective scene in his play *Figures de cire,* some characters who have just attended a performance at the Grand Guignol discuss the fascination the production exerted on them. A woman describes it as 'a strange impression. It grabs you there inside [she points to the pit of her stomach], it stirs you up; you want to leave, you want to stay … it is at the same time disagreeable and … marvellous.'[19]

De Lorde wished to produce an explicitly physical sensation of *trac* or *frisson.* Located in the pit of the stomach, it grabs one from within. There is nothing sublimated about this sensation, no invocation of the exalted power of sight to provide moral vision. The Grand Guignol affects the stomach, not the soul. Further, this physical sensation need have no rational basis. Later in this scene a man discusses the experience of *trac,* cold sweating fear, and emphasises the irrationality of the experience: 'it is not a reasonable business: it is a sensation…. When one is afraid one fears everything and nothing, without reason.'[20]

While this image of a material universe beset by suffering and madness seems at antipodes to the moral occult, the excess it unfolds leads back to melodrama's earliest sources in the Gothic fascination with horror. This early romantic inheritance recalls Brook's analysis of the moral occult's historical and cultural origins, which somewhat complicate its stabilising and meaning-giving function. The moral occult derives from the 'fragmentary and desacralised remnants of sacred myth'.[21] Melodrama for Brooks already proceeds from a world in decay in which the possibility of transcendence is threatened. If melodrama's meanings must be excessive to be legible, it is partly because the signs of virtue are slowly becoming unrecognisable. In Grand Guignol one encounters not simply the collapse of a sacred world, but its liquid putrescence. The moral occult has literally decomposed into elements of sensation.

In classic melodrama the moral occult plays more than an ideological role; it determines dramatic structure. Since the moral order has been occluded behind the deceptive play of signs, melodrama displays not only a fascination with the hidden, with depths, but an epistemania, a desire to know all. Melodramatic protagonists strive to pull things into the light of day, to unearth the truth, even if this requires violence, the pressure applied to the surface of reality which yields its true meaning, like a prisoner under interrogation.[22] In isolating this essential motive force of melodrama, Brooks links the form with the major intellectual trajectory of the 19th century, the faith in the knowledge-yielding gaze. Like the men of medicine described in Foucault's *The Birth of the Clinic,* melodrama undertakes the project of pushing this gaze ever further into the depths of things, seeking truth beneath the surface as vision moves from a reflection upon the appearance of things to become a probing and even destructive tool.[23] This redefinition of the gaze as an incision into the depths is theorised in Foucault's discussion of autopsies and the dissection of corpses as the foundation of modern medicine and, in some sense, modern knowledge.[24]

This determination to unearth the truth behind appearances remains central to de Lorde's theatre and establishes his strong ties to the melodramatic tradition. However, rather than revealing the moral occult, this very obsession with discovering the truth has been reduced to conflicts between reified forms of official discourse. In the place of the rag-and-bone remnants of the great myths, de Lorde deals with a patchwork of the dominant discourses of his time, medicine and law, with medicine exerting the most modern fascination. One could claim that melodrama has always argued for the emotional needs of its characters against the desiccated discourses of established powers: corrupted religion, law or hypocritical morality. But as melodrama enters the 20th century, the discourses of republican law and modern medicine become particularly problematic elements, since they partake of the same ambition as the form itself: exposing and speaking the truth. I believe such conflicts between forms of established discourse may define an essential aspect of twentieth-century melodrama. The central conflicts of later Hollywood melodramas become clearer if we view them as arenas in which opposing discourses with separate claims to the truth contend for legitimation. De Lorde's horror plays give these conflicts particularly modern outcomes, as the final revelations uncover, not moral truth, but the triad that marks the end of *Le Dernier torture*: a corpse, madness and speechlessness.

De Lorde began writing in a society that was negotiating the roles of law and medicine in dealing with deviance. As Robert Nye has shown, the Third Republic fashioned an intersection between legal and medical discourse which sought both to define the threats of deviants (the criminal, the mad, and the perverse) and to establish a basis for treatment and discipline. Although there were debates between masters of the respective discourses (as well as within them), by the end of the 19th century the discussion of crime and madness in France had become the shared responsibility of legal and medical discourse.[25] Through this overlap these specialised discourses strove to produce an official truth. In de Lorde's plays, cases of crime or madness are frequently subjected to this double vision of supposedly compatible discourses, surveying the new terrain which much of later melodramatic cinema would explore. Even in film melodramas that are not as determinedly perverse as de Lorde's, the moral occult becomes harder to trace. In many of these films the revelation of innocence seems to be replaced by an attempt to fix characters and actions in a net of often contradictory discourses, and in de Lorde, as in many film melodramas, the character subjected to these discourses is most often a woman.[26] The persecuted innocent heroine gives way to a more ambiguous figure as films trace the uneasy fit between these problematic women and official discourses.

A number of de Lorde's plays actually stage a sort of battle royal between these two discourses. The central scene in *L'Homme mysterieu* presents a hearing in an asylum as Raymond Bercier (committed by his wife after he tried to kill her) strives to regain his freedom. At the hearing the asylum doctor claims that Raymond suffers from a sort of demi-mania which allows him to appear sane when in fact he still suffers from an intense persecution mania and is extremely dangerous. The magistrate listens sympathetically to the patient, who claims he is being held by a sort of medical tyranny. At one point Raymond exclaims to the doctor, 'If I answer your questions I am mad.... If I remain silent, I am mad.' The magistrate decides that the asylum doctor who wishes to hold Raymond even though he shows few signs of mental disturbance during his examination exerts an arbitrary power, a medical form of the *ancien régime*'s *lettre de cachet*, and orders the man to be released. Returning home, Raymond slashes his wife's face with a knife and strangles his brother.[27]

When the magistrate accuses the doctor of tyranny, he responds by invoking one of the great legal scandals of the Third Republic, the case of Jeanne Weber which shook public faith in legal and medical discourse. Weber was brought to trial twice for strangling infants left in her care (a total of five deaths). However, medical experts testified that their examination of the bodies of her victims could not establish that the children had been murdered and she was acquitted both times. A few years later Weber was caught attempting another infanticide and her final trial brought not only her conviction but public condemnation of medical testimony and court procedures.[28]

Weber inspired the main character of another de Lorde play, *L'Acquittée*. After a woman, Mme Menard, has been acquitted of strangling children, a doctor and the examining magistrate discuss the case in chambers. The judge doubts the woman's guilt, since the crimes have absolutely no motive. Rather than proving her innocent, the doctor replies, this lack of motive simply proves her mad. Frustrated, the magistrate desires the truth: 'The woman knows it.... It is there behind her forehead. If only we could break it open.'[29] We see here de Lorde's particularly modern reshaping of the epistemological impulse of melodrama. The truth lies behind things and violence might be able to lay it bare. Frustration comes from the inadequacy of rational discourses in dealing with irrational events. However metaphorical the magistrate's desire to open the woman's forehead may be, it images the discovery of truth as an autopsy, a probing of the few grams of cerebral matter.

As the doctor and magistrate continue their discussion, they regret the forbidding of torture in examination. However, the magistrate becomes uncomfortable with this nostalgia for pre-Revolutionary methods, claiming he has no love of cruelty. 'Of course, of course,' responds the doctor. 'It is what we call scientific curiosity.'[30] The doctor, a student of Charcot, proposes that when the woman comes to gain her final release he might be able to hyponotise her. When the woman enters, the doctor puts her in a trance and the following exchange takes place:

Doctor: Shouldn't we take advantage of the situation in order to ...

Magistrate: In order to ...
Doctor: In order to know.[31]

In a deep trance the acquitted woman acts out her recent murders before the astonished gentlemen. However, this proof of her guilt has no legal force. The woman is awakened and let go. The play ends with an image

56

that has become a signature of de Lorde, as the two men stand immobile and speechless watching from the window as Mme Menard leaves the building.[32]

De Lorde both invokes and subverts official discourse. This rational discourse is obsessed with the desire to discover the truth from both a legal and scientific perspective. This desire for the truth can become an obsession which pitches these discourses of reason into madness. Dr Gorlitz in *The Laboratory of Hallucinations* expresses this desire to penetrate into the depth of man's newly discovered material being:

Ah, the brain ... what a superb machine. What an extraordinary mechanism.... It is there, at the bottom of this nervous tissue, that all that *is* is played out, as well as all that is not.... Consciousness, without which the exterior world is only a vain word ... and also illusion, fantasies, hallucinations. Oh, this marvellous laboratory of thought, of life ... and of death. And all of that hidden ... no ... veiled. That's it: veiled. And I have lifted the veil.[33]

However, when the veil is lifted, the brain probed, or the guilty made to confess under hypnosis, the truth so discovered has no moral power, no efficacy. The result is only the end of discourse, a stunned silence before the physicality of death or madness's ability to disguise itself. This speechlessness which frequently ends de Lorde's dramas contrasts sharply with the 'text of muteness' that Brooks finds in earlier melodramas,[34] where non-verbal gestures convey a fullness of meaning that words cannot express. De Lorde's horrified silences close on a hollow bereft of meaning. Characters do not speak because there is nothing to say, the world has been drained of expressiveness. De Lorde's plays involving medical authority frequently end with a grim parody of its discourse. In *The Laboratory of Hallucinations*, after Dr Gorlitz has performed his incision on the brain of his wife's lover and rendered him mad, he suddenly finds himself overpowered by the madman he has created, who begins operating on his tormentor. As he brings down a pair of scissors on the doctor's skull, the lover screams: 'I enlarge the opening. I wipe out his intelligence ... there is nothing left ... there is nothing left but suffering ... only suffering.'[35]

More often than not, rational discourse obscures any access to truth in de Lorde's plays, and not infrequently the medical experiments aimed at uncovering the truth are revealed as acts of random cruelty. In his famous drama *Une Leçon à Salpêtrière*, Claire, a woman patient, claims that one of the medical students has subjected her to needless experiments and in the process paralysed her arm. Although a sympathetic intern finds evidence of this, the director, Dr Marbois, diagnoses her claim as a persecution complex and he presents her to the interns as a classic example. Intending to undertake further experiments, the doctor asks an intern to place her under hypnosis. Claire recognises the intern as her former tormentor and throws a basin of acid in his face. The Grand Guignol here employed its most elaborate make-up effects to re-create the horror of a face burned beyond recognition. As the intern goes into convulsions and the terrified interns 'mill about like their insane patients, not knowing what to do', Dr Marbois simply launches into a new lecture, demonstrating medical procedure: 'First one must immediately neutralise the acid, and prevent it from penetrating the tissues.... In cases like this, one generally uses an alkaline solution.' The curtain comes down as he continues to lecture his students, now indistinguishable from those they treat.[36]

The all-knowing gaze of the doctor and the discourse which supports and translates it has become opaque and meaningless. The examining doctor himself suffers from a sort of hysterical blindness in not recognising Claire's persecution. His professional discourse becomes a hysterical symptom, a mechanical response rather than the expression of truth. De Lorde's fascination with madness, deviant sexuality and hypnosis may make him appear as a precursor of the emerging discourse of psychoanalysis, though this would be incorrect. De Lorde stays firmly within the domain of Freud's teacher, Charcot, the head of the Salpêtrière, and sees madness as the result of physical damage to the brain or degenerative heredity. This distance from psychoanalysis is significant, since Brooks makes a convincing case for psychoanalysis as a classic melodramatic discourse, one involved in liberating truth from repression.[37] De Lorde remains within the narrow materialism of the accepted medical discourse of his era, and this partly determines his pessimism, his lack of faith in a moral occult. For de Lorde, the world consists of sensation and its material support. When one probes beyond physical borders, one discovers only death.

L'Horrible expérience, for instance, seems to invoke a Freudian scenography. In the opening scenes Dr Charrier speaks to his future son-in-law Jean of his great love for his daughter Jeanne. When Jeanne is injured in a car accident and dies in her father's surgery, her father insists on trying his latest invention, an electrical contraption which can stimulate the heart after it has stopped. Jean objects to the experiment as a profanation, but the father insists on making the incision into his daughter's breast and inserting his electrical device. The machine seems to revive her heartbeat and her hand moves convulsively. Jean insists this is nothing but the onset of rigor mortis. However, as the father leans over his daughter, her hand catches his throat and squeezes convulsively. They both fall dead.[38]

Clearly de Lorde (consciously or not) supplies material here for a Freudian analysis in which the father's desire to perform the operation on his beloved daughter stands in for a sexual act. This would also explain his son-in-law's and servant's horror at the experiment and their conclusion that the father's death is somehow a fitting punishment. Of course, the beauty of Freudian analysis lies in the fact that it needs no confession of intention from the material it analyses. However, if we take de Lorde on his own terms, we see how unlike psychoanalysis his topology is, and how the lack of psychoanalytical discourse deprives him of a moral occult. Instead, he remains face to face with the corpse, and the *frisson* of an encounter with death.

When Jean objects to the doctor's experiment, the father doubts the moral basis of his objection: 'You are afraid. You claim to have loved her and yet you are afraid of her, afraid of her dead body, and that is perhaps not even fear, but simple disgust.'[39] Charrier speaks the discourse of scientific curiosity, the methodology of the medical autopsy, indicating to his son-in-law that one must 'steel one's nerves'[40] to penetrate into what Foucault calls 'the white brightness of death',[41] and fulfil one's epistemania. What is at issue here is not simply a displaced sex act but an obsessive desire to see, to know and to explain. However, the experiment is brought short by the grip of death. Instead of a revived corpse the experiment produces a pair of cadavers, father and daughter, collapsed on the surgery floor.

This death-dealing gesture goes to the heart of de Lorde's ambiguous but rich relation to melodrama. The suddenly animated hand could be, as Dr Charrier interprets it, the sign of the experiment's success, the doctor's triumph over death. Or it could be, as his sceptical son-in-law says, simply a mechanical convulsive gesture, something which the two doctors had described earlier in the play as an act without consciousness or meaning.[42] Or it could be seen as a melodramatic gesture *par excellence*, excessive significance sliding into another register of signs, a revelation of the moral occult in which, as Jean says in the play's final line, 'Death has revenged itself.' But if death's vengeance is the final meaning revealed, we find transcendence again blocked. The cadaver's final gesture by no means points beyond itself, but rather affirms itself as a terminus, a barrier with no beyond. The drama of signs ends in the contemplation of a corpse.

Nothing beyond itself, except the *frisson*, the shudder, the knot in the pit of the stomach, the sensation experienced by the spectator. De Lorde frequently provides such scenes of death and madness with spectators rendered speechless by what they have seen (if not actually driven mad), and undoubtedly places these astonished witnesses as surrogates for the audience in the theatre. De Lorde's works may present a final vision, but what is seen obstructs any attempt at significance. Instead of a scene arrested at the moment of transparency and significance, de Lorde's tableaux freeze with a paralysing impotence. Their meaning can be summed up by the final stage directions of his madhouse drama *Les Invisibles*: 'the curtain falls slowly on this tableau of sorrow, misery and death'.[43]

De Lorde's work points beyond the limits imposed on a contemporary understanding of melodrama by the very brilliance of Brooks's semiotic dramaturgy. Melodrama not only stages the drama of the moral occult but also its final dissolution, as sensation overwhelms significance. However, in describing this modern form of melodrama one extends rather than contradicts Brooks, who understood melodrama as an attempt to deal with the destruction of a cohesive concept of the sacred and its social representatives. Melodrama's identity as a 'peculiarly modern form'[44] derives as much from its post-sacred nature as its attempt to discover a moral occult in compensation. I would simply maintain that what Brooks sees as the decadence of melodrama is really its necessary trajectory, as the moral occult becomes a tangle of contradictory discourses and the sense of personal identity and integrity on which a new moral order rested becomes dissolved by a growing sense of the precariousness of reason and the materiality of consciousness. In this sense the latest heir of the melodramatic tradition, and certainly of the theatre of de Lorde, would be the horror films of the 70s and 80s which rediscovered a visuality of horror through physical effects and a sensational approach which produced truly grisly works of art.

Notes

1. Peter Brooks, *The Melodramatic Imagination: Balzac, Henry James, Melodrama and the Mode of Excess* (New Haven: Yale University Press, 1976).
2. Ibid., pp. 40–1.
3. Ibid., pp. 46, 57.
4. Ibid., pp. 48–9.
5. Ibid., p. 48.
6. Ibid., p. 62.
7. Ibid., p. 88.
8. Ibid., p. 5.
9. Ibid., p. 89.
10. Frank Rahill, *The World of Melodrama* (University Park: Pennsylvania State University Press, 1967), p. 43. I agree with Mary Ann Doane's extension of some of my work on early cinema to an understanding of melodrama 'as an organization of "thrills" and "sensations"' (Mary Ann Doane, 'Melodrama, Temporality, Recognition: American and Russian Silent Cinema', *Cinefocus* 2, 1, Fall 1991, p. 14. Reprinted from *East-West Film Journal* 4, 2). Ben Singer has reminded us that the primary meaning of the term 'melodrama' around the turn of the century was sensational, fast-paced action dramas typified by early serial films ('The Perils of Empowerment: Agency and Victimization in the Serial-Queen Melodrama, *Camera Obscura* 22, and his forthcoming dissertation, New York University).
11. Rahill, op. cit., p. 189.
12. Ibid., p. 189.
13. Ibid., p. 189.
14. Quoted in Winifred Hughes, *The Maniac in the Cellar: Sensation Novels of the 1860s* (Princeton: Princeton University Press, 1980), p. 18.
15. For a brilliant presentation of 'sensation' as part of the environment of modernity in daily life as reflected in the sensational press, see Ben Singer's 'A New and Urgent Need for Stimuli: Sensational Melodrama and Urban Modernity', a paper delivered at the BFI 1992 Melodrama Conference.
16. Mel Gordon, *The Grand Guignol: Theater of Fear and Terror* (New York: Amok Press, 1988), p. 21.
17. André de Lorde, *Théâtre d'épouvante* (Paris: Librairie Théâtral, Artisque et Littéraire, nd.) pp. 259–95.
18. Ibid., p. 295.
19. Ibid., p. 109 (my translation).
20. Ibid., p. 110 (my translation).
21. Brooks, op. cit., p. 5.
22. See Brooks, op. cit., pp. 1, 19.
23. Michel Foucault, *The Birth of the Clinic: An Archaeology of Medical Perception*, trans. A.M. Sheridan Smith (New York: Vintage Books, 1975), p. 135.
24. Ibid., p. 196–9.
25. Robert A. Nye, *Crime, Madness and Politics in Modern France: The Medical Concept of a National Decline* (Princeton: Princeton University Press, 1984).
26. Mary Ann Doane's discussion of medical discourse in Hollywood melo-

dramas in *The Desire to Desire: The Woman's Film of the 1940s* (Bloomington: Indiana University Press, 1987), pp. 38–69, shows insight into this transformation of the moral occult. Doane does not emphasise the conflict of discourses *per se*, but she demonstrates the role the problematic fit of such discourses plays in these films. I believe *Possessed* (1947) offers a particularly interesting case of an attempt to make legal and medical discourses intersect over the body of a somnolent woman, albeit with a more conformist ending than de Lorde would offer.

27. André de Lorde, *La Folie au théâtre*, (Paris, Fontimoing et Cie, 1913), pp. 3–160.
28. Nye, op. cit., pp. 252–3.
29. André de Lorde, *La Théâtre de la peur* (Paris: Librairie Théâtrale, 1924), p. 168 (my translation).
30. Ibid., p. 168 (my translation).
31. Ibid., pp. 178–9 (my translation).
32. De Lorde's play contrasts with a more conventional melodrama, Leopold David Lewis's *The Bells*, 1871 (based on a French original by Erckmann and Chatrian, *Le Juif polonais*). This drama also uses mesmerism to reveal a murder but, following Brooks's understanding of the moral occult, the revelation also brings a rectification. Mathias's hallucinatory re-enactment of his crime appears as a court inquest with a death sentence pronounced by an imaginary magistrate. The sentence mystically causes Mathias's death, witnessed by a crowd who fall on their knees at this moral example.
33. Gordon, op. cit., pp. 160–1.
34. Brooks, op. cit., pp. 56–80.
35. Gordon, op. cit., p. 188.
36. De Lorde, *Épouvante*, pp. 80–1 (my translation).
37. Brooks, op. cit., pp. 200–1.
38. De Lorde, *Peur*, pp. 20–83.
39. Ibid., p. 74 (my translation).
40. Ibid., p. 78 (my translation).
41. Foucault, op. cit., p. 165.
42. De Lorde, *Peur*, p. 55.
43. De Lorde, *Folie*, p. 322 (my translation).
45. Brooks, op. cit., p. 14.

PART 2
TRANSFORMATIONS

SCATTERED CHIAROSCURO

Melodrama as a Matter of Seeing

MARTIN MEISEL

My title is stolen from Julian Hochberg, a psychologist who has written a great deal on the elements of perception and cognition in film, and is currently thinking about how seeing was constructed in the film melodrama of the 50s. One term in his description is 'scattered chiaroscuro', a phrase that can be stretched to cover a set of dichotomous relationships that provide a grid for the ill-defined, loosely bounded field of melodrama and the melodramatic. From the standpoint of its perceptual base and its cognitive ordering, these are: light and dark; picture and motion; focus and panorama, which have to do with space; succession and recurrence, which have to do with time, and in melodrama of the classic period accommodate a style of punctuated discontinuity, visually marked. Most of these pairs point to the activity of seeing, and I would argue that melodrama and the melodramatic are specially tuned to its pleasures and capacities, not just through elaborate spectacle (a common historical feature) but in a more primitive sense. There is a fit between how eye and mind are equipped to deal with the world and the spectra of melodrama, between the visual receptors and processors and the selective bias in the genre. In that primitive sense we are at home in melodrama, a fish in the water. Though both cognitively and affectively melodrama presents puzzles and often taps deep anxieties, and aims at being stressful through suspense and disconcerting through surprise, the 'reality' it allows us to construct can be reassuringly precisely because it rests on an enhanced aptitude for recognition, and a fundamental and enhanced capacity for sensory, perceptual and cognitive response.

What I have in mind on the visual side are such matters as the complementarity between sensitivity to form and contour and sensitivity to movement; the phenomenon of 'contour enhancement', whereby receptors responding to different intensities of light exaggerate the differences, making for quicker recognition as well as firmer edges and emphatic boundaries between relative dark and light. Then there is the reading and scanning process, selective and discontinuous, favouring angles, edges and sharp curves; and on the level of representation, the habits of 'perceptual defence' (seeing what is likely, what is familiar and probable) and 'perceptual vigilance' (seeing what is anticipated, even dreaded). In all this I take nineteenth-century melodrama in its mid-century flowering as the reference point, but my object is to begin to explore, tentatively, what has happened since to some of the elements of that comfortable fit between melodrama and visuality in how they construct our worlds.

Let us begin where on the very best authority all things begin, with darkness and light. The association of melodrama with elemental contrasts of darkness and light goes far beyond the literal lighting practices of the theatre in which it flourished, though these were by no means irrelevant. From the late 18th century to 1900, the whole period of the rise and flourishing of melodrama as an identifiable, named dramatic form, the theatre's capacity to create and manage light increased exponentially, with the Argand lamp (1780s); gas (from the 1820s) and control plate; limelight (1837) and electric arc (1848); and finally the incandescent lamp (1880s).[1] The capacity to light is also the ability to create contrasts. Consequently – despite the continuing illumination of the house, the dependence on footlights and other general lighting sources, the problems of shadows on painted illusionistic scenery, and the difficulty of creating and managing a focused beam – lighting for atmosphere and time of day, the use of gauzes, cut-outs, masking scenes, coloured glasses, lighting tubes, lenses, for supernatural events, night scenes, storm scenes, forests, gorges, eruptions, explosions, shipwrecks, dream visions, all made a profound contribution to the capacity for visual contrast and for creating an 'effect'. Indeed, early on, the whole art of melodrama, and under its influence drama in general, was conceived as the art of 'effect'. And 'effect' in turn, in the historical language of criticism, was borrowed, not from psychology (though it came to mean something that creates an involuntary response, before reflection) but from painting and drawing, where it spoke especially to the massing of light and shade, to the management of broad contrasts, to emphasis and accent and appropriate feeling of tone. At its most dramatic (that is, contrastive) it bespoke chiaroscuro.[2]

When George Bernard Shaw in his reviewing days gave his general definition for good melodrama, he saw it as 'depending for variety of human character, not on the high comedy idiosyncrasies which individualise people in spite of the closest similarity of age, sex, and circumstance, but on broad contrasts between types of youth and age, sympathy and selfishness, the masculine and the feminine, the serious and the frivolous, the sublime and the ridiculous, and so on'.[3] One result of such oppositions and contrasts is immediate recognition, an easier, quicker match to existing cognitive schema; a process that vision itself is primed to serve. As I have already suggested, in the retina the effect of varying light intensities on different clumps of receptors is to exaggerate difference, and to foster the perception of accented boundaries. The result is an enhanced perception of edges and contours, and an enhanced competence for giving shape to our world.

I stress this aspect of light and dark, this predisposition in seeing, because of that other set of associations between chiaroscuro and, not contrast, but atmosphere; and between obscurity and mystery, the latter the sustaining force in much melodrama. (It is worth remembering

66

Pixérécourt's pregnant title for the play once labelled the ancestral melo-drama, *The Child of Mystery*.[4]) Yet, despite an affective climate of danger, anxiety and impasse, despite an exposure to the buffeting of violent sensations, abrupt discontinuities, and deliberately evoked misapprehension, most melodrama carries with it an assurance of reassurance, of obscurities dispelled, ambiguities resolved, of a vigorously marked binary pattern of coherence.

I shall come back to this matter of light and dark and mystery by way of a modern instance in another medium – film – but I want first to take up another one of those pairs I mentioned initially, picture and motion. I have argued elsewhere that in the 19th century serial discontinuity was a common style, marking the dominant narrative, pictorial, and theatrical forms; and that all these forms were both narrative and pictorial, but that drama, indeed melodrama, was central, with its situational grammar, its punctuating crystallisations into a pictorial configuration with narrative import and accent: often an impasse, sometimes a resolution, typically followed by a cut (a curtain) or a dissolve. Motion in effect was movement to and away from pictures (or, more radically, was the succession of pictures) and even acting theory turned from a discourse based in rhetorical analysis to one that was fundamentally pictorial.[5] It is the pictorialism, with its narrative functions, that now stands out when compared with earlier and later styles; and yet it is clear that the theatre of melodrama called for an athleticism in its performances beyond that of the more traditional forms (though not beyond other popular forms); not just grappling and swordplay and fisticuffs, but climbing, swinging, leaping, tumbling and posing. Moreover, the scene itself was in motion, with fewer generalised settings and swifter changes within the frame, and indeed moving backgrounds, collapsing structures, mechanical devices and scene-transforming light. For all this it was necessary that the pictorial frame (the proscenium window) should stabilise, as it did progressively in tandem with deep lighting and increasing illusionism, to contain both picture and motion. Both required movement in the gaze: where there was motion, to follow and fix action at the centre of attention; where there was picture, to scan stillness for its dynamic instabilities and telling narrative and situational detail.[6]

The other two broadly dichotomous pairs that I mentioned – focus and panorama, which have to do with space, and succession and recurrence, which have to do with time – are perhaps better talked about jointly. To claim the aptness of treating space and time as a continuum in dramatic representations does not require modern physics. Their dependence was already part of the argument for the Unities – and here let me note parenthetically that the means and conventions for achieving representations of space and time vary with the medium, and affect the rhythms of the representation and thereby what Norman Bryson calls 'the content of the form'. Accordingly, the alternating pattern in melodrama of shallow front scenes with deep scenes more elaborately staged and set – and thus of intimate conversations with large, populous scenes of spectacle and action – can be compared with the pattern of establishing-shot and close-in work in film. These are conventional devices serving narrative and responding to different constraints and opportunities in the medium, but they do not represent necessary differences either in those mental constructs of space and time that result, or in the underlying cognitive matrices. Both practices feed whatever it is in us that assembles acceptable wholes out of synechdochic parts, that bridges perceptual gaps with plausible continuities, that accepts synoptic, relativistic and expressive aspects of the representation of time and space as 'real'.

I am arguing here, defensively, that the conditions of seeing in the theatre of melodrama, and the means at hand in the conventions of the form and the minds of the spectators, do not limit the playwright in comparison with the film-maker in the construction of space and time nor even radically differentiate them, and that therefore this construction may be part of the continuity between melodrama in theatre and film. I am arguing in fact with my title contributor, Julian Hochberg, and his collaborator Virginia Brooks, who point to the film-maker's special means for the visual construction of time and space through elision and assemblage, contraction and expansion, through parallel, repeated and multiple images. The film-maker, they write, 'can also juxtapose two events that are separated in space without actually traversing the intervening distance (e.g., a scene in New York and a scene in Paris, the one immediately after the other), and in so doing, he can make clear that the events that are being projected successively in fact occur at the same time' – a passage to be kept in mind when we consider the theatrical form of *The Corsican Brothers*. They continue:

> Unlike a theatrical drama, which *must* present at least some of the events in real time because the actors portraying those events are themselves constrained to act in real time, the motion picture is capable of retaining only those features which are of interest – a matter of economy that is the essence of an art form.[7]

Yet temporal compression and elision are intrinsic in the playwright's and the actor's craft, in scenes as well as between them, even where time is raised to consciousness; as in the last hour of Marlowe's *Faustus* (no less compressed than his opening-scene progress through the human arts and sciences); or Wilder's *Long Christmas Dinner*, or Beckett's day in the life of Vladimir and Estragon, or his montage of the three ages of Krapp. The race against time, functioning as an affective resistance to an approaching catastrophe, is a staple of melodrama of all varieties, complementing its fundamental pattern of peril and deliverance. The race typically unites space and time, and it is no doubt significant that it took its modern shape, along with melodrama, in the age that achieved the triumph of the Bradshaw – space rationalised in the net of railway timetables. A case in point was, in fact, the notorious 'railway effect', where, even in the grip of the mechanically inexorable, time and space and their dramatic management obey an affective imperative and remain elastic constructs. Following a sensational appearance in Augustin Daly's *Under the Gaslight* (1867), the body on the tracks went underground, to the lines beneath the city, in Dion Boucicault's aptly named *After Dark* (1868). Both plays

After Dark (Dion Boucicault, 1868)

exploited a mid-century appetite for domestic perils set in an urban panorama. In *After Dark*, the rescue of the unconscious victim from the oncoming train entails compression, delay, what might properly be called jump-cuts, and both forced and reversed perspective. Such sequences are made possible by a dramaturgy in which neither space nor time are givens; they are constructs, constructs using both tight focus and panorama and succession and recurrence, synthesised by the viewer out of what are essentially fragments, synechdochic elements succeeding each other within a frame.

I have fixed on *The Corsican Brothers* not least because of the remarkable resectioning of time and space its dramatic adapters found within their repertory, on a much grander scale than the effective montage of parts and wholes in multiple perspective that is constructed into coherence by the audience of *After Dark*. The original form was Alexandre Dumas's novella disguised as a traveller's account, with Dumas himself as reporter and witness.[8] The story there unfolds in linear fashion, passing

69

from Corsica to Paris. Travelling in Corsica, Dumas by chance becomes the guest of the de Franchis. There he searches out the special history of the family – its bloody, noble past, its culturally divided present, its hereditary warning apparition, and the uncanny bond between the brothers – and he is witness to the settling of a local vendetta. Lucien, the Corsican brother, deplores the passing of the old ways; Louis, the Parisian brother, has been furthering it – studying French law, and even at a distance getting his reluctant twin to arbitrate the bloody feud. The Corsican brother's room is full of arms and history; the Parisian brother's room is full of literature.

The heart of the story, and its appeal under all transformations, is the material bond between the brothers, a bond that bridges time and transcends distance. They feel and in part know simultaneously. That they were born attached as Siamese twins, one in blood and nervous system, gives a touch of scientific plausibility to the premise of simultaneous sensation and affect, whereby each feels the other's physical pain and mental anxiety at a distance, even to the point that when Louis is wounded to the death in a duel in Paris, Lucien is felled at the same instant in Corsica, and soon after informed by mysterious means as to what has happened. The novella also makes use of a plausible contemporary reality – a specified present (March 1841), a self-authenticating narrator (Dumas is pleased to discover on a bookshelf in Louis's room his own *Impressions de voyage*), and civilised, matter-of-fact discourse – to both legitimate and qualify the uncanny and the romantic in the tale.

In the novella we attend on the perceiving consciousness (Dumas's), a filter that lets through all that stirs the imagination but modulates affective participation. After Corsica, Dumas returns to Paris, where he calls on brother Louis. He also witnesses the first duel, after Louis tells him of the visit of his father's ghost, in accordance with family custom, to announce Louis's mortal hour, which arrives on schedule. Lucien then appears in Paris to avenge his brother before the mails could have reached him. He visits the scene of the first duel, and recognises it, and insists that the second be set in the same place at the same hour, using the same pistols, and seeming to involve the same personnages. The repetition is willed and retributive, and as such is calculated to reverse the original outcome.

Dumas reports the emotions of the actors, but chiefly reports the effect of what he sees and hears on himself. Much of what he tells us is told to him, narrated within his narrative. Despite the fact that characters are allowed foreknowledge, experience (both the narrator's and the reader's) is linear and progressive. Recurrence, as in the duel and its repetition, is part of succession, and works to emphasise difference.

The primary dramatic versions take a bolder approach. The seminal version was that by Grangé and Montépin, with perhaps Dumas taking a hand, since it played in his Théâtre Historique. Here, through direct representation, time and space are reordered, and unhesitatingly deployed for effect. The play version also eliminates Dumas as the filtering sensibility, though he has a vestigial presence in the Parisian traveller who calls on the Corsican branch with Louis's recommendation, and serves in the first act as excuse for the exposition. Melodrama in the theatre tends to elimi-

The Corsican Brothers

nate the middleman. The temporal premise of *The Corsican Brothers* in its theatrical embodiment is that the first two acts occur more or less simultaneously in different parts of Europe, but fuse in their climactic moments in a recurrence that is identity. The multilocal is brought into one cognitive space and moment, where separate actions also converge; and in all this the point of convergence, and the prime repetend, is a picture.

The first act is set in the hall of a château in Corsica where a Parisian traveller, Alfred Meynard, enjoys the hospitality, observes the native character, and receives the expository confidences of Fabien de Franchi. He hears, for one thing, of a family custom whereby apparitions appear to

71

The Opéra ball. Courtesy of Columbia Library.

survivors at the moment a member of the family dies, and of the first such incident 300 years earlier when a Franchi, writing to a distant brother for whom he felt uneasy, was so favoured and had revealed to his sight the spectacle of his brother's assassination. At the end of the act these events, evoked in the previous narration, are embodied for us in the present in full recurrent detail, with letter, apparition (gliding and rising across the stage – the famous 'Corsican trap'), hand, sigh, gesture and finally picture. The present victim is Fabien's brother, Louis. As his spirit directs the attention of Fabien and his mother to the back of the stage and then disappears, *'at the same moment the scene at the back opens and discloses an open clearing in the forest of Fontainebleau'.* On the ground is Louis de Franchi, supported by surgeon and second, and at centre Château-Renaud (Louis's antagonist) wiping his sword.[9]

The second act is set in Paris, beginning in the interior of the Opéra on a *bal masqué* night (and in Kean's production and later in Irving's represented as taking place on the stage and covered pit of the Opéra, with a painted or partly personated and perspectively sized audience in box and gallery mirroring the real one). This act takes Louis through the intrigue that brings him to the clearing in the Forest of Fontainebleau. The culminating discovery is *'an exact reproduction of the* TABLEAU *that terminated the First Act'.* Moreover, after a few words which serve mostly to register the time and lead our attention back to Corsica, *'the bottom of the stage opens slowly – the Chamber of the First Act is discovered, the clock marking the hour, ten minutes after nine;* MADAME DE FRANCHI *and* FABIEN *looking exactly as they did at the end of the First Act'.*[10]

72

The third act is set in the same clearing and provides a further recapitulation, temporally distinct. Château-Renaud, leaving Paris and the possible attentions of the law, has lost a carriage wheel passing through the Forest of Fontainebleau near the very place of the duel. He is shaken by the coincidence – the very same spot, almost the same time – it smacks of an extraordinary fatality, perhaps even the hand of heaven. Fabien appears, having come in pursuit – an apparition, at first sight. But he brings second and swords, and forces Château-Renaud to the field, brushing aside objections based on a code that has already permitted an expert to challenge and kill a tiro. The civilised duel has no superiority over the vendetta. The duel which then takes place passes from the Parisian to the Corsican mode when Château-Renaud's sword breaks, and Fabien forces a continuation with sword-blades tied to their wrists. Château-Renaud recognises the inevitable, and at the end of the hand-to-hand violence he is killed, same place, same hour, destroyed, if ever anyone was, by the return of the repressed. In a final image the ghost reappears on the scene, to console his twin and propose a meeting hereafter.

In the play, the uncanny is absorbed in the retributive and providential patterns that underlay the expectation of coherence in theatrical melodrama, patterns much stronger than in the narrative. The segments, heavily marked and each rising to a cadence – here a pictorial configuration – are composed into an affective whole. The serial discontinuity in what could be an open-ended series of effective, unstable situations resolves into a final stability.

At a point in the 1860s, some productions of the play in Britain were further enhanced by an allusion to a well-known image from paint and print known as *The Duel*, or *A Duel after a Bal Masqué*, or *The Duel in the Snow*, based on Gérôme's painting of 1857. The painting was known to be based on an actual event, and it no doubt provided, in its 'realisation', an extra measure of sensation and of effect. It connected to the scene of the carnival opera ball, and it reinforced that validating union in melodrama between extremity, fantasy and certified, even topical, reality. In its conflation of genre signals, use of colour and light, of contrast and intensity, broad gestures, eloquent readable configuration, pathos and extremity, the painting is a consummation of melodrama and, stylistically as well as thematically, an appropriate partner of the play.[11]

The Corsican Brothers had a long and persistent life in film, and even film for television, starting with George Albert Smith's 1898 display of the art of twinning, exploiting his patented double-exposure techniques, and including versions from André Antoine (1917), Géo Kelber (1938), Ray Nazarro (1953), and even burlesques (which had long been rampant in the theatre) most recently with Cheech and Chong. The best known of film versions is the black-and-white Hollywood version with Douglas Fairbanks Jr, directed by Gregory Ratoff in 1941. The film, like the play, is unmediated, but it has been distanced, or rather left behind, in the world of historical romance. Still set in the early 19th century, and its story played out, not in Paris, but almost entirely in lawless Corsica, it takes on colouring from the costume western and Sherwood Forest. The opening titles appear on slanting parchment pages in pseudo-Gothic

Jean-Léon Gérôme's *Duel After a Masquered Ball.* Courtesy of Walters Art Gallery, Baltimore

letters, followed by a written introduction on a scroll. Billed as 'a free adaptation of the Dumas story', it restores the linearity of the tale, but begins at the time of the birth of the twins and their separation. There is no retrospect, no mid-point entry, no connection to a remoter past or to actual Corsican history as in the novella. The time line is simple, and all is a present that is past – certainly not, as in the play, a complex expanded present, with two acts converging in one climax. The story bridges more than two decades, and the governing condition is an ancient vendetta, now no longer a partly comic feud between others that the de Franchi mediate and settle, but the de Franchis' own war with the nefarious Colonna, led by Akim Tamiroff.

Though happily removed from the present in time and space, the film acknowledges some acute current concerns, and reflects, perhaps inadvertently, some current social thinking. The politics of the early 1940s enter in the characterisation of Tamiroff's and the Colonnas' Fascist take-over of effective power. Even more interesting are the new lines of discrimination between the twins. In this version, the twins are not raised together in Corsica but, having been separated at birth, are raised in ignorance of each other, 'Mario' in an aristocratic Parisian household, 'Lucien' by a peasant servant of their slaughtered parents in the Corsican wilderness. Ideas about class relationships and a popular psychodynamics give a contemporary parabolic turn to the core idea of Siamese twins separated at birth with a persistent sensory and affective bond. Lucien in his unqualified, uninhibited loves and hates is id to Mario's ego, dark to his light.

74

'Has no one told you that I am my brother's shadow?' he asks the woman they both love. When the brothers quarrel, he tries to kill Mario; when Mario is tortured he is glad to feel the pain, for hatred's sake. The curious thing is that the traffic in pain is only one way in this version, from the aristocratic brother to the peasant and brigand. Accordingly, when Mario is drugged into a simulated death, Lucien feels and celebrates an overwhelming freedom. When he later dies in Mario's arms, the old family doctor (with a bow to *A Tale of Two Cities*) pronounces, 'Lucien has found a greater peace than he has ever known.'

Just as the implicit psychodrama and the suggestion of a democratic resistance to Fascism reflect the climate and categories of the time, so do the priority assigned to nurture over nature in the formation of the twins; the unequal distribution of pleasure and pain; the burden on the underclass brother to suffer a displacement of autonomy and inner life; the threat of a needless, vengeful, proletarian violence as a result. Despite all that, Hollywood's *Corsican Brothers* struck contemporary critics as rather retrograde and fossilised. Despite a large investment in familiar forms of spectacular elaboration, a heightened palette for the broadest of moral contrasts and for vivid infusions of comedy and pathos, a rhythm that alternates action and situation, a sacrifice of plausibility to effect, the film strikes me as less the living heir of nineteenth-century melodrama than some strains that implicate themselves in the mythologised realities of modern life, urban especially, and not only bring to the surface melodrama's dependence on the structures of seeing, but engage the difficulties of seeing in modern conditions of heightened insecurity. The assurance implicit in the fit between how we see and make sense of the world and melodrama fades in its efficacy as the assurance fades that there is a genuine congruence between reality and events that can be represented as providential. It takes a more determined will and a specialised consciousness to snatch such coherence from the chaos, to bridge the serial discontinuities, to construct the scattered fragments into a narrative and ontological whole. That is why the detective story is so vigorous a form of modern melodrama, and in its film realisation is the proper heir of the nineteenth-century evolution from Gothic remoteness to the lights and shadows of modern life; a grandchild of *The Child of Mystery*.

At a high-point in this further succession, the detective was almost synonymous with the Private I (for Investigator) or Eye, a fortuitous pun hardly anyone can resist, least of all a self-conscious film-maker. But private (not public) is also important, for denoting the character of the viewing consciousness, the subject seeking a coherence other than that provided by the official versions of reality. And as an eye, active; not just an objective observer and reporter, but rather more like the Romantic accounts of the imagination in its epistemic role: the agent or faculty that reaches out and constitutes a world.

The exemplary instance in my view is Edward Dmytryk's *Murder My Sweet* (1944) as it is known in America, based on Raymond Chandler's *Farewell My Lovely*, a film noir with a surprising Dick Powell as Philip Marlowe. It begins in effect with the *difficulty* of seeing. The opening image (see A), behind the titles, shows from above a group in shadow

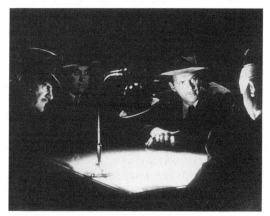

Film stills A–C from *Murder My Sweet*
(Edward Dmytryk, 1944)

seated around a circle of light on a small table lit by a desk lamp. The camera moves in until the background is blank, and then, in the centre of the white screen, under the name of the director, a light appears in a round metal shade which (seen from an angle) appears oval, like an egg or an eye (see B). As the story begins with voices questioning, with only the light to look at, the camera pulls back and we see from face level the waiting group around the lamp and the table, like a Mannerist scene or a Wright of Derby (see C): the centrally lit hatted police and, edging into the foreground and partly from behind, in white bandages that cover his eyes, a blind Philip Marlowe.

For most moviegoers, the primary relevance of any image, though it be there for craft or effect, is to the story. Nevertheless, from the images and movements, the viewer assembles a provisional physical reality, with considerable tolerance for lacunae and ambiguities as to space, location, and viewpoint. The bulb in the round/oval reflector is such an ambiguous image. For when, at the end of the story, it appears again, following hard on the last of Marlowe's many trips into screen blackness and unconsciousness, it becomes retrospectively clear that what we have seen, apparently from below, is not the direct, uncompromising stare of the third degree, but rather a reflection of the desk lamp in the white enamel tabletop that fills the screen. And indeed, as the largely night-time story has shown, light and its dazzle, like wealth and beauty, can be as deceptive, as resistant to penetration, and as dangerous, as darkness.

Marlowe, blind and under suspicion of murder, has to tell his story to the police, not fully knowing its outcome and not able to gauge its reception. The story he tells follows his experience. It is replete with the difficulties of seeing, from when the camera, picking up the voice narration without acknowledging a breach in time, tracks out of the interrogation room window into the vast night city of neon and car lights, mimicking Marlowe's account of a fruitless trek on some old business. The difficulties of seeing then take a literal turn when Marlowe returns to his office in an otherwise deserted building. The camera moves in through the office window and finds him at his desk where he has been telephoning, seeking female company. Facing outwards towards the night, he sees behind him, reflected in the glass, subject to the intermittent neon brightness, a hint and then a sudden apparition (see D): 'the big, ugly, menacing face of a towering figure standing in front of the desk'.[12]

Seen directly and steadily, the visitor turns out to want Marlowe's services, which Marlowe is not in a position to refuse. Returning in the daylight, Marlowe finds another would-be client already in his office, lit by the glare of the sunlight and shadowed by the letters of Marlowe's own name, and here the problems in seeing have more serious consequences. This second client is soon murdered with Marlowe only a few steps away, in a night visit to a canyon rendezvous obscured in mist and underbrush. When Marlowe is felled and slips into what he calls a black pool (at other times a black pit), his recovery begins with a spot of light in the centre of the screen – like the dawn of consciousness – which grows and resolves into his head, followed by a flashlight in his face as he tries to focus on the figure that holds it and then runs off in the dark. On another occa-

77

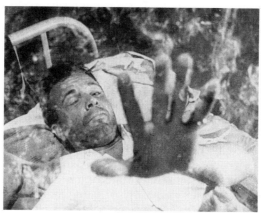

Film stills D–E from *Murder My Sweet*
(Edward Dmytryk, 1944)

sion, when he has been drugged as well as concussed, he wakes up again to a bright light but is beset by a smoke or a grey web that does not go away and threatens consciousness (see E). (We see him through this mottling, this 'smoke', his subjective perception superimposed on ours.)

There is no firm line here between sensation, perception and congnition, ours and his. Marlow is presented with disjointed fragments of experience, apparently unrelated and resistant to explanation. He has been visited successively by two would-be clients from different worlds, one an ex-convict looking for 'Velma', who has disappeared while her lover was doing time (Marlowe cannot see Velma when he meets her because he has a photograph of someone else as a guide); the other an up-market ladies' man wanting an escort for ransoming a friend's stolen necklace. A third visitor misrepresents herself and then tries to persuade Marlowe out of his dead client's case. Eventually (and this is what Marlowe has to figure out) the two seemingly unrelated cases and other disjointed experiences turn out to be all of a piece, part of a plot concerned with conceal-

78

ment and exposure, and much of it directed at removing Marlowe himself.

The mysteries of traditional melodrama often had to do with lost or concealed identities or with hidden crime, revealed or exposed at the critical juncture by the hand of something like Providence. The detective mystery tale, with roots in scientific rationalism, could bring about the same result, but without that apt and marvellous agency of coincidence which fostered the effect of wonder in melodrama, and overcame its diversions and discontinuities (one of the things we have lost in our reception of melodrama is the sense that coincidence *adds* to credibility). It was now the detective's enquiring mind that had to piece together the disjointed fragments of experience, with nothing to go on other than overlooked or misinterpreted traces and a sharp eye; he was the gifted but merely human successor to what was, in classic melodrama, a transcendent bias shaping experience towards a meaningful moral coherence, and expressing itself in ways for all to see.

The premises of rational causality, of material intelligibility (readable phenomena), and penetrable psychology in the detective story are also articles of faith and require affirmation or vindication by the plot. The shift from Providence to the solitary human intelligence, as bearing the burden of eliciting coherence, puts seeing on the line, and at the same time puts to the test the presumption of intelligibility in experience, and finally the whole human episteme, the fit between subject and object. The experience or the dread of a thoroughly arbitrary world (where it is not just the anomalous event or artefact that does not make sense but *nothing* seems to make sense, where fragmentation and disorder are the rule) gives a certain desperate importance to the detective's vocation, adds new shades of peril to the melodrama of his situation, carries him beyond the heroism of intelligence and physical courage to the dogged, stoic quixotism of a dubious Philip Marlowe, persisting in the face of his scepticism. Marlowe's blind virtue is to act as if there is an attainable coherence, despite the fragmentation, the anomie, the corruption, the dangers and deceptions of his melodramatic night world. More exposed by vocation and more knowing, more receptive and more scarred, he is as much the victim of his story as its maker, as much the sacrifice to experience as the stay against chaos.

The film reworks the novel in numerous ways. Among them it nests the narrative within a present situation, Marlowe under suspicion, whose resolution ostensibly depends on his story. Time is a complex manifold, the greater contained in the less, and space has a certain fluidity that responds to the movements of the mind. The novel, on the other hand, is straightforwardly linear, taking the form of Marlowe's retrospective narration. As narrator, Marlowe mediates; but in the film his mediation passes into direct experience. The narrative voice sometimes parallels but most often gives way to unaccompanied scene and action. It does not seem strange that we see Marlowe seeing and we see for ourselves what he saw.

Marlowe's blindess from gunshot blast, a total departure from the novel, is reassuringly stated to be temporary on our return to the framing situation. It could (though not very usefully, to my mind) be construed as a punishment for seeing too much, in an obvious Oedipal situation, or seeing too little. At the end it provides a charming coda in the vein of hard-boiled romance when Marlowe finds his way to his perfumed sexual reward by smell (Powell's disingenuous, 'Would it be all right if I kissed you, Nulty?' – the name of a male detective – would have pleased Shakespeare). But the introduction of a blind Philip Marlowe in John Paxton's screenplay, and its exploitation by Dmytryk, reaches, as I have tried to suggest, beyond the single instance and the plot, to the genre in this modern avatar. If there is still a special congruence between the broad elements of melodrama and what goes into seeing, the significance of that relationship has changed. Some things are no longer to be taken for granted, among them seeing and what is seen, knowing and what is knowable. The result is a Philip Marlowe, officially a Private Eye, but in fact handicapped in his seeing and mostly groping in the dark; protagonist, nevertheless, of a drama rooted in the structures of seeing, whose belated self-conscious action is the effort to elicit from the gaps and fragments of experience a meaningful coherence that can be seen.

Notes

1. See Gösta M. Bergman, *Lighting in the Theatre* (Stockholm: Almqvist & Wiksell, and Totowa, New Jersey: Rowman and Littlefield, 1977), and Terence Rees, *Theatre Lighting in the Age of Gas* (London: Society for Theatre Research, 1978).
2. See the wistful appeal for a stage lighting that could produce powerful chiaroscuro effects in Francesco Algarotti's *Saggio sopra l'opera in musica* (1755), translated as *An Essay on the Opera, Written in Italian by Count Algarotti F.R.S., F.S.A. Etc.* (Glasgow, 1768), p. 89. For the contemporary uses and associations of 'effect', see Chapter 5 of my *Realizations: Narrative, Pictorial, and Theatrical Arts in Nineteenth-Century England* (Princeton: Princeton University Press, 1983).
3. George Bernard Shaw, *Our Theatres in the Nineties*, Standard Edition (London: Constable, 1954), vol. I, p. 93.
4. *Coelina, ou l'Enfant du mystère, drame en 3 actes, en prose et à grand spectacle* (1800).
5. See *Realizations, passim*.
6. For the scene in motion, see, for example, David Mayer, *Harlequin in his Element: The English Pantomine, 1806–1836* (Cambridge, Mass: Harvard University Press, 1969); M. J. Moynet, *L'Envers du théâtre; machines et decorations*, 3rd edn (Paris: Hachette, 1888); Percy Fitzgerald, *The World behind the Scenes* (London: 1881); and A. Nicolas Vardac, *Stage to Screen: Theatrical Method from Garrick to Griffith* (Cambridge, Mass.: Harvard University Press, 1949). For general trends, see Sybil Rosenfield, *A Short History of Scene Design in Great Britain* (Oxford: Blackwell, 1973); and Michael Booth, *Victorian Spectacular Theatre 1850–1910* (London: Routledge, 1981).
7. 'The Perception of Motion Pictures', in *Handbook of Perception*, vol. X, *Perceptual Ecology*, ed. Edward Carterette and Morton P. Friedman (New York: Academic Press, 1978), p. 272.
8. First published in Brussels, in several editions, as *Une Famille corse* (1844), the story's germ is supposed to have been an actual incident of uncanny sympathy between two of Dumas's contemporaries, the brothers Louis and Charles Blanc.
9. I quote from the version in French's Acting Edition, *Les Frères Corses; or, The Corsican Brothers; A Dramatic Romance in Three Acts and Five Tableaux,*

a close translation of Grangé and Montépin. The play proved a triumph for Charles Fechter in France (1850) and Charles Kean in England (1852), whose production is registered in the music-cover lithograph. Irving's lavish revival in 1880 ran for 190 performances.

10. French's Acting Edition. Both the French-language original and a version of the play that Kean had printed (supplied by Boucicault) makes it clear that 'The *back* of the scene opens, and discovers the exact scene of the first act' (my emphasis). The final Act II tableau is then, in effect, a mirror version of the final tableau of Act I.

11. For an informative account of the painting's origins and popularity in the theatre and elsewhere, see Coleman O. Parsons, 'The Wintry Duel: A Victorian Import', *Victorian Studies* 2 (June 1959), pp. 317–22.

12. Edward Dmytryk, *It's a Hell of a Life but not a Bad Living* (New York: Times Books, 1978), p. 60.

OLYMPIAN DREAMSCAPES:
THE PHOTOGRAPHIC CANVAS

The Wide-screen Paintings of Leighton, Poynter and Alma-Tadema

CAROLINE DUNANT

This essay draws on a larger work in progress, and seeks to demonstrate how a particular classical revival not only humanised and domesticated antiquity, providing accessible, emotive images while indulging in size and spectacle, but also challenged the static, two-dimensional nature of the picture frame. It was a style which evolved with the growth of social democratisation in the 19th century, permeated mass culture, and was later taken up by the new medium of cinema, particularly in the epic features of Griffith, DeMille and the Italian pioneers Pastrone, Guazzoni and de Liguoro. In what follows I shall concentrate on the origins of that style and attempt to lay the groundwork for the transformation of these paintings into the bases for moving pictures.

The Victorian classical revival, particularly in painting, tell us more about the contemporary period than it does about antiquity. The patrons of artists such as Frederic Leighton, Edward Poynter and Lawrence Alma-Tadema were not aristocrats, or members of learned society, but the newly rich mercantile class; the industrial barons of the North and Midlands, the merchant princes across the Atlantic, and the bourgeoisie of both continents who bought cheap reproductions of the originals. As Wilkie Collins observed:

> Traders and makers of all kinds of commodities ... started with the new notion of buying a picture which they themselves could admire and appreciate, and for the genuineness of which the artist was still living to vouch. . . . [They had] nothing to lead them by the nose except their own shrewdness, their own interests, and their own tastes – so they turned their backs valiantly on the Old Masters, and marched off in a body to the living men.[1]

The paintings they patronised were of brilliantly coloured, potent and accessible images which drew on traditional, populist, non-verbal, non-literary entertainment forms, such as melodrama, which directly appealed to the emotions. Thus the look, what was presented and shown – the spectacle on display – was all. Erudition was offered in the details, but none was needed to immediately comprehend the universal messages. Often what was portrayed were small moments, trivial incidents, the reactions rather than the actions, private matters, and thus by highlighting everyday sentiment, even in an exotic setting, an immediate affinity was created with the spectator. As Sir Ernst Gombrich pointed out, 'In these pictures, there are none of the problems of iconography that confront the spectator of a Renaissance picture, or the Neo-classical art of the eighteenth century. There is no élitist suggestion of hermetic knowledge.'[2]

These paintings were determinedly democratic in their appeal and marked both a desire to escape from the actual appearance of the world around them, the ugliness of the speedily expanding industrial landscape and the confusion of a society in a state of transition. In their desire to use a distant time in order to clarify the contemporary world, the painters signal the importance of looking to the past in order to anchor and organise the present, and the use of the melodramatic mode in these works, and indeed its cultural prominence in the 19th century, points to the anxiety of this period. As Peter Brooks noted, 'Melodrama became the principal mode for uncovering, demonstrating and making operative the essential moral universe in a post-sacral era.'[3]

The basic convention of melodrama is realism or, rather, naturalism (the representation of the look of a world in all its familiarity), and the principal aim is to show both the façade and the hidden forces behind it, and to bind these two elements together in order to make sense of them and make them clear. Thus visuality carries the full weight of meaning, and by necessity becomes an exaggeration of the natural. This emphasis on spectacle rather than speech, what Peter Brooks termed the 'aesthetic of muteness',[4] is due to melodrama's ancient origins as a form of entertainment or instruction for the people, who were, for the most part, illiterate. Thus, the meaning was required to have a direct and forceful appeal to the senses, a communication to the heart rather than to the head. The depiction of the moment, with the use of tableaux as the climax of gestural action, brings the planes of actuality and signification together, provoking immediate emotional involvement.

Linked to melodrama's visuality are the concerns of John Ruskin, the cultural sage who dominated the Victorian period and believed that art should be of public concern, a social necessity rather than a privilege, a medium that would 'speak' to even the lowest ranks of the populace. He urged a concentration on surface detail, a style of painting that would result from an attentive study of nature – of what is apparent, what is there. In his concern that the canvas must convey this study with clarity, and his demands for an exacting standard of finish, he anticipated both the photograph and, ultimately, the screen.[5]

Paintings were to be easily read, or interpreted. They were to tell a story, to convey a world of the imagination with all the immediacy and familiarity of the actual world, and thus the visualisation, the total look, was all important. As Thomas Elsaesser has stated about film, but it is equally pertinent to the painting of this period:

Considered as an expressive code, melodrama might therefore be described as a particular form of dramatic *mise en scène* ... a sublimation of dramatic conflict into decor, colour, gesture and composition of frame ... an intensified symbolisation of everyday actions, the heightening of the ordinary gesture ... style as meaning.[6]

The *mise en scène* shows and tells and makes things clear. It offers a wordless commentary on what is presented and offers both emotional indulgence and a satisfying coherence. The paintings of the classical revival were prime exponents of spectacle, with elaborate use of tableaux within densely realised compositions in styles displaying a heightened, or superrealist, degree of finish. In contrast to the insularity of other artistic genres in England at that time this movement had European roots, beginning in France with the work of Jean-Léon Gérôme and his circle of the 'Neo-Grecs' in the 1840s[7] and travelling to England in the 1860s, with Leighton, Poynter and Alma-Tadema, all of whom trained in Continental Europe and became the vanguard of the so-called Olympians.[8]

Their work, and that of their followers, does not present any homogeneity, but there are certain shared ideals, the most predominant being a need to reconstruct the ancient world; to realise it as a fully credible, immediately comprehensible and desirable place. The emphasis is on the social rather than the political, the small and incidental rather than the weighty and heroic, and the use of antique settings for scenes of familiar sentiment. Indeed, the paintings bear witness to a close study of ruins and knowledge, usually gained firsthand, of the latest archaeological discoveries. The findings in Herculaneum and Pompeii, in particular, gave birth to a new kind of historical method, giving emphasis to the manners and customs of the past and the study of the lives of ordinary people.

The first official excavation of Herculaneum began in 1733 and Pompeii in 1748, but it was not until 1861[9] that the first fully systematic excavation of the two cities began, with the intention of keeping and preserving the finds *in situ*. What was made swiftly apparent was that Roman society in the first century AD was undergoing a similar social democratisation to that in the nineteenth. There was evidence of rising *nouveaux riches*, a merchant class which was taking over the villas of the declining aristocracy. These cities, particularly Pompeii, were undergoing a rapid expansion of trade, mostly through their freedmen, and there were clear signs of a suburbanisation of the prosperous who were moving from the crowded city to the more pleasant hillsides around.

The most radical aspect of these findings was that the incidental, the trivia, the minutiae of everyday life of a remote period were put on display to the public. As Frederic Leighton said, after visiting Pompeii, 'And what a display it is! Here we are admitted into the most intimate privacy of a multitude of Pompeian houses – the kitchens, the pantries, the cellars of the contemporaries of the Plinies have here no secret from us.'[10]

Alma-Tadema visited Herculaneum and Pompeii in 1863, and took numerous photographs of the excavations. Eventually, he was to fill 164 volumes with his photographs of these and other archaeological sites and ruins, and they became the basis of his work in reconstructing the daily life of antiquity.[11]

In tandem with the growing interest in archaeological discovery of this nature, the historical novel, given respectability earlier in the century by Sir Walter Scott, provided a powerful stimulus to both social history and genre painting. These writers stressed that the lives of unexceptional people were in a way a nobler theme than the exploits of the kings and demigods of heroic poetry. By bringing the past to life, the intention of the historical novel was to humanise history, to use melodrama, which was a particular socially conditioned mode of experience, and to make universal connections. It was part of what the contemporary historian and politician Thomas Macaulay called 'Boswellism':[12] a desire to glimpse the private lives of great men, to catch them off their guard, and to observe their foibles and mannerisms. The Victorians took to 'Boswellising' the past with a vengeance.

History and the novel merged in Becker's *Charicles*, 1866, an account of an Athenian lad's daily life, which was translated into English by Frederick Metcalfe and widely used in schools. However, perhaps the most famous historical novel of the period, and the most relevant to this discussion, was Edward Bulwer-Lytton's *The Last Days of Pompeii*, published in 1834, an established classic by the 1860s, and still in print to this day.[13] The novel has undergone numerous transformations: stage plays; the pyrotheatric spectacles at Alexandra Palace, such as those staged in the summer of 1888 by James Pain Jr, with sets by Joseph Harker; paintings such as Poynter's *Faithful unto Death*, 1865 (Walker Art Gallery, Liverpool), showing a sentry staying at his post; and epic cinema, the first being Luigi Maggi's feature of 1908, *Gli Ultimi Giorni di Pompeii*.

Thackeray detected a strong pictorial element in Lytton's novel, applauding the ingenuity with which he had 'illustrated the place by his text, as if the houses were so many pictures to which he had appended a story'. Thackeray also pointed out that Lytton had presented daily life in Pompeii in a series of tableaux, for example, when the villain, Arbaces, comes upon the hero and heroine, Glaucus and Ione, seated side by side in the peristyle:

> The scene … was stamped by that … ideality of poesy which we yet, not erroneously, imagine to be the distinction of the ancients – the marble columns, the vases of flowers, the statue … closing every vista; and, above all, the two living forms, from which a sculptor might have caught either inspiration or despair! The splashing of a fountain refreshes the sultry heat of noon; handmaids attend at a little distance; a lyre reposes at Glaucus' feet; in short, we seem to have a scene from Tadema before us.[14]

Thackeray's comments indicate the cross-fertilisation that was going on between the different art forms, and the pervasive use of the visuality of the melodramatic mode. It is perhaps Alma-Tadema, after Gérôme,[15] who has been most credited with influencing the new cinematic medium by providing such seductively accessible images of antiquity along with a wealth of archaeological detail presented with great clarity. His work for the stage is outside the scope of this discussion, but a quote by Bram

Stoker, Irving's stage manager at the Lyceum, serves to highlight his contemporary usefulness and importance for dramatisation, which was later taken up by the new medium of cinema. Stoker observed that:

> Alma-Tadema had made a speciality of artistic archaeology of Ancient Rome. . . . He had so studied the life of Old Rome that he had for his own purposes reconstructed it. . . . He was familiar with the kinds of marble and stone used in Roman architecture, statuary, and domestic service. The kinds of glass and crystal; of armour and arms; of furniture; of lighting; sacerdotal and public and domestic service. . . . He was a master of the many ceremonial undertakings which had such a part in Roman Life.[16]

Armed with this knowledge, Alma-Tadema's quest was to humanise antiquity, to reanimate it, and show contemporary spectators that the Romans were much like themselves. Both Leighton and Poynter differed in this quest to a degree, but all shared in the desire to present familiar figures in a story of universal nature, and offer both escapism and erudition in the setting. The buildings and accessories are frequently painted from identifiable models, but treated with a certain amount of artistic licence. As in performed melodrama, the pressure is on the visual to carry the full weight of meaning, and construct a mute but expressive moment: an indulgence in meticulously detailed but imaginative reconstruction both to create dramatic effect and to provoke emotional involvement.

Edward John Poynter, England 1836–1919. *The Visit of the Queen of Sheba to King Solomon* 1884–1890. Oil on canvas 234.5 × 350.5 cm. Art Gallery of New South Wales, purchased 1892.

Edward John Poynter's *Israel in Egypt*. Courtesy of Guildhall Art Gallery, Corporation of London.

Poynter's work employs architectural complexity, frequently departing from strict classical sources, to create extraordinarily solid realisations of a monumental and epic nature. In *The Visit of the Queen of Sheba to King Solomon*, 1890 (Art Gallery of New South Wales, Sydney), he presents a fictional meeting (there is no actual evidence that it took place or, if it did, exactly how and where) but the elaborate reconstruction, the solidity of the architecture and the detail of the setting gives the fiction the force of fact. The story of a wished-for romance in an exotic distant time, and the heightened movement of its inception in a climactically realised tableau, is given weight and credibility. In order to achieve this, Poynter constructed a three-dimensional model, a 'set' complete in every detail and made to scale, from which to paint the picture. As Herbert Sharp observed, this was to 'obtain a great truth of effect'.[17]

Poynter's *Israel in Egypt*, 1867 (Guildhall Art Gallery, London), illustrates lines from Exodus 1: 7–11, and shows the Israelites enslaved by the Egyptians and employed in the building of their cities. The civil engineer Sir John Hawkshaw, who bought the painting, calculated that more manpower was needed to pull the granite lions, prompting Poynter to paint slaves extending out of the frame, thus creating an illusion of an endless procession way beyond the boundaries of the picture. Thus, what the spectator witnesses is a moment in an epic scene, and emotional involvement is reinforced by means of an anecdote placed in the centre foreground, where an Egyptian woman gives a drink of water to a collapsed Israelite, overseen by a harsh taskmaster.

The painting is, in fact, a composite of buildings and objects from different periods and places, but the archaeological detailing, the composition as a whole and its super-realist finish give the picture a completely authentic air. A dream conception is given the force of actuality and familiarity.

Leighton was equally concerned with the credible realisation of a world, but his philosophy inclined more to an aesthetic of timelessness. His paintings recreate moments suspended to infinity: ordinary, everyday sentiments given weight in an exotic setting; attitudes and gestures that speak of a nostalgic longing for an idyllic state of clarity, order and harmony. The scenes fed the spectator's desire to escape the confusion and anxiety of the contemporary nineteenth-century world, but in the manipulation of crowds and depiction of processions Leighton also seeks to defy the boundaries of the frame and more actively engage with the spectator. His tableaux closely follow the Greek frieze form, but the settings have a clarity and solidity, and his figures a bold, corporeal quality, that create an illusion beyond the constraints of the canvas.

This is very aptly demonstrated in *The Syracusan Bride leading the Wild Beasts to the Temple of Diana*, 1866 (private collection). A parade of beautiful girls passes by, fondling flower-bedecked animals who are capable of tearing them to pieces. It is a scene of extraordinary exoticism and sexual suggestion with, furthermore, an overt acknowledgment of the spectator through the introduction of onlookers, a group of men placed at the bottom of the picture, only half in the frame, and on a level with the spectator outside, who gaze up at the girls with rapt attention.

However, it was Alma-Tadema's luxuriantly accessible images which displayed the strongest desire to push at the limitations of the picture plane. To create *The Baths of Caracalla*, 1889 (private collection), he worked from reports of the latest excavations and sought to restore the gigantic dimensions of the ruined Roman baths in a splendidly solid but imaginative reconstruction. The size of the building is first indicated by truncating the immense columns, pediments and arches at the top of the frame and extending it way back to a deep vanishing-point. He then fills the huge space with a mass of figures, many surging in from the sides of the frame, and engaged in busy scenes, seen in full and glimpsed in part, behind the trio of gossiping ladies. The focus is on a moment, a seemingly trivial incident in a story of an everyday nature, but taking place within a very elaborate and fully realised set.

In a later work by Tadema, *Spring*, 1894 (J. Paul Getty Museum, Malibu, California), a procession of servants of the Temple of Flora, to celebrate the Roman festival of Cerealia, come towards the spectator and out of the picture. They emerge from a building, which is only shown in part, as in *The Baths of Caracalla*, although its grandeur and architectural complexity (and a glimpse gained through an arch) indicate that it extends well beyond the frame. The crowd is shown alongside on the street, pushing to the front in the windows, and leaning down from the rooftop, seemingly jutting into the picture from the outside, or as if just caught by the lens. There is a 'snapshot' effect of arrested movement.

Alma-Tadema was greatly interested in photography, and followed the pioneering work in motion pictures, being particularly fascinated by Eadweard Muybridge's studies in recording movement. He used a camera himself both to record information, set up reconstructions and, most particularly, to experiment with pictorial ideas. The latter resulted in his 'photo-like' compositions, with spectacular arrangements of space, partially glimpsed activity, abrupt perspectives, and illusions of deep focus and wide angle.

Tadema's *Antony and Cleopatra*, 1883 (Margaret Brown Collection), is a reconstruction of a historical moment, influenced by Shakespeare's description. While it is a picture of splendid details, its particular interest lies in the composition, which anticipates CinemaScope. Cleopatra reclines in her barge, only part of which is shown, while Antony and Enobarbus's boat lies beyond, partially masked by hers. In a pure melodramatic tableau, what is portrayed is the heightened and telling mute moment of contact; the split second when the moving boats are in the right position for the men to have a first glimpse of her and register amazement. The *mise en scène* shows and tells and makes the whole story clear. The painting is a particularly apt example of the use of spectacle to convey the full weight of meaning, with the tableau merging the planes of actuality and signification in a richly emotional and satisfying coherence. While this melodrama of reaction takes place in the foreground, in an almost claustrophobic space symbolic of the intensity of the emotions, the picture abruptly opens out in the background to show a trireme towering on the left and a fleet extending beyond the horizon.

In these paintings, the past is an identifiable place, with the pleasure principle paramount. The emphasis is on the emotive or melodramatic moment in anecdotal scenes of heightened visuality. The distance of antiquity provided legitimation for indulgence in excess, and for the depiction of spectacles which offered licence for fantasy, for dreaming. These are images that seduce. As Peter Brooks notes, 'The melodramatic utterance breaks through everything that constitutes the "reality" principle. ... Desire cries aloud its language in identification with full states of being. Melodrama partakes of the dream world.'[18]

The paintings are not only to be looked at, watched or gazed upon, but also slipped into, and the ease of slipping into is aided by naturalistic styles which create immediately recognisable, if distant, worlds; the use of meticulous technique achieves a finish akin to photographic, or cinematographic, realism. The intention is to dismantle the barrier and limitations of the object – the picture – and to make the spectator forget that what they are viewing is a confined, flat, static surface. This is what Linda Nochlin refers to as 'the absence – that is to say, the *apparent* absence – of art'.[19]

In this determined eradication of the picture plane – the two-dimensional surface and the actual materials of paint, brushes and canvas – there is a desire to conceal the evidence of the maker in what Roland Barthes calls the creation of the 'reality effect'.[20] These paintings aim (as the screen was later to do) for the achievement of a total visual field as a simple artless reflection of a reality, the fabrication of a world as a space for dreaming, the acknowledgment and feeding of a desire not only to watch, but also to experience – to be 'there'.

These painters produced models of transparent storytelling for the cinema, and the dissemination of the images into popular culture was crucial in the transformation process to the screen. Poynter, Leighton and Alma-Tadema were part of a new climate. They were in the vanguard of the phenomenon of paintings as entertainment, Ruskin's art of public concern, a right available to all rather than a privilege for the few, and they achieved tremendous success and popularity. They were stars, Olympians, and their standing was instrumental in gaining celebrity status for artists and a new non-élitist public for art.

Poynter, Leighton and Alma-Tadema became household names, with their photographs in the magazines of the day, posing in their palatial homes, or in their studios which were like fantastical sets filled with the props that furnished their reconstructions. All three were knighted; Leighton was made a peer in 1896, the only artist ever to have received this honour, and Alma-Tadema was awarded the Order of Merit in 1905.

John Gilbert, a master engraver, employed in the thriving reproduction business in the latter part of the century, summed up the prevailing Victorian attitude to paintings:

> Walls without pictures are like houses without windows; for pictures are loopholes of escape to the mind, leading it to other scenes and spheres, as it were through the frame of an exquisite picture, where the fancy for the moment may revel, refreshed and delighted. Pictures are consolers of loneliness; they are a sweet flattery to the imagination; they are a relief to the jaded mind; they are windows to the imprisoned thought; they are Books; they are Histories and Sermons. They make up for the want of many other enjoyments to those whose life is passed amidst the smoke and din, the bustle and noise of an over-crowded city.[21]

Aiding the popularity of the painters and their paintings was the growth of new exhibition spaces. In the first half of the 19th century there were virtually no independent exhibitions, but this changed with the Great Exhibition mounted in Sir Joseph Paxton's astonishing glasshouse, the 'Crystal Palace', erected in Hyde Park in 1851 (and later moved to the Sydenham site in South London), and the International Exhibition at South Kensington in 1861 (later developed into the Victoria and Albert Museum). These introduced the arts to the masses. Additionally, the development of cheap public transport by omnibus and railway literally brought the arts within reach of the ordinary person.

The growth of provincial cities due to manufacture and trade gave them aspirations to become centres of culture, and galleries were founded with the philanthropic aid of the 'Captains of Industry', as Thomas Carlyle called them. Like the picture houses, or cinemas which came after, these galleries were places to which people could escape. As Charles Kingsley said of them, they 'should be the townsman's paradise of refreshment, transporting him from the grim city world of stone and iron, smokey chimneys and roaring wheels, into the world of beautiful things'.[22]

Rich patrons were not averse to paying enormous prices for well-known pictures, since the purchase added greatly to the prestige of the purchaser, but not every bourgeois household, keen to furnish their walls and provide 'loopholes of escape' or transportation into 'the world of beautiful things' could own an original work of art. The new art dealers, however, saw that the cost of a print was within the reach of many.

By the 1860s, the dealers were a major force in the art market on both sides of the Channel, with links across the Atlantic. The main contenders were the Polish Louis Victor Flatou, the Parisian Goupil brothers and Paul Durand-Ruel, and the acknowledged prince of dealers, the Belgian Ernest

Gambart. They commissioned paintings, acquired them from a studio, and even put artists such as Alma-Tadema under contract. Furthermore, it became the usual practice to tour paintings, and put reproductions on display at home, in order to keep the images before the public and maintain the familiarity of the work and the standing of the artist.

Copyright was a major factor in print-selling, and a painter's reputation was often decided by the careful control and manipulation of it. Gambart, for instance, would seek a percentage of the sale, but more importantly for exhibition, engraving, copying, touring and book illustration rights. The intention was to get as much mileage out of the work as possible, and thus the importance of the original, the act of painting, was being diminished as the image that that act produced was becoming ever more popular and powerful. The actual painting could be regarded as a master negative from which endless prints were made and put into distribution to reach the masses.

There had been many advances in the technology of engraving since the end of the 18th century, but a crucial development was achieved by Thomas Lupton's perfection of the steel plate process in 1822. The copper plate, used previously, had yielded editions of only about 3000 impressions. With the introduction of the method of electrotyping in 1845, however, all limits were removed from the size of editions of engravings. Also contributory was the abolition in 1845 of the duty on glass imported from the continent, thus drastically lowering the cost of framing prints. When photographic methods of reproduction began to replace engravings during the 1870s, prints were circulated more widely than ever before. A steel engraving might cost £2, but photogravures could be sold for a shilling each, thus putting them potentially within the reach of anyone.

In 1847, the Printsellers' Association was established to register and monitor the publication of prints. The printsellers were, to quote Jeremy Maas,

> the unacknowledged legislators of the art world. It was they who carried an artist's reputation into every home in the country and to all four corners of the globe; it was they who brought prosperity to the artists and, of course, to themselves.[23]

The paintings discussed here were endlessly reproduced, and most examples of the genre were known only by this method, the images permeating fashion, advertising, interior décor and household products. The cheap prints, or books of illustrations which could cross the Atlantic in bulk and with relative ease and cheapness, became essential components of the scrapbooks of the early film studios. The look, methods of composition and subject-matter which was appropriate and already familiar and a vital part of mass culture was transposed to the screen. The paintings became moving pictures.

I acknowledge Christopher Wood's pioneering study 'Victorian Classical Painters, 1860–1914' (London: Constable, 1983), which first bound this movement under the title 'Olympian Dreamers'.

Notes

1. Wilkie Collins in Jeremy Maas, *Gambart: Prince of the Victorian Art World* (London: Barrie & Jenkins, 1975), p. 43.
2. Ernst Gombrich, 'Psychoanalysis and the History of Art', lecture given in 1953, printed in *Meditations on a Hobby Horse*, (London: Phaidon, 1963).
3. Peter Brooks, *The Melodramatic Imagination* (New Haven: Yale University Press, 1976), p. 15.
4. Ibid., p. 62.
5. For a fuller discussion of Ruskin's philosophy, see Kenneth Clark, *Ruskin Today* (London: Pelican, 1964); John Ruskin, *Academy Notes 1855–9* (London, 1875); E.T. Cook and Alexander Wedderburn (eds), *The Works of John Ruskin* (London: Library Edition, 1912).
6. Thomas Elsaesser, 'Tales of Sound and Fury: Observations on the Family Melodrama', *Monogram*, no. 4, 1972; revised version in Christine Gledhill (ed.), *Home is Where the Heart Is: Studies in Melodrama and the Women's Film* (London: British Film Institute, 1987).
7. Gérôme's painting *The Cock Fight*, 1847 (Musée d'Orsay, Paris), the first canvas to display domestication of the antique. See also, Charles Moreau-Vauthier, *Gérôme, Peintre et Sculpteur, l'homme et l'artiste* (Paris, 1906), p. 65.
8. Frederick Leighton trained in Frankfurt, Paris and Rome, where Edward Poynter met him in 1853, before going on to study in the studio of Charles Gleyre (master of Gérôme) 1856–9. Lawrence Alma-Tadema, born in Holland, studied in Antwerp and Paris, where he came into close contact with Gérôme; later met Leighton in Brussels, 1866.
9. Until 1861 the sites were at the mercy of treasure-seekers who carted away what they could and covered up the evidence. The new national government (after the *Risorgimento*) assigned Giuseppe Fiorelli to carry out the excavation, and in 1862 he published *Journals of the Excavations at Pompeii*. The same year saw the completion and publication of *Herculaneum and Pompeii*, seven volumes by Henri Roux Sr, of drawings of sculpture, bronzes, household objects, paintings and mosaics which were widely used by these painters.
10. Richard and Leonee Ormond, *Lord Leighton* (New Haven: Yale University Press), 1975.
11. Given to the Victoria and Albert Museum, London, but now housed in the Birmingham University Library.
12. James Boswell, *The Life of Samuel Johnson* (London, 1791). For a discussion of Boswellism, see Richard Jenkyns, *The Victorians and Ancient Greece* (Oxford: Basil Blackwell, 1980), pp. 81–6.
13. For a discussion of Edward Bulwer-Lytton's novel, see Richard Jenkyns, pp. 82–5, 147–9.
14. Ibid., p. 317.
15. Charles Moreau-Vauthier, *Gérôme, Peintre et Sculpteur, l'homme et l'artiste* (Paris, 1906). Gerald Ackerman, *The Life and Work of Jean-Léon Gérôme, with a Catalogue Raisonée* (London: Sotheby's Publications, 1986).
16. Bram Stoker on Alma-Tadema's stage work: 'Art in the Theatre', *Magazine of Art*, no. 12, 1889. See also, Martin Meisel, *Realizations* (New Jersey: Princeton University Press, 1983), chap. 19, pp. 402–32; and Bram Stoker, *Personal Reminiscences of Henry Irving* (London: Macmillan, 1906), pp. 66–7.

17. Herbert Sharp, 'A Short Account of the work of Edward J. Poynter', *The Studio*, 1896, p. 366.

18. Peter Brooks, *The Melodramatic Imagination* (New Haven: Yale University Press, 1976), p. 41.

19. Linda Nochlin, 'The Imaginary Orient', in her *The Politics of Vision, Essays on Nineteenth-century Art and Society* (London: Thames & Hudson, 1991), p. 33.

20. G. Genette and T. Todorov, *Littérature et Réalité*, (Paris: Le Seuil, 1982).

21. Rodney K. Engen, *Victorian Engravings* (London: Academy Editions, 1975), p. 5.

22. E.D.H. Johnson, *Paintings of the British Social Scene: From Hogarth to Sickert* (London: Weidenfeld & Nicolson, 1986), p. 245.

23. Jeremy Maas, *Gambart: Prince of the Victorian Art World* (London: Barrie & Jenkins, 1975), p. 28.

EAST LYNNE TO GAS LIGHT

Hollywood, Melodrama and Twentieth-century Notions of the Victorian

GUY BAREFOOT

My subject is the persistence, transformation, rejection, revival and creation of 'Victorian' melodrama in the 20th century, in particular with how an association between melodrama and 'the Victorian' has been revealed in the medium of the cinema.

I shall focus on two works: *East Lynne* (also known as *Led Astray*) and *Gaslight* (as a play it was *Gas Light* in Britain and *Angel Street* in the USA; the first film version in 1940 was known as *Gaslight* in Britain and *Angel Street* in the USA; the second film version was American, called *Gaslight* (1944), but known as *The Murder in Thornton Square* in Britain). My concern is not with the textual detail of these works, but with the complexities, tensions and contradictions revealed through an examination of their different versions and their changing reception.

One pattern of melodrama's reception has been that of reaction and reassessment. The twentieth-century devaluation of melodrama has often meant that where it has been considered at all it has been castigated, as Christine Gledhill observes, as failed tragedy, and a fall from 'seriousness', dealing in stereotypes, overblown emotions, and a Victorian sentimentality and moral schematization.[1] A disapproval of melodrama even caused it to be seen as non-existent for the purposes of serious study: 'there is little to be said about the drama in our period until its revival in the eighties', noted a 1938 study of *The Victorians and After*, 'To all intents and purposes there was none.'[2]

That view has changed. 'Melodrama, that once ragged waif, has been brought in from the cold,' announced Louis James at the end of the 1970s.[3] Of course, the word 'melodrama' continues to be used as a term of abuse, but the fact of a Melodrama Conference in 1992 was itself evidence of the continued productivity of contemporary melodrama studies, and of a continuing reassessment of the form.

This pattern of reaction and reassessment is relevant not just to the Victorian stage but to the Victorian era itself. Describing the Victorians' own glorification of their era, which was then followed by a period when debunking was in fashion, David Walker Howe wrote in 1975: 'now, it would seem the time is right for a kind of understanding that can go beyond an immediate need to celebrate or derogate'.[4]

A second pattern of reaction and reassessment pays greater attention to more popular notions of the Victorian, and indeed to revivals of it. On the release of the film adaptation of *Little Dorrit* (1987) Raphael Samuel unfavourably compared that film's preservationist aesthetic with the darker melodrama of the 1940s versions of *Great Expectations* (1946) and *Oliver Twist* (1948). While '*Little Dorrit* might speculatively be explained by the rehabilitation of Victorian values which has been such a feature of recent years', the earlier films, he argued, along with other period melodramas of the time, were products of a 'modernist revolt against Victorianism', and were themselves 'highly influential in popularising the notion of the Victorian period as a time of darkness and fear'.[5]

The word 'Victorian' can be used to refer to source material or setting, to when *East Lynne* was first published (1861) and to where *Gas Light* (first performed in 1938) is set (London, in the late 19th century). The word, however, carries a charge over and above these usages. The value of Samuel's model is that it suggests that the need to celebrate or derogate the Victorian past remains present. The Victorian era continues to have a meaning in the context of modern, or post-modern, society. When Patrick Hamilton called his play *Gas Light: A Victorian Thriller*, he was stating that the play takes place during the reign of Queen Victoria, but he was also indicating the nature of the plot, the décor, the characters and the structure of morality within which these were placed. 'Victorian' is a word descriptive of narrative, style, moral codes (and the practices underlying such codes). In a wider sense 'Victorianism' has been seen as a 'cultural complex' that preceded modernism, and its identifying characteristics have not been limited to either Britain or the 19th century.[6]

Melodrama has also remained important beyond the reign of Queen Victoria. Melodrama is by definition a form of theatre, a genre primarily restricted to the 19th century, but beyond this particular meaning 'melodrama' has also accrued wider connotations. The reviewer who wrote that MGM's *Gaslight* 'has kept all the good old Drury Lane melodrama'[7] was invoking the particular association of melodrama as a form of Victorian theatre, but was also invoking the characteristics underlying that form: a structure based on moral polarities, an appeal to excitement and the emotions, a heightened sense of theatre through the use of gesture, staging or music. While Victorianism has been referred to as a cultural complex, melodrama has been seen as a 'mode' rather than a genre, and Peter Brooks has referred to the melodramatic mode as 'a central fact of the modern sensibility'.[8]

Bearing these large claims in mind it can be noted that 'Victorian' has in particular been used in the context of America. Not only is it unexceptional for American historians to speak of 'American Victorian culture' and for design source books to refer to 'American Victorian' as a style, but it has been stated that 'Victorianism had its most successful blossoming in America' and that 'Victorian culture was experienced more fully in the United States than in Victoria's homeland'.[9] Melodrama has also been used in the particular contexts of America and Hollywood. 'While in Europe melodrama was waning, in America the melodramatic project gained new life', notes Gledhill.[10] The moral polarities, excitement, emotional display and accentuation of the nineteenth-century stage were perpetuated but transformed on the Hollywood screen.

East Lynne and *Gas Light* illustrate this persistence and transformation. They are important because of their popularity and because they achieved a level of public awareness not restricted to their specific audiences (hence the parodies such as *East Lynne with Variations* (1919) and *Autolight* (first broadcast on US radio, 1945). Both were English in origin and setting, both had a life on the stage before being adapted for the screen, and both achieved much of their popularity in the United States. *East Lynne* is discussed here as a novel written in the Victorian era which was subsequently adapted for the cinema, *Gas Light* as a work that was from the beginning a re-creation of the Victorian. Both illustrate a cross-media intertextuality that has a transatlantic base.

East Lynne

A discussion of *East Lynne* needs to refer to its enduring popularity as a novel, play and film. It is therefore necessary to discuss both the persistence of its appeal and the transformations that accompanied this persistence. It is also necessary to examine the point at which transformation became rejection.

The novel was reprinted throughout the 19th century, in both three-volume and cheaper editions. It was first dramatised as early as 1862, significantly in America rather than Britain, and one source, confined to nineteenth-century Britain and America, lists 88 different productions of the play.[11] In the 20th century, productions of *East Lynne* ceased to be a feature of the established theatres but travelling companies continued to rely on the catchphrase, 'Next Week – *East Lynne!*' 'Nor does the popularity of the play show any signs of abatement,' noted a reviewer of a 1916 film version, while a stage version published as late as 1941 describes it as 'the most talked of play ever written'.[12]

Allowing for inaccuracy and exaggeration in the above quotations it remains true that, while the popularity of the novel and the play did decline, *East Lynne* continued to live on in the cinema. It was filmed in 1902, 1908 (twice), 1909, 1910, 1912, 1913 (twice), 1915, 1916, 1921, 1922, 1925. Finally, in 1931, Fox Studios in America produced their third adaptation; another American film, *Ex-Flame* (1931) was billed as 'a modernised version of *East Lynne*', while in Britain the burlesque *East Lynne on the Western Front* (1931) followed in the footsteps of earlier film parodies of 1914, 1917 and 1919.

In the years up to 1931 *East Lynne* was not simply adapted for the cinema; it was filmed again and again. The story of Lady Isabel, her elopement and her subsequent suffering passed from print to stage to screen.

Cinema, for all its modernity, was the inheritor of the institutions, the modes of expression, the source material, arguably even the audience of Victorian literature and theatre. The stage provided a link between novel and film, but if, through this theatrical connection, *East Lynne* came down to Hollywood as a melodrama, the novel provided a point of reference for the cinema because of its enduring prestige. It is not only the story that persists but also its prestige value. The respectability of a half-page book review in *The Times* in 1862 can be compared with the Best Picture Academy Award nomination given to the 1931 film version, and this respectability resurfaced in 1982 in a British television version that explicitly attempted to cast off the melodrama of the stage version, and, in the producer's words, to restore the 'book and its author to their former position of eminence'.[13]

In an (American) advertisement for a British film version of 1913 it was announced that *East Lynne* was 'A Fragrant Memory of the Dear Old Past, The "Best Seller" of an Unbroken Half Century of Book History.'[14] Arguably, such continuity has had a similar function to that ascribed by David Cannadine to more ritualistic events such as coronations, which, in a period of change, 'might be deliberately unaltered so as to give an impression of continuity and comfort, despite overwhelming contextual evidence to the contrary'.[15] In the case of *East Lynne*, the notion of 'A Fragrant Memory of the Dear Old Past' was itself a transformation of the novel's near-present-day setting, one that, in an American context, represented not just nostalgia, but the privileging of an Anglo-American lineage.

It was not only the context of *East Lynne* that changed, however. The history of the stage and screen versions is the history of adaptation, of the transformation of both text and context. There was not just one stage version but numerous versions (at least as many as 35, according to Fox Studios in 1930), and in 1931 even the novel was rewritten in the form of a novelisation.[16] A second approach adopted by the film industry was the modernisation of the story. In the 1916 version the literal Victorian furniture has been removed, the setting transported to contemporary America, and Lady Isabel elopes in a motor-car. The 1931 'version', *Ex-Flame*, came complete with the accompaniment of Louis Armstrong's jazz orchestra, and ended, according to the *New York Times*, with, 'a grand reunion, in which Sir Carlyle admits he has been a cad and a bounder', a conclusion that appears to lack the names, the vocabulary and the retribution of the original novel.[17]

A third form of transformation was provided by comedy. The title of the Ben Turpin parody of 1919, *East Lynne with Variations*, is itself suggestive in this respect. It is worth noting also that transformation does not originate in the 20th century; there is a tradition of burlesque versions of *East Lynne* dating almost as far back as the original play.

Comedy represented a transformation of *East Lynne*, but it was a transformation that did not necessarily imply a rejection of melodrama. *East Lynne* represented prestige but also sensation and low comedy: 'Sophisticated audiences probably won't approve, but the masses will love it,' wrote *Variety* of *East Lynne on the Western Front*.[18]

Yet transformation can be rejection as well as persistence, and reports of audience laughter exist as one indication of a reaction against Victorian melodrama. At the Bronx screening of one of the 1913 versions *Variety* noted that 'An irreverent male unit of raucous voice larfed [sic] out loud ... when Sir Francis Levison won his first kiss from Isabel.'[19] Thus, while the film industry continued to recycle the story, these adaptions were by no means always favourably received.

After 1931 Hollywood continued to produce 'maternal melodramas' but the line of film adaptations of *East Lynne* died out. The prestige of the name had apparently become a liability, and the contrast between Victorian literature and modern film production was accompanied by the perception of *East Lynne* as a deeply conservative work, upholding the Victorian, patriarchal values of female forebearance and the sanctity of marriage. More generally, the very word 'Victorian' came to denote the 'old-fashioned': 'It is all very out-moded in this sophisticated world of ours today,' noted one reviewer of the 1931 Fox film version.[20]

Thus the morality of *East Lynne* came to be seen as an aspect of Victorian hypocrisy, and in a shift from 'the Dear Old Past' to 'a time of darkness and fear' the very icons of Victorian morality became subject to iconoclasm. If the Victorian era presented a respectable façade, beneath that façade, it was argued, existed frustrated, occasionally not so frustrated, passions. 'The Great Victorian Myth', complained one writer in 1948, 'has almost succeeded in converting the younger generation to a belief that Victorian domestic life was full of thwarted motherhood, tyrannical husbands and fathers, and spiritual frustration in dark, rambling houses.'[21]

Two points need to be made here. Firstly, this writer traced the darker Victorian myth back to *East Lynne*. However, this notion that *East Lynne* is something more than 'A Fragrant Memory of the Dear Old Past' is, in fact, supported by the textual evidence of the novel. The direct message delivered by Ellen Wood, her appeal to women to 'pray for strength to resist the demon that would urge you to escape',[22] certainly needs to be taken into account, but in its very insistence on endurance and forebearance the novel strongly suggests dissatisfaction. The consequence of Lady Isabel's flight might be suffering and humiliation, but until then her life has been one of petty frustration. The 1925 film version suggested that the heroine is tempted out of an ideal, rural security; but in the novel it is not Eden from which Lady Isabel is driven, but a life of unsatisfying conformity.

The notion of the Victorian era as a time of darkness and fear originates with the Victorians themselves. Anti-Victorianism and Victorian morality inhabit the same territory, and both use the metaphor of melodrama. In *Eminent Victorians* Lytton Strachey stated that the 'saintly' Florence Nightingale was, in reality, possessed by a demon, adding that 'demons, whatever else they may be, are full of interest'.[23] Similarly, Wood's Lady Isabel was also shown to be possessed by a demon urging her to escape; like Strachey's Florence Nightingale, Lady Isabel also became interesting when she did not conform to the Victorian ideal.

Secondly, it should be noted that the reference to 'the Great Victorian Myth' was written in the context of a review of *So Evil My Love* (1948), one of several British and American films from the 40s, including both versions of *Gaslight*, that used a late-Victorian setting for narratives of murder and melodrama.[24] These films were not, like *East Lynne*, based on Victorian sources; rather, they were twentieth-century imitations of Victorian narratives.

98

Gas Light

Gas Light is a clear example of a text which rejects the Victorian past from a contemporary point of view, yet this rejection is complicated in that it takes the form of a return to 'Victorian melodrama'. It is necessary, therefore, to consider both how the different versions of *Gas Light* existed as part of a more general revival of interest in Victorian art and artefacts, and how that revival involved the deliberate construction of a notion of the past rather than simply the persistence of Victorian influences.

The textual changes evident in the different versions of *East Lynne* found an analogous reflection over a more limited period in the shift from the West End play, *Gas Light*, to the MGM film, *Gaslight*. The texts and contexts of *Gas Light* therefore provide a means to explore both the cross-media intertextuality noted in *East Lynne* and the different approaches adopted by Britain and the United States to 'Victorian' melodrama.

The play first opened in 1938. In 1939 it had a successful run in the West End and was subsequently made into a low-budget but again well-received film, produced by British National Pictures. The play then transferred to America, where the text and title were amended to become *Angel Street*. In this form it became one of the most successful Broadway productions of the time, running for 1295 performances. The Broadway production was still running when the second film version, produced by MGM, was released in 1944. This production was also well received; it was voted sixth-best film of the year in the *Film Daily* critics' poll, and won Ingrid Bergman an Oscar. The play has continued to be revived; it was adapted for American television in 1948, 1950, 1952, 1953, 1954 and 1958, and twice parodied by Jack Benny, while in the 60s it was rewritten as a novel.[25]

Evidence of the rewriting of *Gas Light* exists both across and within these different versions, and this rewriting indicates shifting contemporary attitudes to the play's melodramatic nature and Victorian setting. The 20th century's high-brow devaluation of melodrama resulted in its becoming associated in America with the low-brow form of 'ten-twenty-thirty' [cents admission] drama, and in Britain with 'blood and thunder' drama and Hollywood sensationalism. Where *Gas Light* was praised, therefore, it was often distinguished from these 'lower' melodramatic forms.

In Britain *The Times* acknowledged that the play was labelled a 'thriller' but thought it 'unjust to leave it in the same category with pieces that depend on groping hands and phosphorescent faces or, alternatively, on gangsters and G-men'.[26] The original script for the British film was later described by its director, Thorold Dickinson, as 'a real blood and thunder B feature job'; this crude melodrama, stated Dickinson, was then rewritten as a more subtle and detailed re-creation of the Victorian era.[27] In a review of the American film, *Variety* noted 'times when the screen treatment verges on a type of drama that must be linked to the period on which the title is based', but found 'whatever lack of values that element might have sustained' dissipated by the 'sober' screenplay and performances. This *Gaslight*, wrote the reviewer, lacked 'the ten-twenty-thirty element that had been a factor in the stage play'.[28]

Such remarks reveal attitudes to melodrama and Victorianism, and the establishment of distinctions between a British and an American approach. The British reviewer who praised the play at the expense of cruder gangster thrillers can be set against the American reviewer who praised the Hollywood film at the expense of the cruder melodrama of the play. These distinctions took on a more blatantly nationalistic character when it was reported that British National had come to an agreement with MGM stipulating that all prints of the British film be destroyed, an agreement that provoked the British critic C.A. Lejeune to defend 'our' *Gaslight* against America's version.[29]

I refer to the establishment of distinctions because I am concerned here with how *Gaslight* was characterised, that is, with its context rather than its text. Two points need to be added, however.

First, the invocation of national identity masked a more complex set of attitudes; American films were highly popular in Britain, while Lejeune's complaints about the British National–MGM agreement were also made in an article she wrote for the *New York Times*.[30] The Broadway success of *Angel Street* itself suggests not just 'Americanisation' but an East Coast Anglophilia.

Second, there are also textual differences present in these different versions of *Gas Light* which reveal distinctions between British and American approaches. The changes made in the story's setting illustrate such distinctions. The opening stage directions of Patrick Hamilton's play state:

> The scene is a living-room on the first floor of a four-storied house in a gloomy and unfashionable quarter of London, in the latter part of the last century. The room is furnished in all the heavily draped and dingy profusion of the period, and yet, amidst this abundance of paraphernalia, an air is breathed of poverty, wretchedness and age.[31]

The screenplay for the British National film simply refers to 'a typical middle-class drawing-room of the late 1880s', but in the MGM screenplay it is noted that 'Thornton Square should be similar to one of the smaller squares in London, either in Knightsbridge or on the north side of Hyde Park in Paddington, ultra respectable, upper middle class.'[32]

Between 1938 and 1944, between Britain and America, and between stage and screen, *Gas Light* moved up the social scale. The publicity for the American film refers to items of furniture, 'fringed and festooned in typical 1880 elegance [and] so valuable that setting a price for them would be impossible'.[33] Just as the low-budget British National film made way for an expensive MGM production, the theatre's unfashionable Victoriana, its 'poverty, wretchedness and age', became Hollywood's respectability and wealth.

The play's stage directions continue with the instruction: 'THE CURTAIN RISES upon the rather terrifying darkness of the late afternoon.'[34] Samuel's 'darkness and fear' undoubtedly represented one image of the Victorian era present in the different versions of *Gas Light*. 'I'd seen the play and been shaken by it and jumped at this chance to expose the worse side of the Victorian male's attitude to women,' commented Dickinson, and in its

100

review *The Tatler* saw the play as coming 'from a period when wives were more readily intimidated by the dominant male'.[35] 'Everything is middle Victorian,' noted one of the MGM filmscripts of another scene. 'This goes particularly for the pictures on the wall, all English and all bad.'[36]

In their different ways these comments all speak the language of the rejection of Victorianism. The Victorian is identified with tastelessness, with bad art and paraphernalia, and beyond that there exists the misogyny referred to by Dickinson and the 'poverty, wretchedness and age' referred to by Hamilton. The association of age with negative values suggests a validation of modernity. The gloom and claustrophobia of Victorian architecture could be contrasted with the openness and light of a modernist aesthetic. The gloomy Victorian setting acts as a motivation for the action, as a motivation for both misogyny and melodrama. Male intimidation is identified with the past rather than the present.

Yet anti-Victorianism was not exclusively formulated in modernist terms. The Victorian era could also be seen as too tainted with modernity. The era could signify both the old-fashioned and the evils of modernity: with it had come industrialisation, slums, the destruction of an older, rural and craft-based community. While one writer stated that in this period 'the machine was never allowed to do its splendid best', another categorised Victorian furniture as 'heavy, unlovely, machine-influenced'.[37] The rural setting of *East Lynne* can be contrasted with the urban setting of *Gas Light*, a world on the brink of modernity. However, even the original *East Lynne* plays on the perils of mechanisation, using the melodramatic, and proto-cinematic, device of the train crash, while the original *Gas Light* ends with the promise of an idyllic Devon to which its heroine will escape and find sanctuary from the city.

The pattern of association is complex and contradictory: 'Victorian' could imply both the modern and the antiquated, both propriety and impropriety. The British novel *Fanny by Gaslight*, for example, was, according to one reviewer, set in a Victorian London characterised by 'the grossness of its pleasures and the scarcely hidden service of debauchery'.[38] But if *Gas Light*, *Fanny by Gaslight* (published in 1940, filmed in 1944), and other books, articles, plays and films display a reaction against the Victorian era, they were also a return to that era. 'Victorianism is in vogue,' noted one British article, while another asked 'why these novels and novelists of the past, especially of the Victorian past, are so much in demand'.[39] Melodrama such as *The Streets of New York* and *Ten Nights in a Barroom* were being produced almost as frequently as originally, claimed an American article of 1945, and publishers' catalogues were 'filled with imitations of Victorian melodrama'.[40]

One reason for such popularity may have been that the Victorian era could stand in for darkness and fear, whether because of a twentieth-century rejection of the era itself, or because this dark, melodramatic Victorianism allowed the exploration of contemporary fears. A further reason was that the Victorian era in general and Victorian melodrama in particular could be made quaint and comic because it represented another time. Indeed, in so far as melodrama is played for laughs, there is an attitude of condescension in this Victorian revival.

The demand for the Victorian past, however, was also a reaction against modernity, and it was possible to discover a charm even on the underside of Victorian life, and to mourn what George Orwell called the 'Decline of the English Murder'.[41] The characterisation of Victorian life and artefacts in terms of tastelessness and falsity needs to be set against the notion of the era's 'period charm'. Advertisements for 'Old Victorian Oil Lamps' (electrified for modern convenience), 'Victorian "Double Life" curtains – As dainty and Victorian as you please', and claims that 'Charming Women love exquisitely feminine Vanderley Victorian', suggest an explicitly gendered, popular notion of the Victorian that could be contrasted with modern functionalism or austerity.[42] If one myth was of spiritual frustration, another would have nothing to do with this dark side of the Victorians; Queen Victoria's reign, according to another writer, 'was such a long, happy one, it is little wonder that there should be a revival of interest in the Victorian style of furniture, glass, carpets, wallpapers and all sorts of decorative accessories'.[43]

Gas Light, in its different forms, may have represented a rejection of 'Victorian values', but it also existed in the context of a popular interest in Victoriana. Both the British and the American films highlight the sense of period, the British film through the details of morning prayers, a charity concert, and a visit to the music hall, the American film through more ornate furnishings.

As was noted at the time, however, it is inadequate simply to describe this popularity as a revival of Victorian melodrama or Victoriana. Advertisements for 'Victorian' curtains referred to a style rather than a date of origin, publishers catalogues were filled with 'imitations of Victorian melodrama'. The production of *Gas Light* was not the revival of a Victorian melodrama but the twentieth-century creation of one, and the same was true of novels, plays and films such as *Fanny by Gaslight, Pink String and Sealing Wax* and *Ladies in Retirement.* The 1916 film had modernised *East Lynne*, just as *The Woman in White* and *Dracula*, to mention two other Victorian novels, were modernised in 1920 and 1931; in Hollywood in the 40s the reverse process can be noted, as novels with contemporary settings, such as Patrick Hamilton's *Hangover Square*, were pushed back towards (although not quite within) the Victorian era.

Film studies, in tracing the Victorian prehistory of Hollywood melodrama, has discovered connections across texts and contexts, across media, cultures and epochs, and my title, '*East Lynne* to *Gas Light*', can also suggest continuity. One concern of this essay has, indeed, been with the identification of such connections through an examination of the different versions of *East Lynne* and *Gas Light*.

The history of the different versions of *East Lynne*, however, is also the history of a shifting body of material and of changing reactions to its Victorian and melodramatic basis. A reaction against Victorianism provided, in its turn, the basis for the revival of 'Victorian' melodrama, as can be seen in the different versions of *Gas Light*. The connection here involved the twentieth-century construction of a notion of Victorianism rather than the continuation of a direct line of descent.

102

The continuity that is present, therefore, is one of a continuing but shifting significance of the Victorian past. The nature of that significance was subject to change and complicated both across and within individual texts. There is a tension both between and inside the different versions of *East Lynne* and *Gas Light*, a tension between a nostalgia for the past and the rejection of the past, and between prestige and excitement.

Melodrama deals in the material of lived experience. *East Lynne* deals with the relationship and separation of mother and child, and *East Lynne* and *Gas Light* are both domestic melodramas, concerned with conflict within the institution of marriage. Their resonance is rooted in the fact that they present recognisable situations, and their longevity can be attributed to the fact that while their appeal has varied over time it has not been restricted to particular historical circumstances.

However, as well as dealing in the material of lived experience, melodrama deals in the material of popular history and myth. Melodrama had a central place within Victorian culture, but the Victorian has also been returned to and reinterpreted for the purposes of melodrama. It is important to speak of a melodramatic tradition, but also to recognise that in doing so we are speaking of a shifting tradition, a product of the 20th century as well as the 19th century.

Notes

1. Christine Gledhill, 'The Melodramatic Field: An Investigation', in Christine Gledhill (ed.), *Home is Where the Heart Is: Studies in Melodrama and the Woman's Film* (London: British Film Institute, 1987), p. 5.
2. Edith Batho and Bonamy Dobrée, *The Victorians and After, 1830–1914* (London: Cresset Press, 1938), p. 122.
3. Louis James, 'Was Jerrold's Black Ey'd Susan more popular than Wordsworth's Lucy?', in David Bradby, Louis James and Bernard Sharratt (eds), *Performance and Politics in Popular Drama* (Cambridge: Cambridge University Press, 1980), p. 3.
4. David Walker Howe, 'American Victorianism as a Culture', *American Quarterly*, vol. 27, 1975, p. 532.
5. The first quotation comes from Raphael Samuel, 'Little Dickens', *Guardian*, 19 February 1988, the latter two from 'Dickens on Stage and Screen', *History Today*, vol. 39, 1989, p. 50.
6. 'Before post-modernism was "modernism" and before that a cultural complex most historians agree in calling "Victorianism",' states Daniel T. Rodgers in 'Before Postmodernism', *Reviews in American History*, vol. 18, 1990, p. 77.
7. *Los Angeles Examiner*, 19 January 1944.
8. Peter Brooks, *The Melodramatic Imagination: Balzac, Henry James, Melodrama, and the Mode of Excess* (New Haven: Yale University Press, 1976), p. 21.
9. The quotations are taken from Rita Wellman, *Victoria Royal: The Flowering of a Style* (New York and London: Charles Scribner's Sons, 1939), p. 209, and Howe, op. cit., p. 508. An example of a relevant design source book is Lawrence Grow and Dina Van Zwech, *American Victorian: A Style and Source Book* (New York: Harper & Row, 1984).
10. Gledhill, op. cit., p. 25.
11. Nebile Direkcigil, 'An Edition of T.A. Palmer's Dramatisation of Mrs Henry Wood's *East Lynne*, With a Section on the Theatrical Background'. Unpublished PhD thesis, Leeds University, 1975.

12. 'The Drama That Never Fails', *Bioscope*, 7 September 1916; introduction to 'Ned Albert' [pseudonym of Wilbur Braun], *East Lynne* (New York: Samuel French, 1941), p. 3.

13. *The Times*, 25 January 1962; Colin Shindler, 'The Woman Who Wrote *East Lynne* But Not *That* Line', *The Listener*, 23 and 30 December 1982.

14. Clipping file for *East Lynne* (1913), Academy of Motion Picture Arts and Sciences, Los Angeles.

15. David Cannadine, 'The context, performance and meaning of ritual: The British Monarchy and the "Invention of Tradition", *c.*1820–1977', in Eric Hobsbawn and Terence Ranger (eds), *The Invention of Tradition* (Cambridge: Cambridge University Press, 1983), p. 105.

16. The figure is taken from a letter dated 19 June 1930, held in the Fox Legal File for *East Lynne* (1931), Department of Special Collection, Theater Arts Library, University of California, Los Angeles. In 1931 the New York publisher Grosset & Dunlap published '*East Lynne*, by Arline De Haas, Suggested by Mrs Henry Wood's Famous Novel, with Scenes from the Fox Movietone Starring Ann Harding and Clive Brook'.

17. *New York Times*, 24 January 1931.

18. 28 July 1931.

19. 18 July 1913.

20. *Picturegoer Weekly*, 26 September 1931. The earliest usage of 'Victorian' in the sense of 'old-fashioned' cited by the *Oxford English Dictionary* (2nd edn, 1989) is from the 1934 edition of Webster's Dictionary.

21. *Evening News* [London], 27 May 1948.

22. Mrs Henry Wood, *East Lynne* (London: J.M. Dent, 1984), p. 289.

23. Lytton Strachey, *Eminent Victorians* (Harmondsworth: Penguin, 1986), p. 113.

24. As a Hal Wallis production for Paramount that was filmed in England, *So Evil My Love* was a product of both the British and American film industries.

25. '*Gas Light*, Presented on the Stage as "Angel Street", by Patrick Hamilton, novelized by William Drummond' (New York: Paperback Library, 1966) was described by the publishers as 'The greatest Gothic Thriller of all time!' It would appear to have been published at this time due to the current trend for publishing 'paperback Gothics'.

26. 1 February 1939.

27. Quoted in Jeffrey Richards, *Thorold Dickinson: The Man and His Films* (London: Croom Helm, 1986), p. 69.

28. 10 May 1944.

29. Review of *The Murder in Thornton Square*, *The Observer*, 16 July 1944.

30. *New York Times*, 13 August 1944. For the popularity of American films in the period immediately following the war, see Paul Swann, *The Hollywood Feature Film in Postwar Britain* (London: Croom Helm, 1987).

31. Patrick Hamilton, *Gas Light: A Victorian Thriller in Three Acts* (London: Constable, 1939), p. 7.

32. British screenplay dated 12 February 1940, p. 9; American screenplay dated 10 August 1943, p. 1. Both held at the Academy of Motion Picture Arts and Sciences in collections relating to the MGM *Gaslight*.

33. British Film Institute Library microjacket, *Gaslight* (1944). This quote is taken from the British press-book.

34. Hamilton, op. cit., p. 7.

35. Quoted in Richards, op. cit., p. 68; *Tatler*, 22 February 1939.

36. Revised script, dated 16 March 1943, Department of Special Collections, University of Southern California, Los Angeles, p. 63.

37. John Gloag, *The English Tradition in Design* (London and New York: Penguin, 1947), pp. 22–3; *Antiques Yearbook, Encylopedia and Directory 1949–50* (Malvern: Tantivy Press, 1949), p. 135.
38. *The Observer*, 5 May 1940.
39. Willson Disher, 'Melodrama and the Modern Mind', *Theatre World*, vol. 30, 1939, p. 152; Anne Kavan, 'Back to Victoria', *Horizon*, vol. 13, 1946, p. 62.
40. Alan S. Downer, 'A Preface to Melodrama: I. The Less Eminent Victorians', *Players Magazine*, vol. 21, 1945, p. 9.
41. See George Orwell, *Decline of the English Murder and Other Essays* (Harmondsworth: Penguin, 1965), p. 9.
42. *House and Garden* [American edition], December 1940, p. 25; October 1940, p. 68; May 1950, p. 7.
43. Ruth Webb Lee, *Victorian Glass: Specialities of the Nineteenth Century* (Northboro, Mass.: published by the author, 1944), p. 4.

MUSIC AND THE MELODRAMATIC
PAST OF NEW GERMAN CINEMA*

CARYL FLINN

New German Melodrama and Technologies of Muteness

Film melodrama's most famous link to New German Cinema has been made via Douglas Sirk, whose influence on Rainer Werner Fassbinder is apparent in films like *The Merchant of Four Seasons* (1971), *The Bitter Tears of Petra von Kant* (1972) and *Fear Eats the Soul* (1973), Fassbinder's remake of *All That Heaven Allows* (1955). Not coincidentally, Fassbinder remarked that 'Sirk's been in everything I've done,'[1] wrote an article on Sirk in 1971, was interviewed with him in 1979, and was eulogised by Sirk after his death. Scholars, for their part, have highlighted the many similarities between Sirk and Fassbinder, and the term frequently used to describe their work is 'excessive' – a word which just as aptly describes the melodramatic and New German Cinema traditions in which the two directors worked.

Just what is excessive about Hollywood melodrama and New German Cinema? To be sure, the excesses of such different modes of film-making cannot be configured the same way. Within New German Cinema alone there are many ways in which 'excess' may and has been constituted. Nor can melodrama's indulgences be made smooth or coherent, though one highly influential attempt was made in the 70s when Geoffrey Nowell-Smith argued that film melodrama operated according to the same mechanisms as those of conversion hysteria.[2] Hysteria's investment in restaging past events will prove especially crucial to our look at how music operates in Fassbinder's work which, like so much New German Cinema, places considerable emphasis on the role of the past in shaping current conditions. Melodrama too has its own 'magnificent obsession' with the past, with its circular stories and its elaborate (if not compulsive) restagings, longings, and missed opportunities. Given that Freud and Breuer identified hysteria as the 'suffer[ing of] reminiscences', it is small wonder that Nowell-Smith's idea has enjoyed the influence it has. Much of the

---

* This piece is taken from a larger piece on performance, melancholia, and the New German Cinema. For reasons of space, I have concentrated primarily on the role of music in selected films by Rainer Werner Fassbinder.

106

exegetic force of his hysterical model is derived from the assertion that a traumatic event in the past – one which has been subsequently buried beneath the realm of consciousness – cannot be directly expressed, an idea which has obvious ramifications for a cinema obsessed by its cultural and political past such as New German Cinema, as well as for melodrama. The past, in a sense, has been censored, made difficult, rendered mute in the text's body. The repressed traumas reveal themselves only in highly displaced, non-linguistic ways (aphasic conditions, Sirkian colours, scores by Max Steiner). The critic/analyst thus reads the film/body's elaborate, 'excessive' markings back for generative 'causes', which critics have argued had to do with social and ideological contradictions that the text cannot smooth over or maintain. In this fashion melodramas, like so many films read against the grain, have been believed to present ideological critiques by displaying what could not be contained at more manifest, narrative levels.

As it was constructed by critics during the 70s, melodrama appeared to produce a voice where only silence had existed. Peter Brooks famously refers to melodrama as a 'text of muteness'; David Grimsted calls it the 'echo of the historically voiceless'.[3] The same emphasis on silence and expression carries over into the work of Helene Cixous, who comments that 'silence is the mark of hysteria. The great hysterics have lost speech, they are aphonic.'[4] In classical Hollywood melodrama, speechless characters abound (consider the servant in *Letter from an Unknown Woman* (1948) or Jane Wyman in *Johnny Belinda* (1948)), and deaf and mute characters populate a number of early New German films as well, such as *Wrong Movement* (1974), *The Bitter Tears of Petra von Kant*, and *Chinese Roulette* (1976). Richard McCormick has argued that the perceptual disabilities of these latter figures constitute part of the 'inward turn' German literature was taking then, after the grinding disappointments of the late 60s, as part of a larger cultural and political distrust of the senses, direct experience, and language.[5] Clearly, silence and expression are central preoccupations of both melodrama and New German Cinema, but the focus might be better shifted on to the ways in which these texts *break* with silence, how they *make* noise and music, so that we can re-evaluate the applicability of the hysterical model.

The Surfeit of Music

Music has been central to the excesses attributed both to melodrama and to New German Cinema. Its importance in the former was asserted in Elsaesser's classic 'Tales of Sound and Fury', where he argues that, along with other formal elements, it forms a 'system of punctuation, giving expressive colour and chromatic contrast to the story-line, by orchestrating the emotional ups and downs of the intrigue'.[6] The remark indicates how melodrama amplifies – indeed, makes excessive – music's conventional Hollywood function of providing passive, emotional support to film's visual and dramatic activity. For Nowell-Smith, melodrama's

> undischarged emotion which cannot be accommodated within the action, subordinated as it is to the demands of family/lineage/inheri-

tance, is traditionally expressed in the music and, in the case of film, in certain elements of the *mise en scène*. That is to say, music and *mise en scène* do not just heighten the emotionality of an element of the action: to some extent they substitute for it.[7]

The *melos* of melodrama, then, picks up where something else leaves off, veering in the direction of what might appear to be pure surfeit or excess. Now since, as Peter Brooks argues, the motor behind the genre is an impulse to 'express all', a certain shifting of registers is necessary to get past the conventional linguistic constraints, and music (however deceptively) often yields that impression of bypassing or even of preceding language.[8]

Critics have argued that, along with other non-referential signs like performance, gesture and rhythm, music indeed *does* take over for melodrama's linguistic deficiencies. Though not able to operate mimetically, music can, in the words of Richard Dyer, gesture towards a 'something better' that he and others have associated with a Utopian impulse.[9] Although Dyer charts this Utopian function in relation to the Hollywood musical, the idea is most appropriate to melodrama, given music's central (even etymological) position within the genre. In fact, Elsaesser has linked the idea of Utopian both to the musical and to melodrama, arguing that Utopian moments are frozen in the former and continually deferred by the latter.[10] Music thus offers a promise of fantasy and desire, if not its fulfilment.

In his interview with Jon Halliday, Sirk barely mentions the scores to his films, even though Frank Skinner's music saturates most of his work done at Universal. Yet for an earlier film, *Schlussakkord (Final Accord)* (1936), which takes place at the Paris Conservatory, music was not only important in establishing its diegetic world, but in how Sirk conceptualised his melodramatic work more generally. As he told Halliday in reference to the film, 'I am interested in circularity, in the circle – people arriving back at the place they started out from. This is why you will find what I call tragic rondos in many of my films, people going in circles. This is what most of my characters are doing.'[11] The same melodramatic circularity orchestrating Sirk's famous narratives could also be said to shape their scores. In *All That Heaven Allows*, for example, both Rock Hudson and Jane Wyman's characters have brief scenes playing the piano. In Hudson's piano number he sings, introducing into the score a catchy, original song about attracting a lady's eye, no less (what he will literally be doing to her in *Magnificent Obsession* (1954)). In Wyman's scene, on the other hand, she does not sing but (Cixous's perfect aphonic) simply performs a variation of Frank Skinner's endlessly repeated main theme of the film. Though played by her, music expresses nothing really her own, but simply circles back on itself.

Music performs an equally conspicuous role in New German Cinema. Films will quote from earlier texts, and one often gets the sense of the German cinema going on a raid of its national musical past. Kluge's acoustically stunning and complex *The Power of Emotions* (1983), for example, features portions of *Parsifal, The Ring, Aida, Tannhäuser, The*

Makropoulos Affair, and other operas. Hans-Jurgen Syberberg and Werner Schroeter's work could not exist without music or the operatic: Syberberg's well-documented obsession with Wagner is evident not only in his well-known *Our Hitler* (1977), but in his adaptation of *Parsifal* (1982), and in *Ludwig: Requiem for a Virgin King* (1972) – the last, for example, opens with *Das Rheingold,* closes with *Götterdämmerung,* and borrows from *Tristan and Isolde* in the middle. Schroeter's work plays with even more intricate relationships to music in, for example, *The Death of Maria Malibran* (1972), *Palermo* or *Wolfsburg* (1980). Tim Corrigan makes an interesting remark on operatic performance in Schroeter's *Willow Springs (1972–3):* 'the *mise-en-scène* of that scream/song, in short, shifts registers rather imperceptibly so that the anguish of the image becomes at once exaggerated and trivialised, translated along the way into a blend of camp, kitsch, melodrama, and soap opera'.[12] Corrigan's observation about the film evokes the shifting of textual registers that are also at work in melodrama, and can be usefully extended to other New German films which use musical citations in such exaggerated ways that they generate the impression of inculcated, clichéd codes rather than the sense of something 'original' or emotionally expressive.

Elsaesser's argument that music operates as a contrapuntal register to the drama of family melodrama brings to mind any number of film scenes (most vividly for me, the carnival music that blares from a TV set in *Bigger than Life* (1956) as best buddies James Mason and Walter Matthau brawl violently on Mason's staircase). His comment also recalls Hanns Eisler and Theodor Adorno's argument in *Composing for the Film,* where they maintain that film music should not have to provide neat, auditory equivalents of visual information. (To give music a more active role in the cinema, they argue, would help reveal the constructed, material nature of film form rather than naturalise or falsely unify its various elements, as it does in conventional cinematic practice. What Elsaesser's description of film melodrama suggests is that the musical alternative Eisler and Adorno outline for Hollywood might already be working there.)

The distancing of film score from image (and from the dramatic imperatives conventionally associated with the image) also suggests the work of Bertolt Brecht, whose notion an epic theatre requires strategies such as direct address, actors playing multiple roles, flat, unemotional delivery, and unprofessional singers to help destroy the illusion of naturalism or unity. The impact of Brecht's thought is readily apparent in the work of Fassbinder (as in many other post-war German directors), and his influence on Fassbinder is well known. 'With Brecht,' he once maintained, 'you see the emotions and you reflect upon them as you witness them but you never feel them. That's my interpretation and I think I go farther than he did in that I let the audience *feel and think.*'[13] His remark might explain Fassbinder's use of popular film forms like melodrama, despite his complaint that 'The American method of making [melodramas], however, left the audience with emotions and nothing else.'[14] Following (and perhaps even outdoing) Brecht, Fassbinder's scores often *turn in on* the sentimentalisation of musical excess, sometimes by denying it altogether, as in its near total absence in the first three-quarters of *The*

Bitter Tears of Petra von Kant, or by using conspicuously pre-recorded music *with* emotionally excessive moments, as in the end of the same film. By this point of the film, when Petra is deserted by her long-faithful, mute assistant, a decontextualised fragment of Verdi's *La Traviata* plays alongside The Platters, whose 'The Great Pretender' is heard in its entirety. Both pieces are obviously pre-recorded and, although they provide *some* commentary on Petra's distressed condition, there is little which would enable listeners to attach the songs directly to an inner state of her character. The music is borrowed, pasted on from quite different texts and contexts.

Peer Raben, Fassbinder's composer on several films (and his director and fellow actor in Action Theatre), highlights music's intertextual, 'borrowed' role. He maintains that *all* styles of music from *all* periods can accompany *any* story of *any* period. Film music should aim for what he calls an 'additive originality', a concept he links with the Utopian.[15] Despite Raben's assertions to the contrary, it would seem that New German Cinema meets his requirements. Consider the Bach that anachronistically permeates the otherwise 'mod,' post-war industrial diegesis of Kluge's *Yesterday Girl* (1966), where music does less to counter dramatic action than to suggest its emergence from another place, period, genre, or set of circumstances. In a similar way, Werner Herzog's *Nosferatu* (1979) features brief portions of *Das Rheingold* when Jonathan hikes towards the count's castle, when the captain of the infested ship works at his desk, and when the vampire finally leaves the boat, by then its sole survivor. In obvious contrast to its function in *The Ring*, the music here signals not an enthralling, enticing power or glittering discovery, but a complete lack of control, of bodies taken over (outdoing even Alberich's renunciation and curse!). The elliptical, extremely truncated use of the Wagner dispels any unit or fullness that *Nosferatu's* score might provide (additional music by Popul Vuh and composer Florian Fricke splinter things even further). For all the averred excesses and indulgences of some New German Cinema soundtracks, then, music appears in curiously restrained forms, functioning as little more than fleeting, hollowed-out operatic shells in *Petra von Kant*, or hopelessly fragmented as in *Nosferatu*.

The most influential scholarship on Rainer Fassbinder has concerned itself with the ways in which specularity and the gaze operate in his openly exhibitionist films.[16] Fassbinder's masochistic yielding of body and identity to the gaze are, according to Thomas Elsaesser, tied to social and historical particularities, and to Kaja Silverman, to the utterly inaccessible nature of the gaze itself. The impossible, judgmental power of the gaze that bears upon his texts includes not only the gaze of German history but the gaze of Hollywood cinema (especially Sirk's, which weighs heavily upon Fassbinder's *oeuvre* as a master presence and not simply as reference).[17] The externality of such gazes is important here. Writing about post-war German identity, Elsaesser stresses that:

Since 1945 solutions to the German question, official attitudes to German history and many of the moral and political judgements on the War and Fascism had been, as it were, imposed *from outside*. The defeat of Hitler, the creation of West and East Germany, rearmament and the division of the German nation were seen as external interventions, rather than expressions of a national resolve. Germans were liberated from outside, and they were separated into good Germans and bad Germans from outside.'[18]

We should recall that the 'New German Cinema' was not named as such domestically, nor was it commercially successful at home: its definition and existence were established by foreign critics.

Music also avails a foreign 'gaze' of another sort, another constraining discourse or intertextual intrusion that limits not only the power of characters within their diegetic worlds, but the subjectivity they appear to emblematise. The voices, sounds, and music of Fassbinder films do not function as expressions of subjectivity (be they of character, composer, or director), nor do they even reproduce or quote an originating source. Instead, they engage in an exhibition, a playing out of earlier influences. In this light, the notion of stylistic and textual excesses expressing displaced *internal* memory becomes rather difficult to sustain.

Although Fassbinder's films rely on Hollywood's melodramatic model, their use of music avails less a sense of something punctuating or proceeding from within than of something that constrains or comments upon from both within and without (such clear-cut textual boundaries are problematic to begin with, especially in the light of New German Cinema's international circulation). As Peer Raben writes, 'Music's development shouldn't conform to the movements and feelings of the characters depicted, rather it opposes them.' Discussing a melody from *Love is Colder than Death* (1969) that he borrowed from a Spanish madrigal, he writes that the 'melody seemed entirely appropriate to break up Fassbinder's laconic characters and, consequently, made them speak in a different way. At the time I really wasn't aware that they were expressing themselves in Spanish through my music.' Unconcerned with historical, cultural, or thematic 'matching' of music to diegesis, Raben goes on to say (in a space somewhere between the melodramatic and the Utopian) that music 'supports something that isn't yet in the image, nor in the mind either ... that isn't yet *true*'.[19]

Fassbinder's *Fear Eats the Soul* makes patently clear the unwillingness to interiorise musical signs, or, for that matter, to associate them with any kind of simple emotional affect. The film features Emmi, a middle-aged German widow employed as a cleaning woman, who enters into a difficult relationship with Ali, an immigrant worker from Morocco about thirty years her junior. The North African music that appears intermittently in the film's spartan score reasserts the rigid racial boundaries of its diegesis. The music offers no escape to Ali and his friends (who are never depicted without it), for whom it is an auditory reminder of Germany's unwillingness to accept anything beyond their status as *Gastarbeiters*. It proffers Ali, in other words, acoustic signs of his proper cultural identity while simultaneously reminding him of that identity's current uselessness to him. (The owner of the grimly named Asphalt pub tells Emmi there is German music on the jukebox but 'they prefer their own'.)

111

For Emmi, on the other hand, the songs extend the possibility of some kind of refuge. For a middle-aged cleaning woman whose labour is ill paid and whose sexual exchange value has plummeted, the North African music might offer a Utopian alternative, a momentary escape from industrialised Western norms. This is not to say that the music functions as a pure metonym for Ali's non-Western culture or that Emmi's is a simple, open celebration of it. Far from it. She first meets Ali, for instance, at the Asphalt pub, where a jukebox plays some music and their dance initiates their courtship. The tune at this point is not North African but an old, scratchy popular German song (later referred to as 'that gypsy record'), significantly the only time Western music plays in the bar – or most of the film, for that matter.

When the two first dance, they use just enough words to get to know one another (Ali comments, 'German master, Arab dog'). Judith Mayne has commented on Ali's fractured German and Emmi's reliance on popular clichés and platitudes.[20] Language, functioning like a test case of both melodrama and Lacanian theory, offers little here, even to Emmi, the German subject to whom it might come easily. Consider its function as a marker of class: Emmi is distinctly unfamiliar with several terms at an upper-class restaurant she visits with Ali and has trouble negotiating the waiter's queries. In classic melodramatic fashion, words do little except to construct the barest, most superficially symbolic of their identities.

Neither, however, does music come in to redress such representational deficiencies, as it might in a conventional Hollywood melodrama. Indeed, the score offers little stability, providing no extravagance or even sustenance to its characters. Take, for instance, the non-diegetic tune used briefly on three occasions. A short, aimless melody first appears when Ali and Emmi talk in bed the night they meet, then as Ali walks towards the bar after he has walked out on her, and at the end of the film as the image fades to black. Unmotivated, and thoroughly conventional in style, the brief melody appears to be Fassbinder's little wink at music's typical emotional function in melodrama (a similar device appears in *The Merchant of Four Seasons*). The North African record, too, offers little in the way of emotional or identificatory pinning, even though Emmi appears to have more invested in it than in the 'gypsy' German song to which she and Ali first dance. 'Now I'll play our record,' she announces when placing it on the pub's jukebox during their engagement celebration. Yet by the end of the film, the initial promise of the song has been punctured, something literalised on the body of Ali (the ulcers that perforate his stomach will continue to torment him, as the doctor says, because *Gastarbeiters* are never given sufficient time off work to recuperate). The doctor's diagnosis that concludes the film offers a stunning example of the way in which melodrama perpetually defers the Utopian. *All That Heaven Allows*, the film on which *Fear Eats the Soul* was based, ends quite similarly, focusing on the body of the young, ailing male (Rock Hudson). In both films the physical disabilities of the characters are great enough to overpower the sense of a happy ending that might have emerged from the women's reunion with their partners after the men are injured. The closing of *Magnificent Obsession* uses physical infirmity in precisely the same way, darkening any optimism that might be suggested at narrative levels. As Wyman recovers after Hudson (now a doctor) has performed surgery on her to restore her sight, she articulates a desire for immediate pleasure ('Can't we have fun now?'). Yet he, the paternal voice of melodrama, incants 'Tomorrow, tomorrow,' deferring Utopia so as to become, melo-dramatically speaking, impossible.

Fassbinder's *Chinese Roulette* is another movie obsessed with thwarted desire, repetition and the past. Angel, the crippled daughter of bourgeois parents who are both having affairs, brings them together for a retreat in their country château (*à la Rules of the Game* (1939)) – each unaware that the other will also be there, with their lover. The action at the estate is captured through vertiginous camerawork that encircles characters as they assemble for (among few other things) cocktails. Drinks, glasses, mirrors, dildos: the film is filled with objects and signs of identity on the skids. Catalysed by Angel, the characters at the château trek into her family's past. The journey culminates in the playing of the vicious parlour game, Chinese Roulette, which is motivated by Angel's matricidal fantasy. After the game's violent conclusion, the film ends on a long shot of the country estate, over which wedding vows are written and we hear the musical per-formance of it. Though literally 'parallel' to image, the score is highly ironic yet, interestingly, *Chinese Roulette* features one of Fassbinder's more varied and sensual soundtracks. The score is littered with choirs, disco music, opera, a generic 'thriller' motif, a central theme that is repeated several times, and an extended, compositionally varied piece during the playing of the Chinese Roulette game itself. Yet for all this acoustic dis-play, as Angel warns the gardener Gabriel, 'eavesdroppers often hear the wrong truths': the film's soundtrack raises the same epistemological, emo-tional and moral uncertainties as does its mirror-studded imagery. No music lasts very long; *Chinese Roulette* uses the elaborate forms of opera and melodrama only to carve them up and drain them. It opens, for example, with an early nineteenth-century German opera playing, its lavishness overwhelming the motionless sterility of the mother–daughter characters who are visually introduced. The scene melodramatically repeats two separate, static shots of Angel and her mother, as if to advise the filmgoer that some intimacy between the two was forthcoming (per-haps a maternal melodrama?). When the aria accompanying these initial shots comes to an abrupt halt as soon as the girls' father arrives and breaks the dyad, the expectation is heightened all the more. Yet nothing brings them together – one could not ask for a more vitriolic mother–daughter relationship. Music offers no stability, no hope, no sense of future gain.

A Less Hysterical Music

In explaining how the mechanism of conversion hysteria works in melo-drama, Nowell-Smith writes that the

> repressed returns, converted into a bodily symptom.... In the melo-
> drama ... a conversion can take place in the body of the text.... It is
> not just that the characters are often prone to hysteria, but that *the film*

itself somaticises its own unaccommodated excess, which thus appears displaced or in the wrong place.[21]

To psychologise the text 'itself' in such a fashion raises certain questions, and Nowell-Smith is not unaware of them when he notes the difficulty connecting melodrama's 'hysterical moments' to specific sources. Are they produced by the director (the article is on Minnelli, after all)? Are they breakdowns of narrative? of characters? Although Nowell-Smith, like other melodrama scholars, insists that melodrama's excessive, hysterical markings are socially and ideologically driven, in the last instance these instabilities seem to be generated by the text itself, as if some interiority were stable enough to be pressed out.[22] Sirk once remarked vis-à-vis the issue of domestic drama, 'everything happens on the inside'.[23] Yet in what sense does an 'inside' of melodrama or New German Cinema exist? What kind of agency lurks behind melodrama's imperative to 'express all'? Is it stable enough to psychologise?

The question of agency grows more important when considered alongside the characters as they are constructed in New German Cinema and in melodrama. As critics have noted, characters inhabiting melodrama's worlds function in flat, highly emblematical ways, typifying moral extremes, social or class positions rather than three-dimensionalising them (Sirk's *Written on the Wind* (1956) and Fassbinder's *Merchant of Four Seasons* are exemplary in this regard). Characters are powerless (recall Grimsted's reference to melodrama 'as echo of the historically voiceless'); victims of circumstance, they are shaped out of fate and their ideological environs in the same way that, in Elsaesser's words, they are constructed 'out' of the décor, the visual and acoustic moorings which so often overwhelm and exceed them. In this light, then, what film melodrama criticism of the 70s produces is *a psychologised text without psychologised characters*. A text constructed in such a way might work less to destabilise subjectivity than to resecure it, as Laura Mulvey has suggested with regard to Sirk's heavily stylised work: '*Mise en scène*, rather than undercutting the actions and words of the story level, provides a central point of orientation for the spectator'.[24] One might well ask what *kind* of spectator, what form of subjectivity, gets 'oriented' or resecured. Nowell-Smith argued that, as far as gender goes, melodrama reveals an equal disempowerment of male and female characters, and Elsaesser has remarked that both New German Cinema and melodrama emphasise the discrepancy between the social roles and the people asked to fill them. However, to assume a subjectivity under siege is to assume the existence of a 'subject' stable enough to be put at risk. For women, who have yet to reap the full benefits of subjectivity, the assumption is obviously problematic. The issue is even more politically pressing when we consider the fuller intersecting concerns of race, sexual orientation, and ability – issues which melodrama scholars have only recently begun to be explore.

I have stressed that both melodrama and New German Cinema are characterised in terms of their working-out of the past, a past often viewed as an irrepressible force. In the 70s, melodrama criticism accounted for this psychoanalytically by invoking the structures of hyste-

114

ria. To do so required maintaining certain boundaries between inner and outer, surface and depth, and assumed a somewhat stable subjectivity (however hysterically expressed) to be generating the meanings 'behind' melodrama's music and *mise en scène*. Locating that agency has been difficult. I think that the model might be usefully revised by bringing the notions of melancholia, performance, and identity formation into discussions of melodrama and other modes of film-making, like New German Cinema.

Since the 1917 appearance of Freud's 'Mourning and Melancholia' the notion of melancholia has been tied to loss and to coming to terms with the past.[25] Unlike mourning, which succeeds at working through loss, melancholia remains tied to the lost object, refusing to let it go. Moreover, melancholia is quite emphatic about this clinging. As Freud argues, the melancholic shows a distinct proclivity towards 'self-exposure', with its essentially 'shame[less]' exhibitionist tendencies.[26] Melancholia's unabashedly performative nature has obvious resonance for film studies and for the highly stylised ('excessive') films of melodrama and New German Cinema. Some critics have focused on the 'self-hatred of melancholia', yet its lack of 'humility', particularly with regard to the notion of display, might be read as a way of forcing out and even *confronting* culture with the failure of the latter's objects to satisfy the ego.[27] We see these kinds of confrontations all the time in the (often futile) outbursts of characters in both New German Cinema and melodrama, films whose scores feature equally random, often volatile bursts of music. Appropriately, Freud wrote that melancholic behaviour 'proceed[s] from a constellation of revolt', which he often finds 'passed over into the crushed state of melancholia'.[28] Like melodrama, melancholia's difficult relationship to past events cannot be tidied up by stitching on a happy ending; its revolt is one without gain. Nevertheless, what the performative, exhibitionist side of melancholia offers is a set of *strategies* for coming to terms with the past and with the losses continually imposed upon the present. Such strategies are not interested in reproducing lost or rediscovered 'truths', nor in 'expressing' something from within the depths of the subject. In fact, they suggest that such things are impossible in the first place. Although music works quite melodramatically in Fassbinder's work, it is finally less the deferral of Utopia that is so much at stake as the idea of its irretrievability. Think of the pre-recorded pieces at the end of *Petra von Kant*, the fragmented opera in *Chinese Roulette*, the intermittent use of brief 'melodramatic' melody in *Fear Eats the Soul*. All of them are musical 'objects' that distance us from what their earlier contexts, identities or fantasies might have offered.

Conclusion

One of melodrama's great contributions has been to offer the possibility of reading the 'facts' of our everyday existence and identities in informative, new ways. Elsaesser goes so far as to call melodrama the 'literary equivalent of a ... mode of experience'.[29] Initially borne of the middle class at the time of the French Revolution, melodrama was produced out of a constructed group's growing awareness of itself as capable of being dealt with narratively. Two centuries later, in a post-war, post-modern age when history has become imaginable largely as a film (or smoke) screen, when narrative and identity began to offer fewer and fewer 'truths', New German Cinema created in an educated German middle class an awareness that its current identity could be constructed only by understanding its past. It showed the impossibility of reading the present or the everyday without simultaneously rereading the past. As Elsaesser writes in reference to Syberberg's *Our Hitler*, the film is 'concerned with re-enactment, a resurrection, a re-animation of cast-offs and rejects', filled as it is with the kitschy clutter of social and cultural memento.[30] Texts like *Chinese Roulette* and *Fear Eats the Soul* further the issue by interrogating whether the visual and acoustic debris of everyday life really can be internalised as 'ours' to begin with, or as a specific country's. The American popular music in *Petra von Kant*, or in movies like *Sugar Baby* (1985) and *The American Friend* (1977), certainly suggest a larger blurring of cultural and national identities, not unlike the Arab music in *Fear Eats the Soul*. Music in New German Cinema offers no fixity, no boundaries, and certainly no direct route to personal expression. In this way the 'New German Melodrama' externalises the 'inward turn' discussed by Richard McCormick in relation to German literature and challenges the interiority implicitly assumed by melodrama's critics who have, with the help of the hysterical model, 'turned inwards' to excavate stable meanings (be they subversive or not) from within the texts.

The 'excessive', outward displays of New German Cinema are not, however, unconcerned with subjectivity, since they literally *perform* efforts to construct identity, to construct relations with structures and objects outside their (and our) control. My essay has suggested a few of the ways in which music participates in that difficult labour, since music offers one means by which personal and cultural histories are preserved and inscribed. In Fassbinder's films, music works within a fragmented series of lost, foreign, Utopian objects, and because these objects carry with them their own material histories and contexts, they always give the sense of being borrowed, never fully possessed, in the same way that identity is also performed, never really existing on its own. No longer an expressive 'excess', music helps establish current relationships to Germany's history, film history, and the history of other cultures. In this way, the obsessive returns to the past of both New German Cinema and melodrama are less hysterical than they might appear at first sight. It is only the work of culture, holding on affectively – if not quite effectively – to its ghosts.

My thanks are due to the participants of the BFI Interdisciplinary Conference on Melodrama, London, July 1992, for their comments and suggestions, and to Jim Cook at the BFI for his editorial guidance. Special thanks also to Marsha Bryant and Maureen Turim for being such fine readers, friends and colleagues.

Notes

1. Rainer Werner Fassbinder in M. Toeteberg and L. Lensing (eds), *Anarchy of the Imagination* (Baltimore: Johns Hopkins University Press, 1992), p. 12.
2. Geoffrey Nowell-Smith, 'Minnelli and Melodrama', in Christine Gledhill (ed.), *Home is Where the Heart Is: Studies in Melodrama and the Woman's Film* (London: BFI, 1987).
3. Peter Brooks, *The Melodramatic Imagination* (New Haven: Yale University Press, 1976); David Grimsted, 'Melodrama as Echo of the Historically Voiceless,' in Tamara Hareven (ed.), *Anonymous Americans: Explorations in 19th Century Social History* (Englewood Cliffs: Prentice-Hall, 1971), p. 80.
4. Hélène Cixous, 'Castration or Decapitation?' *Signs* 7, 1, 1981, p. 49. For an excellent reading of Ophuls's *Letter from an Unknown Woman* that makes central use of this quote, see Tania Modleski, 'Time and Desire in the Woman's Film', in Gledhill, op.cit., pp. 326–38.
5. Richard McCormick, *Politics of the Self: Post Modernism, Feminism, and German Literature and Film* (Princeton: Princeton University Press, 1991).
6. Thomas Elsaesser, 'Tales of Sound and Fury: Observations on the Family Melodrama' (1972), in Gledhill, op. cit., p. 50.
7. Nowell-Smith, op. cit., p. 73.
8. For a fuller exploration of music's association with earlier states, see Caryl Flinn, *Strains of Utopia: Gender, Nostalgia, and Hollywood Film Music* (Princeton: Princeton University Press, 1992). As if talking about silent film, Elsaesser discusses the strategies of 50s melodramas to 'compensate for the expressiveness, range of inflection and tonality, rhythmic emphasis and tension normally present in the spoken word'. Elsaesser, 'Tales of Sound and Fury (1972), in Gledhill, op. cit., p. 51.
9. Dyer, 'Entertainment and Utopia', in Rick Altman (ed.), *Genre: The Musical* (London: Routledge and Kegan Paul, 1981), pp. 175–89; Ernst Block, *Essays on the Philosophy of Music*, trans P. Palmer (Cambridge: Cambridge University Press, 1985) and *The Utopian Function of Art and Literature* (Cambridge, Mass.: MIT Press, 1988); and Flinn, op. cit.
10. Elsaesser, 'Vincente Minnelli', in Altman, op. cit.
11. John Halliday, *Sirk on Sirk* (New York: Viking Press, 1972), p. 48.
12. Timothy Corrigan, 'Werner Schroeter's Operatic Cinema', *Discourse*, no.3, Spring 1981, p. 52.
13. Norbert Sparrow, 'I Let the Audience Feel and Think: An Interview with Rainer Werner Fassbinder', *Cineaste* 8, 2, 1977, p. 20. For an introduction to the influence of Brechtian concepts on the melodramas of Fassbinder and other European art directors, see Katherine Woodward, 'European Anti-Melodrama: Godard, Truffaut and Fassbinder', *Postscript* 3, 2, 1984, pp. 34–47.
14. Sparrow, op. cit., p. 20.
15. Peer Raben, 'Musique et film, la cantate de Bach dans l'érable', *CinémAction*, 1984, pp. 126, 127.
16. See, for example, Thomas Elsaesser, 'Primary Identification and the Subject ...', Kaja Silverman, 'Fassbinder and Lacan: A Reconsideration of Gaze, Look, and Image', *Camera Obscura*, 19, 1989, pp. 54–85, and Judith Mayne, 'Fassbinder and Spectatorship', *New German Critique*, no. 12, 1977, pp. 61–74, reprinted as 'Fassbinder's *Ali: Fear Eats the Soul* and Spectatorship' in Peter Lehman (ed.), *Close Viewings* (Talahassee: Florida State University Presses, 1990).
17. Elsaesser identifies other 'forefathers' (and one foremother) for New German directors: for Wenders, it is Ray and Fuller; for Herzog, Eisner. See Elsaesser, *New German Cinema: A History* (London: Macmillan/BFI, 1989).
18. Elsaesser, *New German Cinema*, p. 248.

19. Raben, op. cit., pp. 125, 126, 127.
20. See Mayne, op. cit.
21. Nowell-Smith, op. cit., pp. 73–4 (my emphasis).
22. Though rarely named as such, an expressionistic strain informs the way critics have talked about the mechanics of the 'melodramatic imagination'. Given expressionism's etymological root in 'pressing out', it makes immediate sense that it could account for melodrama's generic interest in 'expressing all'. Like the hysterical model, the expressionist one conceives textual excesses (brush strokes and colour in painting; performance in theatre; camerawork and musical accompaniment in film, and so on) as a consequence of internal psychic states and conflicts that are somehow 'pressed out' on to the text. The chief difference is that, whereas expressionism assumes a somewhat direct, unmediated relationship between the inner states and their external representation (e.g., *Caligari's* sets articulate the madness of its narrator), hysteria, like melodrama, struggles against greater repressive forces, and requires disguise and displacement in order to operate. Both assume some form of internalised, organised subjectivity that becomes externalised through representational quirks.
23. Quoted in Ben Singer, 'Female Power and the Serial-Queen Melodrama: The Etiology of an Anomaly,' *Camera Obscura*, 22, 1990, p. 98.
24. Mulvey, 'Notes on Sirk and Melodrama', in Gledhill, op. cit., p. 77.
25. Sigmund Freud, 'Mourning and Melancholia', *Standard Edition of the Complete Psychological Works*, vol. 14 (New York: Norton, 1953), pp. 243–58. Prior to the this, melancholia had been conceptualised in a variety of ways, tied first to bodily humours, then to perturbations of the soul, and finally to psychological responses to loss. For a good overview, see Stanley Jackson, *Melancholia and Depression: From Hippocratic Times to Modern Times* (New Haven: Yale University Press, 1986).ﾟ
26. Freud, op. cit., p. 247.
27. The notion of melancholia'ṣ self-hatred and ₔits lack of humility are taken from Alexander and Margarethe Mitscherlish, *The Inability to Mourn: Principles of Collective Behaviour*, trans B. Placzek (New York: Grove Press, 1975), p. 63.
28. Freud, op. cit., p. 248.
29. Elsaesser, 'Tales of Sound and Fury', in Gledhill, op. cit., p. 49.
30. Elsaesser, 'Myth as the Phantasmagoria of History: H. J. Syberberg, Cinema and Representation', *New German Critique*, nos. 24–5, Fall/Winter 1981–2, p. 136.

PART 3
REVISIONS

'IT WILL BE A MAGNIFICENT OBSESSION'

The Melodrama's Role in the Development of Contemporary Film Theory

LAURA MULVEY

'It will be a magnificent obsession,' says the strange spiritual mentor about the strange spiritual quest he proposes to Rock Hudson in Douglas Sirk's first full-blown melodrama for Universal, *Magnificent Obsession.* The phrase came to my mind when I was preparing this paper as a figure for the persistent but shifting place the Hollywood melodrama has occupied for film theory and criticism. Successive generations with different perspectives and priorities have turned to the melodrama as a critical catalyst, as a medium through which questions and difficulties raised by the aesthetics of Hollywood cinema could find articulation. As a result, any attempt to define the melodrama is more likely to find a critical chameleon than a coherent Hollywood genre, as though the concept 'Hollywood melodrama' emerged more out of an accumulated body of writing than the production system of the Hollywood studios. Melodrama emerged into film critical consciousness bit by bit, first through directors (Sirk, Minnelli and Ray, for instance), through period (Eisenhower's America), through form while denigrating content (*mise en scène* released from action or theme), through form as expressive of content (Thomas Elsaesser's ground-breaking 'Tales of Sound and Fury'), through content (feminist analyses of 'women's pictures'), through origins (Griffith, the silent cinema and the legacy of theatrical melodrama), through psychoanalytic theory (a doubling-up of the interior of the home with the interior of the psyche).

These different approaches to Hollywood melodrama all interweave, overlap and bear witness to the persistent influence of Hollywood in general on the development of film theory and to the influence of the melodrama on contemporary film theory. Hollywood is not the only national, mass-entertainment cinema to have produced a melodrama genre; recent work on European and Indian melodrama, for instance, confirms their intrinsic interest. It was Hollywood, however, that provided a catalyst for mapping out a critical and theoretical terrain. Hollywood was not only a culturally and economically dominant cinema produced by the economically and culturally dominant United States, but also the 'primal scene' of modern mythologies. Its myths were specifically American, historically

121

and ideologically, but it also exported the glamour of America and its Utopian modernity, simultaneously recycling narrative patterns, aspirations and personifications that were close enough to folk tradition to be familiar to most moviegoing audiences. Hollywood thus created a chimeric monster for contemporary cultural theory, turning out movies that both demand and evade politics. In this paper, I want to trace some of the main lines of the debates that developed around the Hollywood melodrama, and suggest that the genre played an important role in the politics of Hollywood-oriented film criticism and that this important role was crucially dependent on the development of feminist film theory, and particularly the alliance between feminist film theory and psychoanalytic theory. The issues raised by theories of melodrama also indicate ways in which psychoanalytic film theory returns to questions of history.

The story of melodrama criticism traces a curve of shifting priorities between form and content and, in the last resort, makes a case for psychoanalytic theory as a conceptual means for merging the two. As the 'melodrama' is the genre of domesticity, aimed at a female audience, early critical neglect of its content has often been attributed to male critics' lack of interest in 'women's pictures'.[1] Two other considerations should be borne in mind here. First of all, the genres that initially exerted the strongest critical appeal, particularly the western and the gangster film, allowed an understanding of Hollywood cinema as a version of myth, as a popularisation and an ideologisation of American history, belonging to the male sphere, exterior and public. The domestic melodrama, once it congealed into something like a genre, lacked this kind of appeal. Thus, secondly, the 'interior' world of the melodrama demanded, and had to wait for, a different kind of critical understanding appropriate for the private and its attendant connotations of femininity, apparently cut off from the course of history. To break out of its feminised ghetto certain conceptual and ideological shifts in cultural methodologies had to take place. First of all, the sphere of the feminine had to find a voice which could provide critical commentary on its genre, the domestic melodrama. At the same time, the 'interiority' of the domestic had to open up to reveal a new terrain, the terrain of the 'unspeakable'. Feminism would provide the voice and vocabulary which could transform the content aspect of the melodrama into material of significance, while psychoanalytic theory (from Thomas Elsaesser's article 'Tales of Sound and Fury' onwards) would provide the concepts which could transform the 'unspeakable' into the unconscious, transforming the stuffy kitschness of the melodrama into the stuff of dreams and desire. Finally, the ahistoricity of the melodrama, as it flourished in the 50s, had be understood as a historical phenomenon. The melodrama is part of American 'myth' but, rather than looking back and retelling and reordering the narratives of the public sphere, it symptomises the history of its own time, an aspiration to retreat into the privacy of the new white suburbs out of the difficulties of contemporary political life.

There is, of course, another aspect to the critical problems raised by the melodrama as a cinematic genre, to which the Melodrama Conference bore witness. The term long predates the coming of cinema, and the melodramatic tradition has stood for the non-literary, the popular and the 'low' in the high/low cultural binary opposition on both sides of the Atlantic. It was the European intellectuals' post-war re-evaluations of Hollywood cinema that helped to erode the value system that supported the hierarchical opposition high/low. So, in the strange, extended romance between European intellectuals and American popular culture, Hollywood cinema of the studio system played a privileged, formative, part. If the United States now, in Robin Wood's words, 'takes Hitchcock seriously' it is partly because the European intellectual fascination with Hollywood, evoked by Thomas Elsaesser as 'two decades in another country', returned American popular culture across the Atlantic, enhanced by the trappings of 'French theory'. It was a two-way movement: European intellectuals embraced the products of American popular culture which were then received back into their homeland and negotiated into academia through another exchange of cultural fantasy, the arrival in the United States of European-grown ideas, particularly those associated, in the first instance, with structuralism and, in the second, with psychoanalysis. While Hollywood studio system cinema as such launched the 'first wave' of European cinephilia, the melodrama, I shall argue, played a privileged part in a 'second wave', in the process also enabling the negotiation of political pitfalls at stake in the first.

The Hollywood cinema that had first fascinated European intellectuals was energetic and cathartic, a cinema of the machine age, streamlined and commodified, able to produce and repeat successful formulas, stories or stars, as Detroit might produce motor-cars. This cinema stood in direct opposition to high cultural values, encrusted with the weight and authority of tradition. European intellectuals took up American cinema partly in a spirit of political polemics with the traditions and values of their own culture. A Hollywood film, brazenly generic, shamelessly star-struck, not even dignified by the presence of a single creative imagination, came to epitomise a binary opposition to the academic appropriation and fossilisation that overwhelmed the high cultures of literature, music, painting and so on. Popular cinema had fascinated the Surrealists and others on the left, in Britain as well as France, in the 20s when Hollywood cinema established itself as world cinema, and this fascination found new life with the rediscovery of Hollywood, this time in the guise of a new film criticism, in France after the Second World War. The new criticism is associated primarily with the *Cahiers du Cinéma*, partly due to its transnational influence, in turn partly, of course, due to the subsequent evolution of many of its critics into film-makers, and also due to the place of André Bazin in the history of film theory.

The legacy of the French critics was not, on the face of it, political, but their legacy was open to a kind of proto-politicisation. Their criticism of passion not only loved and valued Hollywood precisely because it was non-literary and gestural, essentially melodramatic, as Thomas Elsaesser and others have pointed out, but it also led further. Existing critical methodologies could not be appropriately applied to commercial cinema and its particular mode of production, which subordinated individual creative autonomy to the stamp of conventions of all kinds. The *Cahiers* critics' investigative system that came to be known as the '*politique des auteurs*' was not so important as a means of restoring a traditional concept of 'the author' to non-authorial culture, but as a method of critical analysis that could be applied to and evaluate cinema, produced within the formulaic system of genre, and celebrate directors who managed to turn, bend, or mould their material into something cinematically vivid, dramatically direct, and moving.

Cahiers methodology was a painstaking process that searched across the whole range of work to find a command of cinematic language hidden under the surface of the text. The process was a kind of decipherment; its pleasure, as well as in cinema *per se*, was detection, and its method, refusing to hierarchise the good and bad, fascinated by the mythic elements of American genres, provided fertile ground for the implantation of French structuralist theories into film theory. Perhaps strangely, this implantation also involved a transplantation, as the influence of French ideas took root in Britain in the mid-60s, where critics who had previously simply enjoyed the fruits of *Cahiers* criticism, began moving towards theory. The characteristics of Hollywood cinema that had placed it on the 'low' side of the cultural binary opposition (generic plots, stereotypical characters, clichés and melodramatic emotion) could be magically transformed into the vocabulary of myth and into dramatic motifs of cultural meaning and significance. The anti-establishment, anti-high cultural investment in Hollywood cinema became explicitly political in Britain, as a negative gesture directed against Englishness, its élitism, its complacency and its insularity in relation both to the European theory and to US mass culture. British intellectuals in the 60s rejected British cultural traditions and 'value' criticism, applying French theory to American popular culture, first and foremost (again following the French) to Hollywood. It is no accident that the first examples of British auteur criticism appeared in *New Left Review*, and by and large all *Cahiers*-influenced British cinephiles were on the left.[2]

In the last resort, however, it was politics that brought the seeds of decay to the 'two decades in another country'. A critical engagement with Hollywood cinema could easily be seen, not only as a means of liberating British intellectuals from insularity, but also as an unquestioning acceptance of an imperialist cinema. The recuperation of Hollywood in France had taken place in the period of the Marshall Plan, when American investment in the post-war reconstruction of Europe also opened up European markets for its products, in which Hollywood films played an important part, damaging the struggling national cinemas of the post-war years. In the 60s, growing political consciousness leading up to the events of 1968, the American military build-up in Vietnam and awareness of the stifling of indigenous Third World as well as European cinemas under American exports all combined to repoliticise intellectual attitudes to Hollywood. Furthermore, of course, the studio system that had been the source of the westerns, gangster movies, musicals, films noirs, comedies and so on and the B pictures that had provided the stuff out of which the auteur theory developed was itself in crisis. This 1967 statement from Godard, one of the great 'discoverers' and *aficionados* of Hollywood, reflects the changed atmosphere:

On our own modest level, we too should try to provoke two or three Vietnams in the bosom of the vast Hollywood–Cinecittà–Mosfilm–Pinewood, etc., empire, and, both economically and aesthetically, struggling on two fronts as it were, create cinemas which are national, free, brotherly, comradely and bonded in friendships.[3]

The political/historical events of the late 60s created a fissure, if not a crisis, in European left intellectuals' relation to Hollywood.

Needless to say, my account is partial in both senses of the word, both incomplete and personal, a reflection of and on my own shifting relations with Hollywood cinema. I spent the 60s under the influence of the *Cahiers du Cinema* and absorbed in Hollywood. The crisis for me (which was also political) was precipitated by feminism, and feminism irretrievably changed the terms, or the agenda, of debate. Firstly, the question of Hollywood cinema became absorbed, negatively, into polemics against images of women and women as spectacle. Secondly, and consequently, Hollywood could provide a 'pool' of narratives and iconographies symptomatic of patriarchal culture, enabling their analysis. Thirdly, there was a renewed interest in the Hollywood melodrama as a mass-entertainment genre specifically designed for and directed at a female audience. To my mind, these three areas encouraged feminists' engagement with theory which, in combination, produced the second wave of the Hollywood/theory conjuncture, but this time centred primarily around psychoanalysis. Pam Cook and Claire Johnston, in their 1974 article 'The Place of Woman in the Cinema of Raoul Walsh', make this point:

> in the tradition of classic cinema ... the characters are presented as autonomous individuals; but the construction of the discourse contradicts this convention by reducing these 'real' women to images and tokens functioning in a circuit of signs, the values of which have been determined by and for men.[4]

The concept of displacement, which lies behind this quotation, condenses Freudian theory of the language of the unconscious with semiotic theory which turned Hollywood cinema into a rebus for decipherment. The melodrama as a form directed at women raised different problems of displacement and decipherment, so it was eagerly studied for its alternative psychic scenarios, its representations of female desire, its non-cathartic narratives and its suitability for psychoanalytic criticism. In the context of the melodrama, psychoanalytic criticism focused on how material that was beyond conscious or ideological articulation effected 'displacements' in the text, rather than on the image of women itself as a displacement, constituting a sign for the male psyche.

As Elsaesser originally argued, the melodrama is characterised by the presence of a protagonist whose symptomatic behaviour emerges out of irreconcilable or inexpressible internal contradiction, and this 'unspeakable' affects and overflows on to the *mise en scène*. The concept of displacement thus evokes the Freudian unconscious which disguises its irrepressible ideas through its symptoms and also cinema's extension of this displacement into the symptom-like qualities of *mise en scène*. Given that Hollywood cinema of the studio system by and large shares this quality, the spectator of the melodrama is therefore a more than usually 'deciphering' viewer. It is nevertheless further arguable that a popular cinema is symptomatic (or rather shares certain qualities of the symptom) on the wider scale of the social and historical, and especially in the United States which represented the myths, repressions and aspirations of an immigrant society through its cinema.

I am attempting here to articulate a concept of 'collective fantasy' which is neither a reworking of ideology nor a reflective theory of historical representation. Furthermore, the 'symptomology' of collective fantasy or the repressed of a social formation would not depend on any essential or ahistorical concept of the human psyche. This kind of 'collective fantasy' would be evidence of the presence of psychic symptoms within the social, traces of unassimilated historical traumas (in Freud's sense of the word). On the other hand, certain narrative structures, psychic scenarios and character figurations do persist; myths and narratives from traditional Western culture are recognisable, under new names and in new shapes and forms, in Hollywood cinema. One could cite work on narrative that has made use of Propp's *Morphology of the Folk-tale*[5] or Barbara Creed's[6] and Teresa de Lauretis's[7] different citations of the Medusa myth, or the extraordinary reiteration of the Oedipus myth throughout Hollywood cinema, still flourishing in late Hollywood and even in the (perhaps unlikely) setting of Gus van Sant's *My Own Private Idaho*. These narratives and figurations are not transhistorical, except in the sense that, as Propp argued, some powerful stories can outlive the moment of historical contradiction or stress that gave rise to them and survive through storytelling tradition, in a sense almost overdetermining subsequent mythic invention by the sheer force of familiarity and repetition. They also, obviously, may well persist if relevant psychic structures keep them alive, giving private reverie a short cut to a gallery of collective fantasy, inhabited by monsters and heroes, heroines and *femmes fatales*. The short cuts can also act like templates, patterning social identities while also, sometimes, simultaneously acknowledging and indicating their imperfect fit. Distance from daily political reality, the process of displacement itself, may bear witness to the social equivalent of a geological fault, a point where intractable material is in danger of erupting. Narrative conflict, its heroes and villains, supply pattern and order, but also, through the clusters of repetition, recurrence and excess suggest the presence of a 'cultural symptomatic'.

I was recently struck by the following extract from the first of Freud's 'Five Lectures on Psychoanalysis':

Our hysterical patients suffer from reminiscences. Their symptoms are residues and mnemic symbols of particular (traumatic) experiences. We may perhaps obtain a deeper understanding of this kind of symbolism if we compare them with other mnemic symbols in other fields. The monuments and memorials with which large cities are adorned are also mnemic symbols. If you take a walk through the streets of London, you will find, in front of one of the great railway termini, a richly carved Gothic column – Charing Cross. One of the old Plantagenet kings of the thirteenth century ordered the body of his beloved Queen Eleanor to be carried to Westminster; and at every stage at which the coffin rested he erected a Gothic Cross. [Another example is the Monument to the Fire of London.] These monuments, then, resemble hysterical symptoms in being mnemic symbols; up to that point the comparison seems justifiable. But what would we think of a Londoner who paused today in deep melancholy before the memorial of Queen Eleanor's funeral instead of going about his business in the hurry that modern working conditions demand or instead of feeling joy over the youthful queen of his own heart? Or again what would we think of a Londoner who shed tears before the Monument that commemorates the reduction of his beloved city to ashes even though it has long since risen again in far greater brilliance? Yet every single hysteric or neurotic behaves like these unpractical Londoners.[8]

The images and stories of popular cinema can function like collective mnemic symbols, and allow 'ordinary people', us, to stop and wonder or weep, desire or shudder, momentarily touching 'unspeakable' but shared psychic structures. We are licensed to respond, in Freud's terms, 'neurotically'. While most people, perhaps, behave like 'unpractical Londoners' only while actually seated in the cinema, the critic has to foster this unpractical relation to popular cinema in order to decode the collective 'pool' of fantasy and daydream. Popular cinema draws attention to the memorials and mnemic symbols inscribed in collective culture. The events of social and political history erupt into representations, and the significance of the original events are distorted by the processes of condensation, displacement, into signifiers and memorials, scars of social or psychic disorders and of the repressed in history that creates violence, despair, racism and sexual oppression. Freud's use of the public monument as a metaphor for a psychic symptom also allows one to stop and think about the indexical nature of the symptom, its grounding in experience and in the history of the individual.

Old mythic tropes and narrative patterns can find new inflections transposed into the New World. For instance, like many traditional European folk-tales, the Hollywood narrative tends to resolve itself around marriage, as critics and theorists have frequently pointed out. I have argued elsewhere that this form of closure balances the stability of a story's opening, and both are frequently realised in the figuration of 'home' which the hero first leaves and then reconstitutes. Furthermore, the Proppian function W (wedding) is, unlike his other functions including that of the hero, necessarily gender specific. It is marriage that insists that the hero should be male and the 'to be married' should be female. An association between movement and the masculine and the feminine and stasis (that Teresa de Lauretis also notes in the spatial relations between monster and hero) reiterates the formal configuration of narrative closure.

In the western, these spatial relations find new meaning as the colonisation of America is represented as a movement of agriculture against nomadism. The old function 'wedding' acquires another layer of social

127

significance, as gender and colonial conquest fuse in the trope of narrative closure as victory over the villain followed by marriage and formal stasis. The ideas contained in the word 'settlement' slide into and across each other.

In the melodrama, according to Elsaesser's model, the opposition between action and stasis, between catharsis and settlement, breaks down, as though the space of narrative closure realised as the 'home' then becomes the 'container' for a different generic narrative. The concept of settlement is thrown into disarray, as the interior, the sphere of the feminine, overflows on to the 'interiority' of emotion and, particularly, those irrational emotions that evade articulation. The Hollywood melodrama has not been able to displace its irrational on to 'Gothic' topographies that can literally materialise the unconscious into lower depths, spaces below the surface, ancient ruins or the city's underworld. The irrational of the Hollywood melodrama is poised between the interiority of the individual unconscious and the community that contains it. However, the irrational is not exteriorised and personified as 'other', and it is essential to remember that the 50s melodramas existed within the historical context of McCarthyism, the Korean War and the Cold War, when Hollywood (as Michael Rogin conclusively demonstrates[9]) 'demonised' the Communist threat, particularly through its science fiction genre. In this sense, the absence of politics from the melodrama should be understood as an inscribed absence, an erasure of the public enabled by the retreat into the domesticity of the newly formed suburbs with their differently constructed priorities.[10]

I want to end by looking briefly at two Sirk movies that bracket his career as Universal Studios' most successful melodrama director. *Magnificent Obsession* (1954) established his success, and *Imitation of Life* (1959) won an Academy Award for the best picture and was the last Sirk made in Hollywood. I want to try to illustrate some of my arguments with these two very different kinds of melodrama and speculate that the shifts in social and political priorities across the decade contribute to the shifts in films' inscription of the social and polital. While *Magnificent Obsession* erases the external altogether, *Imitation of Life* reflects the effects of racial discrimination and persecution, but as a zone of silence and repression, marked but outside adequate social articulation.

Although *Magnificent Obsession* takes place mainly in the well-to-do milieu of an ideal, semi-rural, semi-small-town America, the setting is atopian rather than social. Always despised by critics, ignored even by Sirk critics and melodrama theorists, the film's interest primarily lies in its unusual reversed Oedipal fantasy. Father/son rivalry, conflict and different forms of reconciliation make up by far the most frequent form of Oedipal narrative, a negotiation into the patriarchal symbolic, which is supposed to involve the subordination of desire to the patriarchal symbolic. In *Magnificent Obsession* desire outwits, as it were, the patriarchal principle, and the narrative topography of constraint and interiority that almost always characterises the melodrama gives way to a narrative topography of movement and journey. While the male hero's journey is one of search or pursuit, the heroine's journey is one of flight and escape. The heroine's flight from her desire, once into blindness, then into a literal journey of escape, leaves her nomadic, unable to settle until the object of her desire has completed his emotional and psychic journey into maturity. Bob Merrick's Oedipal trajectory is internal and more precisely portrayed than in movies whose Oedipality is exteriorised and carried forward by action. Here the plot is fuelled simply by movements generated by desire. In a sense, therefore, it loses the social implications that are of central importance in the domestic melodrama and the women's picture. *All That Heaven Allows*, the direct follow-up to the success of *Magnificent Obsession*, makes thorough use of the social as a delaying mechanism to the movement of desire. The love story between Ron and Cary is disrupted by differences of age and class, and while Ron is seen as a younger man, Cary as an older woman, there is no implied metaphor of mother/son incestuous desire. *Magnificent Obsession*, while obviously unable to depict a literal, blood relationship, creates a kind of sub-text which constantly places the two lovers within an incestuous frame of reference.

The film's opening premise is that Bob Merrick, a very rich and self-indulgent playboy obsessed with the thrill of speed, has an accident through his own irresponsibility, as a result of which Dr Phillips, head of the local hospital and much loved and respected philanthropist, dies. Dr Philips's death is incidental, but the medical equipment he needed in an emergency is tied up saving Bob Merrick, and the film dwells on the cause and effect. The immature and irresponsible younger man causes the death of a man who occupies the place of the law, culture and moral worth invested in the Symbolic Order. Merrick's subsequent behaviour is depicted less as immature than as infantile – in Freud's term, His Majesty the Baby.

His life is changed when he meets Helen, Dr Phillips's widow, with whom he falls instantly and passionately in love. The film's next move is precipitated by Helen's attempt to ward off Merrick's pursuit, when she is knocked down by a passing car and loses her sight. Her blindness allows him to meet her on the beach under an assumed name, where they read the funnies with Helen's minder, a little girl, depicted in a de-gendered latency period, and who in this sense marks Merrick's movement from self-centred infancy into a kind of childhood idyll. In the meantime, Merrick is initiated into a pseudo-symbolic order by Dr Phillips's old friend who teaches him Dr Phillips's own recipe for self-fulfilment: a secret philanthropy which sustains the donor purely through the gift without demand for social recognition in exchange. The ego's wish for recognition is, as it were, subsumed into a higher ideal. Merrick takes up his abandoned medical career and, during the rest of the film, his trajectory is directed towards acquiring the place of the 'father', whose death he has caused, in order to marry his widow. She now passionately reciprocates his love, even acknowledging that she knows that the man she loves caused her husband's death, but she runs away from their love, delaying the resolution of the plot not through the intervention of any exterior force but through her flight, a mechanism based purely on the danger of her desire. It is not until she is at the point of death that Merrick finds her, operates on her himself and restores both her life and her sight. By then all the outraged witnesses of their romance, in particular Dr Phillips's daughter, have also acknowledged that true love has won over past wrongs and the couple are united.

This story, if my argument for its Oedipal implications holds good, fails to subordinate an illicit desire to the law. Merrick successfully assumes the position of the dead doctor, the father figure in my terms, without having to give up his love for the mother figure, the doctor's widow. Without making any great claims for *Magnificent Obsession*, I would use it as an example of how only a little help from psychoanalytic theory brings a story of forbidden love into focus as a vehicle for incestuous daydream. The film strips away any extraneous elements exterior to the love story; the relationship between Bob and Helen is all there is to it. The middle-class, well-to-do social milieu serves two functions. First, as I said earlier, it is atopian, neutral, safe from any possible interference from social or economic pressures. Bob Merrick's money funds the Utopian romance just as money funds a movie. Second, the well-to-do milieu does have social connotations. It puts an idealised American lifestyle and landscape, interior and exterior, on show to a very different America and to the world at a time when American movies were a showcase for this lifestyle. The realisation of an impossible desire condenses with the aspiration to an impossible way of life. Sexuality effaces all contradiction and the surface of the screen is simply that. It is perhaps significant that, when Helen travels to Europe for medical consultations, her destination is Switzerland, unravaged by the aftermath of the Second World War and available for folksy, kitschy representations of village lifestyle that has remained unchanged, and represents some fantasy of an ahistorical Middle Ages. But in the scene in which Bob acts as Helen's eyes and describes the ritual burning of an effigy of a witch, it is hard not to be reminded of the witch-hunts that were taking place in the USA at that time.

Magnificent Obsession is, obviously perhaps in the context of my earlier points, a film of total whiteness. *Imitation of Life* deals specifically with race. The question of race becomes condensed with questions of visibility and invisibility: woman as spectacle and the woman whose labour produces the other woman as spectacle. Both films (and I am not making a polemical case for authorial consistency) revolve around 'blind spots'. Helen, the heroine of *Magnificent Obsession*, literally blind for most of the film, can fall, illicitly, in love under its mask. Lora, in *Imitation of Life*, although literally sighted, is blinded by her ambition to be seen as spectacle and, while the bright lights of stardom shine on her, she is unable to discern, to make out, the emotional events that are taking place around her. Her inability to understand the tragic reality of racial oppression and exploitation is realised under the guise of spectacle which prioritises appearance.

There is a complicating factor here, since the spectacle of the star is offered overtly as a performance and as a construction. In the melodrama, the woman's image, and how it is constructed for female spectators, assumes pre-given awareness of the voyeuristic tendency of Hollywood cinema and turns it upside down. The female protagonist may be depicted as a source of fascination within the diegetic text so that her erotic appeal works within the narrative but is consistently distanced for the spectator. 'To-be-looked-at-ness' becomes a problem. Helen escapes into an accident to avoid Bob Merrik's *coup de foudre*; just as Cary in *All That Heaven Allows* feels humiliated when she sees Ron and his friend looking at her and laughing. When Ron explains later that they were admiring her legs she is partially reassured, but the spectator has shared her embarrassment, not their pleasure. In *Imitation of Life* there is an incident that conforms to this pattern, when the theatrical agent, Loomis, tries to teach Lora how to use her sexual appeal for professional purposes. However, *Imitation of Life* concentrates on how Lora is produced as a star. She is, diagetically, spectacle, but not eroticised for the spectator, while in the story she is clearly an object of desire for the male protagonists, Steve Archer and David Edwards. The place of race within the film is worked through, and subordinated to, the visiblity of whiteness, which is figured through the successful actress/spectacle.

Annie, Lora Meredith's black maid, gradually emerges as the central character in the film, but as both black and worker she cannot achieve the status of the 'spectacular' until her death, in her funeral procession, in which all the trappings are white. Throughout the story to that point she is, first, the labour that initiates Lora's success as an actress, and then the labour that sustains her ascendency as a star. There are two kinds of performance here. Annie's performance of her role as maid allows Lora's career to take off towards stardom. As Lora goes, as she says, 'up and up' she also becomes on the screen whiter and whiter, more and more invested in appearance. Her performance is built on the disavowal of the black woman's labour, which is reconstituted as friendship. Annie understands the true nature of the mistress/maid relationship, but also accepts the social and racial limits that constrain her. Sarah-Jane, Annie's daughter who can pass for white, will not accept the same heritage and questions the relation between appearance and essence. Why, the film asks, does a society that is obsessed by appearance and spectacle suddenly fetishise essence when it come to race. Sarah-Jane follows Lora's path into masquerade as she, too, becomes a performer. But she understands that the masquerade only works if her black mother is wiped out and made invisible once again. To achieve certain whiteness is to achieve the performance of white femininity, to become the product that she had witnessed her mother effacing herself to produce. Lora's production of herself as a star is not only painted, as it were, on the surface of Annie's work as her maid, but the concept of whiteness as spectacle alienates Annie's daughter into a re-performance of that spectacular femininity. In one case, Sarah-Jane's, the blot of race is effaced, on the other, Lora's, it is contained within a power relation of worker and commodity. The commodity is in command.

In this sense *Imitation of Life* could be understood not only as a depiction of race relations through the question of visibility and invisibility, but could also suggest a metaphor for the invisibility of labour as such, erased by the visibility of the commodity it produces. There is a possible series of condensations here: Annie's performance of the role 'maid', her actual labour as cook and backstage dresser, which are both invisible in the final product and familiarised under the guise of friendship. This is not only the role of a particular black woman in relation to a particular star, but also the role of the worker as producer of value in capitalist society. Annie is not only black, she is a worker. Again Sarah-Jane, in her rebellion, insists on this class relationship as one that overdetermines race relations. Black people perform the invisible services that allow white people to achieve visible supremacy. Class disappears under race and race is erased by performance. Power relations become personal and, indeed, melodramatic, in *Imitation of Life*.

Obsession and imitation. These two ideas, at the risk of seeming fanciful, evoke two relevant aspects of psychic processes. First, the irrational psychic energy that activates the unconscious, second, the disguises, substitutions and masquerades that characterise the language of the unconscious. While contemporary intellectuals, especially film theorists, may be accused of an obsession with Hollywood cinema, from the days of auteurism and *mise en scène* analysis onwards, the kind of criticism they produced has been concerned with clues and their decipherment rather than intentional and innate meanings. The melodrama could condense this critical tendency with the methodologies of psychoanalysis and feminist interest in challenging the transcendent power of the visual. While the spectacle of woman, in Hollywood in general, is a symptom that relates back to the male psyche and blocks the understanding of the social, the melodramatic symptom tends to de-eroticise its female spectacle. The 'symptom' can, residually, reflect on its own imitation and acknowledge its own 'blind spot.'

Notes

1. There is, obviously, a legacy left by the nineteenth-century popular theatrical melodrama on Hollywood as such. An aesthetic which exteriorised, rather than psychologised, emotion and conflict and evolved around gesture and tableaux rather than literary verbalisation was reinforced by the cinema's birth in music and silence. The term 'melodrama' as applied to a particular Hollywood genre of domestic-, woman- or family-oriented drama as a precise categorisation is more recent. It is this cinema that I am concerned with here.
2. The '*politique des auteurs*' was translated into English by the American critic Andrew Sarris (whose ultimately successful attempt to return Hollywood to its own country also received at least a decade of bitter resistance) as the 'auteur theory' in the early 60s, and was first published in *Film Culture*, primarily a magazine of underground cinema and the emergent American avant-garde. I mention this to highlight the 'underground' and anti-establishment nature of a critical allegiance to Hollywood cinema at the time.
3. Quoted in Thomas Elsaesser: 'Two Decades in Another Country', in C. Bigsby (ed.), *Superculture* (London: Paul Elek, 1975), p. 216. My argument is influenced by this article, which gives an excellent historical account of European intellectuals' changing relation to American popular culture and, particularly, to Hollywood.
4. Pam Cook and Claire Johnston, 'The Place of Woman in the Cinema of Raoul Walsh', reprinted in Constance Penley (ed.), *Feminism and Film Theory* (London: Routledge/BFI, 1988), p. 26.

5. See, for instance Peter Wollen, '*North By Northwest*: A Morphological Analysis', in *Readings and Writings* (London: Verso, 1982).

6. Barbara Creed, '*Alien* and the Monstrous Feminine', reprinted in A. Kuhn (ed.), *Alien Zone* (London: Verso, 1990).

7. Teresa de Lauretis, 'Desire in Narrative', in *Alice Doesn't* (Bloomington: Indiana University Press, 1984).

8. Sigmund Freud, 'Five Lectures on Psychoanalysis', *Standard Edition*, vol. XI (London: Hogarth Press, 1957), pp. 16–17.

9. Michael Rogin, 'Kiss Me Deadly', in *Ronald Reagan: The Movie* (Berkeley and Los Angeles: California University Press, 1987).

10. See Lynn Spigel, 'Installing the Television Set: Popular Discourses on Television and Domestic Space 1948–1955', *Camera Obscura*, no. 16, 1988.

'LOCAL' GENRES

The Hollywood Adult Film in the 1950s

BARBARA KLINGER

One of the strongest tendencies traditionally driving genre theory and criticism has been to devise 'master' definitions of genres that can explain affiliations between numerous and diverse films. Critics routinely identify formulas and conventions as a means of elaborating the shared character-istics of a body of films. Hence, a film is a musical if its courtship-centred narrative demonstrates *bricolage* and self-reflective revelations about enter-tainment, and a western if its setting, characters, and iconography reflect the historical conflict between wilderness and civilisation rooted in the latter half of the 19th century.[1]

In addition to constituting generic stability, scholars have avidly pur-sued the question of generic change, analysing subgenres and cycles that appear historically in answer to industrial and social developments. Every major genre exhibits such inventions and trends: the operetta, slasher film and woman's film offer variations, respectively, of the musical, horror film, and melodrama, for example.[2] While 'master' characterisations have been helpful in trying to account for family resemblances among hun-dreds of films produced over many decades, subgenres and cycles indicate important differences between films within a class that testify to generic mutability over time.

However, some critics have recently suggested that this interplay of conclusive designation and serial mutation often has not fully explored areas that bear significantly on identifying genres within a historical framework. One of these areas concerns the role non-academic institu-tions, such as the film industry or review journalism, play in creating generic categories that circulate during reception. As Steve Neale writes, 'industrial and journalistic labels ... offer virtually the only available evi-dence for a historical study of the array of genres in circulation, or of the ways in which individual films have been generically perceived at any point in time'.[3] The significance of these non-academic sites is that they demonstrate how certain films were identified historically for popular con-sumption, helping us to assess the mechanisms behind the creation of a film's social image or meaning at particular moments. In addition, studies of industry or review classifications are likely to challenge academic

134

assumptions about the generic status of specific films. Through historical example, these classifications show that what we may consider as a western or gangster film was quite differently categorised for audiences in the past, causing us to query in particular the adequacy of 'master' definitions.

To historicise enquiries into genre more fully it is necessary to consider how films were labelled in the past and, in the process, to grant that generic definition is a potentially volatile or at least contingent phenomenon, conditioned by social, institutional, and historical circumstance. Pursuing this view of genre, I should like to concentrate on a particular case: those films referred to by Thomas Elsaesser as the 'sophisticated family melodramas of the 1940s and 1950s', a subgenre of melodrama directed by Douglas Sirk, Vincente Minnelli, Nicholas Ray and others. For two decades critics have agreed that the post-war family melodrama is exceptional within the landscape of 50s cinema and culture. The genre's concerns with family neurosis and destructive sexuality, as well as its vividly symptomatic *mise en scène*, seem to overtly attack the *status quo* ideology of the Eisenhower years, centred around the complacent image of the suburban, nuclear family. Critical consensus has perpetuated this identity for so long that the films' status seems self-evident and beyond dispute. I shall argue, however, that family melodramas were labelled differently in the 50s, and that, in this former life, they were placed into a complex relationship with certain dominant ideological values of the time concerning sexuality.

Within the original circumstances defining the production and exhibition of post-war melodramas, the films of Sirk, Minnelli and Ray were not exceptional; they were part of a general industry trend towards more 'adult' entertainment. The studios and review establishment alike used the adult film label as a means of identifying certain films with sensationalistic content. The adult film was a 'local' genre, in the sense that it was a historically specific and transitory category that gained steam during the post-war years and faded from view in its Hollywood usage after the 60s. It none the less functioned as a recognised and influential means of classifying films during this time, effectively reorganising the field of existing genres.

The adult film arose as a result of a series of developments within both the film industry itself and society at large. While the industry was in the throes of transformation in the wake of the Paramount Decree of 1948, society was becoming increasingly oriented towards a kind of sexual sensationalism in representation. The adult film category was in this sense multidetermined by a complex succession of institutional and cultural events.

Selling Melodrama

Advertising campaigns in the post-war era routinely called attention to the sensationalistic content of films. As early as 1945 the poster for *The Lost Weekend*, a film about alcoholism, exclaimed, 'How daring can the screen *dare* to be? No adult man or woman can *risk* missing the startling frankness of *The Lost Weekend*.'[4] By the 50s, 'daring', 'shocking', 'frankness', 'adult' and other such terms were common in advertisements. The industry typically defined the adult film through a double language which emphasised its social significance to justify titillating indulgence in the spectacles provided by psychological torment, drugs, sex, and murder. This new standard pervasively affected melodramas. But it defined examples from almost every other genre as well, including *The Searchers* (1956), a western with a theme of miscegenation, *Love Me or Leave Me* (1955), a musical which focused on violent marital relations, *The Detective Story* (1951), a crime film which mentioned abortion, and *The Moon is Blue* (1953), a sex comedy. In this sense, the adult label constituted a powerful cagegory, capable of characterising a large number of films from distinctly different generic traditions.

Selling films through promises of sensationalism was nothing new in film advertising, but in the 50s a number of industry factors converged to create a specific manifestation of this tradition, resulting in both the production and advertisement of films as adult. The contributing factors included competition with television, the import of foreign films, the status of film censorship, and the Paramount Case.

In 1956 *Variety* indicated that, besides blockbusters, 'unusual, off-beat films with adult themes that TV could not handle' represented an effective route of combat with television.[5] While by this time studios had created profitable alliances with television by selling their films for TV broadcast or by producing TV series, industry rhetoric still figured the new medium as a major competitor. By presenting mature narrative situations related to sexual problems, drug abuse, and other sensationalistic subjects, studios attempted to enhance the competitive edge by providing content that the variety shows, family situation comedies, and other TV fare could not. Thus, the family melodrama of the 50s, with its tortured family units and emphasis on psychosexual problematics, featured topics far removed from what television could offer in such sit-coms as *The Adventures of Ozzie and Harriet* (1952–66) or *Father Knows Best* (1954–63).

However, this trend towards mature subject-matter in the Hollywood film cannot be explained as simply a reaction to television content. Indeed, the 50s saw the US exhibition of *La Ronde* (1950), *Summer with Monika* (1952), *Smiles of a Summer Night* (1955), *And God Created Woman* (1956), and other foreign films with sexually explicit content. The admission of such films into the USA was aided by the reorganisation of the film industry after the Paramount case.[6] The separation of exhibition from production and distribution that the Paramount Case dictated loosened the control that the Hays Code and the MPAA (the Motion Picture Association of America) had previously exerted over imported films, and this development helped to create alternative distribution and exhibition circuits which could show such foreign fare. The assumption of mature themes by some Hollywood films allowed them to compete, then, with both foreign imports and television. At the same time, the art film, described as realistic (in other words, providing revelations about the human condition), while offering daring presentations of sex, may have helped supply the vocabulary that studios used to promote their own melodramas.

136

Along with the influence of television and foreign films, the status of film censorship during the post-war era helped to create a felicitous environment for the production of films with mature subject-matter. From the famous MPAA/Howard Hughes dispute over *The Outlaw* in 1946 to United Artists' release of two Otto Preminger films without the MPAA Seal of Approval – *The Moon is Blue* (1953), a sex comedy in which the word 'virgin' was uttered for the first time, and *The Man with the Golden Arm* (1955), which was about drug addiction – the domain and regulations of the MPAA were almost continually challenged.[7]

The Paramount Case, which had played a role in loosening the grip of the MPAA over the distribution and exhibition of imported films, had a similar effect on domestic products in that it enabled a somewhat less authoritative relation between censorship and film production. In addition, because of post-war attendance problems and competition from television, exhibitors and studios put pressure on the MPAA to soften its moral standards to respond to box-office needs.[8] The Code was revised in December 1956 to allow references to previously forbidden subject-matter such as drug addiction, abortion, prostitution, and miscegenation, though topics like sexual perversion were still banned. By the 60s, even this last bastion of censorship was finally overcome.

Shifts in the industry were in accord with significant legal decisions against the censorship of certain subjects handed down during this period. In 1952, after a controversy surrounding the banning of Roberto Rossellini's *The Miracle* on the grounds that it was sacrilegious, the Supreme Court granted the film First Amendment protection (*Joseph Burstyn, Inc.* v *Wilson*, 343 US 475, 1952). In the next few years, the Supreme Court disallowed banning a film because of subject-matter focused on sexual immorality. Such developments in the film industry and legal structure helped, then, to fuel more permissive screen representations.

Interestingly, advertising campaigns often went so far as to call attention to their challenges to censorship as a means of selling a film. *The Rose Tattoo* (1955), for example, was 'The Boldest Story of Love You've Ever Been Permitted to See,' while *The Sun Also Rises* (1957) was a 'Love Story Too Daring to Film until Now,' and *From Here to Eternity* (1953) was 'The Boldest Book of Our Time, Honestly, Fearlessly on The Screen.'[9] Studios thereby made themselves appear as crusaders for the freedom of speech ('honestly, fearlessly') and the right of their audiences to experience mature, realistic content.

Thus, because of developments affecting content, the film industry produced movies that could compete in a market-place tuned to the box-office possibilities of explicit psychodramas. Indeed, many of the biggest-grossing films during this era – *I'll Cry Tomorrow* (1955), *Picnic* (1955), *The Man with the Golden Arm* (1955), *Trapeze* (1956), *Giant* (1956), *Written on the Wind*, and *Peyton Place* (1957) – were melodramas with social, psychological, and/or sexual problems at their core.

For their materials, studios often adapted novels and plays with cele-brated adult profiles, enhancing the prestige as well as the notoriety of the films indebted to these prior works. Tennessee Williams's stories, includ-

Advertisement for *The Rose Tattoo* (Daniel Mann, 1955)

ing *A Streetcar Named Desire* (1951), *The Rose Tattoo*, *Baby Doll* (1956), *Cat on a Hot Tin Roof* (1958), and *Suddenly Last Summer* (1959), were thus converted. So were a host of novels and other plays, including James Jones's *From Here to Eternity*, Lillian Roth's autobiography *I'll Cry Tomorrow*, William Inge's *Picnic*, Robert Anderson's *Tea and Sympathy*, and Grace Metalious's *Peyton Place*. 'Racy' topics in these texts included homosexuality, sexual initiation, prostitution, rape, abortion, adultery, sexual frustration and temptation, alcoholism and murder.

Studios produced and exhibited films by Minnelli, Ray and Sirk to fit within this trend. Minnelli's *The Cobweb* (1955), *Tea and Sympathy* (1956), and *Home From the Hill* (1960), Ray's *Rebel Without a Cause* (1955), and *Bigger Than Life* (1956), and Sirk's *Written on the Wind* (1956) and *Tarnished Angels* (1957) offered their own impressive array of sensationalistic topics. Among these were psychological dysfunction, premarital intercourse, adultery, frigidity, homosexuality, nymphomania, sterility, illegitimate birth, alcoholism, family strife, violence, and drug abuse. Advertising practices secured the adult identity by highlighting narrative components and characters which would broadcast whatever

Advertisement for *Written on the Wind* (Douglas Sirk, 1956)

Advertisement for *Tea and Sympathy* (Vincente Minnelli, 1956)

mature situations the film in question had to offer, helping to characterise the post-war melodrama as a forum for spectacle by ceaselessly chronicling its sensationalistic elements.[10] In this context, film melodramas became one of the means by which the studios could profitably respond to specific industry developments.

However, analysis of the industry provides only a partial view of how and why 'local' genres are constituted. The coining of the adult film was both a symptom of an attempt to capitalise on the rising tide of overt discourses on the sexual and other sensational topics during the 50s. Examining this social context is key to understanding the ideological meaning of adult forms in this era.

The Sexual Display

Film academics studying the 'sophisticated family melodramas' of the 40s and 50s have typically portrayed the Eisenhower years as socially and sexually repressive. This social order is clearly manifested in television situation comedies such as *Father Knows Best*, where family cohesiveness is celebrated, and rigid sex roles portray men as benevolent patriarchs and women as dutiful housewives. From such a monologic perspective, the excesses of the post-war melodrama seem clearly subversive.

However, as Richard Dyer has argued in his work on Marilyn Monroe, we would do well to reconsider the 50s beyond its repressive label.[11] Such a depiction ignores the high visibility and complexity of discourses on sexuality characterising this era, for along with its sedate images of the nuclear family the 50s saw an explosion of discussions and representations of explicit sexuality that made sex an aggressively integral part of public life. With this cultural development in mind, we can rethink the relation between the family melodrama, frequently preoccupied with sexual turmoil, and its original social context.

An examination of the post-war era shows that counter-cultural expressions of sexuality were gaining great currency. Organised gay subcultures, beat generation philosophy, and the routines of the so-called 'sick' comedians attacked, respectively, heterosexist presumptions, marriage and monogamy, and propriety regarding what should be publicly said about intimate relations between the sexes.

Gay subcultures became particularly visible in the post-war era, inspired by same-sex experiences abroad and on the home front during the war, as well as by the Kinsey reports in 1948 and 1953 which found that male and female homosexuality was not uncommon.[12] At the same time, some representations focused with candour on the homosexual experience, including Kenneth Anger's *Fireworks* (1947), lesbian pulp fiction by Ann Bannon and others, and particularly Allen Ginsberg's ode to homosexuality, *Howl*, published in 1956 and one of the most influential volumes of poetry published during the decade.

The beatniks' particular form of anti-conventionalism espoused the notion of 'free love' as opposed to maritally sanctioned intercourse, while 'sick' comedians like Lenny Bruce and Mort Sahl not only assaulted the canons of respectable language but openly joked about problems in sexual relationships.[13]

141

Such marginal expressions of homosexuality, free love, and open, sometimes graphic, depictions of sexual encounters and problems begin to demonstrate how punctuated this era was with sexual discourse. This was true not only in the counter-cultures themselves, but in the massive mainstream culture response that attempted to understand, condemn, censor, or reform these groups. However, sexually explicit issues did not arise solely in relation to counter-cultures. It was in society at large that sexual representation made its most pronounced and pervasive appearance.

In *Intimate Matters*, John D'Amilio and Estelle Freedman describe the 50s as part of the rise of 'sexual liberalism' in the United States that commenced after the Second World War, resulting in more permissive attitudes towards sex among white, middle-class Americans. These attitudes were evident in the 50s in studies of private expectations, public forums discussing sexual morality, and depictions of sex in the media. For instance, whereas premarital sex was still taboo during the 50s, other forms of intimacy – dating, going steady, and heavy petting – were more or less socially acceptable means of premarital sexual expression. Middle-class couples who headed towards marriage, conversant with Freud and aware of the availability of contraception, placed a great deal of emphasis on sex as a marker of well-being at the same time as they separated its pleasurable from its procreative dimensions.[14] According to Elaine Tyler May, the encouragement of 'healthy' heterosexual relations and early marriage by journalists as well as education and psychology experts served as a primary defence against the Cold War demon of homosexuality, interpreted as a distinguishing mark of Communist activity.[15]

In any case, the term 'sexual liberalism' did not connote complete freedom or open-mindedness in this arena of human affairs. Its liberal dimensions, that is to say, a greater and more open emphasis on heterosexual pleasures of certain kinds, were constrained by a series of boundaries, including the oft-mentioned double standard and the demarcation of other sexualities, particularly homosexuality and African-American sexuality, as deviant. However, sexual liberalism did provide a supportive atmosphere for the profusion of sexually frank materials in the media.

Supreme Court decisions allowing greater explicitness in sexual representation for public consumption helped to stem the tide of censorship in relation to most of the media, and as a result, as D'Amilio and Freedman put it, 'sex unconstrained by marriage was put on display'.[16] Among other media, phenomena contributing to the heightened sexual explicitness in the 50s were the Kinsey reports, *Playboy*, the publication of 'adult' novels and suggestive paperbacks, and exposé magazines like *Confidential*.

Both Kinsey reports, *Sexual Behaviour in the Human Male* (1948) and *Sexual Behaviour in the Human Female* (1953), spent several months on the *New York Times* Best Seller List, each selling almost a quarter of a million copies. Kinsey's unmasking of the actual sexual practices of white Americans caused a public furore, since his findings demonstrated how inadequately traditional moral norms described how people actually lived their sexuality. These reports helped to foreground sex and sexual behaviour as very much a part of the public cultural landscape.

Many of the other representations within the 'sexual display' had the visual objectification of women as their express subject. *Playboy*, which began publication in 1953, continued to promote the implicit affiliation between sexual explicitness, sexual liberation, and suggestive representations of the female body. *Playboy* was devoted to an anti-family philosophy of male freedom built on the foundation of a connoisseurship of extramarital pleasures, central among them the image of the sexually available, always 'ready' woman.[17] *Playboy*'s first issue sported the by now famous nude calendar photo of Marilyn Monroe, and a later issue that of Jayne Mansfield, two of the most prominent 'blonde bombshells' in film. By the mid-50s, *Playboy*'s success spawned a number of imitators interested in capitalising on the 'girlie' aspects of its format; these included *Rogue*, *Nugget*, and *Dude*.

The paperback book industry, which was booming by the 50s, also sported sensationalistic covers featuring women in a state of undress or other compromising positions, with such titles as *Three Gorgeous Hussies*, *Women's Barracks*, *I, Libertine*, and *Junkie*. In addition, these and other successful paperbacks at the time, including *From Here to Eternity*, *The Man with the Golden Arm*, Mickey Spillane novels, *Lady Chatterley's Lover*, *From Russia with Love*, and *Peyton Place*, drew obscenity charges from the House of Representatives' Gathings probe into paperback publication for their portrayal of explicit sexual encounters.[18]

While such forums as *Playboy* and paperbacks seem to posit a direct relation between sexual display, the sexual objectification of women, and a predominantly *male* spectator, there were types of explicitness strongly aimed at female readers. Central among these were exposé magazines such as *Confidential*, which appeared in 1952. *Confidential* enjoyed tremendous popularity by indulging in what its publisher called 'sin and sex'. This magazine, like the spin-offs it inspired in the 50s, including *Dare*, *Exposed*, and *Uncensored*, depicted social ills and the private lives of celebrities through lurid innuendo to create maximal sensationalised effects. Incriminating headlines, such as 'Why Robert Wagner Is a Flat Tire in the Boudoir', were common.

Exposé magazines borrowed from the already proven successful story formula of the confession magazine, such as *True Confessions*, that grew in popularity after the Second World War, a time which also saw a revolution in morals and manners creating a more permissive attitude towards sex. The point of the confession story ('I Had to Prove My Love/The Night before the Wedding') was to give the reader 'a glimpse into someone else's most intimate affairs', with sex as a perennial sub-text.[19] Publishers found that women, initially the undereducated working class but increasingly the middle class as this formula found its way into fan magazines and even some general circulation magazines like *Look* and *Life*, particularly enjoyed this combination of 'authentic revelation' tinged with highly emotional problem-oriented scenarios, often sexual in nature.

The growing frankness of sexual discourse during the 50s should not, however, cause us to view the decade as a heretofore unrecognised Sodom and Gomorrah. Despite changing rules of censorship, such media

143

events renewed the fervour of reformists and groups bent on challenging the morality of the sexual display. Similarly, while homosexual subcultures and their representations grew, so did their persecution at the hands of Cold War ideologues; while images of Monroe and Mansfield pervaded the media, so did discussions of the sanctity of the family and traditional sex roles; while *Confidential* flourished, so did *Better Homes and Gardens*. In other words, an emphasis on the sexual display does not redefine the 50s in some new monologic way; instead, it alleviates a simplistic depiction of the decade by revealing how central discursive adventures into explicit sexual territories were. Subsequently, this era appears as one driven by contradictory and sometimes combative representations of sex, manifested in a wide range of popular forms from Monroe and *Playboy* to *Father Knows Best* and Walt Disney films.

Hence, the industry produced and promoted melodramas to dovetail with the decade's interest in sexual display and the sensational. Industry discourse, far from representing some hyperbolic and mendacious Barnum-esque ploy, assumed the task of presenting melodrama in accord with social developments around more permissive representations of sexuality and other potentially volatile topics. Studios attempted to align films with the prevailing winds of discourse, here through generic attribution.

In addition, the manner in which the post-war culture of heterosexual display targeted both genders helps clarify how melodrama was to signify during this time. As we have seen, certain media forms courted men through the explicit representation of the female body, placed in the exhilarating space of pre- or extramarital pleasure. Others, particularly scandal magazines, attempted to appeal to women through the rhetoric of the exposé, which depicted 'private' problems through the lens of sensationalism. Thus, within this genderised intertextual universe of publications, the sexually-tinged sensationalism of the adult melodrama could appeal to both male and female audience members.

The importance of this social background for the 'sophisticated family melodrama' is that it represents what Tony Bennett and Janet Woollacott have called a 'culturally specific' instance of generic construction arising from a particular institutional and social location. Woollacott and Bennett's perspective allows us to examine how texts are drawn into different generic relations depending on specific social and historical situations – how, that is, a text can be associated with various genres over time, which may draw it into 'different social and ideological relations of reading'.[20] Part of the stake of historicising the question of genre lies in realising the influential relation between generic identity and ideological meaning. The various categories a film has belonged to through its history may define its cultural functions in ways at odds with the propositions of 'master' concepts. Even the most transitory of classifications provides clues as to how past social orders made the cinema ideologically intelligible according to the demands of prominent value systems of the time.

During the 50s such a 'culturally specific' instance of generic identity occurred for the family melodrama. It occurred through affiliation with the adult film, a transient 'local' genre forged by a mixture of institutional and social factors. This generic frame selectively activated filmic elements, such as psychosexual conflicts, to foster an ideological identity for melo-dramas which was commensurate with the era's strong emphasis on sexual display. This climate, underwritten by a renewed heterosexual fervour in the anti-Communist post-war years, created a voyeuristic ethos focused on the objectification of women and a lurid sensationalising of social problems and human relationships.

As the strong presence of reformers indicates, increasingly explicit representations of sex were not without subversive implications. If the 'sophisticated family melodrama' attained a transgressive status during this time, it was not because its representations of sexuality proved an exception to the repressive rule of the Eisenhower years; it was because such representations were so much a part of a dominant, and for some objectionable, trend in film-making encompassing films from *From Here to Eternity* to *Peyton Place*. However, the issue of ideological status is not so easily resolved. At the same time as these films may have represented a liberation from the forces of censorship, the climate of sexual display tended to associate sex with traditional patriarchal pleasures, and a domestic ideology that saw women as avid consumers of conflicted romantic narratives in the style of *True Confessions*. The film studios, *Playboy*, *Confidential*, and other mainstream media forums articulated sex for consumption within value systems that ultimately affirmed cultural continuity.

Thus, historical analysis suggests that family melodramas were not always family melodramas; they were once classified as adult fare. In this way, the example of melodrama encourages us to consider generic identity as a series of mutations shaped at the very least by authoritative environments involved in cinema's cultural and historical circulation. These environments are responsible for making films appealing to audiences within the boundaries of specific social systems. Non-academic institutions use generic labelling as a key means of accomplishing this task, though the creation of 'local' genres by these institutions is neither superficial nor inconsequential. This process is, rather, deeply embedded in institutional and social conditions, and capable of defining the significant components of a generic corpus as a means of generating audience expectations. Further, while they may affront 'master' characterisations and the values they impute to certain films, such transient generic affiliations help to clarify how films are made to mean within radically different historical and social conjunctures.

Notes

1. See, for example, Jane Feuer, *The Hollywood Musical* (Bloomington: Indiana University Press, 1982) and John Cawelti, *The Six-Gun Mystique* (Bowling Green: Bowling Green University Press, 1971).
2. Work identifying cycles and subgenres has included Rick Altman, *The American Film Musical* (Bloomington: Indiana University Press, 1989); Robin Wood, *The American Nightmare: Essays on the Horror Film* (Toronto: Festival of Festivals, 1979), and Mary Ann Doane, *The Desire to Desire: The Woman's Film of the 1940s* (Bloomington: Indiana University Press, 1987).
3. Steve Neale, 'Questions of Genre,' *Screen*, vol. 31, no. 1, Spring 1990, p. 52. See also Tony Bennett and Janet Woollacott, *Bond and Beyond: The Political*

Career of a Popular Hero (New York: Methuen, 1987), and Alan Williams, 'Is a Radical Genre Criticism Possible?', *Quarterly Review of Film Studies*, vol. 9, no. 2, Spring 1984.

4. Joe Morella, Edward Z. Epstein, and Eleanor Clark, *Those Great Movie Ads* (New Rochelle: Arlington House, 1972), p. 88.

5. 'Sticks Now on "Hick Pix" Kick', *Variety*, 5 December 1956, p. 1.

6. Steve Neale, 'Art Cinema as Institution', *Screen*, vol. 22, no. 1, 1981, pp. 32–3.

7. For a fuller discussion of censorship and *The Outlaw*, see Mary Beth Haralovich, 'Film Advertising, the Film Industry, and the Pin-up', in Bruce A. Austin (ed.), *Current Research in Film I: Audiences, Economics, and Law* (Norwood, NJ: Ablex Publishing Corporation, 1985), pp. 143–51.

8. *Variety*, 5 December 1956, pp. 1, 86.

9. Morella et al., op. cit., p. 77.

10. See my 'Much Ado About Excess: Genre, *Mise en scène*, and the Woman in *Written on the Wind*', *Wide Angle*, vol. 11, no. 4, 1989, pp. 4–22, for a more detailed discussion of how advertising activated generic frames in an attempt to define the reception of one of these 'adult' films.

11. Richard Dyer, *Heavenly Bodies: Film Stars and Society* (New York: St Martin's, 1986), pp. 19–66.

12. John D'Amilio, *Sexual Politics, Sexual Communities: The Making of a Homosexual Minority in the United States, 1940–70* (Chicago: University of Chicago Press, 1983), pp. 23–39.

13. For discussions of both beatniks and 'sick' comics as incipient forms of the more developed counter-cultures of the 60s, see Marty Jezer, *The Dark Ages: Life in the United States 1945–1960* (Boston: South End Press, 1982), pp. 258–90.

14. John D'Amilio and Estelle B. Freedman, *Intimate Matters: A History of Sexuality in America* (New York: Harper & Row, 1988), pp. 239–74.

15. Elaine Tyler May, *Homeward Bound: American Families in the Cold War Era* (New York: Basic Books, 1988), p. 116.

16. D'Amilio and Freedman, op. cit., p. 277.

17. Barbara Ehrenreich treats the relation of *Playboy* to images of the family and women in the 50s in *The Hearts of Men: American Dreams and the Flight From Commitment* (New York: Anchor Press, 1983), pp. 42–51.

18. Kenneth C. Davis discusses paperback covers and obscenity problems in *Two-Bit Culture: The Paperbacking of America* (Boston: Houghton Mifflin, 1984), pp. 135–41, 216–47.

19. Thomas Peterson, *Magazines in the Twentieth Century* (Urbana: University of Illinois Press, 1964), p. 304; he also analyses the success of exposé magazines in the 50s, pp. 379–82.

20. Bennett and Woollacott, op. cit., p. 81.

HAVING A GOOD CRY OVER
THE COLOR PURPLE

The Problem of Affect and Imperialism in
Feminist Theory

JANE SHATTUC

Recently I came across the following statement about the film *The Color Purple* (1985) while researching a book on affect and feminine pleasure:

> *The Color Purple* has meaning only in the experience of having watched it. ... It simply, in the absolute darkness of the theater, allows one to evoke endlessly a series of absolutely trite responses to a series of emotional, manipulative, trite situations; for the film does indeed trivialize its themes by condemning the modes of irony, ambiquity, and ultimately, realism; so instead of being searing, it is merely heartwarming.[1]

The quotation embodies not only the traditional modernist or 'masculine' disdain for melodrama, it also addresses a problem in theory that feminists have failed to resolve: the affective power of the melodramatic text. Indeed, feminist analysis pushes questions about emotional response to the side, preferring the more intellectual or modernist concepts of excess and contradiction which distance the viewer from the power of the text's conservative morality.

According to Laura Mulvey, there are two theoretical approaches to melodramatic excess in film studies.[2] The first evolves out of work on Douglas Sirk's films where neo-Marxists argue that melodrama's political importance lies in its visual and narrative ruptures and fissures of the film's bourgeois realism and ideology. Melodramatic excess stands as the precursor to Brechtian distanciation. Unfortunately, any identification with melodrama's feminine subject-matter was damned as complicit with bourgeois oppression. Responding to this dismissal of the possible progressive content of a feminine genre, feminists have reread melodrama as a rare site for female identification. Here, Sirk's as well as melodrama's stylisation or excess becomes a method to accentuate the emotional content within the film. Nevertheless, for Mulvey melodrama is still centrally defined by its method of 'working certain contradictions through to the surface and representing them in an aesthetic form'.[3] This position represents the continuing love/hate relationship that feminists have had with melodrama. In order to salvage the feminine subject content, there is a continual return to the modernist view of melodrama as an inherently distancing form. It would, then, seem impossible to have 'a good cry' over *The Color Purple*.

This ambivalence about emotional identification with the melodrama heroine can be traced throughout recent feminist writing. For example, Jane Feuer directly links melodrama's subversive potential with its excessive style when she argues that Joan Collins's hyperbolic performance as Alexis Carrington in *Dynasty* is a comment on the impossibility of a woman's role under capitalism.[4] Working from Thomas Elsaesser's theory of the contrapuntal function of melodrama's *mise en scène*, Tanya Modleski argues that *Letter to an Unknown Woman* takes melodramatic emotion to its exteme, rupturing the text by revealing a different rhythm in the film's hysterical repetitions that evoke a 'feminine' or repressed text.[5]

Even in feminist analyses that mark the importance of affect and identification for a popular feminine appeal, such as E. Ann Kaplan's study of the maternal in melodrama, this affective power becomes secondary to readings of contradiction.[6] Here, the conservative masculine narrative content and the progressive feminine content do not match up, allowing the viewer to see through the dominant patriarchal text. All these analyses are thoughtful elucidations of theoretical debates, but what happens if we read melodramas 'straight' – the way they were intended to be read? This paper investigates feminist criticism's refusal to own up to the political power of affect in melodrama (even in its conservative 'happy ending' form) and, in particular, the racial implications of such a denial for the reception of *The Color Purple*.

Melodrama has been historically a major site of the political struggles for the disempowered, both female and black. Harriet Beecher Stowe's *Uncle Tom's Cabin* remains the single most famous example of a melodramatic book that spawned a political movement. Jane Tompkins defends the emotive power of the melodramatic and sentimental in feminine texts in literature as perhaps some of the most powerful political writings. For her, we need to see

> the sentimental novel, not as an artifact of eternity answerable to certain formal criteria and to certain psychological and philosophical concerns, but as a political enterprise, halfway between sermon and social theory, that both codifies and attempts to mold the values of its times.[7]

Nevertheless, film feminists have more often dismissed the feminine and racial content of melodrama texts as bourgeois ideology or as a sensibility dominated by white masculine values. Therefore *The Color Purple*, a melodrama about a black woman's liberation, is as equally damned as *Stella Dallas* as an example of bourgeois ideology. Most often, it is the visual irony of Stella's clothing and Stanwyck's performance against the backdrop of bourgeois conformity that rescues *Stella Dallas*.[8] Indeed, Alice Walker's novel, has also become the *cause célèbre* in the feminist literary community not only because of its tale of a black woman's journey to empowerment, but also because its epistolary form as a 'womanist' genre is often seen as 'distancing'[9] – whereas the film has been resoundingly denigrated in the critical press as melodramatic simplification of the sophisticated novel, eliminating much of the formal innovation of the written work.[10]

More importantly, the film has received no textual or serious political analysis by feminists – Jacqueline Bobo's analysis of the film remains the exception.[11] Given the fact that such a commercially popular feminist film has been either overlooked, neglected or disdained, I tend to conclude that Suzanne Clark rightfully argues that 'sentiment condenses the way gender still operates as the political unconscious within criticism to trigger shame, embarrassment and disgust'.[12] Ultimately, rather than champion the feminine, racial and political content of these tearjerkers, feminists have preferred to defend melodramas based on their ironic or contradictory value, which, as Christine Gledhill points out, can be a misogynistic approach given the feminine content of these works.[13]

Not only does such use of high theory limit popular feminist understanding, it also involves racial questions. Jane Gaines and Manthia Diawara have argued against the racist implications of psychoanalysis where feminism sees the male/female dichotomy as the founding moment of oppression.[14] Gaines questions the universality of the theory when she writes: 'The theory of the subject as constituted in language imported into US academies seemed able to account for all oppression, expression and socio-sexual functioning'.[15] Psychoanalysis cannot account for the black woman's identification with the black man as based on their shared subordination in a white-dominated patriarchy.

Given genre theory's awareness of historical change, we would expect a greater sensitivity to social difference when investigating melodrama. The defence of formal and narrative excess becomes even more problematic when one considers the racial and class implications of excess – a concept derived from European high modernism, an academic movement in which these disenfranchised groups have not traditionally participated. For is not excess, the self-consciousness of a reading strategy, invented by and taught through the Western academy? Such cultural competency is a class and racial privilege.

Rather, we need to question more closely why blacks and women have been drawn to and have utilised melodrama and sentimental fiction as the chosen form for their narratives of victimisation. These works comprise early slave narratives, such as *Uncle Tom's Cabin*, domestic tearjerkers and, most recently, black feminist fiction such as *The Color Purple*. In literary feminism, Gayatri Spivak has warned of a similar separatist mentality – specifically, in reproducing 'the axioms of imperialism' in its 'isolationist admiration of the female literature in Europe and the high feminist norm'.[16] We too need to look to how 'the intellectual feminine voice' has served to undercut the political power of melodrama texts that invoke the pleasure of tears and political change, rather than the policing effect of intellectual distance. What is it that middle-class feminists fear that causes them to support intellectual distance over emotion? Is it fear of blacks and working-class women being 'out of control' and therefore outside 'our' control?

Before making a case for the affective and political power of the film *The Color Purple*, a film that became the site of powerful debate within the black community, I want to review some of the potential problems that I as a white, middle-class feminist might reproduce in championing the affective power of the film. Pascal Bruckner[17] constructs three potentially imperialist stances involved in the liberal-to-left's writing about the Third World (which includes America's internal colonies of women and blacks). I want to outline them by using potential responses to *The Color Purple* as illustrations.

The Solidarity Stance

Here, a white feminist feels fellowship for the black women in the film because of her own oppression as a woman. Oppression is basically the same everywhere: 'I cry out of the pain of our shared existence.' I cry also because the film has articulated the oppression and rights of African-Americans, thus freeing all oppressed groups a little. But Bruckner would argue that such a position is ultimately indifferent to Celie's particular plight – her problem becomes one of many.

The Pity Stance

Because I am a member of the white middle class, I am rich and they are poor. I am automatically more successful because of the colour of my skin. I am an oppressor. Being white and middle class, I am guilty. Because I consume more, I create their poverty. Ultimately, my well-being is predicated on their misery and oppression. I cry because I feel sorry for their pain and my consciousness has been raised. But Bruckner argues that this sadness only reinforces the idea that I as a white woman do indeed have it better – and *The Color Purple* reinforces my sense of luck and pleasure at being white.

The Imitation Stance

Here, I cry because Celie and the other black women of *The Color Purple* are so noble and have a wisdom that I have lost as a white in the process of my empowerment. I am beside myself with emotion over how Celie, Shug and Nettie are closer to nature as rural blacks than I am. I should be more like black women in order to return to the simplicity and straightforwardness of this black feminine community. To overcome my cry, I will put myself in the place of the 'other' black woman and open myself to non-white cultures. But Bruckner argues that in the end my imitation becomes only a vulgar substitution. I elide social differences between black and white cultures in order to experience black culture.

This typology of 'good cries' points out the difficulties of the Utopian goal of equity for feminism. There are a number of problems: conflating different histories of oppressions, creating scenarios of victimisation that further weaken the power of the 'other' group, and the reductive process of comparing greater injustices. Indeed, with whom do feminists want equity? Is it simply with men? Or is it also an issue of black women having the power of white women? In addition, is there a stable end-point

150

that the concept 'equity' might suggest? Bruckner concludes that, at best, the privileged can swing between the poles of criticism and solidarity. As a result, feminist theory needs to reconcile its attitude to patriarchal oppression with the self-sufficiency of female and black readers to recognise their own oppression.

This paper, an elucidation of the similarity of the feminine and black melodramatic form as powerful political tracts, also falls potentially into this problematic trap of conflating the form and content of racially different histories. By outlining these stances, I am not offering an answer as to how to transcend such power inequities, nor am I shunning feminism as a powerful critique of authority. Moreover, I want to point out how often white liberal-to-left-wing compassion or 'tears' for black culture can lead to contempt, complacency and inaction. I think that there is potentially a form of contempt in arguing for the necessity of excess to produce ideological distance – academic feminists can see through ideology as we critique all kinds of texts, classic realist and excessive. But the 'people' or the masses or the uneducated 'need' to have the constructed nature of ideology telegraphed to them.

Indeed, feminism's hesitance to endorse the affective power of melodrama stems from a traditional leftist vision of false consciousness: tears became the marks of enthrallment not only intellectually but emotionally (the ultimate sign of control) by the bourgeois morality of the film's content. Fredric Jameson critiques this leftist suspicion of direct emotional appeal and ideological control. Turning around Walter Benjamin's pessimistic statement about cultural advancement, Jameson declares that 'There has never been a document of culture which was not at one and the same time a document of barbarism,' and argues that what is 'effectively ideological is also, at the same time, necessarily Utopian'.[18]

This thesis implies in the case of *The Color Purple* (a film based on a black woman's vision filtered through the white masculine ethos of the American film industry) that the text draws its power over the female viewer from its appeal to what Patrocinio Schweickart calls 'authentic desires' which it rouses and then harnesses to the process of white emasculation.[19] The film plays not only on my false consciousness, but also on my authentic liberatory aspirations, those Utopian impulses that have drawn me to both the women's and the civil rights movements.

When a woman identifies with Celie, she performs what Schweickart would call a 'two-stage rereading'. She focuses on Celie's narrative as a metaphor for feminine transcendence of patriarchal control. The film as well as the novel plays on the religious logic of empowerment and transcendence as Celie becomes a near Christ-like figure as she addresses her epistolary pleas to 'God'. In fact, Celie's change is predicated on her discovery and eventual control of her body, first taken from her by men. This action visualises a central tenet of recent feminism which simply expressed the rallying cry of the 80s, 'our bodies, ourselves'. One could argue that when Celie, with Shug's encouragement, stands in front of the mirror, the film visualises the mirror phase as Celie comes to recognise her individuality and narcissistic desire. Instead of a masculine Oedipal trajectory, Celie's sexual desire is initiated by a woman. Although the film as an essentially conservative text destroys the original political power of the overt lesbianism of the novel, the film still retains the separatist logic of women empowering women. As a result, one of the most powerful moments in the film comes when Celie breaks from Mister and declares, 'I'm poor, I'm black, I may be ugly and can't cook.... But I'm here.' Here, my emotional identification is based on the feminist ideology of autonomous selfhood.

In the process, however, I am still drawn into the scapegoating of the black male in the figure of Mister, where the stereotype is the most feared and problematic figure in American society, perpetuating the racist hegemony of the white patriarchy. Manthia Diawara has chronicled the history of similar black male figures in American films such as *The Birth of a Nation* (1915), *Rocky II* (1979), *A Soldier's Story* (1984), and *Forty-Eight Hours* (1982). He argues that these films all stage their narrative around an image of a 'punished and disciplined' black man. In all of them the spectator is denied identification with the black man because the narrative depends on the castration of his power either 'by white domestication of black customs and culture – a process of deracination and isolation – or by stories in which blacks are depicted playing by white rules'.[20] In fact, Mister's attempted rape of Nettie in *The Color Purple* nearly repeats Gus's chase of Little Sister in *The Birth of a Nation* as parallel editing emphasises identification with the female victim.

My point here is that all dominant melodramas produce a dual hermeneutic: a positive hermeneutic of the 'good cry' which recuperates the Utopian moment, the authentic kernel, from which they draw their emotional power, and a negative hermeneutic that discloses their complicity with white patriarchal ideology. If, indeed, the content of melodrama is conservative bourgeois ideology, then its popularity with women signals that it contains the seeds of women's liberation which dominant ideology must stage, contain and diffuse. Herein lies the tradition of positive hermeneutics in black and feminine melodrama – the bourgeois uplift story.

Historically, black sentimental fiction, melodramas and slave narratives, written by the black literate middle class, paralleled the style of nineteenth-century women's sentimental fiction. They centred around liberation myths. According to Henry Louis Gates Jr, slave narratives were structured around the 'overlapping of the slave's arduous journey to freedom and the journey from orality to literacy'. *Our Nig*, one of the first novels written by a black woman, Harriet Wilson, employed the 'women's novel's' use of sentiment to indict social injustice. Additionally, slave narrative writer Harriet Jacobs employed a plot initiated by the sentimental novel (a high-born male seducing a lower-class woman) to structure her story of victimisation as her master seduces her.[21] According to Gates, black writers in the 19th century wrote exclusively about their social and political condition.[22] It is not surprising, then, when blacks turned to filmmaking by the 1900s, that their chosen form was the domestic melodrama. Jane Gaines points out how the early black film (the child of the black bourgeoisie) could accommodate the black 'claim to power yet simultaneously counselling resignation'.[23]

152

The Color Purple, both as a novel as well as a film, follows the Utopian tradition of the black bourgeois uplift literature tradition. The film traces the classic slave narrative structure as Celie is liberated from patriarchal enslavement while simultaneously becoming literate. Jacqueline Bobo offers strong evidence of the positive ideological influence that the film had on black women. They were 'moved' by 'the fact [that] Celie eventually triumphs in the film'. She chronicles how they 'cried', 'became angry', and finally 'became proud' of Celie's liberation.[24] Bobo concludes that 'Black women have discovered something progressive and useful in the film.' This discovery was made through the emotive power of identification with the film's Utopian logic.

Indeed, The Color Purple, along with Uncle Tom's Cabin and Frederick Douglass's autobiographies, represent a long and powerful tradition of political tracts in black and feminine fiction that base their strength in the power of sentimentality. Jameson claims that all effective ideologies, both conservative and radical, must make these emotional claims to Utopian transcendence, no matter how subtle. These black and feminine texts fall openly in a sentimental tradition of American jeremiads which Sacvan Bercovitch describes as 'modes of public exhortation designed to join social criticism to spiritual, public to private identity, the shifting sign of the times to certain traditional metaphors, themes and symbols'.[25] Through the vigour of its representation of the black woman's plight borrowed from the novel, the film The Color Purple represents the essential ideal of hope that motivates any revolutionary movement whether it be Marxist, feminist or black.

Yet for all the emotive power of its transcendence theme, The Color Purple was clearly received by the African–American community with an awareness of Jameson's negative hermeneutic tradition or 'lessons of false consciousness, of class bias and ideological programming'.[26] As is generally known, The Color Purple engendered a significant debate in the black community about gender and dominant ideology. On one level, the film was criticised resoundingly for its simplification of the novel: the racial clichés and stereotypes of a Hollywood spectacle. Additionally, it was criticised for its false representation of the black experience through a landed gentry. But the centre of the debate focused on the image of the black man as the source of Celie's victimisation (and therefore that of black women in general) which echoed white patriarchy's depiction of the black man as 'quintessentially evil'. As a result, black women's pleasure from the film's portrayal of the patriarchy was implicated in the displacement of white racism into a feminist text.

But as copious articles in Ebony, Jet and academic journals as well as Jacqueline Bobo's ethnographic study attest, The Color Purple is a dominant film that elicited both a powerful affirmative reading as well as, simultaneously, a highly critical reading of its dominant ideology. My own personal experience of this debate was as one of the few white female sleeping car porters on Amtrak during the summer after the film's release. The film blossomed into a major discussion topic between the black women porters and me. They tended to talk about the poor black woman's experience and I tended to talk about Celie's victimisation in general.

Inspired by the film, we circulated the Walker novel among us and we were all initially frustrated by the difficulty of following written black dialect. However, the major debate took place in late-night arguments in the dining car between the female and male black porters over who was to blame for the victimisation of black women – black men or white society.

My participation as a white woman was continually contested. I was first told that I knew nothing as a 'white college girl of being poor, black and eating Georgia red clay when hungry'. On the other hand, I was also defended at times as a woman who knew what it felt like to be a 'victim'; as one of my male co-workers put it, 'at least white women do not hate and fear the black man like white men'. Given all my 'white compassion' and tears for the 'black experience', I was placed or 'positioned' both within and outside the black community in all discussions.

For all our self-consciousness of social difference, however, we were all critical of the film and aware of its emotional impact on us as well as society at large. Yet, from an academic perspective, the film was marked by a relatively straightforward melodramatic style offering little or none of the ironic counterpunctuation that recent melodrama criticism has heralded as the source for ideological distance. Here, resistance emanated from the social situation of the black reader (and in my case a white woman) whose 'real' or lived experience contested the dominant ideology of the film.[27]

In conclusion, what I have presented here is a call for a new feminist reading strategy based on a dual awareness of the text as both positive and negative hermeneutics. Feminist reading and writing are interested in building a community of feminists, and one hopes that that community will grow to include all races and genders – the feminist Utopian moment. We need to begin to rewrite the terms of the debate where emotion can be reasoned and tears mean active involvement, not disregarded as trite responses as the opening quote would have it.

Nevertheless, until we break the instrumental logic of reading all ideology as false consciousness and the reproduction of self-serving class and racially bound concepts such as excess, we limit some of the most powerful examples of political resistance and communal beliefs. In the end, tears are not a sign of feminine weakness, as the patriarchy would have it, but they are more than the manifestation of physical pleasure or Barthes's *jouissance*. Having a good cry represents the potential for the disempowered to negotiate the difficult terrain between resistance and involvement.

Notes

1. Gerald Early, '*The Color Purple* as everybody's protest art', *The Antioch Review*, 44, 3 (Summer 1986), p. 264.
2. Laura Mulvey, 'Notes on Sirk and Melodrama', in Christine Gledhill (ed.), *Home is Where the Heart Is: Studies in Melodrama and the Woman's Film* (London: BFI, 1987), pp. 75–9.
3. Ibid., p. 79.

4. Jane Feuer, 'Melodrama, Serial Form and Television Today', *Screen*, 25, 1, pp. 4–16.
5. Tanya Modleski, 'Time and Desire in the Woman's Film', in Gledhill, op. cit., pp. 331–3.
6. E. Ann Kaplan, 'Mothering, Feminism, and Representation', in Gledhill, op. cit., pp. 131–5.
7. Jane Tompkins, 'Sentimental Power: *Uncle Tom's Cabin* and the Politics of Literary History,' in Elaine Showalter (ed.) *The New Feminist Criticism: Essays on Women, Literature and Theory* (New York: Pantheon, 1985), p. 83.
8. For example, after a sympathetic reading of *Stella Dallas*'s identificatory power, Linda Williams champions the film based on the excessiveness of Stanwyck's performance and the resulting female viewer recognition of the impossibility of female 'representation under patriarchal structures of voyeuristic and fetishistic viewing'. See Linda Williams, 'Something Else Besides a Mother', in Gledhill, op. cit., p. 318.
9. Valerie Babb, '*The Color Purple*: Writing to Undo What Writing has Done', *Phylon*, 47, 2 (Summer 1986), pp. 107–16; Henry Louis Gates, 'Color Me Zora: Alice Walker's (Re)Writing of the Speakerly Text', in *Intertextuality and Contemporary American Fiction* (Baltimore: Johns Hopkins University Press, 1989), pp. 144–167; Lindsey Tucker, 'Alice Walker's *The Color Purple*: Emergent Woman, Emergent Text', *Black American Literature Forum*, 22, 1 (Spring 1988), pp. 81–95; and Wendy Hall, 'Lettered Bodies and Corporeal Texts in *The Color Purple*', *American Fiction*, 16 (Spring 1988), pp. 83–97.
10. For examples, see Fred Bruning, 'When E.T. Goes to Georgia', *Maclean's* (24 March 1986), p. 9; *The New Yorker*, 61 (30 December 1985), pp. 68–70; Richard Combs, 'Great Expectations', *Sight and Sound*, vol. 55, no. 2, (1986), pp. 135–6; and Richard Blake, 'Survivors', *America* (1 February 1986), p. 75.
11. Jacqueline Bobo, '*The Color Purple*: Black Women as Cultural Readers', in E. Deidre Pribram (ed.), *Female Spectators: Looking at Film and Television* (London: Verso, 1988), p. 93.
12. Suzanne Clark, *Sentimental Modernism: Women Writers and the Revolution of the Word* (Bloomington: Indiana University Press, 1991), p. 11.
13. Christine Gledhill, 'The Melodramatic Field: An Investigation', in Gledhill, op. cit., p. 12.
14. Manthia Diawara, 'Black Spectatorship: Problems of Identification and Resistance', *Screen*, 29, 4 (Autumn 1988), pp. 67–77; and Jane Gaines, 'White Privilege and Looking Relations: Race and Gender in Feminist Film Theory', *Screen*, 29, 4 (Autumn 1988), pp. 12–25.
15. Gaines, op. cit., p. 14.
16. Gayatri Spivak, 'Three Women's Texts and a Critique of Imperialism', in Catherine Belsey and Jane Moore (eds), *The Feminist Reader: Essays in Gender and Politics of Literary Criticism* (New York: Blackwell's, 1989), p. 175.
17. Pascal Bruckner, *The Tears of the White Man: Compassion as Contempt*, trans. William R. Beer (New York: Free Press, 1986), pp. 1–147.
18. Fredric Jameson, *The Political Unconscious* (Ithaca: Cornell University Press, 1981), p. 286.
19. Patrocinio Schweickart, 'Reading Ourselves – Towards a Feminist Theory of Reading', in Robyn Warhol and Diane Proce Herndl (eds), *Feminisms* (New Brunswick: Rutgers University Press, 1991), pp. 525–50.
20. Ibid, p. 72.
21. Valerie Smith, *Self-Discovery and Authority in Afro-American Narrative* (Cambridge, Mass.: Harvard University Press, 1987), p. 41.

22. Henry Louis Gates, *Figures in Black: Words, Signs and the 'Racial' Self* (New York: Oxford University Press, 1988), pp. 125–63.
23. Gaines, op. cit., p. 6.
24. Jacqueline Bobo, op. cit., p. 93.
25. Sacvan Bercovitch, *The American Jeremiad* (Madison: University of Wisconsin Press, 1978), p. xi.
26. Jameson, op. cit., p. 281.
27. Diawara makes a similar case for what he calls the African–American 'resisting spectator' in 'Black Spectatorship', p. 68. But I differ from him only in that he does not discuss either the divided identification of black women in the case of *The Color Purple* or other cases of resistance, such as women. Alison Light addresses the racial conflict for feminist readers in 'Fear of the Happy Ending: *The Color Purple*, Reading and Racism', in Michael Green (ed.), *Broadening the Context* (London: John Murray, 1987), pp. 103–17.

REALIST MELODRAMA AND THE AFRICAN–AMERICAN FAMILY

Billy Woodberry's Bless Their Little Hearts

CHUCK KLEINHANS

In the aftermath of the Los Angeles Rebellion of 1992, Billy Woodberry's film *Bless Their Little Hearts* of a decade earlier stands as one of the most compelling recent works presenting the dynamics of African–American consciousness. This study of a family facing the economic, social and personal realities of unemployment in the Los Angeles black community shows the private sphere, the domestic side of the public events which erupted in an explosive contest with state power and authority and an assault on commercial property following the acquittal of the police accused of beating Rodney King.

I want to use this film as a reference point for discussing realist melodrama, a film and theatrical form which has been frequently attacked, dismissed, and ignored in recent years. Considered hopelessly bound to the 'monstrous delusion' of realism, to use Peter Wollen's phrase,[1] by proponents of a Brechtian aesthetic, hopelessly old-fashioned by adherents of avant-garde narrative, and forgotten by post-modernists, realist melodrama nevertheless remains one of the perennially popular forms used by artists seeking to depict the unrepresented and misrepresented. Why is this so? The all-too-easy answer is that such dramatists, film- and videomakers naively believe in the power of realism and uncritically accept the narrative logic of melodrama. I find that answer itself naive, however, for it ignores certain demonstrable powers and appeals of the form.

First, a few clarifications. *Bless Their Little Hearts* is a black and white feature film made from a script by Charles Burnett, who is also the film's cinematographer. Burnett is the writer and director of the independent narratives *Killer of Sheep* and *My Brother's Wedding*, and the Hollywood feature *To Sleep With Anger*. *Bless Their Little Hearts* appeared in 1983 at the end of a first wave of new independent film-making in Los Angeles by African–Americans, a movement characterised by critic Clyde Taylor as the 'LA Rebellion'.[2] This aesthetic rebellion against the conventional presentation of African–Americans by Hollywood was influenced by UCLA professor Teshome Gabriel who lectured on, presented, and wrote about Third Cinema in the Third World (in his book of that title), and it produced important films by Haile Gerima, Charles Burnett, Julie Dash, Alile

157

Sharon Larkin, Ben Caldwell, and Larry Clark. Woodberry is also a UCLA graduate and *Bless Their Little Hearts* was his master's degree project. I find the film one of the most accomplished of this group of fascinating and important works.

In summary, the story covers several months in the life of a family, centring on the father, Charlie. Recently unemployed, he finds casual work but no steady job. His wife, Andais, exhausted from her own job, domestic chores, and coping with the reduced income, avoids his sexual advances. Charlie takes up with another woman, but when she demands more time, money and responsibility from him, the affair ends. He returns home to what becomes the film's most highly charged scene: a ten-minute quarrel in a small kitchen filmed with a hand-held continuous wide-angle shot. Charlie later goes fishing and realises that he could sell the fish, and with his buddies does so, hawking them at the roadside, but at the film's end he walks away, providing his answer to the moment of moral decision that he described early in the film: at a certain point in life one has to choose between the material and the spiritual.

Second, I want to narrow the broad term 'melodrama' for this discussion. I see melodrama as a protean form, occupying many different spaces at different times. Without denying recent reminders of the action/adventure/sensation tradition of the form, I am particularly concerned here with the domestic melodrama tradition of the bourgeois era, which has a fairly coherent historical and social existence. In this context, melodrama finds a long and varied expression in paying attention to and validating the significance of personal, familial, and workgroup social relations. Descended from the French *drame* of the 18th century, beginning with Diderot's *Le Père*, the domestic melodrama, while robbed of the awesome destiny of classical and neo-classical tragedy, finds its viewer's fascination in the changing dynamics of human relationships on the everyday scale and with (relatively) ordinary people. As I have argued elsewhere it operates on the unresolved and unresolvable tension between a capitalist society on the one hand and personal and familiar needs and aspirations on the other.[3]

Third, I want to clarify my understanding of the term 'realism'. Realism has a bad name today for some good reasons and a few bad ones. Certainly the current critical catechism with its repeated formula that everything is constructed within discourse, culture, and ideology seems to dismiss the animating base of a realist aesthetic and epistemology. I hardly want to go back to a traditional left politics or aesthetics to justify realism, but the post-structural/post-modernist spin on realism itself contains a certain naiveté and problem which is that it cannot explain the undeniable power of realism except as a 'monstrous delusion' perpetrated by an insidious culture industry, or, in a more whimsical version, as a familiar pleasure, a set of codes producing a happy consciousness.

From such positions it is impossible to see that highly conscious, theoretically knowledgeable, politically critical artists might actually choose realism as an aesthetic strategy (one of many) in order to achieve certain results that cannot be attained by other strategies which themselves have their own limitations. I am thinking here of choices such as the Brecht–Godardian counter-cinema, the avant-garde New Narrative, the punk and post-punk transgression, the post-modern parody and pastiche, the slickly commercial, and so forth. That each of these strategies has potentials and liabilities, that each of them should be or could be part of the repertoire of the culturally current master artist, is a post-modern insight that not all have yet attained.

Bless Their Little Hearts uses various conventional codes of realism in the general style of Italian neo-realism: black and white cinematography, frequent and noticeable use of hand-held camera in location shooting, actual locations, lighting which approximates the location's given illumination, depiction of ordinary characters in ordinary settings, speech marked by dialect, some unprofessional actors, 'unpleasant' topics, and working-class as opposed to middle-class life. It also makes a number of innovations, and we could use these to claim that the film goes beyond the 'referential illusion', to use Barthes's phrase for the discourse of realism. We find frequent use of low camera positions, often approximating that of a child's view, especially in the interiors, as well as static shots held for a significant amount of time after the key action has taken place, resulting in an emphasis on duration and space within the shot (in interviews, cinematographer Burnett has expressed his interest in Ozu). Such techniques complement and extend the realism, but in a way which veers away from conventional shot and editing rhythms. They vary drastically from the norms of classical Hollywood cinema taken as a dominant form of realism, and they also vary from the conventions of Italian neo-realism or British realism. Thus, depending on the viewer's familiarity with codes and adeptness at code-switching, they may be taken as even more 'realistic' (that is, closer to the existing nature of the referent) in foregrounding temporal and spatial matters.

In addition, the film has certain markers of independent, very low-budget, dramatic film-making: some shots are included which are technically flawed, probably in the lab processing, and some of the voicetrack audio is so low that lines are lost. In addition, since no credits are given for the music, one suspects that existing recorded music was used but that rights were not cleared, another typical characteristic of independent low-budget work.[4] To some extent these markers also help to situate the film within the realist mode since they are also familiar to viewers of similar realistic coded works.

All of this fits the close observation of everyday detail in visuals, speech and character actions that remain central to a realist aesthetic. At the same time, it is important to distinguish this use of realism from that version of realism which pushes to a naturalist position. Using many of the same techniques, naturalism proceeds in a steadily, inexorably downward narrative movement, towards stasis and inevitability at the end. Naturalism has been so often maligned by the political right and left and by commercial and avant-garde sectors that we may actually forget its political basis and its current variant manifestations. Of its politics, Bertolt Brecht pointed out that naturalism has a progressive aspect in that it shows that something is profoundly wrong with society, although it cannot provide any insight or perspective on how those problems might change or be changed.[5] Because it effectively evacuates human agency or portrays collective action as finally futile, naturalism comes to a static end-game. In terms of its current versions, I can mention Chantal Akermann's film, *Jeanne Dielmann, 23 rue de commerce,* as a perfect modernist example of naturalist melodrama with a *coup de théâtre* ending.

At moments *Bless Their Little Hearts* could be taken as naturalist, and critic Edward Guerrero gives the film's ending such a reading:

> By the film's close, [Charlie] has replaced his version of dominant ideology, that of middle-class optimism and mobility through individual effort, with its underclass counterpoint, an outlook by which he perceives himself as socially worthless, economically discarded, and psychically defeated.[6]

The clearest statement that the film's dramatic dilemma is due to externals that inexorably wear down the protagonists takes place during the husband–wife quarrel. The fight is based in the double bind of the wife's repeated statement that she is tired of the current situation brought on by unemployment and underemployment and the husband's claim that he cannot make 'the Man' give him a job. Clearly the external situation is the determinant one in the last instance, a point made lyrically in a sequence of Charlie after a casual job clearing weeds from vacant land. As he rides home in a pick-up truck, industrial buildings move past him. One privileged shot shows a half-demolished factory, itself the symbol of an industrial economy in decay, and the emphatic point of the visual sequence which shows his exclusion from relatively well-paying factory work.[7] On the soundtrack we hear a woman singing a blues song: 'Lost in a dream/And I just can't find my way'.

However, the film does not present a consistent downward movement. Some individual episodes reverse the expectation. For example, when Charlie shaves one morning, he looks in the mirror in a conventional narrative symbolisation of self-examination, self-searching. He then completes the cleaning ritual by turning off the water taps (see A). The degree of his frustration is expressed in the force of the closing. His older daughter then enters to wash and, finding the taps impossible to open, gets a huge wrench and lightly hits on the handles to open them. The moment is comic and telling, for here and elsewhere the children function as those who must fit 'in between' the parents' frustrations and stresses. Here they do so successfully, though at many other points it is clear that they end up mimicking the parents' behaviours, and often the most destructive parts.

Bless Their Little Hearts also maintains the dialectical form of realist narration, as opposed to the negative determinism of naturalism, by use of socially significant gesture and detail. In one such moment Angie, the oldest daughter, perhaps nine, helps prepare dinner. She carefully places large potatoes in the oven to bake (see B) and secures the door with a piece of wire. The details are significant in context: mother asleep after work; father out of the house; potatoes an inexpensive but filling carbohydrate; baking them a preparation a child can master; her labour is part of what children in poor families must contribute to domestic work. Finally, the

160

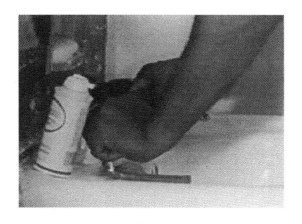

Film stills A–C from *Bless Their Little Hearts*
(Billy Woodberry, 1982)

wire is also telling. This is a family who must use an old stove with a broken door catch and then cope with a serviceable if inelegant repair. In a more extended narrative scene Charlie is shown painting his graffiti-covered garage (see C). He proceeds methodically and one senses the purposefulness of the work and the self-satisfaction at the end of the job. Thus both his willingness to work and pride in accomplishment is demonstrated, underlining the source of his unemployment as the economic structure rather than personal traits.

By placing the quarrel, the deepest moment of crisis, two-thirds into the film, the subsequent episodes serve to redeem the pessimism. Fishing, like the earlier garage painting, is shown as a lyrical moment of self-directed accomplishment. In a key moment, after his daughter has suffered a broken arm (the specific event is not clear, but Charlie's speech at that point makes it clear that he attributes the cause to their neighbourhood), Charlie apologises that he cannot make enough money to have the family live in a better place and breaks down crying. This display of the injury to his pride and exhibition of his frustration provides a cathartic moment which re-establishes the family bonding with children and wife (who comforts him).

The momentum of realism in *Bless Their Little Hearts* is tempered by the dynamics of melodrama. The protagonist's moral decision is frankly indicated at the very beginning when Charlie tells his friends, who casually talk about robbery as a potential source of income, that one must choose between the spiritual and the material (see D). The open expression of emotion and the narrative's repeated presentation of the masculine crisis re-contexted through the effects on the wife and children allows for a greater understanding of family dynamics. The family drama is clear in *Bless Their Little Hearts*, but is also presented as a dilemma. At the end, Charlie sees his friends' antics in trying to stop cars as playing the fool.[8] His choice to reject the pursuit of materialism which turns man into a buffoon is clearly the right thing, but what decisions the rest of the family makes are not examined with the same attention. Because Kaycee Moor who plays Andais, the wife, is the actor with the most screen presence in the film, her character is strong and convincing, but her psychology is barely sketched in. The moral choice is privileged with the husband.

These too are the marks of melodrama: a drama of clear moral choices, appeals to morality and sentiment, the potential pathos of seeing the effects of bad actions on innocent children and defenceless women, a clearly marked villain (the Man), a reconciliation and endorsement of the family, episodic construction, emphasis on emotional moments over narrative explanation, and so forth. Why, then, to return to my earlier question, would some artists choose to use this dramatic form when it seems so quickly dated and artificial and even dishonest when we look at examples from the past? I think the answer is, first, that melodrama is usually so strongly time-bound to its own moment of production because it uses the social commonplaces of its current time as an unthinking referential and moral norm in a way that is both its power and its liability. Second, in extension, it is useful for the dramatic artist precisely because it articulates those social commonplaces so well, so 'naturally' in its construction,

162

Film stills D–E from *Bless Their Little Hearts*
(Billy Woodberry, 1982)

that it gains a profound psychological resonance in the audience of its own time, especially when reinforced by depictions of the audience's own class, gender and ethnicity. It works on the power of recognition and in two ways: in its realist dimension it provides recognition of the familiar, the everyday, the otherwise taken-for-granted, and in its emotional dimension it validates the frequently experienced as well as what is emotionally desirable, but sometimes unattainable. It is gratifying to see that Charlie will do the right thing and leave his friends' materialism behind. It is gratifying to see that a husband's sexual wandering will be set right. It is gratifying to see that a man can cry in front of his family to express and relieve his humiliation.

This realist melodrama form avoids irony and self-reflection. It cannot claim the sophistication of playing stylisation against content to achieve the ironic distanciation claimed for Sirk, for example, but in its plain frankness, in its direct validation of the everyday and everyday desires, it speaks powerfully and directly of that which is unrepresented, misrepresented, and underrepresented in the dominant culture's depiction of the exploited. The film indicates that Charlie must make a moral decision, one that may go against his immediate desires, to bring money home for the family. In this way the film's moral standard, its authorial voice, speaks across to Charlie as an equal, not down to him as a victim. We are not so very far here from the judgment we are asked to pass on Mother Courage.

My understanding of the film differs significantly from Guerrero's analysis. While we agree on the film's value and achievement, Guerrero reads the film as a pessimistic, naturalist story focusing on the theme of African–American manhood as expressed by the character Charlie: 'Woodberry's film relentlessly unfolds to explore a spectrum of shrinking possibilities, foreclosed options and futile actions, occurring between the poles of the ideal and the material, that by the film's end prove Charlie wrong.'[9] Drawing on an analysis of the film as very close in style and spirit to the Italian neo-realist classic *Bicycle Thieves* as centrally presenting the dilemma of, respectively, the working-class and poor African–American male, and drawing on Fredric Jameson's Marxist discussion of the 'political unconscious' in works of narrative art, Guerrero draws a strong conclusion:

> Of course we've seen these black men warehoused on all the corners and vacant lots of America's inner cities and ghettos. That's the familiar. The art of Woodberry's film resides in the fact that by the time of its conclusion, we can no longer deny that we understand how these discarded, black men have come to be at such a hellish, desolate location. For the entire narrative is a crafted irruption of the socially and politically repressed leading out thoughts and emotions in this direction until, finally, we have been forced to see things differently.[10]

I agree with Guerrero that the film does this, but I think it also does more. I find that it functions like *Bicycle Thieves'* ending which affirms the strength of the human spirit, an argument most eloquently developed about De Sica's film by André Bazin.[11]

Of course, Bazin's argument can be extended to a declaration of political quietism: ground down and defeated in the material world, the character triumphs in spiritual consciousness. In the case of *Bless Their Little Hearts*, however, I find that the film expresses the same type of dialectic as the blues. While on the surface about misfortune and hard times in love or life, the blues always also expresses the singer's strength in the face of adversity. The end of Woodberry's film is not a triumph of the spiritual, but simply a coming to terms with life. Charlie has learned, he is stronger, he has his dignity; he does not sell his manhood into the bondage of demeaning public behaviour to make some money. Furthermore, taking a larger narrative view, by looking at the family, at the wife and children, at the domestic space as a counterpoint to the realist drama of men in public space, we can see the film as even richer in its presentation. From the opening shots of Charlie in the unemployment office while 'Nobody Knows You (When You're Down and Out)' plays on the soundtrack, to the final shots with Charlie returning home, where people do know him in all his weakness and strength, the film sings the affirmation of a blues discourse while also depicting the sorrows of South Central Los Angeles life.

Realist melodrama has a recurrent appeal to artists seeking to construct dramatic narratives about and for the oppressed. It has been frequently noted that Italian neo-realism can be easily seen as the dominant style influencing the New Latin American Cinema,[12] and specific examples, such as *Portrait of Teresa* (Cuba, 1979, directed by Pastor Vega), confirm the persistence of the melodramatic form. While it would be foolish to ignore the artistic and political limits of realist melodrama, it would be equally foolish to ignore the potentials. For communities for whom the family in various forms is a basic unit of survival, and yet also a focal point of distress caused by outside forces, realist melodrama provides an often acute political discourse. Caught in a contradiction that does not go away, oscillating between the family as 'haven in a heartless world', and families as 'worlds of pain',[13] realist melodrama can speak profoundly about and to people struggling against capitalism's destruction of human values.

My thanks are due to Billy Woodberry, Charles Burnett, Julia Lesage, John Hess, Angela Martin, JoAnn Elam, Joe Hendrix, Zeinabu Irene Davis, and Christine Gledhill.

The film is available (on videotape) from Billy Woodberry, 1607 S. Shenandoah, Los Angeles CA 90035; phone 213–205–0929.

Notes

1. Peter Wollen, *Signs and Meaning in the Cinema* (London: Secker & Warburg, 1971; Bloomington: Indiana University Press, 1972), p. 166.
2. Taylor used the phrase to label a January 1986 'New American Film-makers Series' he guest curated at the Whitney Museum of American Art, New York. The programme notes were reprinted: 'The LA Rebellion: A Turning Point in Black Cinema', *Black Film Review*, Spring 1986, pp. 4, 29. Taylor provides a useful survey in 'Decolonizing the Image: New US Black Cinema,' in Peter Steven (ed.), *Jump Cut: Hollywood, Politics and Counter-Cinema* (London: BFI, 1985).
3. Chuck Kleinhans, 'Notes on Melodrama and the Family under Capitalism', *Film Reader*, 3, 1978.
4. Without copyright permissions such films can still be easily shown in media art centres, festivals, and classroom screenings. However, for TV broadcast or commercial distribution, fees must be paid and music cleared. The most predominant music track is a saxophone and piano; the sax is played in the style of Sonny Criss, the late LA-based musician.
5. Brecht, quoted by Lee Baxandall, 'Brecht in America, 1935', *TDR: The Drama Review*, vol. 12, no. 1, Fall 1967, p. 84.
6. Edward Guerrero, 'Negotiations of Ideology, Manhood, and Family in Billy Woodberry's *Bless Their Little Hearts*', *Black American Literature Forum*, vol. 25, no. 2, Summer 1991, p. 316.
7. For a concise discussion of the Los Angeles economy and its impact on the African–American community, see Mike Davis, 'The LA Inferno', *Socialist*

Review, vol. 22, no. 1, Jan.–Mar., 1992, pp. 57–80. Davis's book-length study, *City of Quartz: Excavating the Future in Los Angeles* (New York: Random House, Vintage, 1992) provides the full context. Also of interest are Edward W. Soja's two chapters on Los Angeles in his *Post-modern Geographies: The Reassertion of Space in Critical Social Theory* (London: Verso, 1989).

8.   This is the most speculative part of my interpretation. There is no evidence in the dialogue that explains the character's action. Guerrero interprets this action as Charlie seeing himself as worthless and defeated. I read it as marking the moment of moral choice and coming to a new level of awareness and a return to his home, his family. I also differ from Guerrero on Charlie's history: I find dialogue that indicates that his unemployment is relatively recent, while Guerrero cites dialogue to conclude that it has lasted ten years. I see the film as strongly marked by Charles Burnett's screenplay, and I interpret it in relation to Burnett's other films as, for example, in the themes of sleeping and dreaming and the brief vignettes in neighbourhood locations.

9.   Guerrero, op. cit., p. 316.

10. Ibid., p. 321.

11. André Bazin, 'Bicycle Thief', in *What is Cinema?*, vol. 2, trans. Hugh Gray (Berkeley: University of California Press, 1971).

12. For a useful article outlining similarities and decisive differences, see John Hess, 'Neo-realism and the New Latin American Cinema: '*Bicycle Thieves* and *Blood of the Condor*', in Manuel Alvarado, John King and Ana Lopez (eds.), *1492–1992: Mediating Two Worlds* (London: BFI, 1993).

13. Christopher Lasch, *Haven in a Heartless World: The Family Besieged* (New York: Basic Books, 1977); Lillian Breslow Rubin, *Worlds of Pain: Life in the Working-Class Family* (New York: Basic Books, 1976).

SOCIETY AND SUBJECTIVITY

On the Political Economy of Chinese Melodrama

NICK BROWNE

A study of film-making in the People's Republic of China will, almost inevitably, take as its starting-point the figuration of the relation of the character ('the self') to the social space in which it moves. The assumption that this dramatic relation is also, at bottom, an ideological formation is evident in contemporary Chinese cinema through the continuity with and conflict between the pre-Liberation traditions of Confucianism and the post-Liberation ideologies of socialism, a continuity and conflict that turns on the relations among the 'self', the family, the workplace, and the State, the fundamental and constituting terms of any image of the social totality. Starting from these premises, this paper argues that the most complex and compelling popular film form that embodies the negotiation between the traditional ethical system and the new State ideology, one that articulates the range and force of the emotional contradictions between them, is what is known in the West as 'melodrama'. As this category is not part of the Chinese genre system, its use entails a shift of cultural perspective.[1]

The Western critical legacy of melodrama in literature and film is complex and contradictory in its theoretical formulation of the affective foundations of subjectivity. For Elsaesser, melodrama is the representation of the subjectivity of the European bourgeoisie in its struggle against the authority of a declining feudalist system.[2] That is, melodrama is a passionate meditation on the historical experience of bourgeois subjection to the economic authority of the *ancien régime*, an account of action and subjectivity in the social formation from the standpoint of loss and from the point of view of its victims. This representation of historical victimisation as a social catastrophe is registered by narrativising the subjective and ethical aspect of the drama within an economic interpretation of class relations and by viewing the story's individual protagonist as an overdetermined ideological figure. The shape of the story underscores a fate of suffering and of eventual social insistence on reconciliation through conformity that locates this sentimental drama and its protagonist within an ultimately oppressive social order.

The main alternative to Elsaesser's understanding of melodrama emerges from Peter Brooks's psychoanalytic account of the melodramatic

167

imagination.³ On this account, 'melodrama' is founded in the attempt, following the French Revolution, to institute in the Republic a morality founded on an ethical imperative centred around a new and troubled figuration of the self in its relation to the unconscious. Melodrama is a theatre of social misfortune in which personal virtue is contested, hidden, misrecognised, or subverted, a form of theatre that seeks within the confining and largely recalcitrant parameters of the old society to restore and recentre the ethical imperatives required of the bourgeois age. The personification of innocence and villainy constitute the dramatisation of the democratic reverberations of a newly emergent, post-traditional mode of romantic individuality. In this, melodrama is a *mise en scène* whose system of figuration is caught between restoration and reform. For Wylie Sypher, melodrama, seen from a political point of view, is the characteristic form of nineteenth-century bourgeois aesthetic thought that marks out the impasses and the paralysis of Western revolutionary programmes and aspirations, informing even the theatrical metaphors and schemes of Marx's *Kapital*.⁴

For contemporary film studies, melodrama indicates a site of ideological critique centred on the representation of sexual difference.⁵ Its logic as an aesthetic ideology is founded on the contradiction between a potentially transgressive feminine sexuality and a social system that seeks to delimit and contain it. As a transcription of the tragic into the domestic order, melodrama exemplifies the instability of the ideology of private life under capitalism and, from women's perspective, the domains of affect and action within the nuclear family. The dominant explication of the conflict of law and desire is founded on the psychoanalytic paradigm of the (white) bourgeois patriarchal family. The 'social' itself (the workplace, politics) enters the familial configurations of subjectivity through the mediation of the father. The specifically aesthetic impasse of melodrama, and to a certain extent the limitation of its critique, consists of the form's failure to constitute the family in a clear or comprehensive relation to the larger social formation.

From a feminist perspective, melodrama is a dominant mode of mass culture and the site of the central contradictions of patriarchy. Owing to the centrality of its figuration of women's experience, it has been the chosen ground for the delineation of the affective stakes of social constraint and transgression. In the USA, Hollywood melodrama's aesthetic ideology, as distinct from the strongly marked class oppositions characteristic of its European prototypes, reflects the democratising of its cultural scope and generic meaning.

Even with certain ambiguous precedents, the translocation of the critical/aesthetic category of 'melodrama' from its Western inscription to a contemporary Chinese context is hardly unproblematic. On what basis can an aesthetic ideology so embedded in the popular entertainment forms of Western culture – Christian and capitalist – be treated as sigificant, culturally speaking, to the form and meaning of contemporary Chinese film? Strictly speaking, the Chinese system of genre classification and its categories are incommensurable with the Western system. The comparability of critical terms like 'genre' is not simply a question of formal similarity, but one related to recognising both significant similarities and differences in literary *and* cultural contexts.[6] It remains true, however, that important conventions, of both Chinese *spoken drama* and *butterfly fiction*, instances of popular, vernacular entertainment that influenced Chinese film-making in the early decades of the century, are arguably Western influenced.[7] Though the term 'melodrama' and 'family melodrama' have been used rather widely in the 80s in discussion of films from Hong Kong (to emphasise sacrifice for family order),[8] I am unaware of a general account of the cultural or critical genealogy of the term in relation to Chinese aesthetics.

Ma Ning's analysis of contemporary PRC cinema shows how what he calls 'melodrama' renegotiates the relation between tradition and modernisation in a narrative that introduces a justification for a new economic order, represents a transformation of power relations within the family order, and shows this change from the vantage point of an established power structure. This social order, he argues, is ultimately subordinated to the system of hierarchy and patronage that supports the political power of patriarchal socialism and its new, ideological imperatives.[9] The constitution of the family drama calls on a system of family ethics that serves in turn the project of ideological legitimation. Nevertheless, a depiction of the designated conflicts within the family does not, it seems to me, constitute in a sufficiently clear way the melodramatic problematic as it has been enacted in Western cultures. The 'other' can be reduced to the 'same' only at a price. That is, though important elements associated with Western melodrama are present in films in the PRC, these films do not exemplify its distinctive, constitutive features – the form's schematisation of good and evil, its emotional effects, its mode of theatricality and spectacle, its mode of characterising the individual as victim, and its mode of understanding the relation of the individual to the social as a matter of justice. At best, the term 'melodrama' indicates a rough critical analogy.

I express this reservation about the relevance of Western melodrama to an accounting of Chinese film forms for several reasons: in order to motivate a move towards a more specific account of the constitution, function and interpretation of these forms as works functioning within the culture in which they originate; to qualify the colonising power and domination of Western critical theory for an accounting of the specificity of Chinese film and culture; and, within the discipline of film studies, to work towards a new model of figuring melodramatic structure and affect in the Western context, through an alternative to its familial focus, namely through the juridical. To the extent that the Western theory of melodrama has privileged the nuclear family and its psychoanalytic account of the private sphere of 'sexual difference' and 'subjectivity', it has lost sight of the broader social conditions of the meaning of the form. I want to proceed, in other words, on the premise that what has been called the genre of Chinese 'family melodrama' is neither a true analogy nor the exclusive site for the expression of what we might call the 'melodramatic mode'. Cross-cultural exchange and interpretation of what is meant by 'melodrama' may be elaborated by considering the form of what I shall call 'political melodrama' as it is dramatised in the work of the Chinese film director

Xie Jin. In this way, we might treat 'melodrama' as an expression of a mode of injustice whose *mise en scène* is precisely the nexus between public and private life, a mode in which gender as a mark of difference is a limited, mobile term activated by distinctive social powers and historical circumstances.

The political melodrama that I want to consider is best exemplified in Xie Jin's films focused on the figure of the rightist, and concern the nature of his crime, punishment, and the process of political rehabilitation. In the 80s, this thematic is an authorial preoccupation in *The Herdsman (Muma ren,* 1982), *The Legend of Tianyan Mountain (Tianyunshen chuanchi,* 1980), and *Hibiscus Town (Furong zhen,* 1986). Indeed, *Hibiscus Town* addresses the emotional complexity of the central ideological question of the post-Cultural Revolution era: the place accorded to individual entrepreneurship within the socialist order.

Hibiscus Town tells how a young woman laboriously and diligently builds up a small business (a tofu restaurant), and is then denounced by the local party leader jealous of her excessive income. She loses her business, her house and her husband (who is persecuted to death), suffers years of ostracism, becomes sick and slides into despair, falls in love with a fellow street cleaner (an old rightist who cares for her), becomes pregnant, is illegally married, is judged and condemned again by the party (it isolates her and imprisons her new husband), and bears the illegitimate child. At the end of the Cultural Revolution she has her second husband, home and business restored to her. The 'text' of *Hibiscus Town* narrativises these events through a sexual, economic and political description of the organisation of the society of a small Chinese rural town from 1963 to 1979. The film centrally dramatises the relation between 'subjectivity' (self) and society as it is organised and mediated by the Communist Party.

At the very outset of the film, the population of Hibiscus Town consists of three groups: the 'people', the 'bad elements', and the party. The action proper begins with the arrival of local Party Secretary Li, a woman, under the banner of 'class struggle', and the initiation of her investigation of Hu, the small restaurateur. The latter is building a new house with her business profits on land bought from a local party official, Wang, a land-reform expert, who lives elsewhere in a dilapidated section at the edge of town. Party Secretary Li's investigation moves forward with a public accusation of Hu's 'illegal' self-enrichment (realised, it is alleged, through favourable terms she had negotiated with the local manager of the State's granary stores). The State confiscates Hu's property, condemns her as a 'bad element', 'a newly rich peasant', and sets her to work cleaning the town streets. Three years later, with the onset of the Cultural Revolution, Secretary Li is herself stigmatised as a slut (she protests, saying she is a 'leftist') and is publicly humiliated. In 1979, with the close of the Cultural Revolution, Secretary Li returns to the town to carry on Communist politics.

In posing the question of how, fifteen years after the founding of the Socialist Republic, hard work leading to the purchase of a house can be regarded as a crime, the film points quite directly to the contradictory ideology and practices of socialism in the reform years. Indeed, the film's complexity consists of the fact that the sexual, economic and political systems that compose this social network are almost completely imbricated and intermixed. Notwithstanding this, the film is organised around distinctive binarisms, identified and labelled as 'rightist' and 'leftist'.

Most importantly, these political categories (which are also economic categories) intersect with moral categories. That is, in the film's principal reversal, the moral perspective contradicts the long-standing correspondence of 'left' with 'good' and 'right' with 'bad'. Indeed, the film inverts the dogmatic formula of the 50s in which the party leaders come to the small village and liberate the people from an oppressive feudalism by dissolving the forced marriage contracts that serve as the quintessential emblem of feudal patriarchy. *Hibiscus Town* inverts this formula by showing that the party system of population control through classification by type leads to persecution and criminalisation of a marriage between two persons freely choosing each other outside the authority of the party. In *Hibiscus Town* the agents of the party are designated as oppressors.

The personification of the moral and sexual conflict between 'right' and 'left' is realised in a dramatic comparison between two women, Secretary Li and New Rich Peasant Hu. Each woman is authoritative in her own sphere of work. Hu, the younger, is married both at the beginning of the film and at the end; Li is older, more severe, and unmarried throughout. Li's political comrade and lover Wang is a boastful, self-important toady, imperious in his own sphere, but wholly subordinated to her power. The

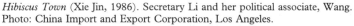

Hibiscus Town (Xie Jin, 1986). Secretary Li and her political associate, Wang.
Photo: China Import and Export Corporation, Los Angeles.

171

Hibiscus Town (Xie Jin, 1986). New rich peasant Hu and husband.
Photo: China Import and Export Corporation, Los Angeles

film's evident inversions of traditionally subordinated power relations between women and men underscore and thematise male masochism.

In conjunction with the moral evaluation of political positions is a moral evaluation of sexual relations. In this way, the personal and sexual characteristics of the two leading women contribute to an understanding of the legitimacy, and even the rectitude, of their political status. In one central difference – not of gender but of politics – the film points up the superiority of Confucian morality over socialist pragmatism; that is, the ethical perspective at work in the film contends with the political system.

The narrative of *Hibiscus Town* is organised around three major clusters of events that can be summarised as crime, punishment and restitution. Hu's trajectory through the film marks them out: the allegation of criminal self-enrichment through the sale of State property; her punishment and suffering through the loss of business, house and husband; and the restitution and restoration of her home, a new husband (for the dead one), and, in addition, the birth of a son. The film supplies a quite detailed and comprehensive literal accounting of the economic foundations of Hu's tofu business that includes the cost of raw materials, gross sales, and so forth. Indeed, her product is explicitly analysed as a commodity. The fact that the business is part of the food cycle puts the enterprise in close proximity to a biological understanding of the requirements of maintenance of life. Indeed, attention to food – both its lack and its abundance, its necessity and its symbolism (as in the wedding feast) – grounds this film, linking it to one of the dominant preoccupations of Chinese cinema and underlining its foundations in the representation of scarcity. This sequence of narrative events, then, is the figuration of a political interpretation of economic events: acquisition, loss, and return of objects of value (literal and symbolic).

Hibiscus Town shows a fundamental and strict understanding of the political economy of the social order: its modes and relations of production organising both goods and social relations, and, indeed, 'subjectivity' within the framework of the same system. The narrative intelligibility of this Chinese text as a system of signs is predicated not only on a series of motivated consequences, but also upon a system that correlates its objects with modes of subjectivity. In this sense, the political classification scheme is co-extensive with the order and hierarchy of the social body and serves as a mode of mapping that decides individual obligations and privileges. Social positions and subjectivity are named and determined by the political system; the party's political criteria provide a legal justification for the assignment of persons to social ranks. The film shows in methodical, narrative detail the deprivation of life and goods by a political machine that serves at the same time as a judicial apparatus.

In the Chinese political melodrama, the political process is narrativised as a trial that occupies the thematic centre in the way that the family conflict does in the family melodrama. Here, the drama arises from the Chinese institution of crime and punishment worked out through socialist culture. The film represents the party's action on the social body, but in the contemporary period a political perspective vies with and is contested by the ethical one. In this sense Xie Jin's narration and point of view include a perspective on the world of the characters that includes a historical critique. At stake in this form of melodrama is a definition of the self and the figuration of the relation of the individual to the social as a fully public matter. Melodrama is the mode of representation of a historical experience that inscribes 'subjectivity' in a position between the expectations of an ethical system (Confucianism) and the demands of a political system (socialism), a condition that typifies the Chinese dilemma of modernisation.[10] The form's principal significance is in the registration of the affective dimension of the self's relation to the social order, catalysing two affective regimes that are acted out in the narrative as intensified performances of betrayal, disappointment or defeat. Chinese melodrama's mode of arbitrating the relation of subjectivity and society is, in other words, a specific cultural formation.

Confucianism's traditional ethical doctrine linked the social body at all levels, modelling the responsibilities and duties of self, family and State on an analogical 'great chain of being'. Socialism has undertaken to remodel these relations without abandoning them, recruiting film as a State ideological apparatus for the representation of this new, ethical system and its corresponding prescriptions on subjectivity. In this sense, Xie Jin's films work quite explicitly to monitor and readjust these new ideological premises to old ethical standards, and, through a cultural critique of con-

173

tinuing anti-rightist violence, to explore the limits of the political administration of socialist justice. *Hibiscus Town* lays out the political process of justice – crime and punishment – but it also subjects that process to a kind of critique that puts politicisation itself on trial from an ethical standpoint. For its audience, the film takes the form of a kind of judicial hearing with its own rules of evidence and argument. The film, both as a narrative institution and as a critique of politics, mediates the relation of the audience to the abuses, disturbances and injustices of the real, continuing events of the Cultural Revolution.

In what way, we must ask, can the representation of the experience of Western capitalism viewed from a Christian perspective be analogous to the representation of the experience of contemporary Chinese socialism viewed from a Confucian perspective? The cultural specification of 'subjectivity' and of victimisation in melodrama implies, from the first, the concept of the 'person'. In the ethical and political writings of these two religious traditions, the treatment of the concept of 'person' is traceable to the difference between (Western) 'subjectivity' as the private, personal, and perspectival representation of a single mind and the (Chinese) definition of the person as a set of conventions, social relations, and transactions within the group (mind serving as the ground of social relatedness).[11] The Kantian foundation of ethics in individual responsibility defines the moral autonomy of the self as a matter of choice grounded in a universal faculty of reason beyond or above social convention. What grounds this personal ethical autonomy, legally speaking, is an acknowledgement of rights. Western individuality is treated as a freedom from social and governmental control, surveillance and the like, and hence individual autonomy is closely associated with the sphere of privacy. In its ideal form, the law guarantees and institutionalises these freedoms and rights.

In Chinese culture, traditional writings on Confucian individuality underscore the transitive obligations between subjective terms within a hierarchy that regards the person as a social function, a position placed within the five cardinal relations of domination and subordination that draws its meaning and its codes from hierarchically organised social practice, and not from the status of the person as an agent of free choice. This tradition of ethics as the co-operation of person and group as institutionalised by social practice is the basis of Confucian legal and administrative theory, a theory that posits human improvement through the exemplification of virtue and correction through education. Confucian legal doctrine[12] was elaborated over several centuries in conflict with an alternative, secular 'legalist' theory that called for equal treatment of all before a uniform law, and an ethical system backed up by rewards and punishments. Confucian ethics, on the other hand, was constituted almost entirely as a code regulating *hierarchical* social relations within and beyond the family. It was the basis of the legal theory in one fashion or another that was inherited by the Communist social administration. Legalist theory, however, with its democratic instincts and its doctrine of reform through punishment provided in some measure, I suppose, one of the intellectual resources for Communist administrative reform of Confucian feudalism.

174

We might ask, then, about the form of individualism implied in Xie Jin's political melodrama, and how it stands in relation to Chinese models of justice. Who are Xie Jin's characters? What is his mode of characterisation? First, the mapping of persons in the social field is done by designation of titles: Secretary Li, Director Gu, and so on. These are markers of official political status, positioning persons within the classificatory space of social hierarchy. The society understands the importance but also the superficiality of identity through this kind of symbolic positioning, and the posing of the problem of personal identity by the film is articulated around a cinematic topos constructed through distinguishing between the space of the house and the street. The spatial co-ordinates of personal identity are 'inside' and 'outside', 'home' and 'workplace'. Xie Jin's revisionist mode of socialist spatialisation, of construction of the lived relation person/environment, both deconstructs and institutes the frontier between private and public spaces and the equivalent distinction within the *mentalité* of the social subject. In this sense, the project of revising established conventions of socialist spatialisation (that is, there is *only* public space) seeks to locate the self both in the spaces of the house and of the street. In *Hibiscus Town* cinematic *découpage* articulates the revision of the political valence of space.

The main question and interest of the film, then, can be located in the problematic of the marginal characters, the social and political outsiders. What is the form of their social non-being? *Hibiscus Town* provides significant instances of the representation of the life of these outsiders. For a long time, one feels, they live in the streets. Indeed, in the long mid-section of the film that traces the development of Hu and Qin's relationship, exterior social space and its representation is transformed lyrically. Bodily movement of the work of sweeping becomes the dance of the courtship ritual. This part of the film opens on to a strangely isolated cultural space that is roughly divided in equal part between the street and Hu's room, between long shots of alleyways receding into the distance (largely bluish-grey in colour) that serve as the narrowed space of romantic choreography and the smallish rose-tinted scenes of the interior, nondescript private space in which the bed and the hearth are the most evident furnishings, the site of passion and its consummation. Outside this room, at the side of the door, are two posters announcing the place to the public as the residence of a 'black couple', that is, the place of the outsiders explicitly signed as a space apart is the space of a criminalised marriage. Thus, the space of the social outsider is, in a way, indifferent to the discrimination between house and street. At the same time, there is a single space of romance, of song, and, indeed, of sexual pleasure. This middle section of the film is composed through what we might think of as a romantic comedy centred around the formation of the transgressive couple.

Politically speaking, however, the spatialisation of this interlude is contradictory and paradoxical and stands as the film's central instance of a mode of subjectivity at the margin of official discourse. It is the space of unauthorised and, indeed, transgressive assertion of individual choice. It, alone, is the space abandoned to the private and is explicitly, I think, the 'space of human rights' as it might be understood in the West.

Hibiscus Town (Xie Jin, 1986). The outsiders in the Cultural Revolution.
Photo: China Import and Export Corporation, Los Angeles.

The theme of the rights of political outcasts to marry is repeated and underlined in Xie Jin's work in the 80s. In *Hibiscus Town*, with Hu's announcement to Qin that she is pregnant, the couple seek permission from the party authorities to marry. The request is received by Wang with astonishment at 'class enemies screwing on the sly!' and is refused. Qin protests that even members of the 'five bad elements' have the right to marry and have children. Qin's assertion of this right is assigned special status – differentiating the human as such. Marriage, however, requires legitimation by civil authority. Old Gu, formerly party secretary, observing that no one else would dare to attend the wedding of a 'black couple', performs this office. Subsequently, the couple are condemned by the Military Commission for 'threatening the dictatorship of the proletariat' and are sent to gaol. The space of romantic privatisation is illusory and short-lived, and is soon rearticulated with the larger public space of the *mise en scène* of trial and punishment. The dark results, announced on the steps of a municipal building in the rain to the assembled community, underlines the party's real power – if not over biology itself, then over the definition of the social status of human relations. It is part of Xie Jin's humanism to depict the injustice of this eclipse of the space of the human.

There are two scenes that underline the authority of the party to decide the propriety of individual action: the early night scene of Secretary Li's

176

public denunciation of New Rich Peasant Hu, and the late scene pronouncing the verdict on the couple. Both have a similar formal design traceable to the explicit theatricalisation of juridical politics: the official speaker is centre stage and points out the accused either to incriminate or to condemn. The scene of judicial decisions is presented theatrically to an assembled audience as a public lesson for didactic purposes. The *mise en scène* of human rights exists in the relation between the empty streets of political non-being and the private room, and the administrative display of public and formalized deprivation and castigation. The two spaces, of being and administration, are dialectically related.

The subjective state of the victims that corresponds to these public sanctions is ambiguous. Generally, Confucian punishment rests on the premise of corrective re-education through shame rather than guilt as a *social* means for the production of conformity. Guilt, a private emotion, seems more consistent with the punitive theories of Western individualism. The film depicts the couple's refusal to accede to either punitive state. Rightist Qin, the town's artist manqué and poster-maker, having had more experience of being an outcast, teaches Hu the way to bear this public sanction when he writes and then posts outside their own door the signs announcing the residence of a 'black couple' to the assembled public. Qin's comic resilience, bemused distance and elevated indifference to these self-authored critiques (an attitude carried equally in the movement, gesture and carriage of his body) gives form to a personal style of Chinese autonomy. It is a style of resistance to public sanction. He must bear the injustice, but it does not touch him or alter his fundamentally comic and ironic outlook on life.

This is a form of melodrama founded on the concept of the 'person' apart from gender *per se*. The chief antagonists are both women, though one is 'masculinised'. In both Xie Jin's *The Legend of Tianyun Mountain* and *The Herdsman*, the political victims are men, although the women are both the active figures and the ones who sacrifice themselves to maintain the man. The evident victim in *Hibiscus Town*, the one whose misfortunes are recounted, is the woman, Hu, while it is the man, already stigmatised, who supports her. The dynamics of Xie Jin's victimised couples, between male and female, passive and active, are not irrevocably fixed. The woman suffers, as does the man, but neither sacrifices themselves for the other. Both characters adopt an ethic of survival, living when necessary like animals. Although in *Hibisbus Town* the woman is victimised, the man, the rightist, is the reference point for Xie Jin's humanist critique. The two figures are in a sense condensed in an emblem of social injustice. The party's general amnesty returns Hu's confiscated property and provides her with a legitimate husband. With his return, the family as a social unit is reformed and the tofu business resumed. The formation of the family, with child, however, stands outside the strict terms of literal accountability. No price can be put on their suffering. In Xie Jin's hands the political melodrama concludes with the restoration of the family, embedded in a profitable, small, entrepreneurial business.

The humanist ideology of the film is simultaneously transparent and complex in its relation both to the processes of socialist revolution and

177

modernisation in China in the 80s. Contemporary Western film criticism, since 1968 heavily invested in ideological critique, has not generally confronted the problem of the critique of socialist representation. Following Althusser, Western Marxism in its cultural criticism has treated ideology as a discourse of mystification justifying the capitalist order by naturalisation. The spectator on this account is forced to subscribe to an implicit agreement with the terms of the text's construction, one that precludes a critical reading. This process of ideological interpellation is literalised by an account of the functioning of cinematographic apparatus.[13] This paradigm has become an article of critical faith across a range of 'progressive' perspectives. Yet what can the Western critique of bourgeois ideology and its associated critical technology achieve when applied to Chinese film? More to the point, what from a Western point of view constitutes an adequate critical model of the relation of film and ideology in the PRC? Socialist 'ideology', it would seem, is hardly secret and in need of demystification – it is explicit and taught as such. This fundamental difference of perspective indicates that a politcal reading of *Hibiscus Town* as melodrama and as ideology should proceed in close relation to the political time and culture in which it is embedded and not simply as the transcription of a Western critical problematic.

Soviet analysts of China in the 20s and 30s were undecided about the terms for analysis for the potential for Marxist revolution in China because of its complicated and entrenched mix of feudalism and capitalism.[14] *Hibiscus Town*, however, appears in a post-revolutionary culture, after the Liberation. It is a given that the feudal order so evident in many PRC films (especially those in the leftist tradition of the 30s and 40s) has been dismantled. Indeed, in this earlier period there was another version of Chinese political melodrama in which the central antagonist that victimised the main characters was the feudal order itself, but in *Hibiscus Town* 'class struggle' is waged by the socialist victors against the defeated remnants, practices and personnel of the pre-revoluntionary period.

Melodrama centred around such persons as Hu and Qin as victims seems possible only retrospectively – *after* the socialist revolution and after the shift of policy that permitted in the 80s what was prohibited in the 60s. 'Modernisation' as it was understood in China in the 80s necessitated a change of ideology and, in particular, the process of de-Maoification. The new socialism borrows a moral perspective from Confucianism in order to critique the old ways and to justify a new concept of the self appropriate to the new economic order. However, the film argues that this mode of subjectivity is *not* new, but is found in the villages of the past. What is new is the ideological task of negotiating and legitimating individual entrepreneurship.

The Cultural Revolution in the film is a negative political reference mobilised as a framework in which to present the case for a more local and particular change – the process of 'modernisation'. The relationship of the form of 'political melodrama' to the process of 'modernisation' is as complex as its relation to 'revolution'. This fact puts the form of Chinese socialist melodrama, and *Hibiscus Town* in particular, in relation to a certain historiography. The fictional form of the film is articulated around the contrast between past and present, by the process, told in multiple interrupting flashbacks, of Hu's remembering scenes from an earlier and happier life. The narrative itself is marked out by a series of designated dates – 1963, 1965, 1979 – that organise the entire film and put this melodramatic form in relation to the audience's popular memory of contemporary history. The film restates the problems of the Civil War and Liberation through its figuration of the Cultural Revolution and its aftermath. In this, socialist historiography confronts the ambiguities of the post-Liberation period. Assistant Party Secretary Wang, driven crazy by events, is left wandering the streets, banging a gong and shouting his prophetic announcement of the return of another 'movement'. History, as seen by the film, threatens social dismemberment by repetition of the constituting struggles that led to Liberation.

It is difficult to consider the film as fully a part of the new ideological campaigns of the 80s. It looks backwards and in Xie Jin's account the party is assigned responsibility for the strife and suffering of the past. Yet the film stages an alteration of the social category of the 'individual' that answers both to the needs of the past and to the present. It is precisely the redefinition of human rights of citizens (that is, civil rights), that Xie Jin formulates in the film.

I have detailed the system for figuring the emotional content of the experience of the depicted characters in terms of the relation of personal 'subjectivity' to social structure, and treated it as a matter of victimisation. The film explores the scope and content of the 'space' of human rights through an analysis of complicating relations between the two large systems of ethical and political thought, Confucianism and socialism, that operate in some composite form in contemporary Chinese society. In this, the film indicates the affective basis of Chinese 'political melodrama'. Suffering is linked ultimately to the injustices of the political administration of social power. In this sense 'subjectivity' is recovered as part of a new political language of the post-Cultural Revolution period. It indicates an aspect of the 'person' beyond that of the 'citizen'. From this perspective we can see the justice of designating Xie Jin's project, as Esther Yau has aptly suggested, 'rehumanisation'. Economic 'modernisation', to the extent that it includes a cultural redefinition of the sphere of the personal or the private, indicates a future, yet to be realised, of both rights and desires.

The film's fundamental choice to proceed by dramatising the central conflicts of a certain historical moment through representation of women indicates the contradictory cultural symbolism of the figure of Chinese woman.[15] Secretary Li is a personification, no doubt, of the detested figure of Jiang Qing, Mao's wife, the leader of the Gang of Four, and the film puts the blame on her for the persecution of the couple. In this regard, the film depicts the disfiguration of the social caused by the 'phallic woman'. By contrast, peasant Hu carries the extraordinary virtues of her type. In depicting cultural and economic change through the tropological opposition of two women, Xie Jin continues and extends the Chinese practice of representing socialist ideological change by a reduction of 'sexual difference' to an epiphenomenon of the social formation. 'Woman' is

179

an ambiguous figure of the Chinese cinema: the figure of the woman liberated by the party has been a traditional justification of Chinese socialist domination. Xie Jin's critique of social deformation in the past neither excuses the party nor supports a call for dismantling it. The film is situated on the cultural horizon of the 80s in quite a different way from many of the radically conceived films of the Fifth Generation in their refiguration of the role of the political. Xie Jin remains squarely within the recognisable terrain of Han culture and the familiar contours and problematics of a socialist vision of life, while succeeding in formulating an ethical discourse that works closely in the space between popular sentiments of disappointment or cynicism and the regime of the politically possible. For some Chinese critics and film-makers this form of socialist humanism and the Hollywood mode that supports it constitute a cultural monument to the past and designates the limits of sustainable cultural critique.

Notes

1. For important contemporary statements on the question of cross-cultural method, see Esther Yau, '*Yellow Earth*: Western Analysis and a Non-Western Text', *Film Quarterly*, vol. XLI, no. 2, 1987–8; Fredric Jameson, 'Third World Literature in the Era of Multinational Capitalism', *Social Text*, no. 15, Fall 1986; and the response, Rey Chow, 'Rereading Mandarin Ducks and Butterflies: A Response to the "Post-Modern" Condition', *Cultural Critique*, no. 5, Winter 1986–7.
2. Thomas Elsaesser, 'Tales of Sound and Fury: Observations on the Family Melodrama' (1972), in Bill Nichols (ed.), *Movies and Methods*, vol. II (Berkeley: University of California Press, 1985).
3. Peter Brooks, *The Melodramatic Imagination* (New York: Columbia University Press, 1985).
4. Wylie Sypher, 'Aesthetic of Revolution: the Marxist Melodrama', in Robert Corrigan (ed.), *Tragedy: Vision and Form* (Scranton, Pa.: Chandler Publishing Co., 1965).
5. A thorough orientation and survey of the field from this point of view is Christine Gledhill (ed.), *Home is Where the Heart Is: Studies in Melodrama and the Woman's Film* (London: BFI, 1987).
6. Andrew H. Plaks, 'Towards a Critical Theory of Chinese Narrative', in Andrew H. Plaks (ed.), *Chinese Narrative: Critical and Theoretical Essays* (Princeton: Princeton University Press, 1977). For a justification of the use of the term melodrama in relation to Chinese fiction, see C. T. Hsia, 'Hsu Chen-Ya's Yu-li-hum: An Essay in Literary History and Criticism', in Liu Ts'un-yan (ed.), *Chinese Middlebrow Fiction from the Ch'ing and Early Republican Eras* (Hong Kong: The Chinese University Press, 1984). As it relates to tragedy, see in the same volume Ping-cheung Cheung, '*Tou O yuan* as Tragedy'. On the relation of literature to film more generally, see Leo-ou-fan Lee, 'The Tradition of Modern Chinese Cinema: Some Preliminary Exploration and Hypotheses', in Chris Berry (ed.), *Perspectives on Chinese Cinema*, Cornell University East Asia Papers, no. 39. For a general study of the performing arts, see Bonnie S. McDougall (ed.), *Popular Chinese Literature and Performing Arts in the People's Republic of China 1949–1979* (Berkeley: University of California Press, 1984).
7. See Perry Link, *Mandarin Ducks and Butterflies: Popular Fiction in Early Twentieth-Century Chinese Cities* (Berkeley: University of California Press, 1981).

8. See the remarkable documentation in Li-Cheuk-to (ed.), *Cantonese Melodrama: 1950–1969* (Hong Kong: The Tenth Hong Kong International Film Festival, 1986).

9. Ma Ning, 'Symbolic Representation and Symbolic Violence: Chinese Family Melodrama of the Early 80s', *East–West Film Journal*, vol. 4, no. 1, 1989. After the completion of the present paper, I read Ma's PhD dissertation, *Culture and Politics in Chinese Film Melodrama: Traditional Sacred, Moral Economy and the Xie Jin Mode* (Department of Visual Arts, Monash University, Australia, 1992). He argues that 'although Chinese film melodrama in its development in this century was subject to Western influences, it also embodies a culturally specific mode of imagination related to Chinese metaphysical, ethical, aesthetic and political traditions'. It is the site in which the moral economy of traditional Chinese culture (an economy rooted in traditional Chinese cosmology and ethics) asserts itself in the area of mass cultural production. Ma argues for the specifically Chinese way of ideological domination.

10. The interaction between these two ideologies is the main theme of Judith Stacey's *Patriarchy and Socialist Revolution in China* (Berkeley: University of California Press, 1983).

11. The traditions are discussed at length in Donald Munro, *Individualism and Holism: Studies in Confucian and Taoist Values* (Ann Arbor: Center for Chinese Studies, University of Michigan, 1985).

12. The classic study is T'ung-tsu Ch'ü, *Law and Society in Traditional China* (The Hague: Mouton, 1961). See also, M. H. Van Der Valk, *Conservatism in Modern Chinese Family Law* (Leiden: E. J. Brill, 1956). For a penetrating account of the status of rights within the liberal framework, see Mark Kelman, *A Guide to Critical Legal Studies* (Cambridge, Mass.: Harvard University Press, 1987).

13. Jean Louis Baudry, 'The Ideological Effects of the Basic Cinematographic Apparatus', in Bill Nichols (ed.), *Movies and Methods*, vol. II (Berkeley: University of California Press, 1985).

14. Arif Dirlik, *Revolution and History: Origins of Marxist Historiography in China, 1919–1937* (Berkeley: University of California Press, 1978).

15. For recent analyses of Chinese women by women, see Esther Yau, 'Cultural and Economic Dislocations: Filmic Phantasies of Chinese Women in the 1980s', *Wide Angle*, vol. XI, no. 2, Spring 1989, and 'Is China the End of Hermeneutics? Or, Political and Cultural Usage of Non-Han Women in Mainland Chinese Films', *Discourse*, vol. XI, no. 2, Spring/Summer 1989; E. Ann Kaplan, 'Problematizing Cross-Cultural Analysis: The Case of Women in Recent Chinese Cinema', *Wide Angle*, vol. XI, no. 2, 1989. On non-white women more generally, see Teresa de Lauretis, 'Displacing Hegemonic Discourses: Reflections on Feminist Theory in the 1980s', *Inscriptions* (Santa Cruz), no. 3/4, 1988.

PART 4
POLITICS

MELODRAMA AND REVOLUTION

DANIEL GEROULD

Although melodrama is usually assumed to be morally conservative and supportive of the political *status quo*, the theatrical left has repeatedly turned to the genre as the most effective means of conveying revolutionary sentiments to mass audiences. I wish to examine this attraction through selected instances of revolutionary melodrama and melodrama dealing with revolution in both nineteenth-century French and twentieth-century Russian theatre. In other words, my aim is to trace the genealogy of one sub-genre of melodrama: that dealing with revolution and violent social change.

Granted, the melodrama of revolution has been a minor strain, often passing unnoticed within the vast expanses of conformist plays, but it has, I think, an importance out of proportion to its statistical frequency because it reveals something fundamental about the nature of the genre. Since the poor and downtrodden are its protagonists of choice, melodrama tends to favour the cause of the dispossessed rather than of those in power, even when its plot structure ultimately brings about accommodation to the reigning order. Thus melodrama's central theme of oppressed innocence has regularly been perceived as an incitement to rebellion against tyranny by audiences suffering similar victimisation.

Melodrama, in fact, originated in France with the overthrow of the *ancien régime*. As a form of theatre, it is legally the offspring of the French Revolution. The decree of 13 January 1791 by the National Assembly giving freedom to the theatres and their repertories made melodrama possible – it liberated authors, actors, audiences, and genres from the old rules and restrictions. The abolition of censorship opened the way for a new subject-matter, a new ethos, and a new sensibility.[1]

We should nevertheless remember that the 'classic' melodrama created by Guilbert de Pixérécourt, which held sway from 1800 to the mid-1820s and coloured all later conceptions of the genre, extolled the civic virtues and shared the Revolution's didactic goal of instructing the people in patriotism and military heroism. As at a tribunal, evil was punished and providence justified. Pixérécourt's friend and champion Charles Nodier, in his defence of the genre, declared that 'Melodrama was the morality of the Revolution.'[2]

In its earliest manifestations, during the Empire and the restoration of the monarchy, melodrama upheld the social hierarchy and its values of work, courage, and rectitude. It was only after subsequent revolutions – in 1830, 1848, and 1871 – that the subversive, agitational potential of melodrama was eventually realised. The violent social upheavals that periodically shook France produced brief periods of political freedom (followed by renewed repression) in which the genre could openly explore the revolutionary past and present.

When the constraints of censorship were relaxed after 1830 and 1848, melodrama immediately took as its material daring new subjects from contemporary life: the working classes in their homes, at their places of work, and in the streets. Furthermore, it was then that melodrama first dealt with the subject of revolution itself. Throughout the 19th century no major literary, 'high culture' French dramatists wrote plays about the French Revolution or put on stage Danton, Robespierre, and Saint-Just. The melodramatists did. The elemental passions and spectacular crowd scenes of revolution were effectively represented in the theatre by the gestural language and stage technology of melodrama. Whenever censorship was abandoned or significantly lessened in nineteenth-century France, radical melodramas were produced in the theatre, inspiring fear in the ruling classes. The very presence on stage of the people as an active force was seen as a grave threat to public order.

Nineteenth-century French Melodrama of Revolution

After the fall of the Bourbons in July 1830, the melodramatists made use of their new liberties to denounce anti-republican forces. With the abolition of censorship, they were free to treat subjects from political actuality or historical themes from 1789. The great men and the repertory of the Revolution were resuscitated. There were revivals of celebrated ur-melodramas from the First Republic, such as the anti-clerical *Les Victimes cloîtrées* (1791) and *Robert, Chef de brigands* (1792), as well as productions of new melodramas dealing with figures from the Revolution and Empire, who had been banned from the stage for thirty years. Kings and priests could once again be attacked on-stage.[3]

During December 1830 and January 1831 Anicet-Bourgeois's historical melodrama *Robespierre* played at the Ambigu-Comique for forty performances. Prior to the July Revolution, it would have been impossible to stage a play portraying the heroes of 1789. The popularity of Anicet-Bourgeois's drama was ensured by its republican message (and topical allusions) as well as by its exciting scenes depicting the previously banned French Revolution. Robespierre was, of course, the villain, conceived as a gloomy, guilt-ridden tyrant and self-terrified fanatic. But Anicet-Bourgeois's melodrama was equally anti-royalist, pointedly hostile to the deposed Bourbons. The play's special appeal lay in its spectacular scenes, including an elaborate reconstruction, as tableau vivant, of the Festival of the Supreme Being.[4]

A number of other historical melodramas about the French Revolution voicing republican sentiments were staged in the 1840s, including *Madame Roland* by Virginie Ancelot at the Théâtre Vaudeville in 1843.

Madame Ancelot, a successful author of melodramas, comedies, and a feminist drama,[5] was married to Jacques Ancelot, himself an author of tragedies and melodramas – the only husband and wife team of melodramatists that I know.

After 1830, subversive melodramas, highly popular with audiences but attacked by the establishment critics, made villains of the clergy and the rich. The nineteenth-century playwright and theatre historian Alphonse Royer called these new melodramas 'intellectual poison', 'the apostolate of evil', and 'the systematic inversion of public morality'.[6]

A radical change in sensibility had indeed become evident. Melodramas of social protest were played in both the boulevard and the minor theatres. The traditional values of classic Pixérécourtian melodrama were turned upside down. Convicts, bandits and asocial figures, who had previously been villains, now became heroes. These new protagonists served as sardonic and embittered commentators, ironically lamenting that virtue went unrewarded and crime unpunished.

The most literally incendiary of the rabidly anti-clerical melodramas was *L'Incendiaire ou la curé de l'achevêché* by Alexis Decomberousse and Benjamin Antier, staged at the Porte-St-Martin in March 1831. The play takes its subject from a series of recent fires in Normandy, suspected of being arson directed against liberals by royalist fanatics. The arrogant, luxury-loving archbishop forces a young working-class woman to torch the farm of a liberal on pain of being denied the sacrament and a church marriage because she has sinned with her fiancé. Theatrically exciting is the sensation scene of the arson itself (a favourite device of later melodramas from *The Poor of New York* and *Lady Audley's Secret* to Méliès's *History of a Crime*).

Félix Pyat, a journalist, socialist politician, and later Communard, systematically cultivated a revolutionary brand of melodrama that may actually have influenced the course of political events and certainly helped to shape working-class consciousness of social injustice. In 1834 Pyat's *The Brigand and the Philosopher* presented speculators on the Stock Exchange as no better than highway robbers. His greatest success, *The Ragpicker of Paris* (which the author later novelised), contrasts an honest worker and a corrupt banker. It opened at the Porte-St-Martin in 1847 and moved to the Ambigu where it was playing to tumultuous crowds at the time of the Revolution of 1848, which Pyat claimed that his melodrama incited. At a free performance of *The Ragpicker* given on 26 February, two days after the outbreak of the Revolution, Frédérick Lemaître, the great popular performer playing the title role, emptied his ragbag on the stage and out rolled a crown. The entire theatre went wild with enthusiasm; actors and spectators together sang the 'Marseillaise' and cried 'Vive la République!'[7]

In fact, it was Frédérick Lemaître, a truly revolutionary actor, who had first transformed conventional moral melodramas into socially inflammatory plays. The character Robert Macaire in *L'Auberge des adrets* (1824) had been drastically reshaped by Lemaître into an expression of the mob's rage against society's injustices. Embodying the spirit of anarchy and revolt, the sarcastic and subversive Macaire seemed to justify the use of crime to fight social inequities. In *L'Auberge des adrets* there was a couplet about 'Killing policemen', and one night Lemaître directly addressed the audience to explain: 'This evening we shall not be able to kill a policeman, the actor is sick. Tomorrow night we'll kill two.' After the eightieth performance, the censor intervened and the play was forbidden. Continuing to develop this almost mythical comic figure who changed the course of melodrama, Lemaître in 1834 created his own new play called *Robert Macaire*.[8]

Censorship was re-established in 1835, but it did not succeed in discouraging the writing and performing of social melodramas. Adolphe Thiers, a former journalist, historian of the French Revolution, and now Minister of the Interior, summoned the Paris censors to his office and told them that he wanted *Robert Macaire* and Dumas père's *La Tour de Nesle* kept off the stage for ever. (Thiers will appear later in our story as a dramatic character and the villain of the bloody suppression of the Commune.) The censor was particularly afraid of two melodramas: *Robert Macaire* and *The Mysteries of Paris*, adapted from Eugène Sue's novel. In 1843 *The Mysteries of Paris*, seen as dangerous because of its radical depiction of social misery, was temporarily stopped by the censor, but eventually authorised for performance.

The censor also held up Dumas père's *La Chevalier de Maison-Rouge* which dealt with the fall of the Girondins and a failed attempt to free Marie Antoinette from imprisonment in the Temple. It was eventually passed by the censor (with some cuts) for performance at Dumas's own Théâtre Historique in 1847. Contrary to Dumas's professed intentions of reproving violence, the playwright, the censor argued, used the occasion to exploit revolutionary turmoil on-stage.[9] Dumas's melodrama was temporarily forbidden because of its scenes of collective action, above all the famous concluding tableau of the Girondins' final banquet at the prison of the Conciergerie. The authorities found particularly inflammatory and objectionable the singing of *Le Chant des Girondins* (a contemporary revolutionary song of the 1840s): '*Mourir pour la patrie,/ C'est le sort le plus beau, le plus digne d'envie.*' Thus it was the powerful conjunction of tableau, music and song that brought *La Chevalier de Maison-Rouge* to a dangerously revolutionary denouement.[10]

Dumas's *The Whites and the Blues*, presented at the Châtelet in 1869, experienced similar problems with the censor because the revolutionary extremist Saint-Just is its principal hero. *The Whites and the Blues* grew out of an unusual posthumous collaboration with Dumas's friend Charles Nodier, who had died in 1844 (the year of Pixérécourt's death). Both the novel and the play versions of *The Whites and the Blues* are based directly on Nodier's written recollections of the Revolution as well as on his conversations with Dumas. The dedication of the novel is 'To my illustrious friend and collaborator.' The adolescent Nodier actually appears in the melodrama as an important (and historically accurate) character, played (as were most boys' roles) by an actress.

In 1794 Nodier's father sent his fourteen-year-old son to Strasbourg to study Greek with Euloge Schneider (known as the 'Marat of Strasbourg'), an eminent German classical scholar who had been a professor at the University of Bonn and formerly a monk, but who had given up the church and gone to France because of his fanatical zeal for the Revolution. Now the public prosecutor of Strasbourg, the renegade priest and his 'hussars of death' (with crossbones on their shakos, rows of white braid resembling ribs on their jackets, and skulls on their tobacco pouches) travelled about Alsace with a nomadic guillotine, dispatching 'enemies of the people' to the scaffold.

A central episode in Dumas's melodrama concerns Schneider's wooing of Clotilde, the beautiful daughter of the wealthiest aristocrat in Strasbourg. The public prosecutor has the count arrested and condemned to death as an *émigré* unlawfully present on French soil. Before asking for Clotilde's hand in marriage, Schneider sets up his guillotine, bedecked with flowers and ribbons, outside the count's living-room. When the public prosecutor opens the window and shows his beloved the waiting scaffold, Clotilde – 'a poor defenceless young girl' – agrees to marry her eager suitor in order to save her father's life, but secretly clutches a small dagger behind her back. After the hurried ceremony, the bride directs the wedding cortège (including the hussars of death, the executioner, and his portable guillotine) to the Hôtel de Ville where Saint-Just, who has come to Strasbourg to establish justice and ensure military victory, is haranguing young volunteers on the need to serve the nation in its hour of danger. The spectacular climax of *The Whites and the Blues* takes place on the public square in front of the Hôtel de Ville. Leaping from the carriage, Clotilde denounces her loathsome husband's monstrous abuses to the Representative of the People. Producing the dagger from her bosom, the bride-to-be declares that if she could not obtain justice, she would kill the 'Marat of Strasbourg' that night in bed. The embodiment of melodramatic providence, Saint-Just saves 'old age and innocence': he pardons the count and unites Clotilde with her young fiancé. In a final battle tableau, Saint-Just grabs the tricolour from a standard-bearer and leads the French army to fight triumphal wars of conquest for the new Republic. At the last moment Dumas subordinates the revolutionary theme of his drama to the patriotic bravura of military pageantry.[11]

Unlike 1789, the Paris Commune was a proletarian revolution in which ordinary working women and men made up the front ranks. I stress women, because the Commune entailed 'the massive, extraordinary, momentous participation of women'.[12] In 1871, after the shameful defeat of the French army and capitulation to the Prussians, the working classes of Paris seized power for themselves, having been cheated of the prize in so many previous uprisings that were appropriated by the bourgeoisie. The extreme polarities of class antagonism engendered by the Commune and its cruel defeat provided exciting material for melodrama, but the immediate reimposition of censorship rendered any direct treatment of the commune on the stage impossible. The Paris Commune was a subject off limits for drama in France for almost a century, at first because of political censorship lasting until 1905 and then because of the prevailing social and political prejudices that made the Commune a taboo subject virtually until 1968. Almost all major French writers fiercely opposed the Commune as a threat to civilisation and private property, and many enthusiastically applauded its bloody suppression.[13]

189

A number of Communards, however, were playwrights, including Félix Pyat, the author of the earlier *Ragpicker of Paris*. Two Communards, Louise Michel and Maxime Lisbonne, used the theatre, and specifically melodrama, to keep the memory of the Commune alive.

The schoolteacher Louise Michel became one of the leaders of the Commune and a later heroine of the French left. For her activities in the Commune she was deported to New Caledonia in 1873, but after her return from imprisonment in 1880 she wrote several revolutionary melodramas. In 1882 her play *Nadine* was given at the Bouffes du Nord, a working-class theatre, directed by the manager of the theatre, Maxime Lisbonne. *Nadine* was ostensibly about the Polish uprising against Tsarist oppression, but of course it actually dealt with the Commune, a subject forbidden by the censor. Recognising the kinship of political and theatrical activities, Michel often gave lectures to proletarian audiences in the theatre auditorium itself. As a militant anarchist, she felt that melodrama would reach the audience she wanted to address, and she returned to the genre in 1890 with her play *The Strike* staged at the Théâtre de la Villette. The action takes place in Warsaw in 1860, the year of the tragic rebellion against the Tsar. In all Louise Michel's melodramas the revolutionaries are finally crushed, as they had been in the Commune, amid apocalyptic flames, but their dying hope is that others will continue the struggle and finally realise their Utopian dreams.[14]

Louise Michel's friend Maxime Lisbonne was a man of the theatre, the manager of the Folies Saint-Antoine, and an actor who had played d'Artagnan in *Les Trois Mousquetaires* and Buridan in *La Tour de Nesle*. Lisbonne (a flamboyant ex-soldier who walked the streets of Paris in a fantastic uniform like a performer from the Cirque Olympic, wearing oriental spurs, sword and scabbard, huge boots, a Zouave's tunic, wide trousers, black hat, and red plume) rose to the rank of colonel during the Commune. Known as 'the d'Artagnan of the Commune', he fought heroically at the barricades, lost a leg, was condemned to death, and then reprieved and sent to New Caledonia. Finally repatriated in 1881, he staged plays by Louise Michel and Victor Hugo, Zola's *Germinal*, and wrote a revolutionary drama himself which was forbidden by the censor.

As a self-styled '*farceur et cabotin*', Lisbonne engaged in various paratheatrical activities of a melodramatic nature celebrating the Commune. He even ran for the legislature in 1889 as a *saltimbanque* and ex-convict from the Commune, turning politics into a form of theatrical entertainment. He operated theatrical cabarets and brasseries that presented tableaux vivants of episodes from the Commune. In 1885 Lisbonne opened his Café for Convicts, where the customers were received by a prisoner guard, where the waiters were dressed as convicts (yellow trousers and red caps for the life-termers), and where the walls were hung with pictures of Nouméa, the place of his exile. Twice a week Lisbonne presided over the ceremony of riveting the chains on the ankles of the prisoners. While Lisbonne described the suffering of the convicts and explained the aims of the Commune, the prisoners re-enacted the tortures of New Caledonia under portraits of Communards massacred in 1871. In 1886 Lisbonne started his Taverne de la Révolution Française where the great patriots of the Republic were glorified. In 1888 he opened his Brasserie des Frites Révolutionnaires where he staged tableaux, such as *La Mort de Delescluze*. Lisbonne lectured on the Commune, appeared in music hall and revues, and turned the pathos and irony of his life as a Communard and deportee into theatre. His visiting card read: 'Maxime Lisbonne: Ex-convict – actor.'[15]

For their propagandistic purposes in educating working-class audiences, Michel and Lisbonne made idiosyncratic use of the techniques and ethos of melodrama, but in 1874 the extraordinary success with the general public of Dennery's *The Two Orphans* had re-established the vogue for traditional melodrama – sentimental, moralistic, and intricately plotted. By the 1890s, however, the genre once again became a vehicle for socialist ideas.[16] For example, in 1892 at the Bouffes du Nord, an unusual revolutionary melodrama, *IX Thermidor*, by Jean La Rode, Georges Rolle and Albert Crémieux, was played to the loud and prolonged applause of working-class audiences. *IX Thermidor* is the first performed French drama that totally rehabilitates Robespierre (previously cast as the darkest villain of the French Revolution) by making him an innocent and idealistic hero pitted against the evil, sensual adulteress, Mme Theresa Tallien ('Notre-Dame de Thermidor'), who, rebuffed in her attempts to seduce the Incorruptible, vows to destroy him. Robespierre, surrounded by enemies but absolutely dedicated to justice and legality, wants to end the terror and bring about a reconciliation among all French citizens. His austere devotion to virtue is tempered by his love for the pure young daughter of his landlord, Eleonore Duplay, whom Robespierre plans to marry. Unfortunately, a strict sense of duty does not allow the Incorruptible to assume dictatorial powers and crush his opponents, as his friend Saint-Just urges.

For their positive portrayal of Robespierre, the authors of *IX Thermidor* drew upon the recent writings of the revisionist historian Alphonse Aulard. I should mention that in 1922 Aulard attacked Griffith's *Orphans of the Storm* for giving a totally false picture of the French Revolution, which would do great harm to France's reputation in the world and must therefore be refuted.[17]

The Soviet Experiment with Melodrama

Marxist theorists in the USSR recognised French nineteenth-century melodrama as a model for a popular propaganda theatre that would speak to the masses. Melodrama flourished in Russia after 1917, just as it had in France after 1789. It addressed the same kind of new public and it identified many of the same enemies: priests, aristocrats, profiteers and former rulers. It adopted the same Manichean view of the world, voiced the same need for heroes and villains, and preached the same simplistic moral lessons.

For a few years in the 20s, Soviet melodrama was officially promoted and financed by the state as a means of furthering the revolution. There was even a temporary fusion of melodrama and avante-garde experimentalism that produced lively intellectual debate and theorising about the genre by first-rate talents in the Soviet performing arts.

191

In January 1919 the People's Commissar of Education, Anatolii Lunacharsky, himself a playwright and drama critic who knew the French theatre well, wrote an influential article, 'What Kind of Melodrama Do We Need?' In it, Lunacharsky declared: 'Melodrama simply as theatre is superior to other dramatic genres.'[18]

In 1922, writing of the newly formed Romanesque Theatre in Moscow, dedicated to the performance of romantic melodramas and during its one year of existence presenting Dumas's *La Tour de Nesle* and *The Count of Monte Cristo*, Lunacharsky wrote: 'I say that in the field of theatre we must go back to Dumas père, and in the field of the novel back to Sue.'[19]

Following Lunacharsky's lead, ideologists of Soviet culture became seriously interested in melodrama as the theatrical genre that could best express revolutionary ideology, and leading theatre artists experimented with its themes and techniques in the 20s.

Soviet melodrama was every bit as teleological as its nineteenth-century capitalist ancestor, replacing a providential Christian world view with dialectical materialism which ensured the eventual triumph of the working class.

Soviet children's theatre in the 20s, highly subsidised by the state as a means of ideological indoctrination, developed melodramas for young spectators, who were the perfect audiences for the genre. The Leningrad Theatre for Young Spectators was specially organised for the children of the Revolution and Civil War, which had made many of them destitute orphans. A number of the young teenage actresses, who specialised in travesty roles, were themselves orphans. Here, then, was a theatre of orphans that performed revolutionary melodramas for orphans.

In 1925 the Theatre for Young Spectators turned to revolutionary historical themes, and many world classics were adapted to suit the times. Among these was Dickens's *A Tale of Two Cities* which the playwright, actor, director and teacher Leonid Makariev renamed *Citizen Darnay*.

Makariev felt that in a melodrama for children the spectator must be directly involved:

> In the spectator's active responses is rooted the life nerve of the stage action. Empathy, delight, rage, sympathy, or resentment permeate the amphitheatre. In the course of the performance the spectator performs complicated emotional work as he seeks the answer to the all-important questions: who is right? who is guilty? who is good? who is bad?[20]

Anglo-American readers of Dickens's novel will be surprised to learn that Makariev solved the problem of adapting *A Tale of Two Cities* to Bolshevik ideology by simply omitting Sidney Carton and his noble sacrifice. The Soviet playwright has retained the melodramatic form of *A Tale of Two Cities*, but substituted a different set of melodramatic values. The absolutes of melodrama differ from culture to culture and from one historic moment to another. According to the melodramatic rhetoric of 1917, service to the revolution is the highest value. Monsieur and Madame Defarge, the three Jacques, and the inhabitants of the street are the new collective hero – the people. Sidney Carton, so crucial to Dickens's conservative, sentimental ideology, proves totally detachable from the story of the French Revolution as seen through Soviet eyes.

Neither the Terror nor the guillotine is ever mentioned in Makariev's version of *A Tale of Two Cities*. The drama unfolds at the time of the storming of the Bastille, when revolutionary consciousness first reaches a high level of emotional intensity. In *Citizen Darnay*, the people disarm members of the guard and convert them to the revolution. A choral character, the washerwoman Barbier, whose child was run over by the Marquis de St-Evremonde's carriage, interposes herself between the soldiers and the inhabitants of the *quartier*: 'Stop, soldiers – think what you're doing! Whose side are you on? With the people or against them?' The spectacle of government troops being won over to the side of the people is a classic scene in Soviet revolutionary melodrama. Trotsky described such an event in his *History of the Russian Revolution*, and in his 1925 film Eisenstein recreated the episode on the deck of the battleship Potemkin when the sailors cry out to the guard, 'Brothers! Who are you shooting at?'

The youthful spectators watching *Citizen Darnay* were invited to admire the power and energy of the people and to emulate the revolutionary virtues of courage and steadfastness. As the crowd chants, 'Death to the traitors!' and 'Enemies of the people!' the spy Barsad, in the pay of St-Evremonde, denounces Charles to the Revolutionary Tribunal as an aristocratic *emigré* working for the counter-revolution. But justice triumphs – Darnay is exonerated and freed as the new troops from Marseilles arrive. The noble martyr of the *ancien régime*, Dr Manette, declares that the revolution is just beginning and hails its victory in future generations. Everyone sings the 'Marseillaise', and instead of Sidney Carton's 'It is a far, far better thing that I do,' the Soviet *Tale of Two Cities* concludes with the rousing cry of 'Long Live the Revolution!'

As a dramatic subject, Soviet theoreticians and playwrights much preferred the failed Paris Commune of 1871 to the successful bourgeois revolution of 1789, which led only to Napoleon and the Empire. The first true proletarian revolution, the Commune had as its innocent hero/heroine the generic working people of Paris. Their story is a harrowing melodrama full of all the pathos of revolution. Happy, joyous, content with simple pleasures, the virtuous people are persecuted by the evil old capitalist Thiers, allied with the foreign Prussian army and the reactionary military–clerical establishment. The sadistic, treacherous bourgeoisie delight in the people's sufferings and defeat. The ultimate happy outcome comes with the last-minute recognition that the triumphant Russian Revolution of 1917 is the long-lost child of the Commune. Here is the *voix du sang* of all Soviet Commune plays.

Hundreds of Commune plays were written and performed in the USSR after 1917, celebrating its way of life and egalitarian values, praising it as the beginning of the World Revolution, and linking it directly to the Bolshevik Revolution. These plays were often written by amateurs as contest entries for festive performances at clubs and factories or in army units on 18 March, the day of the establishment of the Paris Commune and a Soviet holiday.[21]

The hundreds of spectacles about the Paris Commune were part of a system of secular rituals instituted by the new Soviet authorities to replace the old sacred religious holidays with commemorations of the various stages in the history of world revolution. Patterned after the great festivals of the French Revolution, the largest of these mass spectacles involved immense casts of amateurs and huge audiences who became participants in the events being re-enacted.[22]

Soviet scriptwriters and film theorists such as Viktor Shklovsky and Adrian Piotrovsky wrote Commune scenarios that were staged in the early 20s. Piotrovsky (1898–1938) was a classical scholar and translator of Aristophanes, Aeschylus and Sophocles, and a critic, director, writer and theorist of mass spectacles, melodrama and film genres. He was also a practical man of the theatre, director of the Theatre Workshop of the Red Army, literary advisor of the Kirov Opera and Ballet Theatre, and artistic director of the Lenfilm Studio. His *The Paris Commune* was presented in Leningrad on 17 March 1924 for the anniversary of the establishment of the Commune. It belongs to a sub-genre of agit-drama known as *inst-senirovka*. These dramas are frescoes of great events in the revolutionary history of the people, depicting many historical figures, their famous speeches, and other information about the period. They feature declamation, music and song, especially choral chant. We might say that these dramas are twentieth-century Soviet versions (utilising formalist abstraction) of the nineteenth-century French *drames historiques à grand spectacle* – the military–patriotic spectacles that played at the Cirque Olympique. They are certainly melodramas in their ethos and structure.

In Piotrovsky's text the noble old man Delescluze (consumed by a passion for justice) is pitted against the villain Thiers. The people and their city, Paris, are the innocent, anonymous heroine/hero who wish to spread their Utopian revolution everywhere, but who have been abandoned and orphaned by the world they hoped to remake. The old order is reasserted as the Commune drowns in a sea of blood and 20,000 Communards are shot. Was the Commune a vain dream? We jump ahead in time. Workers in contemporary Paris sing *The Internationale*. The French working class recognises in Lenin and the Soviet state their own offspring, whom they must now emulate; in that way the massacred Communards will be avenged.

In an article entitled 'Melodrama or Tragedy?' written in early 1924 at exactly the same time as his play on the Commune, Piotrovsky asks whether melodrama rather than tragedy can deal with the recent experiences of revolution, social upheaval, and civil war. He concludes his theoretical reflections on the genre with the following assessment:

Melodrama is the child of transitional epochs. Chance and relative morality, these are its driving forces.

Melodrama is by its very nature individualistic. There is no fatality.

Short-sighted optimism, easily attained self-satisfaction – these are the psychological roots of the contemporary propaganda offered by melodrama.[23]

These brilliant insights offer pointed criticism of the topical and temporal parochialism of melodrama. In a scenario like *The Paris Commune* Piotrovsky attempted to enrich his drama through the employment of more timeless and universal techniques. He considered the mass spectacle to be a revival of ancient Greek theatre, and he regarded Aeschylus as the model for a new post-revolutionary theatre addressed to the masses. In the use of platforms, massed groups and choral chanting we can also detect the influence of Expressionism. Piotrovsky talks of the 'cinefication of theatre', in which we have the 'sphere of synthetic arts'. According to Piotrovsky, mass spectacles and agit-montages 'deploy every medium of intellectual and emotional influence'.[24]

Piotrovsky made a pioneering application of Formalist principles to cinema in his essay 'Towards a Theory of Cinema Genres'. Fascinated with melodrama as a film genre, he experimented with the form himself. In 1926, the same year as his essay, Piotrovsky composed the scenario for *The Devil's Wheel* by Kozintsev and Trauberg, about a sailor from the *Aurora* in the clutches of gangsters in a sinister amusement park. According to Piotrovsky in 'Towards a Theory of Cinema Genres', film melodrama uses the compositional principle 'catastrophe – chance – rescue'. The Griffith 'catastrophe' is the core of film melodrama, as a creation of montage. The 'elemental catastrophe' in film melodrama shows the parity of human wills and natural forces; 'man' and 'nature' are equally important and play similar roles. It is easier to provide motivation by natural forces and disasters than through human conduct, always so difficult to explain on film (then solely dependent on the image without the spoken word).[25]

In 1929 Piotrovsky wrote that 'Griffith's formula for melodrama' had been decisive in the formative first years of Soviet cinema, but that this formula had then been rejected as bourgeois imitation. According to Piotrovsky, Soviet film-makers should again look at the new American films from which they still have something to learn about the values of melodrama and irony.[26] Unfortunately, Adrian Piotrovsky paid with his life for his Formalist enthusiasms, his interest in American cinema, and his devotion to revolutionary art. He illustrates the saying of Pierre Vergniaud, guillotined in 1793, that 'The revolution devours its own children.' Piotrovsky was eliminated in 1938 at the age of forty in the grim Stalinist melodrama of exterminating class enemies of the people. He was posthumously rehabilitated.

In October 1926 Aleksander Taïrov staged *Rosita* (by Andrei Globa) starring Alisa Koonen at the Kamerny Theatre. Globa's play is based on Ernst Lubitsch's first Hollywood film, *Rosita* (1923, originally to be called *The Singer of Seville*), in which Mary Pickford plays a street singer in nineteenth-century Spain who becomes involved in court intrigues as the result of a song lampooning the king. The film itself is an adaptation by Lubitsch's scenario writer Hans Kraly of a famous nineteenth-century melodrama, *Don César de Bazen*, by Dennery and Dumanoir (1844, Porte-St-Martin, with Frédérick Lemaître), extremely popular in pre-revolutionary Russia. In the French original, the singer is named Maritana, the action takes place in the Renaissance during the reign of Charles II, and the swashbuckling hero is taken from Hugo's *Ruy Blas*. (A second American film version of the same play, called *The Spanish Dancer*, with Pola Negri, Adolphe Menjou and Wallace Beery, also appeared in 1923.) The Soviet Rosita is an anarchist who climbs on top of barrels in poor quarters and sings songs that not only tug at the heart strings, but also offer the people hope and challenge them to fight against oppression. In an address to his company Taïrov declared:

> Melodrama is in origin and in essence a revolutionary type of drama. Its fundamental laws are mockery and abuse of evil, philistinism, and meanness of spirit, and affirmation of justice and truth. . . . The development of the action must be swift, and the rhythm precise. The performance must be fiery and thrilling.[27]

Dennery and Cormon's *The Two Orphans* had been popular in the pre-revolutionary Russian theatre, and in 1919 it was successfully produced at the Free Theatre of Moscow, founded to further the revival of melodrama. In October 1927 a new version, called *The Sisters Gerard*, was presented on the small stage of the Moscow Art Theatre, directed by Nikolai Gorchakov, with Pavel Markov as literary manager. The text was rewritten by Vladimir Mass, who drew upon D.W. Griffith's *Orphans of the Storm* (first shown in the USSR in 1925) in giving his play a historical setting at the time of the French Revolution, but who made the melodrama pre-revolutionary. Attacked by Soviet critics as an obsolete specimen of bourgeois culture, *The Sisters Gerard* was popular with audiences and stayed in the repertory for several years.[28]

Stanislavsky attended rehearsals of *The Sisters Gerard*, and in his remarks to the actors made a number of important observations on the theatrical values of the genre and the proper techniques of melodramatic acting:

> In melodrama the actor must absolutely believe in everything that takes place. No matter what the author has devised, the actor must assume that it has all actually happened. Then and only then will the audience believe all of it. . . .
>
> Melodrama has always arisen when audiences were filled to the brim with lofty and noble feelings and needed ways to express them and find an outlet for their emotions. . . . Now, after the revolution, many beautiful sentiments have been aroused in our audiences, and the public wants to see exactly the same fine and noble things and just such strong emotions coming from the stage.[29]

After 1928, as the Soviet state became a monolithic dictatorship under Stalin, the previous plurality of approaches to theatre was rejected in favour of a single dogma – Socialist Realism (officially proclaimed at the First Soviet Writers' Conference in 1934). The bourgeois Western origins of melodrama and its ties to American film, as well as its sheer exuberance and entertaining qualities, rendered the genre suspect to the party ideologues who were now in charge of the Soviet theatre. The Russian experiment with heroic and revolutionary melodrama came to an inglorious end.

My conclusions may appear gloomy for those who would like to envisage a hopeful future for the revolutionary potential of melodrama. With the failure of world communism and the demise of the Soviet Union, it is widely asserted that after 200 years the revolutionary impetus begun in 1789 has reached its final point of rest and that the very concept of revolution has now been discredited. It seems doubtful that any left-leaning melodramatist in the foreseeable future will write a play like Piotrovsky's that can look back passionately to 1789, 1871, or 1917 and claim that the goals of the Commune or Lenin are now just about to be realised. Except in the Third World it is unlikely that socialist intellectuals will flirt with revolutionary melodrama again except in parodistic forms, such as those pioneered by Frédérick Lemaître on the stage and by Maxime Lisbonne in the streets and cabarets. The bitter, mocking, and flamboyantly theatrical distortions of the genre by these actor–authors suggest rich possibilities for revolutionary melodrama as post-modern parody.

Notes

1. Marc Regaldo, 'Mélodrame et Révolution française', *Le Mélodrame/Europe*, nos. 703/704, November/December, 1987, pp. 6–8.
2. Gérard Gengembre, *A vos plumes, citoyen!* (Paris: Découvertes Gallimard, 1988), p. 78, and Jean-Marie Thomasseau, *Le Mélodrame* (Paris: Presses Universitaires de France, 1984), p. 30.
3. Maurice Albert, *Les Théâtres des Boulevard, 1902* (Geneva: Slatkine, 1969), p. 319.
4. Patrick Berthier, 'Robespierre revu par Anicet-Bourgeois', in Patrick Berthier (ed.), *Robespierre saisi par le théâtre* (Arras: Centre Culturel Noroit, 1991), pp. 24–8.
5. *Marie, ou Les Trois époques*, given at the Théâtre-Française, 1836.
6. Alphonse Royer, *Histoire Universelle du Théâtre*, vol. 5, (Paris: Ollendorff, 1878), pp. 383, 385.
7. Philippe Vigier, 'Le Mélodrama social dans les années 1840', in *Le Mélodrame/Europe*, nos. 703/704, November/December, 1987, p. 79.
8. Frederick Brown, *Theater and Revolution: The Culture of the French Stage* (New York: Viking, 1980), p. 116.
9. Odile Krakovitch, *Hugo Censuré: La Liberté au théâtre au XIXe siècle* (Paris: Calmann-Lévy, 1985), pp. 116–18.
10. Boucicault's adaptation, *Genevieve, or The Reign of Terror*, played at the Adelphi in 1853.
11. Daniel Gerould, *Guillotine: Its Legend and Lore* (New York: Blast Books, 1992), pp. 43–6.
12. Edith Thomas, *The Women Incendiaries*, trans. James and Starr Atkinson (New York: George Braziller, 1966), p. xii.
13. Daniel Gerould, 'Terror, the Modern State and the Dramatic Imagination', in John Orr and Dragan Klaić (eds), *Terrorism and Modern Drama* (Edinburgh: University of Edinburgh Press, 1992), pp. 38–9.
14. Monique Surel-Tupin, 'Une écriture dramatique au service de "la sociale"', in Claudine Amiard-Chervel (ed.), *L'Ouvrier au théâtre de 1871 à nos jours*, *Cahiers Théâtre Louvain* (Belgium), nos. 58/59, 1987, pp. 46–57.

15. Yurii Danilin, 'Maxime Lisbonne', *Oktyabr*, no. 3, 1941, pp. 116–32.
16. Thomasseau, op. cit., p. 85.
17. Alphonse Aulard, 'L'Ancien régime et la Révolution au cinéma' (October, 1922), in *Etudes et leçons sur la Révolution française* (Paris: Félix Alcan, 1924), pp. 183–7.
18. Daniel Gerould and Julia Przyboś, 'Melodrama in the Soviet Theater 1917–1928: An Annotated Chronology', in Daniel Gerould (ed.), *Melodrama*, vol. 7 (New York: New York Literary Forum, 1980), p. 78.
19. Ibid., p. 83.
20. Leonid Makariev, 'How It All Began at the Leningrad Theatre for Young Spectators', in Miriam Morton (ed. and trans.), *Through the Magic Curtain: Theater for Children, Adolescents and Youth in the USSR* (New Orleans: Anchorage Press, 1979), p. 66.
21. Gerould, op. cit., p. 39.
22. Christel Lane, 'The mass political holidays of the revolutionary tradition: a historical review 1918–1978', in *The Rites of Rulers: Ritual in Industrial Society – The Soviet Case* (Cambridge: Cambridge University Press, 1981), pp. 153–88.
23. Gerould and Przyboś, op. cit., p. 85.
24. Richard Taylor and Ian Christie (eds.), *The Film Factory: Russian and Soviet Cinema in Documents* (Cambridge, Mass.: Harvard University Press, 1988), p. 178.
25. Daniel Gerould, 'Russian Formalist Theories of Melodrama', in Marcia Landy (ed.), *Imitations of Life: A Reader on Film and Television Melodrama* (Detroit: Wayne State University Press, 1991), pp. 131–3.
26. Taylor and Christie, op. cit., pp. 267, 269.
27. Gerould and Przyboś, op. cit., p. 88.
28. Alma Law, 'The Two Orphans in Revolutionary Disguise', in *Melodrama*, vol. 7. (New York: New York Literary Forum, 1980), p. 106.
29. Gerould and Przyboś, op. cit., pp. 88–9.

VIGILANTE CHRONICLE

The Politics of Melodrama Brought to Life

DAVID GRIMSTED

The politics of melodrama remain more veiled than its aesthetics or morality, though the form's power and appeal was clearly built on a superstructure of service to democratic-bourgeois society, while surely one of its commonest literary embodiments has been, and remains, the rhetoric of party struggles. Those political writings that represent purest melodrama are the series of vigilante chronicles of the mid-nineteenth century United States, the glory days of these heroic mobs and of the literary genre that they spawned, with 'plots that thrilled' – as well as killed. To look at the rhetoric, structure and argument of these tales is to encounter melodramatic politics in its most theatrical guise, and to gain some clues about melodrama's more disguised role in comparatively everyday politics.

The ties between melodrama and the great democratic-bourgeois revolutions of the last quarter of the 18th century are self-evident truths. The melodrama came of age at the time the French Revolution approached its Napoleonic climax. The relation of the dramatic form to earlier English sentimental plays and novels of the 18th century suggests ties as well to the Glorious Revolution and the world's first industrial revolution. The varied involvement with the French Revolution of the leading French perfecters of melodrama was strong, as were, in a more theoretical way, the ideas of Jean Jacques Rousseau, who named the dramatic form and whose political philosphy influenced directly the best of American vigilante chronicles and, indirectly, all of them. The German August von Kotzebue, highly popular in both England and America, wrote his influential plays under the impact of hopes stirred by the American and French Revolutions. New Yorker William Dunlap, who as adaptor and manager did most to translate German and French melodrama to the American stage, was centrally committed to a social-aesthetic order to complement 'the common sense and democracy' of the American Revolution.[1]

By the time Alexis de Tocqueville and Karl Marx were launching their classic analyses of the new democratic-bourgeois world order, melodrama's political critique had shifted from simply deriding all hierarchy separated from moral worth to attacks on clearly specific bourgeois villains tied to land speculating, industrial, banking, and urban sources of power.[2] It was no accident that the threat of the railroad and of the mortgage-holder provided the most lasting memory of late theatrical melodrama, nor is it surprising that the literary genre of vigilante chronicle developed at the same time as the works of Marx and Tocqueville and of melodrama's overt emphasis on bourgeois power. All the writings were an attempt to understand and to offer hope of control over the threatening aspects of what was a new Western world order. American vigilantes distinguished themselves from rioters largely by their literary productions, 'histories' that particpants or panderers wrote to prove to the world their heroic victory over villainous vice. Like the 'asides' of good characters in melodramas, vigilante chronicles were intended directly to 'spell out its ethical forces and imperatives in broad characters', and to proclaim that they were not mobs but somehow their opposite, disinterested heroes victorious in battle against demonic forces threatening to subvert all moral order.[3]

The parallels between theatrical and political melodramas can be explored by looking at an example of each, both of them suggestive of the good naive average of their genre. *Rosina Meadows, The Village Maiden; or, Temptations Unveiled* and *A History of the Regulators of Northern Indiana* were both based 'on real incidents, well known to local citizens', by authors whose primary careers lay elsewhere. Charles Saunders was an actor who often supplemented his income by writing plays, and M.H. Mott was probably a farmer and certainly a vigilante, his single known literary work published to glorify his single known political act. Both works grounded their literary structure in sacred myth, most clearly the central one of the Judeo-Christian tradition of Eden, fall, and restoration, the evil within being, as always in melodrama, externalised into the villains who bedevil the virtuous.

The starting-point of the two stories is different, with Mott offering only passing reference to the 'happy and peaceful' community that came before his climactic moral struggle. The first scene of *The Village Maiden* takes place on the village green in the middle of a May Day celebration where the town's fairest flower, Rosina Meadows, is to be crowned Queen of the May before making her first journey away from her 'humble cottage' to the city. Into this Eden the villain enters on 'the railroad's iron arm', the sinews of wealth and power in the new order contrasted throughout with the father's arms of protective human decency. Establishing that Boston is but twenty miles away, the villain most glibly quotes the play's scripture of Edenic myth: 'God made the country; man made the town; there vice is clothed in the temptations that brought sin and death into the world. Heaven forfend that so fair a blossom as Rosina Meadows should be untimely nipped' – while he plots her nipping. The happy and loving song of the villagers as Rosina leaves rings in the audience's ears as both plea and dirge:

Farewell to Rosina, the sweet village maiden!
The word must be spoken, Farewell, O, farewell.[4]

200

Innocent youth in Mott's farm country of northern Indiana did not have to go to the city to be similarly endangered. Here, Mott tells us, the attraction of 'swamps' drew and provided a fetid hiding place for large gangs of criminals who were on the brink of destroying all local virtue. Not only had the public been 'outraged' and 'houses and barns pillaged and burnt', Mott rhetorically declared, but their sons had been 'decoyed into the vortex of ruin; the virtue of their daughters blasted forever; and the only alternative that now remained was to challenge the enemy to mortal combat'. 'The crisis was a fearful one,' Mott concluded, ' ... upon which hung in awful suspense the dignity, character, and future doom of Northern Indiana.'[5]

Rosina also realised the horrible evil and possible future doom surrounding her. 'Temptations will be thrown in my way – vice is there to deceive the young and innocent!' In Boston, 'every avenue', as in Noble County 'every swamp', was distilling its destructive poison. The villain soon deceives Rosina: letters are forged and an imposter in 'the habiliments of the man of God' performs a false marriage. The villain having taken 'the jewel' and discarded 'the casket' and driven Rosina from the 'roof of virtue to the house of vice', Rosina is left to die in Boston's streets: 'My limbs grow weak – faint – who'll give a cup of water to the lost Rosina?'[6]

Prostitutes lured the good young men and women of northern Indiana to their ruin as well, with mere law unable to protect either persons or property 'against the depredations of the vampires, who curse the earth with their presence'. Boston's forged letters had their counterpart in rural Indiana's forged banknotes, both of them imitating the era's moral currency, the solid virtue of good fathers and banks. In Indiana, Regulators formed 'as the life-boat to save society from the dashing waves of the whirlpool of infamy and shame'. Mott's melodramatic image of miraculous rescue accorded with his political argument. If outlaws threatened 'to prostitute and blast forever the character of every young man and woman that comes within the range of their damning influence', Mott declared that every person had the right and responsibility to destroy evil 'by virtue of the Declaration of Independence' as well as 'the charter given him by the God of the universe'.[7]

This latter charter of 'he who sits in majesty upon the high throne of heaven' was also invoked in Boston, but providential justice in Boston depended, as in Indiana, on the activity of the virtuous. The dying Rosina begs and gains her father's forgiveness. A policeman brings in the villain, now a disinherited drunk and thief. Old Meadows says, 'Villain! Seducer! – Die! die!' (*Music. He strangles him*). The play ends in a moral tableau, the good man standing over the bodies of forgiven virtue and punished vice, while the watchman points out literally the play's transcendent moral, one arm extended towards heaven and the other towards Rosina. Justice on earth is again made visible.[8]

Mott's melodramatic chronicle also climaxed in edifying tableau, this one enacted on a sunny 26 January 1858, when the Regulators hanged their one victim, Gregory McDougle, a 'villain' perhaps guilty of petty crimes, but hanged for the murder of a gaoler's wife in Canada. Mott claimed that there could be 'no doubt' of his guilt since a jury not just of twelve but of hundreds unanimously convicted him. A rope stretched between the limb of a tree and his neck, McDougle stood on the propped-up tailgate of a wagon and was allowed to offer the drama's moral. Mott quoted a local paper's account which had McDougle praise the work of the Regulators and hang cheerfully after telling his gratifyingly large audience, 'I am happy to see such a crowd around me, and I hope all young men will take a warning from me.' At the midday execution, the audience saw above their victim's head, Mott wrote, 'the star of hope – the omen of better days to Northern Indiana'.[9]

One feature of theatrical melodrama excluded from the vigilante chronicle was the comic middle, those humorous characters allowed to show normal, or even extreme, interest in sex, money and aggression without being morally debased. A Yankee farm girl and a pedlar gave *Rosina Meadows* its 'centre' of decent egoism between the wholly disinterested virtue or superego of the high characters and the totally destructive selfishness or id of the villain. These 'middle characters,' naive but shrewdly capable of self-protection, formed an essential aspect of melodrama's metaphysics, related to the dualism of the elevated and ordinary in much nineteenth-century moral philosophy.[10] Laughter served in the theatre as realistic counterweight to the central moralism, but melodramatic politics would die laughing if humour were admitted to its world of vampires, monster banks and evil empires opposed by wholly disinterested and courageous heroes.

Vigilante chroniclers always avoided the human 'realism' of this humour, though there certainly was enough comic ambiguity in Indiana, as in other vigilante actions, if the evidence is looked at with an honest rather than a melodramatic eye. In fact, that gaoler's wife whom these vigilantes avenged had been killed not by McDougle but by rumour: she was alive and well in Canada.[11] The wordy moralism of melodramatic rhetoric, in chronicle as in play, was intended to paper-over gross improbabilities of plot.

The use of the rhetoric of melodrama to provide absolute clarity and to deny the always morally messy realities of life is clearest in the climax of Mott's drama, which closed with McDougle's edifying last words before the tableau of the final solution illustrating justice restored. The elderly curator of a local historical society told me in 1974 the story his grandfather had told him as a boy. As a fifteen-year-old youth the grandfather went to witness the excitement, and remembered McDougle's last words as much more colloquially American: 'I never did no murder. As for horse-stealing, well, maybe I am guilty, but there's lots here as guilty as me, an' I can name them –', at which point Regulator Chris Heltzell kicked the prop from under the tailgate, so that McDougle breathed and, more to the point, spoke his last.[12]

If Mott's writing represented the typical vigilante chronicle, Alexandre Barde's book was the richest, juiciest, and most engrossing version of the basic tale. Since theatrical melodrama as a clear formula came to the fore first in France, perhaps aesthetic tradition had something to do with making the great American vigilante chronicle a work in French about a group of committees that flourished in the French-speaking sections of Louisiana in 1859. While incorporating all the usual gross myth and exaggeration of vigilante melodrama, Barde did so with rich detail and passionate conviction in contrast to the coarsely calculational narratives of more sober American chroniclers, and with less moral camouflage of the sado-sexual chords of the genre.

In the beginning, Barde explained, Louisiana's Attakapas country was Eden where 'courage, probity, and honour flourished openly as orange blossoms under the tropical sun' during 'a golden age, when society was composed of primitive virtues'. The serpent of greed and apathy, however, led to crimes committed 'every day, every hour, every minute' by a Satanic 'army of generals, officers, soldiers' who gave evil its greatest sway, in all its forms from forgery to murder to lust to lawsuits. This 'net of invisible enemies' made even 'rape and infanticide rampant'. At this juncture, however, honest men, happily untouched by this gross corruption, their very names 'certificates of probity and honour', acted with hands wholly 'pure and disinterested' and hearts braving all danger. Once such men rose up and destroyed corruption, all was again happy, all 'the mire' was removed, so that once again 'ladies may venture out in their satin slippers for they no longer fear the rabble'. Barde's concluding scriptural blessing was that of all vigilante chroniclers: 'Blessed be the Committees of Vigilance which have leaned over the coffee of Public Opinion and drawn it from the tomb as Christ did Lazarus.'[13] The reign of virtue was reborn.

Barde's account is remarkably detailed, if even longer on rhetoric than fact. He tells of 41 beatings, 90 exilings and 7 killings by the vigilantes between the beginning of February and September 1859, when a mass beating of political-vigilante opponents with four deaths ended the movement. Yet this data is subordinated to Barde's rich evocations of melodrama's moral and emotive trappings. His drama opens by establishing the moral polarity essential to the form: 'On February 1, 1859, society found itself divided into two camps … : the first camp was that of honest men, the other was that of bandits.' He shortly provides songs, in poetry and prose, that effectively serve as verbal 'music' underlining his meaning and emotion, similar to that which the orchestra provided for the melodramatic theatre:

> Too many lepers defile our land,
> > Public opinion has condemned them all.
> O, Vigilantes, to war, quickly to war
> > That all bandits be exterminated.

The poem's repeated refrain extolling extermination is even stronger in Barde's prose prologue to action where he announces the 'mad, merciless hunt' about to begin, and pictures the criminals as helpless animals about to be destroyed:

In vain do the beasts flee, like bucks, like deer, like rabbits. They hear already the hot breath of the hounds that chase them. At them, my

203

dogs! At the fugitives! At the deer! At the rabbit! One last effort and the pursued prey will bleed between your white teeth![14]

In melodramatic settings of 'ulcerous rot' and 'leprous air', Barde paraded his history of crime and punishment. His most extended sketch concerned one of the earliest chastisements. Young August Gudbeer, surrounded by vigilantes at 2.00 a.m. in the February moonlight,

> undressed slowly, as a young girl who fears to show to the indiscrete the charms which her bashfulness keeps hidden and which will be seen only by the spouse she sees in her dreams. A shiver ran at times over his body, and imparted a nervous trembling to his hands, frail and delicate.'

Naked in the circle of vigilante eyes, Gudbeer asked why he was being punished. No answer come when he looked at Paul Broussard, then at Desiré Bernard, but Aurelian St-Julien finally replied at length:

> You have been arrested because for twenty years our population, so rich and so industrious, has been exploited, robbed, set on fire by vagabonds who have a sworn hatred for work. ... You have been arrested by us because you are a thief, an incendiarist, perhaps an assassin. ... May this punishment resound in the hearts of all the Attakapas rabble. Strike then, my men.

Each of the twenty-two vigilantes gave the naked Gudbeer, stretched on the ground, two strokes with a large paddle, instructed to announce a crime with each blow. Mixed with the young mans's screams were the charges – arson, theft, insults, perjury, a lawsuit – but no detail of anything specific. It is a good example of vigilante justice: a sketch of horrendous social evils so extreme, including flouting of the work ethic in this slave community, that guilt was by acclamation rather than by whatever petty specific crimes were charged. Proof lay in vigilante conviction. At the end of the ordeal, St-Julien told the twenty-one-year-old victim, 'You have taken part in all the crimes that desolated the country for years.'

The Gudbeer 'crime' Barde most stressed was one that runs through his narrative like a twisted thread: a crude racism integrated to sexual fascination. Crimes are mentioned, but interracial sexual dalliance is lingered over. In Gudbeer's pocket a vigilante found a picture of a daughter of Coco, 'a beauty with woolly hair, thick lips, and saffron complexion'. Barde proceeded to detail the mulatto woman's 'monumental' hands and feet that 'seemed to have been sculpted with an axe, perhaps because God, having spent the whole day creating the white race, had created the negro the following night which was moonless'. Despite his racist theology, in Barde's vision the moonlit white boy, trembling like a virgin, and the moonless black girl are joined in a union monstrously attractive. In ordinary melodrama, the villain's 'fascination', grounded in his uninhibited thrust to power, was checked by constant insistence on his vileness; with no lessening of moralism, Barde much more richly suggested the sharing of fear and desire between the good, the bad, the audience, and the author.[15]

Like the *Mysteries of ...* subgenre of melodrama in mid-century, Barde's account is especially rich in sub-plots, the most fascinating of which involve the twisted racism and the casual viciousness of his slave society.[16] Barde's intensity of belief in his tale encouraged him to include unusually honest detail about the underside of vigilante motivation. He admitted that not all vigilante opponents were really outlaws, but some of them honest opponents of extralegality. He agreed that the vigilantes bought up much land from the victims they drove off, though he argued, quite improbably, that the vigilantes always gave a 'good price' to these people who had no choice, as well as provided generous subsidies to 'widows and orphans' when the vicious victims perforce 'abandoned their families in misery'. Barde's account also makes clear the racist and ethnic thrust of the movement: the vigilantes were almost all of French background, as were a majority of the victims, but a sizeable part of the latter were black or Bohemian/German.[17] The political goals of the vigilantes were also clear: they worked to stamp out the vestiges of the Know-Nothing Party and to restore devotedly pro-slavery Democrats to power. Leader Alexandre Mouton, who had been a Democratic governor and US senator, moved directly from vigilante chief to become chair of the Louisana secessionist convention, which Barde said was to usher in a broader reign of the righteous under 'the majestic Committee of Vigilance' which South Carolina initiated in 1860.[18]

Yet none of this detail shakes Barde's central melodramatic myth grounded in Eden, the fall and millennium through apocalypse worked out by casts of humans who represent the perfectly pure and the totally vile. Most melodramas make gestures of verbal or symbolic reference to this mythology – Eden, gardens, serpents, crosses, rebirth – such as Saunders's 'the Eden of her thoughts' or 'who will give a cup of water to the lost Rosina?' or even Mott's reference to one vigilante group, the 'Eden Police'.[19] Barde's account more systematically brings in these references, with its parade of allusions to Jesus, Mary, Lazarus, Pilate, Lucifer, Eden, crucifixion, redemption, and this rhetoric is fitted to a politics characterised by a sense of deep moral decay that craves correction by expulsion or extermination of all evil. In Attakapas, crime, relaxation of customs, the weakening of religious beliefs, and above all 'venality, cowardice, and the impotency of justice, that triple leper', had leached society of all decency until the pure finally recognised that 'the time has come when the nations who do not wish to die must prepare by a struggle the heroic remedies that will cure them'.[20] What is haunting about this melodramatic rhetoric is how recently one has heard it from the mouths of Ronald Reagan, Jerry Brown, David Duke and H. Ross Perot who promise escape from black decay to daybreak so long as the virtuous follow them in crushing evil empires, evil politicians and all the evil people who resist their march to the millennium.

While melodrama and vigilante chronicle followed precisely the same plot of perfect moral dichotomy and final restoration, the politics of the two genres differed profoundly. In line with the practice of encasing the hero in all the virtues, vigilante chroniclers insisted that their groups acted upon the favoured American clichés of 'self-preservation, the right of revolution, and the will of the people'.[21] While the sound of such truisms was wholly sanctified and traditional, vigilante storytellers used the terms in ways widely divergent from their usual American meanings. The democracy in all this talk was not American democracy, but a variant of Rousseau's authoritarian general will, deeply scornful as that was of mere procedural majoritarianism. Vigilantes all lived and acted in communities wholly majoritarian, while they defied officials that the plurality chose and mocked juries the citizenry composed.

Of vigilante glorifiers, only Barde bothered to think about this essential rejection of procedural majoritarianism. His vigilantes, like all others, were 'the people', ordained with the right to be 'the sovereign judges' of all issues, with their power proof enough of their virtue, since 'success comes only to causes that have the sympathy of the masses'. Yet the dominion of deviltry which caused vigilantes to act also had its mass, even majority, support, Barde argued. Criminals ruled by crime but also 'sometimes and in certain localities by the influence of their votes'. Vermillion Parish, for example, had precisely 100 honest families, but many more bandits or rabble who thus had 'a free hand in all elections'. The committees in fact proved 'the limitations of the seducing dogma of popular sovereignty', and replaced it with armed associations representing the true general will who 'reign and govern and everyone finds the yoke light'. Vigilante victory, Barde predicted, would 'assure forever the dictatorship of the Associations'.[22] No other vigilante defender spoke dictatorship, but their theories in fact proclaimed it pro tem.

The vigilantes' temporary dictatorship of the general will also mocked all procedural rights. If legal rights were the most obvious object of vigilante scorn, rights of free speech, of a free press, of assembly and petition, these chronicles argued, should never protect the vile when they used them to complicate the sway of virtue. Those who blathered about 'rights', vigilantes claimed steadily, cared only about criminals and not their victims or communities. The only rights these groups praised were those of property – except, of course, the property of the villains which they often chose to pocket and appropriate.[23]

Although theatrical melodrama very rarely touched governmental theories, the greatest difference in political argument between the two genres involved their diametrically opposed ideas about a central concern in both, class hierarchy. In melodrama, the relation between class and virtue was amorphously inverse. Saunders's class structure is typical: the good live in a 'humble cottage' and eat a 'humble repast', and the villain, a Boston aristocrat of inherited wealth, lives in a 'proud mansion' and 'feasts' regularly. While some of the 'class élite' in melodrama share in moral decency, the vile are almost invariably the powerful determined to victimise those who are commonly their socio-economic inferiors as much as they are their moral betters.[24]

Melodramatic plays politically provided a theatrical home for the new world order associated with the coming of democratic and bourgeois life.

Ordinary people were the centre of dignity in this life, where the threats and uncertainties they faced were presented in a framework that insisted on a universe of moral meaning if one adhered to a code of kindness, honesty, decency and generosity (indeed, an ethic of love that approached *agape*) in a world where, through most of its long acts, such qualities were threatened and sometimes destroyed by those dedicated to an ethic of power and aggrandisement, a gospel of grab, both financial and sexual.[25]

Those who argue that melodrama was a socially protective, 'unsubversive' form are surely right; like all aesthetic forms, it dwells within, as well as explores, the world that seems possible for its creators and its audience.[26] At the same time, its ideololgical function was homiletic: like the good sermon, reform tract, philosophic or political disquisition, or radical manifesto, it insisted on what morally ought to be by denunciatory exposure of what often was. Its criticisms of the bourgeois world were also quite similar to those of Karl Marx – a passionate hatred of all who pursued a policy of self-aggrandising gain and power that involved harm to the full humanity and just hopes of others – while the elements of fear and anger in the visions of society in both melodrama and Marx led each to theories of social apocalypse and millenium. This is not to question the immense differences grown of the grounding of the one in ersatz religion and the other in ersatz science, and especially in melodrama's personal and Marx's social answer, but such oppositions leave intact the similarities in concern and in dramatic structure.[27]

The class–moral divisions in vigilante melodrama are the mirror image of that of the plays. While not all the poor are inevitably bad, the vigilante vicious are the scum of society and the virtuous are 'the best men' in the community. Barde used the galaxy of favoured vigilante terms for their victims that reek of low social status: 'scum', 'muck', 'mire', 'rabble', 'lepers', 'canaille'. He probably emphasised a middle status for his vigilantes partly because it was true, partly because he wished to refute charges, often made in this case, that his vigilantes were rich men warring on the poor. This attack struck, Barde reported, like an 'alarm bell in the heart of the district' whose prairies had 'their aristocracy and their proletariat'.[28]

The vigilante association of their community's proletariat with those they killed and exiled is clear in historian Richard Maxwell Brown's 'standard' picture of social hierarchy in places where vigilantism erupted. Brown claims that there were always three classes: the highly respectable upper class which provided riotous leadership, the middling sort who made up the vigilante rank and file, and 'the lower orders' who were 'viewed with contempt and loathing' by the other two groups because they were dirty, lazy, immoral, unfamilial, and often wanted 'to burst their subordinate bounds and take over new communities' from their decent betters. To dispel this 'real threat' from the socially debased, upper and middling men resorted to vigilantism, Brown concludes.[29]

American communities, like all others, had their pecking orders, based primarily though never wholly on wealth, but whatever classes there were tended to be less clear-cut, more fluid, much less anchored to moral worth, and more richly criss-crossed with ethnic, religious, political, associational and occupational groupings – and rivalries – than Brown's

Top: Illustration one from *Specimens of Show Printing, Being Facsimiles of Poster Cuts* (Philadelphia, 1868)

Bottom: Illustration two from *Illustrated Police News* reprinted in Lucius Beebe and Charles Clegg, *The American West: A Pictorial Epic of a Continent* (New York: E.P. Dutton, 1955)

Illustration three from Alfred W. Arrington, *The Desperadoes of the Old Southwest* (New York, 1849)

The climactic visual violence of most stage melodramas created sympathy for the victims, one reason vigilante chronicles were seldom illustrated. Illustration one shows the attempted last-minute rescue of the innocent in the mid-century play *Too Late*. Illustration two is of extra-legal Montana hangings of 1836, its visual melodrama contradicted by its vigilante text. When Louis Beebe and Charles Clegg reproduced it in 1955 they resolved the contradiction by claiming inventively that the women begging for mercy who 'ornamented the Montana landscape' proved to 'be local prostitutes enacting a role of respectable domesticity'. The third illustration depicts the efforts of two women to obstruct the five death sentences that vigilantes meted out at Cane Hill, Arkansas in 1839. It paralleled the visual effects of stage melodrama because the author repeated the general vigilante myth, but was convinced of the victims' innocence in this case, although he dared not voice his doubts to their executioners.

schema allows.[30] In part, the appeal of the vigilante tradition, to both its members and its historians, was that it allowed a comforting connection between class and moral position that democratic society and scholarship eschewed in more sober moments and on less picturesque subjects. The strong strand of class consciousness, of deep sympathy for society's poor and disadvantaged and of distrust of the conspicuously wealthy, the proudly powerful and the ostentatiously respectable in theatrical melodrama disappears wholly in the complacent equation of social position with moral worth in vigilante chronicle and subsequent history.

One wonders how much the class concern of melodramatic plays and the class complacency of vigilante chronicles may have contributed to their very different reputations. The judgment on theatrical melodrama has, of course, commonly been harsh or condescending; critics use it as ready-made villain, by definition vulgar and duplicitous, to contrast with the virtue of heroic tragedy or honest realism or politically correct post-structuralism's exposé of capitalist-patriarchal hegemony. Such melodramatic criticism has only recently been countered by those who would tidy it towards ambiguous respectability, largely because they see its genealogical ties to literature unambiguously canonised.[31]

On the other hand, the way historians have accepted at face value chronicles that are grossly melodramatic and interpretively preposterous suggests the deep appeal of a politics of melodrama that screams decadence and promises easy restoration of both virtue and firmer hierarchy. There is no doubt that what historian Robert Senkewicz observed wittily about historians of San Francisco's vigilantes is even truer for many of those who have written about other such groups of citizen-saviours: most historians 'seemed intent on standing Santayana's celebrated axiom on its head: the more they studied the past, the more they tended to repeat it'.[32] Nothing underlines the emotive attraction of the politics of melodrama better than the survival for 150 years in sober history of the plot established in the 'factions' of vigilante chronicle: thrilling and blood-filled tales of perfectly disinterested heroes rescuing at the last moment helpless Society from rape by the fiendish villains whom they so happily hanged, whipped, exiled, burnt, and butchered.

Fact and fiction, art and action, life and literature, story and history less imitate one another than grow from the same seed of human need to round miscellaneous experience towards meaning, planted in the soil of socio-cultural realities that define and confine an individual's deeds and sense of the promises and possibilities that life has to offer and has to frustrate. Melodramatic plays offered exhortations to decency and mutual respect in society, though in personal and religious terms that blunted and beclouded structural realities. Vigilante melodrama possessed all the weaknesses of these plays' politics in a more deadly serious context and a more hierarchical structure. The sources of its appeal are much clearer than are its contributions and dangers.

The vocabulary of American life is absolutist; people talk about democracy, justice, law, Constitution, freedom, order, right, rights, individualism, community, as if they were self-evident and perfect, translucently clear. Yet the grammar of its life, the way such terms become the sentences of American society, is realistic, muddled, majoritarian, some version of the best thing someone can think of and most agree on at the moment. Little wonder that a people fed on such transcendent vocabulary and sentenced to such compromising reality often despise the system they accept, and sometimes seek escape. Vigilantism was the local version of the United States' and the world's frequent politics of simple-minded self-righteousness, the attempt or the pretence of inaugurating the ideal by hanging the real.

Humans find comfort in escaping the ambiguities of personal and social life by entering a morally simple world of perfect virtue and total vice, the latter always painted black enough to allow even the conspicuously shoddy to see themselves as among the children of light. In melodramatic drama, where the prolonged emphasis was on suffering and sympathy, people left the theatre perhaps a touch more caring towards those who bore the greatest social burdens. At least everyone, including

210

the villain, left the theatre. In melodramatic politics, of which vigilante chronicle is a sub-genre, the stress was always on the self-righteous pleasure of the blood atonement needed for communal cleansing, where heroes proved their virtue by their enthusiasm for killing vice: through capital punishment, war, genocide, or the more modest murdering by vigilante groups. Not everyone, however, lived to read the rave reviews the victors wrote.

Notes

1. Peter Brooks, *The Melodramatic Imagination: Balzac, Henry James, Melodrama and the Mode of Excess* (New Haven: Yale University Press, 1976), pp. 20–2, 14–15, passingly ties melodrama to the politics of the French Revolution and of Watergate, pp. 203–4, while Raymond Williams developed the social argument more intensively in the first section of his book *Modern Tragedy* (Stanford: Stanford University Press, 1966). Works on melodrama that explore the political connections and implications of the form are my *Melodrama Unveiled: American Theatre and Culture, 1800–1850* (Berkeley: University of California Press, 1968, 1987); Bruce McConachie, *Melodramatic Formations: American Theatre and Society, 1820–1870* (Iowa City: University of Iowa, 1992); and an excellent study by Paul Ginisty, *Le Mélodrame* (Paris: Louis-Michaud, 1910) which argues that 'le genre théâtral est intimement lié a l'histoire des temps qu'il a traversés' and 'la conscience populaire', pp. 7, 18. He handles well the politics of Pixérécourt, Caigniez, and Ducange, pp. 40–180. William Dunlap, *The History of the Rise and Progress of the Arts of Design in the United States* (Boston: C.E. Goodspeed, 1981 (first pub. 1834)), 1, p. 338.
2. On bourgeois reformist melodrama after the 1830s, see *Melodrama Unveiled*, pp. 158–65, 195–202; McConachie, op. cit., pp. 161–96; Maurice W. Disher, *Blood and Thunder: Mid-Victorian Melodrama and its Origins* (London: Rockliff, 1949), pp. 101–59; Michael Booth, *English Melodrama* (London: H. Jenkins, 1965), pp. 118–42; Frank Rahill, *The World of Melodrama* (University Park, Pa.: State University of Pennsylvania Press, 1967), pp. 240–53; James L. Smith, *Melodrama* (London: Methuen, 1973), pp. 41–2, 73–7.
3. Brooks, op. cit., p. 42.
4. M.H. Mott, *History of the Regulators of Northern Indiana* (Indianapolis: Indianapolis Journal Co., 1859); Charles Saunders, *Rosina Meadows, The Village Maid; or, Temptations Unveiled* (Boston: W.V. Spencer, 1855), pp. iv, 3–18. Mott's account is one of at least a dozen books and pamphlets published to proclaim the virtue of such groups' extralegal activities. There are many more such vigilante chronicles published in newspapers or recorded by local historians from participant accounts later on. For a fuller look at these movements and chronicles, see my 'Né d'Hier: American Vigilantism, Communal Rebirth and Political Traditions', in Loretta Valtz Mannucci (ed.), *People and Power; Rights, Citizenship and Violence* (Milan: University of Milan, 1990), pp. 75–113.
5. Mott, op. cit., pp. 5–16.
6. Saunders, op. cit., pp. 14, 26, 33–4.
7. Mott, op. cit., pp. 8–9, 16, 63.
8. Saunders, op. cit., pp. 28, 40–2.
9. Mott, op. cit., pp. 17, 21–32.
10. The neglect of comedy as an integral part of the moral structure of melodrama is a central weakness in many thoughtful handlings of the topic. This

211

humour was not simply relief, but the creation of the everyday moral world to be encased in transcendent or higher moral truth (Grimsted, op. cit., pp. 183–99, 234–40, 243–5). Central to nineteenth-century thought was a philosophic or cultural dualism that substituted Natural Law for Divine Providence or God, and insisted that everyday reality – or the 'seeming' – was not the only truth but was encased in a higher moral reality that assured, in the *very* long run or long view, that moral justice and reward would finally prevail. Such was the dualism of Emerson's transcendentalism with its encasing Oversoul or Kant's idealism with its protective categorical imperative. Such (on more popular and vague cultural levels) were the 'Victorian' or 'genteel' tradition that divided reality in various ways (everyday and eternal, lower and higher, business and home, male and female, comic and serious) in an attempt to keep the nastier realities and possibilities of democratic-bourgeois society in harness to its moral and humane hopes.

11. A local chronicler who repeated Mott's version of events argued that the Regulators had made no mistake since they had only claimed (with his emphasis) 'unmistakable evidence *charging* him with murder'. *Counties of Lagrange and Noble, Indiana: Historical and Biographical* (Chicago: F.A. Battey, 1882), 2, p. 73.

12. Interview with Lloyd Bender, 26 June 1974.

13. Alexandre Barde, *L'Histoire des Comités de la Vigilance des Attakapas* (1861) translated and edited by Henrietta G. Rogers (MA thesis, Louisiana State University, 1936), pp. 70–1, 356–8, 378–82. Rogers covers Barde's background and gives some citations to his other writings in her helpful introduction to her translation, pp. iv–ix.

14. Ibid., pp. 9, 31, 34–5, 37, 170. Barde apologised for his verse, explaining, 'one cannot meditate over eclogues or bucolic poems when one is sitting on the crater of a volcano', p. 37.

15. Ibid., pp. 65–9, 230–4. Christopher Prendergast talks interestingly of the complicated interplay, so strong in Barde, of fascination with and fear of violence/order in melodrama: *Balzac: Fiction and Melodrama* (London: Arnold, 1978), pp. 11–14.

16. Eugène Sue's *Mysteries of Paris* (1842–43) was the most famous of these, but that book spawned a series of imitative novels and plays in France, England and the United States: Rahill, op. cit., pp. 85–92; Disher, op. cit., pp. 160–76; George Lippard, *The Quaker City; or The Monks of Mork Hall* (Philadelphia: by the author, 1846). Peter Brooks and Daniel S. Burt have articles on the French and British prototypes in Daniel Geroud (ed.), *Melodrama* (New York: New York Literary Forum, 1980), pp. 125–58.

17. Barde, op. cit., pp. 361–2, 432. Barde accused one German the vigilantes drove out of everything from drunkenness to theft, but his worst offence was that he 'jabbered French with the strange, impossible accent which is peculiar to that race beyond the Rhine', p. 197.

18. Ibid., pp. 42–2, 425, 50; *Biographical and Historical Memoirs of Louisiana*, (Chicago: Goodspeed, 1892), 2, pp. 425–9.

19. Saunders, op. cit., p. 34; Mott, op. cit., p. 67.

20. Barde, op. cit., p. 5.

21. Richard Maxwell Brown, *Strain of Violence: Historical Studies of American Violence and Vigilantism* (New York: Oxford University Press, 1975), p. 115.

22. Barde, op. cit., pp. 166, 36, 30, 422, 191, 41–3, 29, 107. Barde used 'dictatorship' in two other places and always with positive enthusiasm, pp. 10, 47.

23. Mobbing to gain land was central in several of the Illinois, Iowa and Missouri vigilante groups, while much of the vigilantism in the far west,

1856–65, had essentially political motives, usually to destroy the power of the Democratic Party.

24. Saunders, op. cit., p. 14; Booth, op. cit., pp. 123–6; Books, op. cit., p. 44; Grimsted, op. cit., pp. 203–10.

25. The stress on success or money as the goal in nineteenth-century popular culture in everything from *McGuffey's Reader* to Horotio Alger's novels is a misreading. There are usually modest rewards not for hard work but for moral generosity, as in melodrama. Robertson Davies argues well melodrama's contribution to creating a general sense of all people's equal worth: *The Mirror of Nature* (Toronto: University of Toronto Press, 1983), especially pp. 11–27.

26. Stephen Neale, *Genre* (London: British Film Institute, 1980), p. 22. Julia Przyboś strongly argues melodrama's conservatism, largely because it urged the individual's subordinance to moral, familial, communal, and national obligations, *L'Entreprise Mélodramatique* (Paris: Corti, 1987), pp. 59–96, 191–4.

27. Marx's bruising wit, angry at everyone, creates a comedy in his one history, *The Eighteenth Brumaire of Louis Bonaparte*. In some sense, this is similar to the function of comedy in melodrama, an incorporation into his work of an everyday world that does not exactly fit, but also does not fight, his theoretical 'scientific' moral patterns.

28. Barde, op. cit., pp. 361–2.

29. Brown, op. cit., pp. 104–5. There is a somewhat parallel tendency to claim that the melodramatic theatre in England (in contrast to that in France or the United States) was poor *because* it catered to 'the mob' or the new industrial lower classes: Brooks, op. cit., p. 12; Booth, op. cit., p. 16; Smith, op. cit., pp. 16–17.

30. Commonly there was little difference in social class between the perpetrators and victims of vigilante action, but the chronicles always suggested a class corollary of their moral Manicheism. On the reality of class insecurity, see the ablest of vigilante studies both in clarity of prose and understanding: Robert M. Senkewicz, *Vigilantes in Gold Rush San Francisco* (Stanford: Stanford University Press, 1985).

31. Good examples are the works by Prendergast, op. cit., Brooks, op. cit., and Smith, op. cit., and George J. Worth, *Dickensian Melodrama: A Reading of the Novels* (Lawrence: University of Kansas, 1978).

32. Senkewicz, op. cit., p. 203. Those historians who, along with Brown, have generally passed on vigilantes' versions of their history include: Hubert Howe Bancroft's California study, *Popular Tribunals*, 2 vols (San Francisco: The History Co., 1887); James G. Leyburn, *Frontier Folkways* (New Haven: Yale University Press, 1935); Wayne Gard, *Frontier Justice* (Norman: University of Oklahoma Press, 1949); W. Eugene Hollen, *Frontier Violence: Another Look* (New York: Oxford University Press, 1974); Philip Jordan, *Frontier Law and Order: Ten Essays* (Lincoln: University of Nebraska Press, 1970); and, with some ambiguity, William C. Culberson, *Vigilantism: Political History of Private Power in America* (New York: Greenwood Press, 1990).

THE SOCIAL EVIL, THE MORAL
ORDER AND THE MELODRAMATIC
IMAGINATION, 1890–1915

RICHARD MALTBY

In 1932, after William Fox had lost his business empire to Harley Clarke and the Chase National Bank, he told his life story to radical novelist Upton Sinclair. In Sinclair's hands, it became

> A Melodrama of Fortune, Conflict and Triumph. Packed with Thrills and Heart Throbs. East Side Boy Conquers Fame and Power. The Masters of Millions Envy His Triumph and Plot His Downfall. The Octopus Battles the Fox. The Duel of a Century! The Sensation of a Lifetime![1]

Upton Sinclair Presents William Fox is a story of ethnic struggle, written with the express purpose of vindicating Fox's good name. In describing Fox's conflicts with the villains of this tale, 'the elegant and cultured New York bankers with the carnations in their buttonholes', Sinclair repeatedly emphasises the fact of Fox's Jewishness and the undercurrent of anti-Semitism in their villainy.[2] One instance is particularly revealing in the connections it makes to other melodramatic narratives. According to Fox, when the General Film Company tried to revoke his exchange licence in the autumn of 1911, they charged that he had permitted their pictures to be shown in a house of prostitution. 'The Trust' had bribed an exhibitor in Paterson, New Jersey, to take films rented from Fox's exchange to a Hoboken brothel, where they had installed a projector and screened the films.[3] This part of Fox's tale is, in all probability, a fiction, but there are several senses in which this melodramatic narrative mode was appropriate to the American cinema's cultural project. The formal mechanisms of a drama of 'muteness' were bound to propose relevant solutions to the narrative and cultural problematics of silent cinema. My interest in Fox's tale, however, draws me less to these formal properties than to pursue the larger claim Peter Brooks makes for melodrama as 'the principal mode for uncovering, demonstrating, and making operative the essential moral universe in a post-sacred era'. A 'dramaturgy of virtue misprized and eventually recognised'[4] was metaphorically appropriate to the cultural position of the early cinema, itself engaged in a struggle for the recognition of its virtue. Whether 'the Trust' actually accused him of pandering or not, William Fox was personally engaged in a drama of recognition, a narrative of virtue made visible and acknowledged.

The charge against Fox was (or was not) made at the height of the 'white slavery' panic, a year in which the United States Immigration Commission report observed that 'There are a large number of Jews scattered throughout the United States who seduce and keep girls.'[5] The report picked up a vein of specifically anti-Semitic nativism present in the white slavery hysteria, and particularly visible in a series of articles by George Kibbe Turner published in *McClure's Magazine* during the New York mayoral election campaign of 1909.[6] It was, declared Turner, 'the Jewish dealer in women, a product of New York politics, who has vitiated, more than any other single agency, the moral life of the great cities of America in the past ten years'. The traffic in women was largely in the hands of 'Austrian, Russian and Hungarian Jews', whose activities were protected by Tammany Hall, the city's Democratic political machine.[7]

The Progressive investigation of prostitution perfectly illustrates Michel Foucault's suggestion that the incitement to discourse about sex places us 'under the spell of an immense curiosity about sex, bent on questioning it, with an insatiable desire to hear it speak and be spoken about'.[8] By 1914, over a billion pages of research and publicity into the 'social evil' had been published in the United States. These studies, however, largely avoided any investigation of the prostitutes' clientele. In the place of a sustained exploration of the social implications of a vice economy that, according to one estimate, maintained one prostitute for every twelve sexually active men, the 'white slavery' scenario accounted for prostitution through its narrative of the degradation of native-born agrarian purity by the 'foreign' city. Its plot was encapsulated in a 1902 movie called *The Downward Path*, in which a naive country girl is seduced into prostitution by a travelling book agent. Abandoned by him, she poisons herself before her aged parents can rescue her.[9] The explanatory power of this scenario lay in the way it articulated and displaced assumptions about the relationship of sexuality, race and power in late nineteenth-century America.[10]

Discussions of the social evil of prostitution were seldom free of racial undertones. The term 'white slavery' itself was both a displacement and an act of regulation, an oxymoron that at the same time denied the specifics of racial sexual abuse under slavery and implied their inversion.[11] The psychological inheritance of racial patriarchy in slavery required that 'white civilisation' be held in (dis)place by the public repression of white female sexuality and the public projection of white male sexuality on to an Other, allowing the contradictions of this displacement to find expression in violence, in what W.J. Cash termed the Southern rape complex.[12] The white slavery scenario provided a means of mediating patriarchal anxieties through its displacement of guilt from customer to panderer, to a male sexual Other, whose Otherness was defined by racial characteristics, and thus it provided an alternative account to the class overtones of earlier melodramatic accounts of despoliation.[13] For both feminists and male reformers, the white slavery explanation of prostitution maintained an identification of sexuality and degradation, and allowed them to see themselves as rescuers of slaves, heirs to an abolitionist tradition. The parable of white slavery broadened the application of the Southern rape complex, substituting ethnicity for race while maintaining the virulence of racial antagonism and preserving its mythology of female sexual passivity.[14]

In 1910, Congress enacted legislation that permitted the deportation of any alien 'who is employed by, in or in connection with any ... music or dance hall or other place of amusement habitually frequented by prostitues'.[15] In the rhetoric of the anti-prostitution campaign, the movie theatre was a 'similar place' to the dance hall as a site for the enactment of the recurrent nativist fantasy of white slavery. That fantasy located the site of sexuality, pleasure, guilt and excess geographically, in the red-light districts of American cites, and it indicted the commercialisation of pleasure in movie theatres, dance halls and cabarets because they encouraged sexual pleasure to escape its geographical bounds and confuse the Victorian dichotomy of public and private.[16] As a place of commercialised pleasure, the cinema was both social space and the site of narrative, and both those activities came under scrutiny. A Jewish motion picture exhibitor, with close business connections with Big Tim Sullivan, Tammany Hall's 'boss of the Bowery' and the most powerful Democratic politician in Manhattan,[17] was undoubtedly vulnerable to the slurs of nativist rhetoric; if General Filmco was going to trump up a charge against Fox, it might as well be as sordid and suggestive as they could manage.

The white slavery scenario also provided an exaggerated account of a normative understanding of relations between the sexes, which, as dance hall reformer Belle Israels explained, were a matter of 'pursuit and capture'. 'The man is ever on the hunt,' she wrote, 'and the girl is ever needing to flee.'[18] Rendering this struggle in fictional form most frequently resulted in the adoption of melodramatic conventions of villainy and victimisation in a narrative of heroic repression, which climaxes in the prevention of an event.[19] In these scenarios the melodramatic cinema borrowed a narrative vehicle for the staging and restraint of desire from the stage and literature. In D. W. Griffith's *To Save Her Soul* (1909), for instance, the clergyman hero prepares to shoot the heroine when he finds her singing and drinking champagne in a nightclub. 'Crazed by jealous love,' reads an intertitle, 'he would kill her that her soul may remain pure.'[20] Seldom, in the event, was such passion spent in a consummation in death; rather, the conventional plot describes the escalation of a bestial threat to a climax of self-restraint. Griffith's own description of his idealised plot read as if it were a sequence of unconsummated sexual encounters. Alternating the action between characters lighted 'like archangels or devils', he sought to 'arouse' his audience to a moral cause:

The pace must be quickened from beginning to end. That is not, however, a steady ascent. The action must quicken to a height in a minor climax which should be faster than the first, and retard again and build to the third which should be faster than the second, and on to the final climax where the pace should be the fastest. Through all the big moments of the story, the pace should build like an excited pulse.[21]

216

'The final climax', the 'consummation of all romantic and adventurous dreams', involved the rescue of the passive heroine from men, or 'devils dressed like men' embodying lust, greed, or tyranny. The narrative's division of masculinity needed women to be nothing more than corruptible vessels of spiritual virtue, over whose purity the man at war with himself might constantly battle. Narrative embodied evil in a recognisable, separate, corporeal entity. On occasion, as in Griffith's *The Avenging Conscience* (1914), the bodies of male good and evil were the same, but the evil existed only in the desiring dreams of the hero. More conventionally, the evil Other was another body, marked by icons of difference, hated and destroyed for enacting desire.[22] Griffith, most notoriously, would return this narrative to the full-blown articulation of the Southern rape complex in *Birth of a Nation* in 1915.[23]

The two great crusades to impose a bourgeois morality on the new urban masses, the attempts to control liquor and prostitution, cloaked a concern for political order beneath moral anxieties, and obsessively declared the villain of their melodramas of souls 'ruined' by drunkenness and white slavery to be the city, a city as sad, dangerous, and imaginary as that of George Lippard fifty years before or Robert Warshow fifty years later.[24] According to the Reverend Charles H. Parkhurst, New York was 'an industrialised Sodom, where prostitution, gambling and illegal Sabbath carousing in the city's saloons were administered by the police through a wondrously intricate discipline of graft, bribes, blackmail, bought promotions and kickbacks'.[25] Parkhurst was a leading figure in the 'fusion' reform campaigns that defeated Tammany in 1894 and 1901. Founder of the City Vigilance League, president of the Society for the Prevention of Crime, he was the 'vice crusader' *in extremis*, stentorian advocate of the coercive approach to urban reform.[26]

The excess moral energy of Progressive reform, not channelled into budgetary efficiency and good city government, was directed into campaigns against 'vice' and small-time 'corruption' that fuelled bourgeois fantasies of urban decadence while having little effect on the substantial causes of urban ills. As Paul Boyer argues, in much reform discourse 'the saloon' and 'the brothel' were drained of concrete meaning and became 'simply code words for the larger menace of urban social change', reducing the complexities of urbanisation to the more manageable proposition that sinister but identifiable evil forces were responsible for social and moral disorder. Vice crusaders like Parkhurst conjured up an 'invisible government' of inordinate, corrupting power that had brought into being and was now exploiting the web of liquor, prostitution and graft.[27] It could only be defeated by what anti-prostitution campaigner Maude Miner called the 'new scientific and humanitarian spirit' of Progressivism. That spirit held that 'since nothing that is necessary is evil, nothing that is evil can be necessary'. Before it, 'the traditional methods of vice' would 'totter and fall'.[28] In its anticipated denouement as well as in its dramatis personae, the anti-prostitution campaign, and the coercive reform movement in general, exercised a melodramatic imagination.

The rhetoric of Progressive reform used the discursive conventions of melodrama as a means of maintaining clear moral distinctions when describing an urban environment where the bourgeois certainties of a Victorian moral order no longer obtained. Movies, amusement parks and dance halls created a heterosocial environment that provided young women with access to a wider range of evening pleasures,[29] and produced a commercial relationship between the sexes that rendered more ambiguous the connection between the exchange of money and the granting of sexual favours than the processes of direct purchase assumed in the red-light districts.[30] Coercive reformers viewed such transactions within the Victorian moral paradigm of the 'fallen woman', and thus identified these new public sites as excrescences of immorality, evidence that vice could not be contained within the confines of red-light districts.[31] In 1913, in search of *The Social Evil in Syracuse*, the Syracuse Moral Survey Committee reported dolefully that 'the commercialization of practically every human interest in the past thirty years has completely transformed daily life.... Prior to 1880 the ... main business of living was living.... The main business of life now is pleasure.'[32] The vice of pleasure particularly affected the working-class young, who were

> filled with vanity and youthful indulgence.... Youth is extravagant to prodigality with itself. . . . It is drunk with its own intoxicating perfume ... and we surround that young, passionate, bursting blossom with every temptation to break down its resistant power, lure it into sentiment, pulsating desire and eroticism by lurid literature, moving pictures, tango dances, suggestive songs, cabaret, noise, music, light, life, rhythm, everywhere, until the senses are throbbing with leashed-in physical passion.[33]

Such language pulsated with a barely veiled eroticism of its own, evidence of the processes of repression and sublimation in the reformers' descriptions of Other sexualities almost or completely out of control. They constructed a vision of a hidden city of concealed, unlimited, unlicensed sexuality while, to their despair, they succeeded in seeing depravity wherever they looked, even in the darkest of places.[34] The Syracuse Vice Commission described a 'secluded spot' frequented by the city's youth as being 'so dark there that you can scarcely see your hand before your face. As you go slowly along you can *see* nothing, but you can *hear* whisperings all about.'[35] The rhetoric of coercive reform grew more exaggerated and vituperative through the first decade of the century, in parallel not with the growth of 'commercialised vice' so much as with the 'commercialised amusements' that were in practice coming to replace it. Absorbing most of the small surpluses over subsistence income in working-class wages, these concerns – penny arcades, dance halls, amusement parks, vaudeville and burlesque houses, anatomical museums and saloons – were the principal manifestations of the more general emergence of a culture of consumption visible and accessible to the working class. They were also complexly intertwined with the political as well as the neighbourhood life of urban America, embedded in the matrix of favours, accommodations, indulgences and influence that made up the compromised benevolence of a city's political machine. Few coercive reformers distinguished between the institutions of commercialised vice and commercialised amusement. Movie theatres were indicted along with dance halls as 'breeding places of vice'.[36] Nickelodeon operators were no better than saloon-keepers: 'dull, ignorant, or vicious men, hungry for money and unscrupulous in the getting of it',[37] and according to the *New York Tribune*, foreign to a man, 'the greater portion' of them 'Jewish Americans, who practically control the whole enterprise'.[38]

Reform anxiety was initially provoked by the nickelodeon boom, which led the People's Institute to conclude in February 1908 that New York's 'moving picture variety shows' had become 'an unwieldy excrescence on the body politic', often 'openly immoral in influence', threatening church activities, school attendance and the use of libraries.[39] Far more than any concern with film content, it was the phenomenon of motion picture attendance, together with the material conditions under which audiences saw films, that preoccupied reformers. Their principal anxieties were created by the fact that nickelodeons were hot, dark places. The dust, the crowds, the heat and the lack of ventilation made them prime sites for the spread of disease.[40] Disease, however, was also a metaphor, and behind such reasonable concerns about the possible spread of tuberculosis lurked others, occasioned by 'instances where children have been influenced for evil by the *conditions surrounding* some of these shows'. The Chicago Vice Commission cited one such instance, where 'a proprietor of one of these nickel theatres assaulted fourteen young girls', and another in which 'the stage manager committed a serious offence with several little boys'.[41] In these investigations, the regulation of content was an element in the regulation of exhibition, alongside the establishment of fire and safety codes and the enforcement of Sunday closing laws,[42] but to assume that the principal cause for objection had to do with the content of the films exhibited is comparable to suggesting that the Anti-Saloon League were concerned that saloons sold poor-quality beer. The analogy also suggests the scale of the task which liberal reformers and exhibitors shared, of persuading the more conservative reform elements to regard the motion picture theatre as a redemptive substitute for the saloon, and not just an equivalent to it.

The National Board of Censorship of Motion Pictures came into being in early 1909, after Mayor George B. McClellan closed the New York motion picture theatres in December 1908. Its early history embodied a struggle between manufacturers and exhibitors for control over a public discourse on film that engaged issues of economic control as well as questions of who and what was to be regulated.[43] The Motion Picture Patents Company, the industry's first oligopoly of manufacturers, tried to exercise its economic power by identifying the movie problem as being caused by unlicensed theatres showing unlicensed films, in circumstances likely to be both morally and physically unhealthy. By way of response, the New York exhibitors, led by Fox, called for censorship to 'protect them from the film manufacturers who foisted improper pictures'[44] featuring crime and vulgarity on them. The formation of the National Board was a strategy in the exhibitors' struggle against the oligopoly power of the Patents Company. Crucially for the exhibitors, this moved the central subject of

219

concern in 'the movie problem' from the theatre itself to the movies shown in them. As the physical conditions of viewing improved to accommodate the middle classes during the 1910s, attention increasingly focused on what was on the screen, and what the audience's relationship was to it. The specifics of these concerns were attached to the formal properties of moving pictures as medium and subsequently as narrative form.

Early cinema had to negotiate the cultural acceptability of its mechanisms of representation against the anxieties generated by the commodification of desire.[45] Motion pictures had to overcome the objection that they were not a 'safe and sane' form of recreation if they were to escape a peripheral and pariah state, and gain access to a middle-class market. Their deployment of the mechanisms of desire necessarily led the movies into areas of cultural taboo and anxiety around sexuality, criminal behaviour, and psychological influence, and around the unhealthy transfer of emotional affect between viewer and viewed object. As Scott Simmon suggests, the moral didacticism of *To Save Her Soul* and other Griffith melodramas was in irresolvable conflict with the 'public display of women' necessarily promoted by the filmgoing situation.[46] The culture of consumption required extensive renegotiations of the ways in which women occupied public spaces, but for cinema the anxieties provoked by these renegotiations concentrated around 'realism' and imitation.[47] Films were censorially criticised for the excessive adequacy of their representations of the real, while it was their 'mesmeric' powers of influence that provoked concern over imitative behaviour.

Progressive reformers such as Jane Addams regarded the screen as transparent and its imitation of reality as unmediated by the audience's recognition of the fictive status of what they viewed. The screen's 'realism' was identified not as a quality of dramatic or narrative structure but as an ontological characteristic of the apparatus. The pro-censorship argument that the medium had the power to influence behaviour relied on an undeclared play on the idea of imitation. Its transparent imitation of reality was regarded as inherently dangerous because of its capacity itself to inspire the imitation of screen behaviour. Newspapers and reformers alike persistently conflated juvenile imitation of the movies with juvenile crime in a cycle that explicitly invoked the addiction of attendance and the hypnosis of the screen: children watched movies in which criminal acts were committed, and then stole in order to raise money to attend movies. This deviant response to 'realism' was not attributed to all viewers, but only to the incompletely or inadequately socialised viewer who was, paradigmatically, the delinquent adolescent.[48]

One solution to these anxieties was the firm declaration of the motion picture's status as fiction. The adoption of fictional narrative as the overwhelmingly dominant form from 1908 was primarily motivated by the material necessities of increased volume production, but it also served other ideological and industrial purposes.[49] If it was the cinema's 'reality effect' that so disconcerted as well as enthused its earliest theorists and critics, the imposition of conventionalised narrative structures on it can in itself be recognised as an instrument of social control. Through narrative, the realism of the screen could be harnessed into a means of inculcating a moral lesson – in effect, the same moral lesson constantly repeated. The producer's obligation included the construction of 'a dramatic story' as a protection for the audience from the 'reality effect'. Fiction itself was presented as an instrument of audience protection and regulation, as part of the means by which the cinema declared itself to be 'merely' an amusement. If it was to remain in the hands of commercial operators, rather than become an instrument of education, its reality effect and capacity to inspire imitation had to be blunted – mediated – by the imposition of regulatory codes that would protect both the audience and the larger society by suitably directing the viewer's gratification. The institutional function of the National Board of Censorship was to develop these regulatory codes, which made assumptions not only about content but also about the organisation and treatment of content. These codes were not merely a list of prohibited actions or representations. They encouraged the construction of narratives relying on a set of conventions which became insistently, and restrictively, familiar to spectators. Section 41 of the Board's Standards declared that

> under no circumstances will the board pass a picture where apparent approval is given of any cause for crime. The results of the crime should be in the long run disastrous to the criminal, so that the impression carried is that crime will inevitably find one out, soon or late, and bring on a catastrophe which causes the temporary gain from the crime to sink into insignificance. The results should spring logically and convincingly from the crime, and the results should take a reasonable proportion of the film.[50]

Audiences were offered the comforts of consolation from familiar and recurring forms that embodied contradictions, rather than the pleasures of contestation coming from forms which articulated contradictions.[51]

A social order was being reinforced in the successful integration of a 'real' (in the form of topical subject-matter and recognisable settings) with the narrative conventions of melodrama. The formulaic narrative that would accommodate and naturalise any subject-matter processed through it was the subject of general social approval; one director claimed in 1914 that he got the 'best points ... from the newspapers' when he applied the formulas of comedy or melodrama to social issues.[52] Kay Sloan argues that early reformist films, such as *The Girl Strike Leader* (Thanhauser, 1913), reorganised the contemporary American milieu by representing social crisis in terms of romance, coincidence and individual redemption, exposing discontent only to exorcise it with a restoration of authority and an assertion of the restorative power of 'heart interest' – 'the ultimate democratiser in America'.[53] These films, and the narrative strategies by which they provided individualist narrative solutions to social problems, did more than simply contain a body of subject-matter. They demonstrated the 'respectability' of moving pictures as an instrument for both ordering and explaining a dominant ideology. The myths of consumer capitalism were given narrative shape as a realism of surfaces was attached to melodramatic conventions of wish-fulfilment and the transcendence of everyday life: 'real' problems were provided with fantastic solutions as the cinema constructed itself as the site of consumer capitalism's desire. The National Board of Censorship played a prominent role in the devising of this cultural function, and in the narratives of containment by which it was achieved. During a period in which the industry exhibited few other signs of unity, the Board became the instrument of the cinema's unified project of 'uplift'. With the Board as its adviser, the industry had by 1915 developed its essential strategy for avoiding external censorship: a narrative system of containment, overseen by an internal regulation more subtly compulsory and pervasive than any legal prior censorship might be.

The melodramatic has structured this account of the Progressive imagination in a number of senses. Coercive reformers, for whom evil was not a swarthy man in a black cape but an Irish–American politician living off the protection money he took from Jewish pimps and saloon-keepers, constructed the city in Manichean terms to retain their comprehension of an urban environment of increasing moral ambiguity. The melodramatic imagination of Charles Parkhurst or Maude Miner sought a confirmation of the existing moral order, a final triumph of virtue in the re-forming of 'the old society of innocence, which has now driven out the threat to its existence and reaffirmed its values'.[54] Melodrama's 'ambition to stage a drama of articulation, a drama that has as its true stakes the recognition and triumph of the sign of virtue',[55] exactly fitted the silent cinema's obligation to provide a morally acceptable overarching framework for the presentation of narratives of desire.

The intersection of these imaginings can be seen in one of the Board's earliest crises of representation, in 1913, which also constituted a significant development of diegetic structure in the American feature film, and conveniently returns me to any starting-point of the representation of white slavery: *Traffic in Souls*.[56] Curiously, the melodramatic convention of the principal villain being a dissembling hypocritical reformer seems to have drawn less criticism than might have been expected.[57] The narrative utilises the established conventions of melodramas involving reformist heroines, in this case an older sister who, together with her policeman sweetheart, rescues her younger sister after she has been kidnapped, but, fortunately, before she is 'ruined'. Acceptably reserved as to quite what 'ruination' involves, the film emphasises its pattern of closure through an excessive neatness of detail. In publicity accompanying the film's release, Universal described the film as a 'sermon', and declared that the company would not 'pander to sensationalism or the cravings of the masses for a glimpse in picture form of the so-called "red-light" district'.[58] When the National Board reviewed the film, they invited the assistance of representatives of other reform organisations, whose chief complaint was that the melodramatic conventions detracted from its realism, and hence its deterrent effect. One reviewer suggested that more accurate detail of procurers' techniques would give the film greater value.[59] Universal and the National Board dissented out of their fear of imitation, and the deletions required by the Board were in the event concentrated in what Ben Brewster describes as the 'quasi-documentary' prologue establishing the white slavers' organisation and methods.[60]

The Board's strategy was confirmed by its response to *The Inside of the White Slave Traffic*, produced by Samuel London in imitation of *Traffic in Souls*.[61] Although it claimed to be an authoritative factual account and stressed its lack of 'exaggeration or fictional indulgence', the Board were highly suspicious of the film's 'documentary' mode, arguing that in depicting the details of commercialised vice the film merely appealed to the prurient because it lacked a strong enough dramatic or narrative line to maintain a moral 'motive running through the picture'.[62]

By 1914, even the 'social evil' could be represented in the movies, as long as it remained within the expected confines of a moral order provided by melodramatic convention.[63] The adoption of such conventions addressed not only formal and aesthetic questions in the development of the American feature film, but also issues dealing with its place in the public sphere and the representational order. The melodramatic imagination of Progressive reform constituted what Jonathan Loesberg has called an 'ideology of narrative', within which silent cinema determined its discursive operations and functions.[64] Economically committed as it necessarily was to the reproduction of its conditions of production, the American cinema recognised the value, in a variety of sites, of regulatory convention. Most important among these sites was the movie theatre itself, where the proprietor succeeded in escaping from the evil stereotypes of coercive reform. By 1914, both inside and outside the cinematic diegesis, the melodramatic imagination had enabled men such as William Fox to stage a drama of articulation, in which the sign of their virtue was made visible and recognised.

Notes

1. Upton Sinclair, *Upton Sinclair Presents William Fox* (Los Angeles: published by the author, 1933), p. v.
2. Ibid., p. 3.
3. Ibid., p. 40.
4. Peter Brooks, *The Melodramatic Imagination: Balzac, Henry James, Melodrama and the Mode of Excess* (New Haven: Yale University Press, 1976), p. 27.
5. United States Immigration Commission, *Abstracts of Reports of the Immigration Commission*, II, 61st Congress, 3rd Sess., Washington, DC, 1911, pp. 342–3, quoted in Egal Feldman, 'Prostitution, the Alien Woman and the Progressive Imagination, 1910–1915', *American Quarterly*, 19, Summer 1967, p. 196.
6. Edward J. Bristow, *Prostitution and Prejudice: The Jewish Fight Against White Slavery 1870–1939* (Oxford: Clarendon Press, 1982), pp. 42, 175.
7. George Kibbe Turner, 'The Daughters of the Poor', *McClure's Magazine*, 34, 1909, pp. 57–8. Quoted in Feldman, op. cit., p. 195. For an account of the electoral politics, see Arthur A. Goren, *New York Jews and the Quest for Community: The Kehillah Experiment, 1908–1922* (New York: Columbia University Press, 1970), pp. 138–9.
8. Michel Foucault, *The History of Sexuality: An Introduction*, trans. Robert Hurley (Harmondsworth: Penguin, 1981), p. 77. Barbara Meil Hobson notes both the limited police action against customers of prostitutes and, as impor-

tantly in this context, the absence of inquiries or investigations into their motivations. Barbara Meil Hobson, *Uneasy Virtue: The Politics of Prostitution and the American Reform Tradition* (Chicago: University of Chicago Press, 1990), p. 159.

9. Leslie Fishbein suggests that before 1915, 'films treating fallen womanhood viewed the peril to women as largely physical and sexual, with no hope of rescue apart from timely male intervention prior to ravishment'. Leslie Fishbein, 'The Fallen Woman as Victim in Early American Film: Soma Versus Psyche', *Film and History*, 17, 1987, pp. 51–2, 54.

10. Bristow, op. cit., p. 23. Statistics about the number of prostitutes are problematic because prostitution did not correspond to the expected stereotypes of the reformers' melodramatic imaginations. Barbara Meil Hobson concludes that Victorian prostitution was a transitory occupation for most women in it, that they moved between prostitution and other employment, and that the majority worked as prostitutes occasionally, seasonally, or in addition to other work. Rather than being a pathological condition, as late nineteenth-century theories of female sexual deviance proposed, prostitution was 'a natural outgrowth of women's social dependencies and weak economic position'. Hobson, op. cit., p. 109. For a discussion of contemporary representations of prostitution in other media, see Suzanne L. Kinser, 'Prostitutes in the Art of John Sloan', *Prospects*, 9, 1984, pp. 231–54.

11. 'After attending the 1914 convention of the National Association of Colored Women, white feminist Zona Gale wrote of black women's efforts to work "against the traffic in women" (which I hope I shall never again call the 'white slave' traffic).' Ellen Carol DuBois and Linda Gordon, 'Seeking Ecstasy on the Battlefield: Danger and Pleasure in Nineteenth-Century Feminist Sexual Thought', in Carol S. Vance (ed.), *Pleasure and Danger: Exploring Female Sexuality* (London: Routledge and Kegan Paul, 1984), p. 45, n. 5. Ruth Rosen provides convincing evidence for the existence of trafficking in coerced women for sexual purposes, and notes that these included a proportion of foreign women imported into the United States, including a large number of Chinese and Japanese women on the West Coast. Ruth Rosen, *The Lost Sisterhood – Prostitution in America, 1900–1918* (Baltimore: Johns Hopkins University Press, 1982), p. 122. See also Hobson, op. cit., pp. 140–3.

12. W.J. Cash, *The Mind of the South* (Harmondsworth: Penguin, 1971), p. 133. The idea of the Southern rape complex is elaborated in Jacquelyn Dowd Hall, '"The Mind that Burns in Each Body": Women, Rape, and Racial Violence', in Ann Snitow, Christine Stansell and Sharon Thompson (eds.), *Powers of Desire: The Politics of Sexuality* (New York: Monthly Review Press, 1983), pp. 333–4; and Hazel V. Canby, '"On the Threshold of Woman's Era": Lynching, Empire, and Sexuality in Black Feminst Theory', *Critical Inquiry*, 12, 1985, pp. 262–77. Its application to cinema is discussed in Jane Gaines, 'White Privilege and Looking Relations: Race and Gender in Feminist Film Theory', *Screen*, 29, 4, Autumn 1988, p. 24. See also John D'Emilio and Estelle B. Freedman, *Intimate Matters: A History of Sexuality in America* (New York: Harper & Row, 1988), pp. 215–21; Angela Davis, 'Rape, Racism and the Myth of the Black Rapist', in *Women Race and Class* (London: The Women's Press, 1982), pp. 172–201; Eric Lott, 'Love and Theft: The Racial Unconscious of Blackface Minstrelsy', *Representations*, 39, Summer 1992, pp. 23–50.

13. For a richly insightful analysis of the melodramatic tradition of the aristocratic seducer and its metamorphosis into narratives of white slavery, see

Judith R. Walkowitz, *City of Dreadful Delight: Narratives of Sexual Danger in Later Victorian London* (London: Virago, 1992), pp. 81–134.

14. The New York Committee of Fifteen, for instance, suggested in 1902 that many females entered prostitution 'before they were old enough to be responsible for their acts'. Quoted in Timothy J. Gilfoyle, *City of Eros: New York City, Prostitution, and the Commercialisation of Sex, 1790–1920* (New York: Norton, 1992) p. 275. The ready mobility of the racial component in this complex was gruesomely illustrated in 1913 when Leo Frank, a Jewish factory manager in Atlanta, was convicted on dubious evidence of the sexually-motivated murder of a thirteen-year-old factory worker, Mary Phelan, and subsequently lynched.

Drawing attention to the intensity with which Frank's opponents insisted that Phelan died 'in defense of her virtue' as a way of camouflaging their anxiety about the active sexual agency of young women, Nancy MacLean suggests that a wealthy Northern Jew, representing the penetration of the South's virtue by the industrial revolution, better fitted the melodramatic narrative required by his lynchers than a black worker would have done. Nancy MacLean, 'The Leo Frank Case Reconsidered: Gender and Sexual Politics in the Making of Reactionary Populism', *Journal of American History*, 78, December 1991, pp. 917–48. See also Shearer West, 'The Construction of Racial Type: Caricature, Ethnography and Jewish Physiognomy in Fin-de-siècle Melodrama', *Nineteenth Century Theatre*, vol. 21, no. 1 (Summer 1993), pp. 5–40.

15. Quoted in D'Emilio and Freedman, op. cit., p. 210.

16. Joanne Meyerowitz, 'Sexual Geography and Gender Economy: The Furnished Room Districts of Chicago, 1890–1930', in Barbara Melosh (ed.), *Gender and American History Since 1890* (London: Routledge, 1993), pp. 43–71; Gilfoyle, op. cit., p. 247.

17. Sullivan ran the East Side for Tammany Hall bosses Richard Croker and Charles F. Murphy. Accused by the Hearst press and reform groups of being a keeper of pool-rooms, a protector of gamblers and 'the dirtiest crook in the city', Sullivan was part-owner of a very successful vaudeville circuit. Harold C. Syrett (ed.), *The Gentleman and the Tiger: The Autobiography of George B. McClellan Jr* (Philadelphia: Lippincott, 1956), pp. 251–2, contains one of the more entertaining accounts of Big Tim's reputation; so does Luc Sante, *Low Life: Lures and Snares of Old New York* (New York: Farrar, Strauss & Giroux, 1991), pp. 251–77. A full reassessment of Sullivan's career appears in Daniel Czitrom, 'Underworlds and Underdogs: Big Tim Sullivan and Metropolitan Politics in New York, 1889–1913', *Journal of American History*, 78, September 1991, pp. 536–8.

18. Elisabeth I. Perry, 'The General Motherhood of the Commonwealth: Dance Hall Reform in the Progressive Era', *American Quarterly*, 37, 5, Winter 1985, p. 724. For accounts of masculinity in the period, see E. Anthony Rotundo, 'Learning about Manhood: Gender Ideals and the Middle-Class Family in Nineteenth-Century America', in J. A. Mangan and James Walvin (eds), *Manliness and Morality: Middle-Class Masculinity in Britain and America, 1800–1940*, (Manchester: Manchester University Press, 1987), pp. 7–51; Lesley A. Hall, *Hidden Anxieties: Male Sexuality, 1900–1950* (London: Polity Press, 1991), pp. 15–39; D'Emilio and Freedman, op. cit., pp. 179–80. On femininity, see Christina Simmons, 'Modern Sexuality and the Myth of Victorian Repression', in Melosh, op. cit., pp. 17–42; Christina Smith-Rosenberg, *Disorderly Conduct: Visions of Gender in Victorian America* (New York: Oxford University Press, 1985); Marta Banta, *Imaging American Women: Idea and Ideals in Cultural History* (New York: Columbia University

Press, 1987); Lois W. Banner, *American Beauty* (Chicago: University of Chicago Press, 1983).

19. For comparable literary accounts, see Christopher Craft, 'Kiss Me with Those Red Lips': Gender and Inversion in Bram Stoker's *Dracula'*, *Representations*, 8, Fall 1984, pp. 107–33; and Elaine Showalter, *Sexual Anarchy: Gender and Culture at the Fin de Siècle* (London: Bloomsbury, 1991), pp. 76–95. Joanne Meyerowitz discusses comparable conventions in 'working girl' romances such as those of Laura Jean Libbey: Meyerowitz, op. cit., pp. 56–7.

20. Kay Sloan, *The Loud Silents: Origins of the Social Problem Film* (Urbana: University of Illinois Press, 1988), p. 81.

21. D.W. Griffith, 'Pace in the Movies', *Liberty*, 13 November 1926, pp. 19–23. Quoted in Lary May, *Screening Out the Past: The Birth of Mass Culture and the Motion Picture Industry* (New York: Oxford University Press, 1980), p. 77.

22. For an account of this function in the western see Richard Maltby, 'John Ford and the Indians; or, Tom Doniphon's History Lesson', in Mick Gidley (ed.), *Representing Others: White Views of Indigenous Peoples* (Exeter: University of Exeter Press, 1992), pp. 120–44.

23. An exploration of the route by which this repressed returned would require at least a cursory account of both black activism and the radiation northward of racist sentiment in the Progressive period. It might focus particularly on Jack Johnson, who became the first black heavyweight boxing champion of the world in 1908. Johnson's relationships with white women brought him legal persecution – a trial for abduction in 1912 and a prison sentence under the Mann Act in 1913, which he evaded by fleeing the country – as well as denunciation from the black press for giving credence to racist mythology about black male sexuality. His defeat of Jim Jeffries in 1910 provoked race riots across the nation, and led, two years later, to an Act of Congress prohibiting interstate traffic in prizefight films. Although the Act's southern sponsors were inspired at least as much by Johnson's sexual activities as by his pugilistic ones, it rendered invisible what would otherwise have been the most prominent version of assertive black masculinity on the screen. It might be argued that 'the Great White Hope' longed for in saloons across the country finally appeared in 1915: not Jess Willard, who defeated Johnson in Havana in July, but Henry B. Walthall, D. W. Griffith's Little Colonel.

24. Micheal Denning describes George Lippard as 'the leading American writer of the "mysteries of the city", and the most overtly political dime novelist of his or subsequent generations ... a key figure in the history of the dime novel. ... The D.W. Griffith of cheap stories.' Michael Denning, *Mechanic Accents: Dime Novels and Working-Class Culture in America* (London: Verso, 1987), p. 87. Robert Warshow, 'The Gangster as Tragic Hero', in *The Immediate Experience* (New York: Athaneum, 1970), pp. 127–33.

25. Justin Kaplan, *Lincoln Steffens: A Biography* (London: Jonathan Cape, 1975), p. 67.

26. Paul Boyer draws a valuable distinction between the two 'environmentalist' approaches to urban reform. Negative environmentalists 'pursued a coercive and moralistic approach, concentrating on eradicating two institutions that for them had come to epitomise urban moral and social breakdown: the brothel and the saloon'. Positive environmentalists aimed 'to create in the city the kind of physical environment that would gently but irresistibly mold a population of cultivated, moral and socially responsible city dwellers'. Both positions, however, 'shared certain fundamental moral-control purposes: the elevation of character, the inculcation of a "higher" standard of individual

behaviour, the placing of social duty above private desire, the re-creation of the urban masses in the reformer's own image'. Paul Boyer, *Urban Masses and Moral Order in America, 1820–1920* (Cambridge, Mass.: Harvard University Press, 1978), p. 190.

27. Timothy Gilfoyle suggests that coercive reformers 'viewed the city as the frontier', and cast themselves in the role of vigilantes. Gilfoyle, op. cit., p. 188, and see also David Grimsted's essay in this volume.

28. Quoted in Hobson, op. cit., p. 156.

29. D'Emilio and Freedman, op. cit., p. 197.

30. The changes in the forms of public display of female sexuality, and the shifting relationships and boundaries between prostitution, entertainment forms and leisure activities, are discussed in Gilfoyle, op. cit., p. 225; Meyerowitz, op. cit., pp. 52–3, 59; and Robert C. Allen, *Horrible Prettiness: Burlesque and American Culture* (Chapel Hill: University of North Carolina Press, 1991), pp. 76, 127.

31. Quoted in Kathy Peiss, *Cheap Amusements: Working Women and Leisure in Turn-of-the-Century New York* (Philadelphia: Temple University Press, 1986), p. 110. In analysing the Victorian fallen woman paradigm, Barbara Meil Hobson suggests that it identified sexual passion as 'a sign of pathology in the female sex', exemplified in the mythology of vampirism by which 'the awakening of female passion comes from an evil source outside the woman', but 'once initiated she becomes a slave to the erotic and a destroyer of others. ... By arguing that female purity represented an advance in human civilisation and, conversely, that the sensual and promiscuous woman was a reversion to a primitive type, [evolutionary theorists] widened the fissure between normal (natural) and abnormal (unnatural) women implied in the fallen woman paradigm. ... A woman's fall meant not only a fall from grace but also a descent into a lower, more savage order of beings.' Hobson, op. cit., p. 111–13. See also Rosen, op. cit., p. 29.

32. Quoted in D'Emilio and Freedman, op. cit., p. 189. Ruth Rosen quotes similar sentiments from the Louisville Vice Commission in 1917; Rosen, op. cit., p. 41.

33. Cecile G. Greil, quoted in Rosen, op. cit., p. 42.

34. Walkowitz explores the relationship between the privileged gaze of the aristocratic or bourgeois *flâneur* and reform activity; Walkowitz, op. cit., pp. 15–39. See also Sante, op. cit., pp. 289–99.

35. Boyer, op. cit., p. 208.

36. *Report of the Vice Commission of Philadelphia*, 1913, quoted in D'Emilio and Freedman, op. cit., p. 210.

37. William Inglis, 'Morals and Moving Pictures', *Harper's Weekly*, 54, 10 July 1910, p. 12. Quoted in Daniel Czitrom, 'The Redemption of Leisure: The National Board of Censorship and the Rise of Motion Pictures in New York City, 1900–1920', *Studies in Visual Communication*, 10, 4, Fall 1984, p. 3.

38. Quoted in May, op. cit., p. 44, and Czitrom, op. cit., p. 3.

39. 'New York's Problem of the Nickelodeon', *New York Press*, 23 February 1908, quoted in Kenneth R. Philp, *John Collier's Crusade for Indian Reform, 1920–1954* (Tucson: University of Arizona Press, 1977), p. 12.

40. 'Moving Pictures and Health', *The Independent*, 68, 17 March 1910, p. 591, quoted in Kathleen D. McCarthy, 'Nickel Vice and Virtue: Movie Censorship in Chicago, 1907–1915,' *Journal of Popular Film*, 5, 1976, p. 40; Jane Addams, *The Spirit of Youth and the City Streets* (New York: Macmillan, 1909), reprinted in Gerald Mast (ed.), *The Movies in Our Midst: Documents in the Cultural History of Film in America* (Chicago: University of Chicago Press, 1982), p. 77.

41. Chicago Vice Commission, *The Social Evil in Chicago* (1911), in Mast, op. cit., p. 62.

42. These activities were paralleled by the regulation of theatrical sites according to the kind of entertainment they provided and the audiences to whom they appealed. Lawrence Levine argues that this regulation was part of the decline of a shared public culture in the late 19th and early 20th centuries, as theatres and other auditoria filtered their clientèle and their progammes to segregate audiences and create a new hierarchy of cultural value, in which the movies, along with professional sport, would at best occupy an ambiguous position. Lawrence W. Levine, *Highbrow, Lowbrow: The Emergence of Cultural Hierarchy in America* (Cambridge, Mass.: Harvard University Press, 1988), pp. 71–9, 207–8, 224–5, 231–4. See also Allen, op. cit., pp. 185–93, 225–46.

43. Two recent articles reassess the early history of the National Board: Daniel Czitrom, 'The Politics of Performance: From Theater Licensing to Movie Censorship in Turn-of-the-Century New York', *American Quarterly*, 44, December 1992, pp. 525–53; and Nancy J. Rosenbloom, 'In Defense of the Moving Pictures: The People's Institute, the National Board of Censorship, and the Problem of Leisure in Urban America', *American Studies*, 33, 2, Fall 1992, pp. 41–60.

44. *New York Times*, 24 February 1909, p. 6, quoted in Charles M. Feldman, *The National Board of Censorship (Review) of Motion Pictures, 1909–1922* (New York: Arno, 1977), p. 23.

45. Linda Williams discusses the coincidence of the inventions of cinema and psychoanalysis as 'mutually reinforcing discourses of sexuality producing particular forms of knowledge and pleasure', and means by which 'fetishism and voyeurism gained new importance and normality through their link to the positivist quest for the truth of visible phenomena'. Linda Williams, *Hard Core: Power, Pleasure, and the 'Frenzy of the Visible'* (London: Pandora, 1990), pp. 36, 45–6. Robert Allen provides an exemplary discussion of Williams's argument in his account of the Edison Company's 'smoking concert' films and the 'spicy' Mutoscope subjects produced by Biograph between 1895 and 1905 (some of them possibly directed by D.W. Griffith); Allen, op. cit., pp. 265–71.

46. Scott Simmon, '"The Female of the Species": D.W. Griffith, Father of the Woman's Film', *Film Quarterly*, 46, 2, Winter 1992–3, pp. 9–10.

47. In his analysis of urban etiquette and its fictional representations, Guy Szuberla suggests that etiquette manuals envisioned city streets as 'the set for a melodrama whose character and sexual types were marked by clear, unmistakable signs'. A respectable woman would pass through the urban environment 'wrapped in a mantle of proper reserve ... seeing and hearing nothing that she ought not to see and hear', and doing nothing 'to attract the attention of the passers-by'. Guy Szuberla, 'Ladies, Gentlemen, Flirts, Mashers, Snoozers, and the Breaking of Etiquette's Code', *Prospects*, 15, 1990, p. 169. See also Levine, op. cit., p. 199; John F. Kasson, 'Civility and Rudeness: Etiquette and the Bourgeois Social Order in Nineteenth-Century America', *Prospects*, 9, 1984, pp. 143–67. By contrast, Lauren Rabinowitz discusses the ways in which women moviegoers 'were positioned on and off the screen as both the subject and the object of "the gaze"', and in her discussion of *Stagestruck* (1906) provides a cinematic example of the pleasures and dangers involved in women being framed as spectacle for an audience, acquiring independence through sexual commodification. Lauren Rabinowitz, 'Temptations of Pleasure: Nickelodeons, Amusement Parks, and the Sights of Female Sexuality', *Camera Obscura* 23, May 1990, pp. 72, 83. Robert

Allen summarises the debate in his comment that 'the struggle over the appearance of women onstage ... was a struggle between spectacle and mimesis, display and drama, desire and repression'. Allen, op. cit., p. 81. For a discussion of new forms of public privacy in the early 20th century, see Louis A. Erenberg, *Steppin' Out: New York Nightlife and the Transformation of American Culture, 1890–1920* (Chicago: University of Chicago Press, 1984).

48. This 'other viewer', the figure of misinterpretation, has remained an archetype of the censorship argument, and is as frequently present in contemporary debates over the regulation of television and pornography as in the early years of cinema. It has also been an important figure in high cultural critiques of popular culture. It is often identified as a child, the figure towards whom the idea of moral guardianship can most unproblematically be extended. Its essential perceptual feature is its inability to distinguish fiction.

49. Robert C. Allen, *Vaudeville and Film, 1895–1915: A Study in Media Interaction* (New York: Arno, 1980), pp. 214–15; Bordwell, Staiger and Thompson, *Classic Hollywood Cinema – Film Style and Mode of Production to 1960* (London: Routledge and Kegan Paul, 1985), pp. 85–141, 155–213.

50. 'The Policy and Standard of the National Board of Censorship of Motion Pictures, Reissued Oct. 1, 1915', reprinted in *Hearings Before the Committee on Education, House of Representatives, 64, 1, on H.R. 456, a Bill to Create a New Division of the Bureau of Education, to be Known as the Federal Motion Picture Commission, and Defining its Powers and Duties* (Washington, DC: Government Printing Office, 1916), p. 290.

51. Michael Hays argues that English stage melodrama of the 1860s fulfilled a similar ideological function. Michael Hays, 'To Delight and Discipline: Melodrama as Cultural Mediator,' paper presented at the BFI Melodrama Conference, London, 1992.

52. Quoted in Sloan, op. cit., p. 7.

53. Ibid., pp. 51, 125–6.

54. Brooks, op. cit., p. 32.

55. Ibid., p. 49.

56. Ben Brewster, '*Traffic in Souls*: An Experiment in Feature-Length Narrative Construction', *Cinema Journal*, 31, 1, Fall 1991, pp. 37, 47.

57. Although *The Outlook* reported on 14 February 1914 that the Board's deletions included 'eliminating the idea that the ringleader was a hypocritical reformer', as well as reducing several scenes inside brothels to one brief scene. Francis G. Couvares and Kathy Peiss, 'Censoring the Movies: The Problem of Youth in the 1920s' (unpublished paper), p. 9.

58. Quoted in Couvares and Peiss, op. cit., p. 8.

59. Quoted in Couvares and Peiss, op. cit., p. 8.

60. Brewster, op.cit., p.43.

61. London is identified in the film's titles as a 'noted sociologist'. He had at one time been an El Paso lawyer who 'had been nothing less than the chief legal counsel for many of the procurers in the south-west', had subsequently been reformed by a guilty conscience and gained the support of several Jewish reform groups. In 1911 and 1912 he worked for the Justice Department and, as an investigator, on the Rockefeller Grand Jury investigations of white slavery in New York. Bristow, op. cit., p. 161.

62. Couvares and Peiss, op. cit., p. 7. However, several members of the Board, including its secretary Frederick Howe, were listed in the film's titles as endorsing its representation of the Traffic. The film also claimed the endorsement of such prominent figures as Carrie Chapman Catt, Charlotte Perkins Gilman, Mrs. O.H.P. Belmont, several judges and sociologists 'from

the Atlantic to the Pacific'. The film's plot follows the conventional line of development in the 'fallen woman' genre, but it is presented without any melodramatic emphasis. Its moral lesson is directed less at young women than at their parents, who are explicitly warned to 'beware the "out of my house" policy' towards their errant daughters.

63. It could similarly be staged under restricted conditions. In the summer of 1913 Lee and J.J. Schubert staged a white slavery melodrama, *The Lure*, by George Scarborough, to have it closed on the grounds of 'indecency and a tendency to corrupt public morals'. The Schuberts agreed to have the play rewritten to accommodate the jurors' objections, and it reopened to a very successful four-and-a-half-month run. Brooks McNamara, *The Schuberts of Broadway: A History Drawn from the Collections of the Schubert Archive* (New York: Oxford University Press, 1990), p. 65.

64. Jonathan Loesberg, 'The Ideology of Narrative Form in Sensation Fiction', *Representations*, 13, Winter 1986, p. 116.

FIRE AND DESIRE

Race, Melodrama, and Oscar Micheaux

JANE GAINES

If D.W. Griffith's *The Birth of a Nation* (1915) was history 'written with lightning', Oscar Micheaux's *Within our Gates* (1919) was history written in smoke.[1] When the African–American independent film producer's second feature was first exhibited in major American cities, black as well as white communities treated it like a time bomb. The very black communities that had welcomed Micheaux's first film, *The Homesteader* (1918), and applauded the success of the Micheaux Book and Film Company, protested against *Within our Gates*. In Chicago, the Methodist Episcopal Ministers' Alliance committee, comprised of representatives of both races, took their case against exhibiting the film to the mayor and the chief of police.

The request for a permit to show the film had been denied after the first screening, but a more liberal group arguing for the social value of the film's subject-matter prevailed after a second screening. The film opened at the Vendome Theatre in Chicago on 12 January 1920, but the protest against it continued until the hour before the film opened. Why? What kinds of scenes could represent such a danger to public safety in 1920? And what issue could unify white and black churches in this way?

In January 1920 *Within our Gates* was caught up in a riot and lynching linkage which characterised American race relations in the 1920s. Because of this linkage (both real and imagined), the film's release offers another case study of the way symbolic events (inflected as socially dangerous) can become inextricably bound up with the events themselves, especially during racially sensitised moments in history. Micheaux's film included a sequence depicting the hanging and burning of two innocent African–Americans, a man and his wife. The sequence may have been no more than a short scene in a flashback filling in the history of mulatta heroine Sylvia Landry, and may have only had minor relevance to the central narrative, but the relation of such a controversial segment to the narrative whole often becomes irrelevant when such a moving image is singled out by public discourse in this way. Released in the USA the year after the 'red summer' of 1919, the film encountered especially active resistance in Chicago where, in July 1919, police indifference to a white gang's drowning of a black teenager set off a chain of South Side riots.[2] In Shreveport, Louisiana, the Star Theatre refused to book the film because of its 'nasty story'. Even in Omaha, Nebraska, Lincoln Motion Pictures head George P. Johnson explained the poor attendance at an August return engagement of the film as due to the fact that the film reminded people of the events of the year before.[3]

In several cities, Micheaux was required by officials to edit out parts of the film, but even this continual recutting does not explain the wild discrepancies in viewers' reports.[4] The groups that wanted an outright ban on exhibiting Micheaux's film saw little results from their direct appeals to city officials whose peace-making solution was to require these cuts. But the case of *Within our Gates* brings home one of the lessons of the NAACP campaign against *The Birth of a Nation*. Whereas *protest* against a film in this period did not mean that it would be banned (and it might even ensure that it drew crowds), the threat of a race *riot* meant that exhibitors and city officials would co-operate to keep a film off the screen.

What suggests comparison between *Within our Gates* and *The Birth of a Nation* is, of course, primarily the cauldron of protest around racial imagery into which both films were flung. However, in almost every other way, Micheaux's film is the antithesis of *Birth*, especially in its middle-class, black-centred view of American society. Also, in contrast to the NAACP protest around *The Birth of a Nation* (centred upon a notion of falsehood in representation), the *Within our Gates* controversy implicitly focused on the fear of 'too much truth'. This *status quo* discourse on 'truth', however, made no reference to the political realities of Southern lynch mob justice. Such mob justice, it should be remembered, had actually contributed to the instability of Northern cities, crowded in 1919 with blacks who had left Southern towns in the aftermath of lynchings. The attempt to ban screenings of Micheaux's film, then, was an attempt to silence the protest against lynching, but also a law and order move to suppress active protest against worsening housing and employment conditions in the North. *Within our Gates* was thus historically linked to fear of cataclysmic social change, a linkage obfuscated by the smokescreen of 'race riot', and this is where the difference between the fate of this film and that of *The Birth of a Nation* is so revealing. While Griffith's 'masterpiece' was enshrined, Micheaux's answer to it was 'run out of town', so to speak. While the white supremacist version of the Civil War survived, Micheaux's African–American history lesson disappeared and was classified by film scholars as 'lost'. Seventy years later, a 35mm print version of *Within our Gates*, now called *La Negra*, was finally returned to the Library of Congress from Europe.

So what follows is an analysis of *La Negra*, the only extant version of *Within our Gates*. This is a work which has had two cultural lives: the first, in the USA in the troubled year of its early exhibition, and the second, on the continent where Spanish audiences would have seen it as a 'strange tale of the American South'. Somewhat like the trade in abolitionist literature which fled an inhospitable climate of race terror to seek publication in Britain, this film is part of that traffic of banned discourse which has historically crossed the Atlantic along with African–American intellectuals, themselves fleeing discrimination. In 1990, the film returned to the USA with Spanish intertitles, producing our estranged culture as a very strange text. In this account, the controversy is sufficient justification for focusing on the lynching story. My exaggeration of its relative importance in the narrative should be understood as a reprise of that earlier exaggeration.

This is not to say that the lynching story (which is not integral to the narrative) is not connected to the whole in any way. As told by Sylvia's cousin Alma to her suitor Dr Vivian, the lynching story is offered as an explanation for Sylvia's reluctance to marry the successful black doctor. Rather than serving any direct narrative purpose, then, the story functions as a kind of exorcism of the past. Tagged on as it is to the end of the film, it seems structurally tangential rather than central. Once Sylvia's history is told, the film cuts to final shots of the heroine with Dr Vivian who reconciles her to a more optimistic point of view, arguing that black participation in the First World War has changed the meaning of American patriotism for blacks. The optimistic nationalism that ends the film, then, depends upon seeing the scenes of racial injustice as relegated to the past, not conceivable in the present of the film's contemporary story, ostensibly the present of the film's year of release.

We are supposing that *La Negra* is structurally similar to the film that was shown in the USA in 1920. However, this assumption still presents us with some mysteries. Why, despite the controversy, was the film promoted by Micheaux himself in terms of the minor lynching story in city after city? Why do none of the existing publicity materials mention the 'uplift' narrative dealing with Sylvia Landry's efforts to raise money for a school in the South? Instead of featuring this respectable narrative, the advertising for the film stressed 'Who Killed Phillip Girdlestone?' and promises, in addition to the solution of the mystery, a 'Spectacular Screen Version of the Most Sensational Story on the Race Question Since *Uncle Tom's Cabin'*.[5] This, then, must be the key – lynching as spectacular attraction – for, more than anything, Micheaux was an accomplished showman.

But in the tradition of *Uncle Tom's Cabin*, spectacle and emotion go hand in hand.[6] The film-within-the-film of *La Negra* is also a small sentimental melodrama – so complete, it is as though one were viewing an entire D.W. Griffith short dropped down within a silent feature. Not surprisingly, the lynching narrative owes its basic formal structure to Griffith, even while its rhetorical structure produces the antithesis of *The Birth of a Nation* – that is, the history of Reconstruction from the black point of view. Wealthy planter Felipe Gridlstone (Philip Girdlestone) is unwilling to settle accounts with black sharecropper Gaspar (Jasper) Landry who has earned the $685 needed to repay his debt to the planter. A fight ensues when Landry urges the villain Gridlstone to treat him fairly. We see, however, that Landry is not alone in his feeling of animosity towards the cruel landowner. A poor white cracker, seeing his opportunity to get rid of the hated Gridlstone, shoots the aristocrat through the window, and the blame falls on Landry. Gridlstone's meddlesome black butler Efrain ('Eph'/Ephrain) has been watching the interview with the

233

sharecropper, but has not seen the shooting and thus sounds the alarm that it is Landry who has murdered old Gridlstone. Landry, his wife, his young son Emilio (Emil), and his grown daughter Sylvia flee to the woods with the lynch mob on their trail.

Lynching as Peculiarly American

Seldom have African–American and Euro–American versions of social reality been more at odds than in the historical case of lynching. In white American popular mythology, a lynching is a hanging, punishment meted out to Negro men who had sexual relations with white women. Technically, however, lynching refers to an enforcement of justice outside the law that could involve any number of brutal punishments from burning to tarring and feathering. Even despite the attempts to educate whites about the full implications of lynching, first by black journalist Ida B. Wells in the 1880s and later by white reformers like Southerner Jessie Daniel Ames, the post-Civil War rape and lynching mythology has persisted for whites even into the present. For black Americans, however, the situation is significantly different since from the 1880s there has been a strong literary and journalistic effort to write lynching sagas as a form of protest against the practice. A comparison of Micheaux's banned version of Southern injustice with the white mythology, then, needs to locate the terms of this dialogue, this ideological battle in the realm of representation.

The act of lynching can be seen as a classic displacement, a radical adjustment in which something of peripheral importance comes to occupy a central position. Here, the central economic concern is shifted on to the sexual, or the threat to real property gets transposed as the threat to symbolic property – white womanhood. To follow the Freudian dream metaphor further, it is not the taboo *sexual* thought that is repressed, it is the *economic* motive that is unspeakable. Sex (even when there was none) was historically asserted and 'money' was denied. To figure the economic basis of lynching too abstractly, however, risks overlooking the unusual mix of the multiple causes of the phenomenon, for lynching can be productively seen as overdetermined in both the Freudian and the Marxian senses.[7] However, in the 1920s, the scattershot determinations of a lynching climate cluster around four main social developments: the extension of voting rights to black men and the question of votes for women; returning First World War veterans seeking jobs; black competition for jobs and black economic successes; and consensual interracial sexual relations.

I also say scattershot 'causes' to emphasise the way mob justice came down – the utter arbitrariness of the trumped-up justifications for lynching – and the nonsense of the charges against Southern Negroes. Micheaux gives us this view of the lynch mob in his portrait of the victimisation of Gridlstone's servant Eph who, having encouraged the mob to look for Landry, is himself grabbed as a substitute when they fail to find the accused.

Perhaps Micheaux's portrait of the lynch mob is his signal achievement in this film, for he chooses to show what blacks knew and Northern whites refused to believe. He shows the total barbarism of the white mob. The more astounding reports collected by Ida B. Wells confirm that lynch mobs decapitated bodies and took parts as trophies, invented obscene tortures, and burned victims after hanging them. Women and children were not sheltered from these horrors, but participated in the horrid revelry,[8] and here is where Micheaux is at his boldest – the mob he gives us is not the usual cadre of town bullies. White women and children also wield sticks and torches in some of the most unsettlingly beautiful scenes in silent cinema of the late teens. Micheaux's day-for-night shooting renders a grotesque black silhouette against a light sky – a kind of multi-limbed spiked monster spirals from background to foreground – attacking and receding in a dynamic use of screen depth. It is all the better that these scenes are also shot in such crisp focus, for what they portray is nothing more nor less than white people as savages. The accusation of 'primitivism' is turned back on to white Southern culture.

This is certainly lynching as sensational spectacle, but we should consider how it is significantly different from lynching as public spectacle, the gruesome ritual that functioned as social control and warning to blacks. In contrast with the white-staged ritual, Micheaux's screen representation of Southern lynching was intended to work in the opposite way on the same black public. For Micheaux, to reveal these horrors was *not* to contain and control through terror. As his publicity asserted, this 'Preachment of Race Prejudice and the Glaring Injustices Practised Upon Our People' was to 'Hold you Spellbound' and offer you details that would make you 'Grit Your Teeth in Silent Indignation'.[9] In the same spirit as *Uncle Tom's Cabin*, Micheaux's film was meant less to inspire action or race solidarity than to work as a kind of moral self-affirmation. As I have argued before, much of the appeal of 'race movies' had to do with their melodramatic structure, that is, the fictional scheme of things in which the power structure is inverted.[10] Melodrama elevates the weak above the powerful by putting them on a higher moral ground. Micheaux's spectacle of lynching, then, was rhetorically organised to encourage the feeling of righteous indignation in the black spectator.

The Politics of Cross-cutting
To these ends, Micheaux makes exceedingly haunting use of cross-cutting, alternating the lynching scene with the attempted rape of Sylvia, and it is this pattern that I want to discuss in detail since it tells us so much about the way African–American artists have historically used melodramatic devices. As I have noted, Micheaux characterises the white mob as crazed and barbarically cruel, so cruel that even innocents – women and children – are its victims. Landry's wife is dragged forward and beaten by the mob, and the noose is placed around her neck and the neck of her young son, although the boy wriggles out of it and narrowly escapes on a horse. That the man and wife are to be hanged together is signalled by one of the most unsettling images in the history of African–American cinema: a low-angle close-up of a wooden bar frames two dangling ropes against a cloudy sky. This abstraction, as it stands in for the horrible tragedy, is then used by Micheaux as a kind of gruesome punctuation in the cross-cut sequence that culminates the lynching scenario.

The fate of the family is thus established as one line of action, a line which splits into two when the film cuts from the lynchers starting a fire to Sylvia Landry, returning to the family's house for provisions, unaware of the plight of her family. In the same shot of Sylvia gathering supplies, she is discovered by Felipe Gridlstone's elderly brother Armando (Armand) who has joined the search for his brother's killer. From the shot establishing Sylvia's danger, the film cuts back to the shot of the ghostly post, this time seen with one noose cut and the other still dangling. Even more strange, a second shot of the noose being cut is upside down, producing an eerie defiance of gravity – the rope stretching towards the sky. Between the shot of the one rope cut and the next shot of both ropes cut is an intertitle: 'Still not satisfied with the poor victims burned in the bonfire, Gridlstone goes looking for Sylvia.' That is, before the victims have been represented as hanged and burned, Gridlstone has examined their bodies. I shall return to the 'error' of this title since it is interesting for the way in which this contradicts the temporal rule conventionally associated with cross-cutting – the assumption that this form of shot alternation indicates simultaneity. Following this assumption the sequence represents a time frame in which Sylvia is being molested *at the same moment* in which her parents are being executed for crimes they did not commit.

Although Armando Gridlstone's taunting of Sylvia is alternated with shots of the hanging, the systematic cross-cutting pattern begins with the conflict between the characters. Here, the struggle is interrupted five times with shots of the mob burning the bodies in a raging bonfire. I say 'interrupted', but there are any number of other ways in which the relationship between the two or more lines of action in a parallel editing pattern can be described. We might say, for instance, that they are 'interwoven', which could indicate that the lines of action are measured out more or less equally. But here I want to emphasise how the parallel narration really works to produce a contrast between the two events. Although a strict reading of the time relations set up by the intertitle tells us that the mob has already completed its terrible work by the time Armando reaches Sylvia, the hanging segment renders moot any rigid linearity of this kind. What matters is that Micheaux has used the connotations of simultaneity to give the attack on Sylvia an additional charge. Yes, the narration tells us that the rape and the lynching are coincidental, but it also says that there is an even closer connection between the fire and the desire. In the struggle, Sylvia and her attacker circle the table, her clothes are ripped from her shoulder, she throws a vase at him, and finally she faints. The scene is thus symbolically charged as a re-enactment of the white patriarch's ravishment of black womanhood, reminding viewers of all of the clandestine forced sexual acts that produced the mulatto population of the American South.

The issue of the temporal order of the lynching sequence gives us an opportunity to ask some additional questions about cross-cutting as melodramatic form. What does it contribute to the affect? How does this device manage melodramatic material? It is arguable that cross-cutting as a form may have special meaning for the disenfranchised because of the way the device inscribes power relationships. Although it is often noted, as I have said, that melodrama empowers the socially inferior by awarding them moral superiority, there are ways in which, contrary to this, cross-cutting puts the viewer in a helpless position. Which is it in this case? As Tom Gunning discusses the technique of cross-cutting, it is clearly marked by the intervention of a storyteller who is in a position to manipulate the narrative, and especially to play on audience sensibilities by 'withholding' parts of the story.[11] In this case, however, if 'withholding' pieces of narrative information does not put black spectators in a controlling position, perhaps it puts them in a familiar position, which would mean that Sylvia's fate (in which they cannot intervene) allows a replay of the futility of the African–American historical condition. Once more, blacks look on while the white patriarch exerts his sexual prerogative. But the scene may still afford pleasure for blacks because, although the white master appears to be prevailing, Sylvia effectively resists and eludes him again and again.

Characteristic of much African–American and abolitionist literature of the late 19th and early 20th centuries is this narrative 'piling on' of the overwhelming odds against freedom and safety (which is not to suggest that this is not an accurate portrayal of the condition of enslaved peoples whose lives were daily defined by attempts to survive humanly impossible tests). One of the features abolitionist fiction borrows most effectively from the melodrama form that predates it is this almost mathematical measurement of outcomes. Life's agonies are cast as the embattled forces of virtue against the vile antagonists of virtue, a confrontation *timed* to the second and rhythmically orchestrated. No device exemplifies this mathematical feature of melodrama more than narrative coincidence, and cross-cutting at its most effective is really an exercise in coincidence.

To return to coincidence, however, and by so doing to take it seriously, is to return to the very device that has been cited so often as proof of the 'lowness' of melodrama form. Was the form maligned because audiences (readers as well as viewers) were insulted by what they thought was the affront to realism that narrative coincidence represents? Does the use of coincidence for some imply a naive reader? In spite of the critical dismissal of such narrative manoeuvres, theatre critic Eric Bentley, in a relatively early defence of theatre melodrama, has claimed that 'outrageous coincidence' is the 'essence of melodrama'.[12] It is, he says, like farce because of the way in which it 'revels in absurdity'. While I approve of Bentley's championing of 'outrageous coincidence', I am not sure that 'absurdity' best describes the amazing coincidences in Griffith's last-minute rescues or the many astounding lucky moments in both the novels and films of Oscar Micheaux. I suspect that the swift turn of events that equalises the unequal and the symmetrical plot development which evens scores may only be absurd and nonsensical to those in power. In his list of melodramatic devices which might be seen by some film theorists as exceeding the constraints of classical narrative economy, Rick Altman mentions a reliance on coincidence along with spectacle and episodic presentation.[13] If he is right that 'coincidence' is problematic excess, that it is not characteristic of classical text construction (and I think he is), does he mean that it is seen as illogical, overblown, or just indulgent, because, in terms of narrative theory, coincidence is not an overindulgence but rather a highly economical solution for the storyteller. Thematic designs and narrative lines can be neatly unified through a coincidental unforeseen intersection of events (for that is what coincidence is), incidents coinciding to bring about swift change. And here, 'swift' needs as much emphasis as 'change', for coincidence brings about that astonishing narrative quickening that Todorov says is produced most effectively by supernatural forces.[14]

Coincidence may be 'excess' but not because it exceeds narrative economy. It must be 'excess', then, for some other reason. Consider that coincidence is perceived as 'low' and 'outrageous' (sometimes illogical) when it is surprising and miraculous, when it is sudden and unmotivated (that is, without justification or preparation). To continue my argument about the appeal to the powerless, consider also how coincidence is really a secular version of divine intervention, the only intervention that can rescue the powerless in the unjust world of social realist fiction. To illustrate this from *La Negra*, I might point to the series of coincidences by which Sylvia comes to receive the much-needed money to keep open Piney Woods School for Negroes in the South. On a fund-raising trip to Boston, a tramp steals her purse and is quickly seen and apprehended by Dr Vivian, the man to whom she becomes romantically attached. Next, Sylvia is hit by a car as she dashes to save a child who has run into the street. Coincidentally, the woman to whom the car belongs is an extremely wealthy suffragette who is sympathetic to Sylvia's cause. Although a visiting Southern matron tries to dissuade her friend, the Boston suffragette decides to give the school not just the needed $5000 but $50,000.

The miracle of coincidence is indifferent to market-place measures of merit and worth. Instead, melodramatic coincidence dispenses rewards and punishments according to the motives of the heart, a standard directly at odds with work-world values. It may thus be that the redistribution of rewards according to this alternative scheme drags melodrama down in the cultural regard. Could it be that this is one of those places where what we have come to call the 'contradictions of capitalism' may be manifest? That the deep asymmetry of a culture that espouses two systems of reward (corresponding with the old public/private sphere division) shows up when the reward systems are seen to be at odds with one another? African–Americans have historically stood a better chance of triumphing in fictional worlds (certainly since the publication of William Wells Brown's *Clotel: Or, the President's Daughter* in 1853). In the fictional world of *La Negra*, Sylvia, the tragic mulatta, survives unscathed and is rewarded with a $50,000 gift from heaven.

Melodrama Form and African–American Fiction

There is still some question as to whether Griffith's parallelism is equal to the job the form will need to do for a socially conscious African–American cinema. With these issues in mind, let us return to Sylvia, cornered by the white patriarch. Micheaux's scene uses the classic double play of silent film melodrama, that is, a parallel concurrence of events (the 'rape' and the lynching) as well as a coincidence that unifes the two lines of action. This is, moreover, a coincidence that asks viewers to accept an improbability which is so far-fetched that it could *only* be seen to happen if it were, indeed, 'the truth', which the adage tells us is 'always stranger than fiction'. So it is that in the act of ripping Sylvia's dress, Gridlstone discovers a telling birthmark on her breast: the mark is proof that he may be sexually assaulting his own daughter. I say 'may be' because the wording of the Spanish title following is somewhat oblique: 'Una cicatriz que tenia en el pecho la salvo de la legitimo matrimonio con una mujer de su raza y luego adoptada por los Landry.' The ambiguity of the pronoun is still not resolved in English translation: 'A scar that she had on her chest saved her dishonour because on discovering it Gridlstone knew that Sylvia was his daughter which he had in legitimate marriage with a woman of her race and later adopted by the Landrys.' Is Sylvia, then, saved from incestual rape?

Conventions of interpretation dictate that we not take intertitles at their word, especially since in this period titles are so often at odds with the dramatic thrust of the silent scenes within which they are inserted. Interpreting Micheaux's scene as 'rape', however, also has a certain political significance since it can be understood as a reaction to that other controversial interracial sex scene, the 'Gus chase scene' from *The Birth of a Nation*. Since the scene of Flora Cameron's flight from the free black man Gus and her leap to death from the edge of a cliff has been historically called the 'rape scene' (although she would jump rather than submit), it seems only fair that we should not hesitate to call Micheaux's point of view a representation of 'rape'.[15] This allows us to see it as the long-muffled African–American retort to what Ida B. Wells condemned in 1892 as the 'old threadbare lie that Negro men rape white women'.[16] Even more pertinently, the parallelism of the rape and the lynching scenes assert the historical connection between the rape of the black woman and the lynching of the black man, the double reaction of the US Reconstruction period to whites' nightmare vision of blacks voting and owning property.

Nevertheless, in representing Sylvia's deflowering as incest, *La Negra* goes deeper than the specific historical moment of lynching, attacking as it does the connecting roots of race, gender and sexuality. For Gridlstone's attack on Sylvia stands in as protest against *all* of the master's sexual encounters with his own slave women, representing each and every encounter as an act of symbolic incest, since the paternalism of the plantation master always encircled slaves in a concept of 'my family, white and black'.[17] Note, also, that Micheaux gives us a rescue sequence with no heroic rescue, no race to protect family honour and female purity. In place of such a Griffithesque rescue, Micheaux's film gives us a title telling us that Gridlstone had paid for Sylvia's education but that, even after his attack on her, he did not reveal that he was her father. Neither is it clear from the one shot of Armando in the contemporary portion of the film (an argument in Sylvia's bedroom) that he has revealed his identity to her. The abrupt cut from this title to the end of Alma's conversation with Dr Vivian in the present suggests that the doctor is offered as saviour, that is, the new professional class (with education provided by philanthropic whites) would 'rescue' the black race. This means that although

239

the white patriarch cannot ride to the rescue when he himself is the real threat to the sanctity of the family, paradoxically (in the strategy of the black middle class), he can still 'save the day'.

Am I making an argument for the radical nature of *La Negra* that I am gradually taking back? I have argued that Micheaux's film counters the white supremacist ideology of *The Birth of a Nation* in its images of the white lynch mob and the white patriarch's sexual assault on black women. We have as well the historical evidence of the attempts to ban the film which suggest that the hanging of innocent Negros was incendiary imagery for blacks as well as whites, although in different ways. Clearly the film troubled ideological waters, yet I want to ask whether there is a kind of formal tempering of this material which is the work of the devices of melodrama in the hands of the black bourgeois. The most obvious criticism of the use of the tradition of *Uncle Tom's Cabin* (in which the nineteenth-century African–American novelists all worked) has been that its sentimentality is dishonest and that its catalogue of brutal acts is without justification, a criticism identified with James Baldwin whose fury at Harriet Beecher Stowe had to do with the way, he said, she left 'unanswered and unnoticed the only important question: what was it, after all, that moved her people to such deeds?'[18]

However, without subtracting anything from the significance of Baldwin's questions, we still need to ask if sentimental fiction is structurally equipped to answer this kind of question at all. Eisenstein, of course, wondered in 1944 if Griffith's parallel editing technique, with its contrasts of rich and poor (to which I have referred above), was capable of anything more than 'liberal, slightly sentimental humanism'. For Eisenstein, scenes paralleled through cross-cutting stood for a dualistic understanding of social class inequality that imagined poor and rich as moving towards 'reconciliation'. This visualised reconciliation, he argued, was as inaccessible and distant as the point of 'infinity' where the parallel lines crossed.[19] What Eisenstein had in mind, of course, was a formal equivalent of Marxist dialectics – graphic clashes (mismatches) within and between his shot units – which could convey a 'unity of opposites', the perfect symmetry of contradiction. To give an example closer to African–American history, the cinema that goes beyond Griffith's humanism would represent something more like Fanon's three 'incongruent knowledges': body, race, ancestors.[20] Such incongruence (which defines race and class relations in US history) cannot be represented by means of Griffiths' 'mechanical parallelism' with its false reconciliation of the irreconcilable.[21]

Eisenstein's early attempt to define bourgeois cinema has been eclipsed by a more contemporary Marxist aesthetics that defines bourgeois form in terms of the illusionism of Hollywood-style continuity editing. Where what Eisenstein called bourgeois form was parallel montage (seen as a microcosm of the US class structure), what later Marxist theorists saw as bourgeois was the denial of cinematic formal devices. Following the logic of Jean-Luc Godard and others, if illusionistic cinema was bourgeois, radical cinema had to be anti-illusionistic – that is, it had to foreground its devices and, ideally, it also had to evidence the material conditions of its production. For Eisenstein, however, Griffith's early cinema was bourgeois because (although it represented class) it could not represent class struggle. It was also patriarchal, but not in any of the ways patriarchal form has been identified by early feminist film theory, for Griffith's patriarchal provincialism was inherited from nineteenth-century melodrama and from Dickens in particular. For Eisenstein, the patriarchal as well as the bourgeois, then, was epitomised in the parallel montage sequence where traditional sentiment was harnessed to the mechanics of shot alternation.[22]

The most I would hope for here is that Micheaux might force a reconsideration of Eisenstein as well as D.W. Griffith. Eisenstein's position has been taken to mean that borrowing such a corrupted form means automatically reproducing the politics it embodies, and I would not want to abandon this argument entirely, especially since so much productive work in the last ten years of film theory has been premised on the 'form equals politics' equation. Nevertheless, the orthodoxy of counter-cinema's antidote to Hollywood has been challenged recently, and no more emphatically than by new black British film-makers,[23] and one can add to this the increasing theoretical importance of a developing Third Cinema whose early manifesto writers embraced a range of forms including the unfinished and 'imperfect', the transitional and the 'incomplete'.[24] This move within the field represents such a total shuffling that it is almost as though we are left with no parameters. One would hope that this state of things will invite attempts to develop new classification schemes as we begin again to ask the same questions about politics and aesthetics. That the overdue consideration of Micheaux's film-making practice comes at this moment is fortunate, since these challenges to the counter-cinema model may stave off attempts to pigeonhole him in pre-existing categories, attempts that could pre-empt exploration into the ways in which his own aesthetic might shape new paradigms. Fortunately, recent considerations of Micheaux suggest that his maverick style confounds complacent assumptions about the connection between race, class, and aesthetic form, and I want to turn next to the task of situating that existing work in Micheaux's film *oeuvre*.

African–American Culture and Bourgeois Cinema

The new Micheaux criticism suggests inventive ways to move beyond the film-maker's reputation for creating unflattering characterisations of blacks, as well as his reputation for technical amateurism and aesthetic poverty. In a bold move, Jay Hoberman has located Micheaux in an avant-garde tradition, claiming that the results of his low-budget shooting produced 'surreal' effects and comparing his indifference to actors to Warhol's famous non-direction. Hoberman would like to place Micheaux outside the Hollywood tradition since the director is seemingly 'oblivious to the laws of cinematic continuity',[25] but here I would differ with Hoberman, arguing as I have that Micheaux should be situated in the classical Hollywood tradition which, after all, he so carefully studied and emulated. It is not so much that he broke with Hollywood conventions (as Hoberman argues) or even that he fell short of mastering them, but that he played 'fast and loose' with classical style. As master of the unmotivated cut, it is almost as though he is saying that if by 1918 audiences had learned to see discontinuous shots as fictional continuous space (always an approximation), then why could they not make sense of shots in a *really* rough approximation of that space?

Clearly, Micheaux's editing style was an ambitious improvisation with the few takes he had left after shooting at a low ratio, and this meant taking temporal licence with the material, even pushing the limits of conventional temporalities. Here, *Body and Soul* (1924), one of the few surviving examples of Micheaux's silent work, is exemplary for the way in which the director gives us not only the entire film as a dream flashback, but two consecutive flashbacks within that dream. Thus, we are doubly deceived by the beautiful mulatta Isabelle's flashback 'confessions' to her mother that the Reverend Isaiah Jenkins (Paul Robeson) raped her and stole her mother's money. The 'confessions' within the dream are two steps removed from the over-protective mother's real fears for her daughter.[26] In addition, within this structure the temporal transitions are relatively unmarked, making it difficult for the viewer to be certain where scenes are located in time.

There is something about Micheaux's unmarked transitions and his temporal ambiguities as well as his unmotivated cuts that suggests that he is working in another mode. Does this mean that he is responding to the 'call' of an indigenous African–American culture? I think not, and here I am as wary of linking Micheaux's unconventional style with any hint of an essential black culture as I am with calling it prescient modernism. Perhaps to elude any attempt to essentialise it, we could treat this style as more of an ingenious solution to the impossible demands of the conventions of classical Hollywood style, short cuts produced by the exigencies of economics, certainly, but also modifications produced by an independent who had nothing at stake in strict adherence to Hollywood grammar; and I do mean grammar, for if any comparison with African–American culture is useful, it may be with the black usage of standard English which linguists have argued is a short cut that often produces refinements of an awkward and illogical standard usage, in which people with less invested in rigid 'rules' simplify them to their own ends. Thus it is my feeling that the key to Micheaux's cinematic formal style as well as to his thematics is to be found in the way he transformed the existing without changing it. To some degree this is the same as the fate of the black bourgeois class which has historically striven for a new order but an order that is not substantially different from the one already in place.

However, there is much to be gained by an approach to Micheaux that insists upon qualifying his African-American heritage with his class position. First, understanding Micheaux's class position gives us a way around the prevalent charges of his own race hatred, the kind of charges that led to the Communist Party's boycott of *God's Stepchildren* (1937) on the basis of its damning portrait of a light-skinned mulatta whose deceitful attempts to reject her family and pass as white end in her tragic suicide.[27] In the work of contemporary African-American theorists, however, such contempt is the product of internal conflict set in motion by the dual motors of dominant and subordinated cultures. The African–American intellectual, says Cornel West, has been historically prone to this 'double consciousness', a theorisation that seems close to the same 'peculiar sensation' which W.E.B. Dubois called by the same name, that 'sense of always looking at one's self through the eyes of others, of measuring one's soul by the tape of a world that looks on in amused contempt and pity'.[28] It is not, then, that this consciousness is one's own or that the voice heard speaks for one's own culture; rather, it speaks for the other culture which, in the case of the black bourgeois, is also his own to the degree that he has been assimilated. It is really no wonder that the cultural products of an aspiring black intellectual in this period gave us black men as scoundrels, religious hypocrites, gamblers and sluggards, and black women as madames, seductresses, and cheats, for he was seeing this black culture through the eyes of the white culture for which this vision of an irredeemable black underclass was flattering and entirely functional.

While the operation of 'double consciousness' seems a fairly obvious way to explain Micheaux's 'offences', it may be less obvious that the critique needs to be applied two ways. That is, we need to consider that the early black culture critics were part of this same divided consciousness which produced the arguments that blacks were really just like whites and that Micheaux was at fault for showing negative images. This criticism, which had its most publicly visible moment in the protest around *The Birth of a Nation*, has been voided by recent work on the problem of the positive/negative formulation.[29] One would think that the popularisation of Gramsci's concept of hegemony would have swept away this earlier formulation, would have rendered it out of date for, as a theory of hegemony explains how the oppressor's point of view is embraced by the oppressed (all the while this point of view does not serve them), the theory could also be said to lift all blame for negative self-imaging from colonised subjects themselves. Discussing the value of Gramsci for ethnic studies, Stuart Hall emphasises that the utility of the concept is in the way hegemony explains the 'subjection' of the victims of racism to the mystification of the very racist ideologies which imprison and define them.[30] Thus it seems to me that there is sufficient theoretical justification for going beyond the early dismissal of Micheaux on the basis of race hatred. The jury is still out on Oscar Micheaux.

What I have suggested here is an approach to this important early African–American film-maker and novelist which allows us to redeem him as well as critique him. Yet in some ways, to try to explain Micheaux in terms of melodramatic form is entirely too tidy. As I have shown, the doubleness of black bourgeois consciousness finds its perfect expression in melodrama, the conflicted mode, the only mode within which (according to recent feminist theories) we can have classical realism and 'progressive' subversion simultaneously. Still, Micheaux introduces a new set of problems for melodrama as the mode of the disenfranchised, not the least of which is the question of what it meant historically for middle-class white women and middle-class blacks to profit from fictions marketed to the less fortunate.

243

My thanks are due to Todd Boyd for the title, Ron Green for the George P. Johnson leads and Celeste Fraser and Kathleen Newman for help with the intertitle translation.

Notes

1. The reference is to the famous quote from Woodrow Wilson.
2. See David Burner, Elizabeth Fox-Genovese, Eugene D. Genovese, and Forrest McDonald, *An American Portrait: A History of the United States*, vol. 2, 2nd edn (New York: Charles Scribner's Sons, 1985), pp. 595–7, for placement of the 1919 Chicago race riot in the context of the year of the 'Red Scare'. Carl Sandburg, *The Chicago Race Riots: July 1919* (New York: Harcourt, Brace and Howe, 1919).
3. Letter to Oscar Micheaux, Chicago, Illinois, from George P. Johnson, Omaha, Nebraska, 10 August 1920. This is in the George P. Johnson Collection, UCLA Special Collections.
4. The primary sources in the George P. Johnson Collection make numerous references to sections of *Within our Gates* as either cut out or replaced for one showing or another.
5. George P. Johnson Collection.
6. On Harriet Beecher Stowe's novel as sentimental fiction see Jane Tompkins, 'Sentimental Power: *Uncle Tom's Cabin* and the Politics of Literary History', in Elaine Showalter (ed.), *Feminist Criticism: Essays on Women, Literature, Theory* (New York: Pantheon Books, 1985).
7. See Sigmund Freud, 'Jokes and Their Relation to the Unconscious', in *The Standard Edition of the Complete Psychological Works*, vol. 8, trans. James Strachey (London: the Hogarth Press, 1959), p. 163; see also Louis Althusser, For Marx, trans. Ben Brewster (London: New Left Books, 1977), part 3.
8. Ida B. Wells-Barnett, 'Southern Horrors: Lynch Law in all its Phases' (1892) in *On Lynchings* (New York: Arno Press, 1969).
9. George P. Johnson Collection.
10. See my '*Scar of Shame*: Skin Color and Caste in Black Silent Melodrama', *Cinema Journal*, 26, 4, Summer 1987, pp. 3–21, reprinted in Marcia Landy (ed.), *Imitations of Life: A Reader on Film and Television Melodrama* (Detroit: Wayne State University Press, 1991).
11. Tom Gunning, 'Weaving a Narrative: Style and Economic Background in Griffith's Biograph Films', in Elsaesser and Barker (eds), *Early Cinema Space, Frame, Narrative* (London: British Film Institute, 1990).
12. Eric Bentley, *The Life of the Drama* (New York: Atheneum, 1964), p. 201.
13. Rick Altman, 'Dickens, Griffith, and Film Theory Today', *South Atlantic Quarterly*, 88, 2, Spring 1989, p. 342.
14. Tzvetan Todorov, *The Fantastic: A Structural Approach to a Literary Genre*, trans. Richard Howard (Ithaca: Cornell University Press, 1975), p. 166.
15. Russell Merritt, 'D. W. Griffith's *The Birth of a Nation*: Going After Little Sister', in Pete Lehman (ed.), *Close Viewings: An Anthology of New Film Criticism* (Tallahassee: Florida State University Press, 1990). For an important analysis of why the black spectator, although set up to view this scene as a 'rape', might resist this reading, see Manthia Diawara, 'Black Spectatorship: Problems of Identification and Resistance', *Screen*, 29, 4, Autumn 1988, pp. 67–70.
16. Wells-Barnett, op. cit., p. 11.
17. Elizabeth Fox-Genovese, *Within the Plantation Household: Black and White Women of the Old South* (Chapel Hill and London: The University of North Carolina Press, 1988), p. 101.

18. James Baldwin, *Notes of a Native Son* (New York: 1949), p. 14.
19. Sergi Eisenstein, *Film Form* (1949; reprinted New York: Harcourt Brace, 1977), p. 235.
20. Franz Fanon, *Black Skin, White Masks*, trans. Charles Lam Markmann (New York: Grove Weidenfeld, 1967), p.79.
21. Eisenstein, op. cit., pp. 233–5.
22. Eisenstein, op. cit., p. 198.
23. See Isaac Julien, as quoted in Coco Fusco, *Young, British, and Black: The Work of Sankofa and Black Audio Film Collective* (Buffalo, NY: Hallwalls/Contemporary Arts Center, 1988), p. 32.
24. Paul Willemen, 'The Third Cinema Question: Notes and Reflections', in Jim Pines and Paul Willemen (eds), *Questions of Third Cinema* (London: British Film Institute, 1989), p. 9. See also Kobena Mercer, 'Diaspora Culture and the Dialogic Imagination: The Aesthetics of Black Independent Film in Britain', in Claire Andrade-Watkins and Mbye Cham (eds) *Blackframes: Critical Perspectives on Black Independent Cinema* (London and Cambridge, Mass.: MIT Press, 1988), p. 59; Julio Garcia Espinosa, 'For an Imperfect Cinema', in Michael Chanan (ed.), *Twenty-Five Years of the New Latin American Cinema* (London: BFI/Channel 4 Television, 1983).
25. Jay Hoberman, 'A Forgotten Black Cinema Resurfaces', *Village Voice*, 17 November 1975, pp. 86–7.
26. Richard Dyer, *Heavenly Bodies: Film Stars and Society* (London: Macmillan, 1987), p. 115, interprets the film this way.
27. Hoberman, op. cit., p. 88.
28. Cornel West, 'The New Cultural Politics of Difference', in Russell Ferguson, Martha Gever, Trinh T. Minh-ha, and Cornel West (eds), *Out There: Marginalization and Contemporary Cultures* (Cambridge, Mass., and London: MIT Press, 1990), p. 28; W.E. Burghardt Du Bois (1903, reprinted New York: Signet, 1969), p. 45.
29. See, for instance, Steve Neale, 'The Same Old Story: Stereotypes and Differences', *Screen Education*, 32/33, Autumn/Winter 1979–80.
30. Stuart Hall, 'Gramsci's Relevance for the Study of Race and Ethnicity', *Journal of Communication Inquiry*, 10, 2, Summer 1986, p. 27.

INDEX

246

247

249